SECTIO

D0118202

MANAGEMENT
THEORY, PRACTICE, AND APPLICATION

Taken from

Management: Leading People and Organizations in the 21st Century
Second Edition
by Gary Dessler

Custom Edition for University of Phoenix

Pearson
Custom
Publishing

Taken from:

Management: Leading People and Organizations in the 21st Century, Second Edition
by Gary Dessler
Copyright © 2001 by Prentice-Hall, Inc.
A Pearson Education Company
Upper Saddle River, New Jersey 07458

Compilation copyright © 2003 by Pearson Custom Publishing

All rights reserved. No part of this book may be reproduced, in any form or by any means, without permission in writing from the publisher.

This special edition published in cooperation with Pearson Custom Publishing.

Published in the United States of America

10 9 8 7 6 5 4 3 2 1

Please visit our web site at www.pearsoncustom.com

ISBN 0–536–72164–5

BA 996418

PEARSON CUSTOM PUBLISHING
75 Arlington Street, Suite 300, Boston, MA 02116
A Pearson Education Company

B R I E F   C O N T E N T S

MANAGING IN THE 21ST CENTURY

WHAT'S AHEAD?

It looked like trail's end for Apple Computer. Sales and market share were dropping fast. Expenses were soaring, the firm had just lost $1 billion, and Apple was in a "death watch," according to some employees.[1] Then Steve Jobs came back on the scene. Jobs—who had founded Apple years earlier and then been pushed out of the firm—returned as interim president. He slashed costs, refocused Apple on 4 product lines (down from 15), reduced bloated inventories, revamped distribution, spearheaded the new iMac computer, and raised morale. And now here he was, at the Flint Center in California, announcing that Apple's profits had surged to $309 million and were heading higher. The employees stood and cheered.

THIS SECTION FOCUSES ON THE FOLLOWING:

- What managers do
- Why the people side of managing is so important
- The main trends in how modern organizations are managed

▶ WHAT MANAGERS DO

Managers can have the most remarkable effects on organizations. IBM floundered through much of the 1980s and early 1990s, losing market share, seeing costs rise, and watching its stock price dwindle from almost $180 per share to barely $50. Within three years, new CEO Louis Gerstner revamped the company's product line, dramatically lowered costs, changed the company's culture, and oversaw a quadrupling of IBM's stock price.[2] Dell CEO Michael Dell created a $12 billion company in just 13 years by instituting one of the world's most sophisticated direct-sales operations, eliminating resellers' markups and the need for large inventories, and keeping a vise-like grip on costs while dozens of his competitors were going down the drain.[3] And Steve Jobs (as we saw on the opening page) totally revitalized Apple Computer in barely a year.

And "manager" effects like these don't happen just at giant corporations. At this moment—as you read these words—managers at thousands of small businesses—diners, drycleaning stores, motels—are running their business well, with courteous, prompt, and first-class service, high-morale employees, and a minimum of problems like "My dinner's cold," or "You didn't press my pants." What do you think would happen if you took the competent managers out of those businesses and dropped in managers without training or skills? You know the answer because you've probably experienced the effects yourself—businesses with untrained or unprepared staff, orders not prepared on time, lost reservations, dirty rooms. About 90% of the new businesses started this year will fail within five years, and Dun & Bradstreet says the reason is generally poor management. Management is as—or more—important for the tiny start-up as it is for the giant firm.

The effect of good management is nothing short of amazing. Take an underperforming—even chaotic—organization and install a skilled manager, and he or she can soon get the enterprise humming. Take a successful enterprise that's been managed well for years—say, a neighborhood stationery store—and watch as a new, less-competent manager takes over. Shelves are suddenly in disarray, products are out of stock, bills go unpaid.

All these enterprises—IBM, Dell, the diner, the drycleaner, and the stationery store—are organizations. An **organization** consists of people with formally assigned roles who must work together to achieve stated goals. All organizations have several things in common. First, organizations needn't just be business firms; the definition applies equally well to colleges, local governments, and nonprofits like the American Red Cross. The U.S. government is an organization—certainly a not-for-profit one—and its head manager, or chief executive officer, is the president.

Organizations are, also (hopefully) "organized": Even your corner drycleaners has an organizational structure that lays out who does what (pressers press, and cleaners clean, for instance), and how the work (in this case the incoming clothes) will flow through the store and get done. An organization should also have policies that lay out how decisions will be made, such as how to reimburse a customer whose blouse has been lost, and what times and days the store will be open.

An organization that's not organized won't be much of a business (or much of a college, or local government, or what have you). To see why, think about the most disorganized person (professor?) you've ever known: lectures are unprepared and rambling, your test is always lost in some stack when you want to discuss it, and grades are never done on time and are based on unknown standards. Neither the professor nor the course are very well organized, and as a result, nothing ever goes entirely right.

Indeed, organizations, by their nature, cannot simply run themselves. Review the definition of an organization again, and you'll see why. Who would ensure that each of the people actually knew what to do? Who would see that they are trained? Who would hire them? Who would ensure that they work together, more or less harmoniously? Who would decide what the organization's goals would be, and then monitor whether each employee was doing his or her share to reach those goals?

The answer is "the manager." A **manager** is someone who plans, organizes, leads, and controls the people and the work of the organization in such a way that the organization achieves its goals. **Management** refers to two things: (1) collectively to the managers of an organization; and (2) to the study of what managers do. This is a text about management. Studying it carefully should put you well on the road to being a good manager.

The Management Process

Management writers traditionally refer to the manager's four basic functions—planning, organizing, leading, and controlling—as the **management process**. The rest of the text covers these in detail, but the following is a synopsis of each:

- *Planning.* Planning is setting goals and deciding on courses of action, developing rules and procedures, developing plans (both for the organization and for those who work in it), and forecasting (predicting or projecting what the future holds for the firm).
- *Organizing.* Organizing is identifying jobs to be done, hiring people to do them, establishing departments, delegating or pushing authority down to subordinates, establishing a chain of command (in other words, channels of authority and communication), and coordinating the work of subordinates.
- *Leading.* Leading means influencing other people to get the job done, maintaining morale, molding company culture, and managing conflicts and communication.
- *Controlling.* Controlling is setting standards (such as sales quotas or quality standards), comparing actual performance with these standards, and then taking corrective action as required.

You Too Are a Manager

Just as organizations needn't be business firms, managers needn't be businesspeople. In fact it's likely that you've already been (or may soon be) in the position of managing others. Let's suppose that you and some friends have decided to spend next summer abroad, say in France. None of you know very much about France or how to get there, so you've been elected "summer tour master" and asked to manage the trip. Where would you start? (Resist the temptation to call a travel agent and delegate the whole job to him or her, please.)

You might start by thinking through what you need to do in terms of planning, organizing, leading, and controlling. What sorts of plans will you need? Among other things, you'll need to plan the dates your group is leaving and returning, the cities and towns in France you'll visit, the airline you'll take there and back, how the group will get around in France, and where you'll stay when you're there. As you can imagine, plans like these are very important: You would not want to arrive at Orly Airport with a group of friends depending on you, and not know what you're doing next.

Developing all those plans will itself be quite a job, so you'll probably want to get some help. In other words, you'll need to divide up the work and create an organization. For example, you might delegate to Rosa—put her in charge of—checking airline schedules and prices, and Ned in charge of checking hotels, and Ruth in charge of checking the sites to see in various cities as well as the means of transportation between them. However, the job won't get done with Rosa, Ned, and Ruth simply working by themselves. Each requires guidance and coordination from you: Rosa obviously can't make any decisions on airline schedules unless she knows what city you're starting and ending with, and Ned can't really schedule any hotels unless he knows from Ruth what sites you'll be seeing and when. You'll either have to schedule weekly manager's meetings, or coordinate the work of these three people yourself.

Leadership could be a challenge, too: Ned and Ruth don't get along too well, so you'll have to make sure conflicts don't get out of hand. Rosa is a genius with numbers, but tends to get discouraged quickly, so you'll also have to make sure she stays focused and motivated.

And of course you'll have to ensure that the whole project stays "in control." If something can go wrong, it often will, and that's certainly the case when a group of people is traveling together. At a minimum, all those airline tickets, hotel reservations, and itineraries will have to be checked and checked again to make sure there are no mistakes. If you're wise, you may even ask another friend to double-check just before you leave to ensure that your group's hotel reservations are confirmed.

In other words, managing is something we all do almost every day, often without even knowing it.

Types of Managers

Most organizations contain several types of managers. In your college, for instance, there are presidents, vice presidents, deans, associate deans, and department chairs, as well as various administrators, like human resource managers. At your place of work (if you work) you might find supervisors, financial controllers, sales managers, plant managers, and a president and vice presidents. These people are managers because they all plan, organize, lead, and control the workers and the work of that particular organization in such a way that the organization achieves its goals.

There are many ways to classify managers. For example, we can distinguish managers based on their organization level, position, and functional title (see Table 1-1).

The managers at the top, of course, are the firm's top management. They are usually referred to as **executives**. Functional titles include president, chief executive officer (CEO), vice president, and chief financial officer (CFO).

Beneath this management level (and reporting to it) may be one or more levels of middle managers, positions that typically have the term *manager* or *director* in their titles. (Particularly in larger companies like IBM, managers report to directors, who in turn report to top managers, like vice presidents.) Examples of functional titles here include production manager, sales director, HR manager, and finance manager.

First-line managers are at the lowest rung of the management ladder. These managers are often called supervisors, and might include the production supervisors who actually supervise the assembly-line employees at Toyota.

All managers have a lot in common. They all plan, organize, lead, and control the people and the work of their organizations. And all managers at all levels and with every functional title spend an enormous part of each day with people—talking, listening, influencing, motivating, and attending one-on-one conferences and committee meetings.[4] In fact, even chief executives (whom you might expect to be somewhat insulated from other people, up there in their executive suites) reportedly spend about three-fourths of their time dealing directly with other people.[5]

However, there are two big differences among the management levels. First, top and middle managers both have managers for subordinates; in other words, they are in charge of other managers. Supervisors have workers—nonmanagers—

as subordinates. Managers at different levels also use their time somewhat differently. Top managers tend to spend a lot of time planning and setting goals (like "double sales in the next two years"). Middle managers then translate these goals into specific projects (like "hire two new salespeople and introduce three new products") for their subordinates to execute. First-line supervisors then concentrate on directing and controlling the employees who work on these projects.

Managing @ the Speed of Thought
■ The E-CEO

What is it like being an e-CEO, the chief executive of one of the hot new e-commerce companies? To hear the executives themselves tell it, *speed* is the word that sums up their experience best. For example, Roger Siboni, CEO of epiphany, a company which creates the software that helps e-corporations get the most from their customer data, says, "You're driving too fast—you feel the exhilaration—you must turn left and right at death-defying speed without blinking—never blink—if you go up and down with the news, you'll never make it."[6] E-CEOs must also be "brutally, brutally honest with yourself and others, because if you let a problem fester a day or two, you'll see someone in your rearview mirror coming after you."

With their markets changing so fast, e-CEOs must also constantly focus their companies' and their employees' attention on the company's mission. These companies are constantly deluged with competitive information and new ideas, so it's relatively easy for the employees to become distracted. It's the e-CEO's job to keep employees focused.

Table 1-1 summarizes why these e-CEOs are in fact a new breed. For example, they're not just younger and richer than traditional CEOs, they're also more comfortable with ambiguity and speed. They're also nearly paranoid about monitoring market trends and competitors' moves, to ensure their companies aren't blindsided by unanticipated events.

T A B L E   1 - 1   **E-CEOs Are a Brand-New Breed...**

Operating at breakneck speed in a world with little or no margin for error, e-CEOs need a new set of qualities to thrive.

Traditional CEO	e-CEO
encouraging	evangelizing
alert	paranoid
cordial	brutally frank
infotech semiliterate (at best)	infotech literate (at least)
clearly focused	intensely focused
fast moving	faster moving
hates ambiguity	likes ambiguity
suffers from technology-confrontation anxiety	suffers from bandwidth-separation anxiety
a paragon of good judgment	a paragon of good judgment
age: 57	age: 38
rich	really rich

Source: Fortune, 24 May 1999, p. 107. © 1999 Time Inc. Reprinted by permission.

The Manager's Changing Role

Yet the manager's job is changing so fast that some—like management guru Peter Drucker—say, "I'm not comfortable with the word *manager* anymore, because it implies subordinates."[7] What's wrong with having subordinates? Nothing, and most managers still do. But as we'll see later in this section, the "old style" manager who expects to give orders and be obeyed is in many situations a relic of the past. How far do you think you'd get by barking orders at the group you'd chosen to help you manage your group's trip abroad? Probably not very far. Similarly, intense competition and rapid change mean most companies today must depend more than ever on their employees' being willing to contribute. Very often, a manager today has to be more a team leader and facilitator than a traditional command-and-control person.

The People Side of Management

Managing has always been a decidedly behavioral or people-oriented occupation, since by definition managers do their work by interacting with others. Yet the people side of managing has taken on increased importance today.

Several years ago the accounting and consulting firm PricewaterhouseCoopers interviewed 400 CEOs whose companies were in the top 2,000 in global size.[8] Their results are summarized in Figure 1-1. As you might expect, a majority of these CEOs devoted a lot of personal time to things like setting corporate strategy, exploring mergers and acquisitions, and monitoring corporate financial results. Surprisingly, about half actually spent as much or more time personally trying to shape and influence the people or behavioral side of their businesses as they did on monitoring financial results.

Why is the people side of managing so important today? Perhaps the best way to answer that is with an example.

What Else Do Managers Do?

There are, of course, many other ways to "slice and dice" what managers do. For example, some time ago, Professor Henry Mintzberg conducted a study of what managers actually do, in part by walking around and watching them as they worked. Mintzberg found that as they went from task to task, managers didn't just plan, organize, lead, and control. Instead, they wore various hats, including:

► **FIGURE 1-1**

What Has the CEO's Attention?

Source: Adapted from "What Has The CEO's Attention?" *Management Review*, American Management Association International, September 1998, from the cover story, p.12.

ACTION	ALL CEOs	U.S. and CANADA	EUROPE and ASIA
Setting vision and strategy	66%	67%	65%
Exploring M&As	51%	51%	51%
Reshaping corporate culture and employee behavior	47%	48%	45%
Monitoring corporate financial information	45%	47%	43%

- *The* figurehead *role*. Every manager spends some time performing ceremonial duties. For example, the president of the United States might have to greet representatives of the state legislature, a supervisor might attend the wedding of a clerk, or the sales manager might take an important client to lunch.
- *The* leader *role*. Every manager must function as a leader, motivating and encouraging employees.[16]

The People Side of Managing

■ Allied-Signal

Honeywell Corporation and Allied-Signal merged in 1999, forming a new, much larger Honeywell Corporation. The merger was made possible by the rising fortunes of Allied-Signal, which had vastly improved under its chairman and CEO, Lawrence A. Bossidy.[9]

How did Bossidy turn Allied-Signal around? Interestingly, Bossidy's people skills had a remarkable effect on this huge industrial supplier of aerospace systems, automotive parts, and chemical products.[10] He took over a troubled company that was "hemorrhaging cash."[11] After just three years under Bossidy, Allied-Signal's net income (profits) had doubled to $708 million, profit margins had doubled, and the company's market value (the total value of its shares) had more than doubled as well, to almost $10 billion.

What did Bossidy do to bring about such a dramatic transformation in just three years? A lot of his changes were operational: Under his guidance the company merged business units, closed factories, reduced suppliers from 9,000 to 3,000, and cut 19,000 salaried jobs from the payroll, for instance.[12]

But much of what Bossidy focused on was behavioral in nature. In other words, he focused on applying his knowledge of how people, as individuals and groups, act within organizations to help bring about change. For example, in his first two months on the job, "I talked to probably 5,000 employees. I would go to Los Angeles and speak to 500 people, then to Phoenix and talk to another 500. I would stand on a loading dock and speak to people and answer their questions. We talked about what was wrong and what we should do about it."[13] His job, as he saw it, was not just to cut jobs and merge operations, since actions like these would have only short-term effects on profitability. In the longer run, Bossidy knew, he had to excite his giant firm's many employees by promoting "our employees' ability to win," by uniting the top management team "with vision and values," and in general by convincing all his employees that there was a tremendous need to change—that their "platform was burning," as Bossidy put it.[14]

Trends like technological innovation, global competition, and deregulation have created an environment that's merciless to companies and organizations whose employees aren't fully committed to doing even more than their best, every day. That's why Bossidy says that when he looks for managers, he looks for those who have a gift for working with and turning on employees. As he put it:

> Today's corporation is a far cry from the old authoritarian vertical hierarchy I grew up in. The cross-functional ties among individuals and groups are increasingly important. There are channels of activity and communication. The traditional bases of managerial authority are eroding. In the past, we used to reward the lone rangers in the corner offices because their achievements were brilliant even though their behavior was destructive. That day is gone. We need people who are better at persuading than at barking orders, who know how to coach and build consensus. Today, managers add value by brokering with people, not by presiding over empires.[15]

- *The* liaison *role.* Managers spend a lot of time in contact with people outside their own departments, essentially acting as the liaison between their departments and other people within and outside the organization. The assembly-line supervisor might field a question from the sales manager about how a new order is coming. Or, the vice president of sales might meet with the vice president of finance to make sure a new customer has the credit required to place an order.

- *The* spokesperson *role.* The manager is often the spokesperson for his or her organization. The supervisor may have to keep the plant manager informed about the flow of work through the shop, or the president may make a speech to lobby the local county commissioners for permission to build a new plant on some unused land.

- *The* negotiator *role.* Managers spend a lot of time negotiating; the head of the airline tries to negotiate a new contract with the pilots' union, or the first-line supervisor negotiates a settlement to a grievance with the union's representative.

More recently, two management experts, Sumantra Ghoshal and Christopher Bartlett, emphasized the importance of managers in creating a responsive and change-oriented company.[17] Successful managers today, say Bartlett and Ghoshal, can't afford to focus just on the mechanical aspects of managing, like designing organization charts or drawing up plans. Instead, successful managers cultivate three processes aimed at getting employees to focus their attention on creating change: *the entrepreneurial process, the competence-building process*, and the *renewal process*.

- *The* entrepreneurial *process.* Entrepreneurship, say Bartlett and Ghoshal, refers to "the externally-oriented, opportunity-seeking attitudes that motivate employees to run their operations as if they own them."[18] In their study of 20 companies in Japan, the United States, and Europe, they found that successful managers focused much of their time and energy on getting employees to think of themselves as entrepreneurs. To do this, managers emphasized giving employees the authority, support, and rewards that self-disciplined and self-directed people needed to run their operations as their own.

- *The* competence-building *process.* Bartlett and Ghoshal also found that "in a world of converging technologies, large companies have to do more than match their smaller competitors' flexibility and responsiveness. They must also exploit their big-company advantages, which lie not only in scale economies but also in the depth and breadth of employees' talents and knowledge."[19]

  Successful managers therefore also devote much effort to creating an environment that lets employees really take charge. This means: encouraging them to take on more responsibility; providing the education and training they need to build self-confidence; and allowing them to make mistakes without fear of punishment, while coaching them and supporting them to learn from their mistakes.[20]

- *The* renewal *process.* Successful managers also concentrate on fostering what Bartlett and Ghoshal call a renewal process, one "designed to challenge a company's strategies and the assumptions behind them."[21] In other words, managers have to make sure they and all their employees guard against complacency. Employees should develop the habit of questioning why things are done as they are and whether it might not be better to do things differently.

The People Side of the Management Process

To get another perspective on how managers manage, consider the behavioral or people aspects of the things managers do. Managers plan, organize, lead, and control. Obviously, leading is a very people-oriented activity, since it involves tasks like motivating employees and resolving conflicts. But, as summarized in Table 1-2, also keep in mind that the people side of managing is important to planning, organizing, and controlling, too. For instance, planning involves getting department heads to work together to craft a new plan; controlling may involve getting subordinates to correct "out of control" behavior. The people side of managing thus affects everything that managers do. We'll illustrate this in each section with a feature called "The People Side of Managing" that shows the people aspects of that section's topic.

Do You Want to Be a Manager?

If you're thinking of being a manager, there's a wealth of research to help you to decide whether that's the occupation for you.

Personality and Interests Career counseling expert John Holland says that personality (including values, motives, and needs) is an important determinant of career choice. Specifically, he says six basic "personal orientations" determine the sorts of careers to which people are drawn. Research with his Vocational Preference Test (VPT) suggests that almost all successful managers fit at least one of two personality types or orientations from that group:

- *Social orientation.* Social people are attracted to careers that involve working with others in a helpful or facilitative way (managers as well as others like clinical psychologists and social workers would exhibit this orientation). Generally speaking, socially oriented people find it easy to talk with all kinds of people, are good at helping people who are upset or troubled, are skilled at explaining things to

TABLE 1-2 **Everything a Manager Does Requires Leading**

Management Function	The People or Leadership Side of the Management Function
Planning	Getting department heads to work together to craft a new strategic plan; working with small groups of employees to encourage more creative ways of looking at the company's situation; dealing with the interdepartmental conflicts that may arise when one department's plans conflict with another's.
Organizing	Dealing with the questions of power and company politics that arise as employees in various departments jockey for positions of dominance; encouraging communication across departmental lines; understanding how personality, motivation, and skills can influence who should or should not be put in charge of various departments.
Controlling	Influencing subordinates to correct "out of control" behavior; dealing with the fact that employees may be motivated to subvert the control system to make themselves look better in the short run; and using effective interpersonal communication skills to encourage employees to change the way they do things.

Note: Leading, the management function that focuses on the people aspects of what managers do, is not just another step in the management process, but an integral part of everything managers do.

others, and enjoy doing social things like helping others with their personal problems, teaching, and meeting new people.[22]

■ *Enterprising orientation.* Enterprising people tend to like working with people in a supervisory or persuasive way in order to achieve some goal. They especially enjoy verbal activities aimed at influencing others (lawyers and public relations executives would also exhibit this orientation). Enterprising people often characterize themselves as being good public speakers, as having reputations for being able to deal with difficult people, as successfully organizing the work of others, and as being ambitious and assertive. They enjoy influencing others, selling things, serving as officers of groups, and supervising the work of others.

Competencies   Your competencies also will help determine how successful you might be at managing others. Professor Edgar Schein says career planning is a continuing process of discovery in which a person slowly develops a clearer occupational self-concept in terms of what his or her talents, abilities, motives, and values are. Schein also says that as you learn more about yourself, it becomes apparent that you have a dominant **career anchor**, a concern or value that you will not give up if a choice has to be made.

Based on his study of MIT graduates, Schein concluded that managers have a strong **managerial competence** career anchor.[23] They show a strong motivation to become managers, "and their career experience enables them to believe that they have the skills and values necessary to rise to such general management positions." A management position of high responsibility is their ultimate goal. When pressed to explain why they believed they had the skills required to gain such positions, many said they saw themselves as competent in three areas: (1) analytical competence (the ability to identify, analyze, and solve problems under conditions of incomplete information and uncertainty); (2) interpersonal competence (the ability to influence, supervise, lead, manipulate, and control people at all levels); and (3) emotional competence (the capacity to be stimulated by emotional and interpersonal crises rather than exhausted or debilitated by them, and the capacity to bear high levels of responsibility without becoming paralyzed).

Achievements   Research also suggests that you might gain some insight into your prospects by looking closely at your achievements to date. Industrial/organizational psychologists at AT&T conducted two long-term studies of managers to determine how their pre-management achievements were related to their success on the job.[24]

Some of their findings were not too surprising. Employees who had gone to college showed much greater potential when first hired for middle- and upper-management positions than did those who had not gone to college; eight years later the differences between these two groups were even more pronounced. Specifically, those who went to college rose (on average) much faster and higher in management than did those in the noncollege sample. College grades were important, too: People with higher college grades showed greater potential for promotion early in their careers, and they rose higher in management than did those with lower grades.

Also, perhaps not too surprisingly, the quality of the college attended meant a lot more early in the person's management career than it did later. Those who had attended what were considered to be better-quality colleges at first ranked higher as potential managers. But within several years college quality seemed to have little effect on who was promoted.

College major did seem to have a big effect, however, and here there were some surprises. Managers who had majored in humanities and social sciences initially scored higher as potential managers and eventually moved faster and further up the corporate ladder.[25] Business administration majors ranked second, and math, science, and engineering majors ranked third.

What accounted for the surprising performance of the humanities and social science majors? At least in this study, conducted in one company, they scored the highest in decision making, intellectual ability, written communication skills, creativity in solving business problems, and motivation for advancement. Both the humanities and social science majors and the business administration majors ranked higher in leadership ability, oral communication skills, interpersonal skills, and flexibility than did the math, science, and engineering majors.[26] Findings like these obviously don't suggest that business and science majors are lost; they may just be unique to this specific group of managers, or to AT&T. However, the findings may suggest that, whatever your major, it's important to work on improving things like decision making, creativity, and written communication skills.

▶ WHY MANAGERS TODAY FACE INCREASED COMPETITION AND CHANGE

If there are two issues that characterize the challenges twenty-first-century managers face today, those issues can be summarized as "competition and change." A handful of forces—most notably technological advances such as the Internet, and the tendency for companies to expand their sales and manufacturing worldwide—have raised dramatically both the competition companies face and the speed with which they must cope with change. And, as a result, the way that managers manage and firms organize have both changed significantly. It is no coincidence that we've subtitled this text "Leading People and Organizations in the Twenty-First Century." We'll explain some of these forces and how they affect managers on the next few pages.

Examples of how such forces influence companies are not hard to find. For example, after more than 230 years in business, Encyclopaedia Britannica was almost put out of business in the early 1990s by Microsoft's *Encarta* CD-ROM. After selling its thirty-two-volume set of encyclopedias (and, subsequently its *Encyclopaedia Britannica* CD-ROMs) for as much as $1,200 per set, Britannica found itself on the brink of extinction, made almost obsolete by Microsoft's relatively costless *Encarta*. Today, Britannica has disbanded its door-to-door sales force and is offering its encyclopedia without charge via the Internet, and hoping that revenue from on-line ads and sponsorships will be enough to make the company grow again.

Indeed, no industry has been immune from these kinds of changes. Today, for instance, many local personnel agencies have found revenues dropping as companies search for employees via the Internet, and prospective employees list their résumés on Internet sites like hotjobs.com. And in the last few years, both Ford and General Motors announced that they are moving their entire (and enormous) purchasing operations onto the Internet, so that suppliers will be able to sell these two giant firms their supplies automatically.[27]

Similarly, in June 1999, Wall Street giant Merrill Lynch made an announcement that rocked its 14,000-member sales force and the rest of the brokerage industry: Rather than pay what often amounted to hundreds of dollars in commissions per trade, Merrill Lynch's customers would soon be able to trade on-line, for about $30 per trade. The idea was to keep Merrill Lynch's customers from jumping to low-fee on-line competitors. Said one Merrill Lynch broker, "There's a lot of very, very sore egos around here . . . we have been insulted one too many times. They basically called us dinosaurs."[28] The changes had, of course, been triggered by the rise of the Internet.

The new on-line competition spawned by the Internet thus set in motion a whole series of organizational changes at Merrill Lynch: a new on-line trading division was created, managers were reassigned, new computer systems were installed, and new plans were developed for the company, for instance. Even within the company, competition between brokers increased. The commissions Merrill Lynch brokers earned would drop, and many would have to leave. Those who remained would have to work harder to provide improved services so their customers would stay loyal and pay commissions.

Such changes were not limited to Merrill Lynch. To stay competitive, other brokers would follow suit. Throughout the industry, lower fees would lead to fewer brokers, general downsizing, and more productivity and competitiveness. With giant industry mergers—such as Traveler's Group and Citibank combining to form Citigroup—added to the mix, managers today must move fast and smartly if their companies are to stay out in front.

Not all managers were able to move as quickly or smartly as those at Merrill Lynch or as Apple's Steve Jobs. In the past few years hundreds of banks, airlines, computer firms, and other businesses have failed or been gobbled up by stronger competitors. Even some of the strongest brands in the world have not been immune. After spending almost $1 billion in an unsuccessful attempt to make the company more efficient and responsive, management found that sales at Levi Strauss were heading down instead of up. Faced with smart and fast-moving global competitors like Gap and Calvin Klein, Levi's sales "fell apart" as its share in the U.S. jeans market dropped from 48% in 1990 to 25% in 1998. As this book was being written, the plans, organization, leadership, and controls of Levi's top managers were increasingly under critical scrutiny.[29]

What forces are causing such turbulence and change for companies and managers around the world today? We'll look briefly at some important ones: technological innovation, globalization, deregulation, changing political systems, category killers, the new global workforce, and new service-oriented jobs.

Technological Innovation

Technological innovations are changing the way companies are managed, and that's not just true for industry giants like Merrill Lynch. For instance, Inter-Design of Ohio sells plastic clocks, refrigerator magnets, soap dishes, and similar products. Its president explains the impact of **information technology**, which merges communications systems with computers, this way: "In the seventies we went to the post office to pick up our orders. In the early 80s, we put in an 800 number. In the late 80s, we got a fax machine. In 1991, pressured by Target [stores, a customer], we added electronic data interchange." Now, more than half of Inter-Design's orders arrive via modem, straight into company computers. Errors in order entry and shipping have all but disappeared, and both Target and Inter-Design have been able to slash finished goods inventories and therefore costs.[30]

Information technology like this has been a boon to many companies, but a near disaster for others. Wal-Mart became the industry leader in the 1990s in part because its managers used information technology to link stores with suppliers: Levi Strauss, for instance, always knew exactly how many size-10, 501-style jeans were being sold and could replenish stores' supplies almost at once. But Wal-Mart's technology advantage almost ruined K-Mart, which struggled for years without the speed and cost-effectiveness of such a system.

The Internet is having similar effects. Without physical stores and staffs, many Internet sellers like Amazon.com can offer much lower prices than local stores. And the availability of easily accessible price information means that retailers of thousands of products from books to boats must now drive down their own costs in order to match Internet sellers' prices. The result is continuing pressure to drive down costs and to manage firms in the most efficient and flexible manner. That's one of the reasons more conventional computer makers like Apple and Compaq have their work cut out for them in competing with the likes of Dell, which is super efficient at marketing its computers via the Internet.

Globalization

Globalization—the extension of a firm's sales or manufacturing to new markets abroad—is also boosting competition. For instance, in the early 1980s GE, long accustomed to being the dominant lighting manufacturer in the United States, had a rude awakening. Its relatively weak competitor, Westinghouse, sold its lamp operations to Dutch electric powerhouse Philips Electronics; overnight GE's competitive picture changed. As one GE executive put it, "Suddenly we have bigger, stronger competition. They're coming into our market, but we're not in theirs. So we're on the defensive."[31]

GE did not stay there for long. It soon bought Hungary's Tungstram electronics, and is fast moving into Asia through a partnership with Hitachi.[32] In 1990 GE lighting got less than 20% of its sales from abroad; by 1993 the figure was 40%; today the estimate is more than 50%.

Production is becoming globalized too as manufacturers around the world put manufacturing facilities in the most advantageous locations. Thus, the Toyota Camry is produced in Georgetown, Kentucky, and contains almost 80% U.S.-made parts, while the Pontiac LeMans contains about two-thirds foreign-made parts.[33]

For managers, globalization is important in part because it means increased competition. In every city and town throughout the world, firms that once competed only with local firms—from airlines to car makers to banks—have discovered they must now face an onslaught of new and efficient foreign competitors. And more competition means you have to manage better and smarter to make your company succeed.

Many firms have responded successfully to this new competition, while others have failed. For instance, when Swedish furniture retailer IKEA built its first U.S. furniture superstore near Philadelphia, its unique styles and management systems grabbed market share from numerous local competitors.

But global competition is a two-way street. Ford and GM have huge market shares in Europe, for instance, while IBM, Microsoft, and Apple (thanks to those great management moves by Jobs) have major market shares around the world. As one international business expert puts it, "The bottom line is that the growing integration of the world economy into a single, huge marketplace is increasing the intensity of competition in a wide range of manufacturing and service industries."[34]

Deregulation

Competition is also keener today because the protection provided to thousands of businesses around the world by government regulation has been stripped away in many countries. In the United States hundreds of airlines, banks, and other companies have had to merge, sell out, or disappear, as deregulation exposed inefficiencies that some simply couldn't eliminate. In 1999 AT&T—formerly only a long-distance phone service provider—was poised to invade the regional Bells' local phone service turf through its purchases of various cable companies. Meanwhile, Bell Atlantic—formerly just a local service provider—was allowed to introduce long-distance service. Congress had earlier approved sweeping deregulation of local and long-distance phone service, allowing carriers to invade each other's markets. Competition in dozens of industries soared, and with it the challenge of managing the newly deregulated companies.[35]

Changing Political Systems

As nations ranging from the Philippines to Argentina, Russia, and Chile joined the ranks of democracies, central planning and communism were often replaced by capitalism. Such political changes have in turn triggered the opening of new markets, with hundreds of millions of potential customers. For business firms, the opportunities are enormous. But the burgeoning demand for goods and services also means increased global competition, as firms in more and more countries gain the wherewithal to compete in the global arena.

Category Killers

Where does a 1,000-pound gorilla sit? A 1,000-pound gorilla sits wherever it wants to, just like category killers such as Office Depot, Comp USA, and Circuit City. These mammoth stores rely on economies of scale and wide selections to drive down costs and prices and to attract huge numbers of buyers. Most small competitors—neighborhood hardware stores, stationery stores, and bookstores, for instance—can't get their costs or prices low enough to compete and haven't the product range to do so anyway. Most are squeezed out of business by the relentless competition, unless their managers and proprietors are smart enough to know how to react.

Department stores illustrate this theme too. Over the past few years many smaller retail chains like Macy's have been absorbed into giant chains like Federated Department Stores. These giant chains have powerful centralized purchasing departments that pressure clothing manufacturers to lower their prices. When the manufacturers were dealing with dozens of smaller chains, it was easier for them to negotiate. But when one giant chain accounts for half your company's sales (or more), it's much harder to resist. Manufacturers are therefore squeezed to reduce their costs, and only the most efficient and best managed survive.

The New Global Workforce

More U.S. firms are transferring their operations abroad, not just to seek cheaper labor, but also to tap what *Fortune* magazine calls "a vast new supply of skilled labor around the world."[36] Even today, for instance, most multinational firms set up manufacturing plants abroad not just to establish beachheads in promising markets, but also to utilize other countries' professionals and engineers. For example, Asea Brown Boveri (ABB; a $30 billion-per-year Swiss builder of transportation and electric generation systems) has 25,000 new employees in former Communist countries and has shifted many jobs from western to eastern Europe.

Tapping such overseas labor markets is a two-edged sword for employers. Employers gain thousands of potential new highly skilled employees, but also face the challenge of competing for and managing a geographically dispersed workforce. And for employees—especially those in the United States—it means competing for jobs with a worldwide labor force, many of whom (such as software engineers in India) may earn much lower wages than their counterparts in the U.S.

A Shift to Service and Knowledge Work

Managing today is also changing because what workers do is changing. This fact reflects several trends in the business environment. One is the growing importance of service work.[37] More than two-thirds of the U.S. workforce is now involved in producing services, not things. And of the 21 million jobs added to the U.S. economy in the 1990s, virtually all were in service industries like retailing, consulting, teaching, and law.[38] Service jobs like these put a bigger premium on worker education and knowledge than do traditional jobs, and thus they add more to a company's "human capital"—the knowledge, training, skills, and expertise of a firm's workers—at the expense of physical capital like equipment, machinery, and the physical plant.[39] As James Brian Quinn, an expert in this area, puts it, "Intellect is the core resource in producing and delivering services."[40]

Human capital is also more important today because manufacturing jobs are changing. Particularly in the United States, jobs in the steel, auto, rubber, and textile industries are being replaced by knowledge-intensive, high-tech manufacturing in such industries as aerospace, computers, and telecommunications.[41] At Alcoa Aluminum's Davenport, Iowa, plant, for instance, computers at each workstation help employees control their machines or communicate data. As *Fortune* magazine put it, "Practically every package deliverer, bank teller, retail clerk, telephone operator, and bill collector in America works with a computer [today]."[42] Here is how Microsoft Corporation CEO Bill Gates put it:

> In the new organization the worker is no longer a cog in a machine but is an intelligent part of the overall process. Welders at some steel jobs now have to know algebra and geometry to figure weld angles from computer-generated designs . . . new digital photocopiers require the service personnel to have an understanding of computers and the Internet, not just skills with a screwdriver.[43]

Innovation, driven by competition, demands more highly skilled employees, too. It is not unusual for more than one-fourth of many firms' sales to come from products less than five years old. As a result, "innovating—creating new products, new services, new ways of turning out goods more cheaply—has become the most urgent concern of corporations everywhere."[44] Companies are therefore relying more on employees' creativity and skills, thus placing more stress on employees' brain power.

For managers, the challenge of human capital is that these "knowledge workers" must be managed differently than workers of previous generations. "The center of gravity in employment is shifting fast from manual and clerical workers to knowledge workers, who resist the command and control model that business took from the military 100 years ago."[45] Knowledge workers, in other words, can't just be ordered around and closely monitored. New management skills are required to turn these highly trained workers into partners in the company-building process. As a manager, you'll need to know how to lead people and organizations in the twenty-first century, in part because these people are doing jobs—designing Web sites, for instance—that workers have never done before.

▶ THE FUTURE IS NOW

The Modern Organization

Let's summarize where we are. Things are moving superfast in the world of business today; in fact, they're moving "at the speed of business," to quote a recent UPS ad. Technology, globalization, deregulation, changing political systems, the new workforce, and a shift to service and knowledge work are putting companies under tremendous pressure to respond faster and to be ever more cost-effective and competitive. What does this mean for how companies are managed? Perhaps the best way to answer that is to look at a few snapshots of how superfast businesses are being managed today. For some, being superfast means using the Internet for "Managing @ the Speed of Thought," as the following box about Dell illustrates.

Managing @ the Speed of Thought

■ Virtual Integration at Dell Computer

How do you build a $12 billion company in just 13 years?[46] For Dell Computer the answer meant using technology and information to "blur the traditional boundaries in the value chain among suppliers, manufacturers, and the end users."[47] What does this mean? As summarized in Figure 1-2, it basically means that there are no intermediaries like wholesalers or retailers to come between Dell and its customers and suppliers, so that Dell can be a much faster-moving company than it

▼ FIGURE 1-2

The Evolution of a Faster Business Model

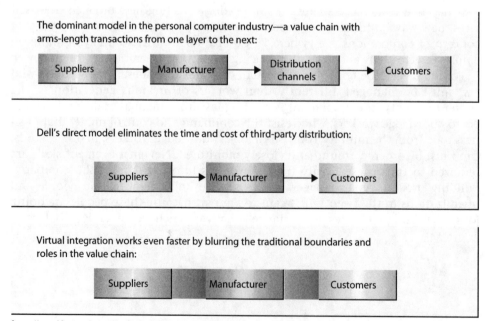

Source: Harvard Business Review, March–April 1998, p. 82. Copyright © 1998 by the President and Fellows of Harvard College. All rights reserved.

might otherwise be.[48] For most computer companies, the manufacturing process is like a relay race: Components come in from suppliers; these components are assembled into computers; and the computers are then handed off to be distributed through wholesalers and retailers (such as CompUSA) to the ultimate customers. Dell's system changes all that. For example, (see Figure 1-2) Dell interacts with and sells to customers directly, so it eliminates the activities of the wholesalers and retailers in the traditional distribution chain.[49]

"Virtual integration"—linking Dell with its suppliers and customers via the Internet—speeds things up even more. As one example, computerized information from Dell continually updates suppliers regarding the number of components to be delivered every morning, so the "outside" supplier actually starts to look and act more like an "inside" part of Dell. Similarly, instead of stocking its own monitors,

> We tell Airborne Express or UPS to come to Austin and pick up 10,000 computers a day and go over to the Sony factory in Mexico and pick up the corresponding number of monitors. And while we're all sleeping, they match up the computers and the monitors, and deliver them to the customers . . . of course, this requires sophisticated data exchange.[50]

The result of what Michael Dell calls "this virtual integration" of suppliers, manufacturing, and customers is a lean, efficient, and fast-moving operation that can turn on a dime if the products demanded by customers change:

> There are fewer things to manage, fewer things to go wrong. You don't have the drag effect of taking 50,000 people with you. . . . If we had to build our own factories for every single component of the system, growing at 57% per year just would not be possible. I would spend 500% of my time interviewing prospective vice-presidents because the company would have not 15,000 employees but 80,000. Indirectly, we employ something like that many people today. . . but only a small number of them work for us. Their contract is with other firms. . . . The vast majority [of customers] think [those people] work for us, which is just great. That's part of virtual integration.[51]

The New Management

We've seen on the last few pages that forces like technological change, globalized competition, deregulation, political instability, and trends toward service jobs and the information age have altered the playing field on which firms must now compete. They have done this by dramatically raising the need for firms to be efficient, responsive, flexible, and capable of competing and reacting rapidly to competitive and technological changes.

Firms like ABB and Cisco are in vanguard of thousands of others that are re-creating themselves to fit these new conditions, by implementing new management methods that enable them to cope with great competition and rapid change. An overview is presented in Figure 1-3. Forces such as technological innovation, globalization, and deregulation mean that companies today must cope with much greater levels of competition, change, and unpredictability than ever before. As a result, to succeed, companies like Dell, ABB, Cisco, and Saturn have instituted new management methods (such as mini-units, Internet-based financial controls, and team-based organizations) that enable these companies to be more efficient, and also much more effective at reacting quickly to competitive and technological change. We'll see how managers actually do this in the rest of the text. But from their experiences, and from those of others, here is a summary of what the new management looks like.

▼ **FIGURE 1-3**

Fundamental Changes Facing Managers   A series of forces—globalized competition, technology revolution, new competitors, and changing tastes—are creating outcomes that include more uncertainty, more choices, and more complexity. The result is that the organizational winners of today and tomorrow will have to be responsive, smaller, flatter, and oriented toward adding value through people.

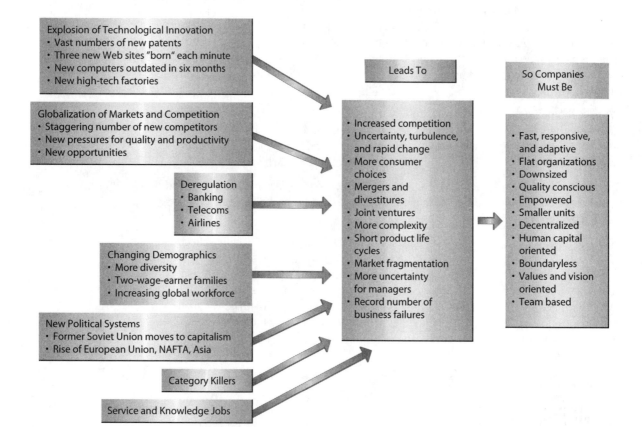

Smaller Organizational Units   First, one way or another, the actual operating units in most companies are getting smaller. For one thing, there's been an explosion of new small ventures, with thousands and thousands of "e-entrepreneurs" setting up their own new firms. And even in big firms (recall ABB), the work is increasingly organized around mini-units.

Cypress Semiconductor is another example. T. J. Rogers, president of this California firm, believes that large companies stifle innovation. So when a new product must be developed, he doesn't do it within the existing corporation. Instead, he creates a separate start-up company under the Cypress umbrella. "I would rather see our billion-dollar company of the 1990s be 10 $100 million companies, all strong, growing, healthy and aggressive as hell," Rogers says. "The alternative is an aging billion-dollar company that spends more time defending its turf than growing." True to his words, Rogers already has four successful start-ups under development.[52]

Team-Based Organizations   As at Saturn, todays' new organizations stress cross-functional teams and interdepartmental communication. There is also a corresponding de-emphasis on sticking to the chain of command to get decisions made. GE's, former Chairman Jack Welch has talked of the boundaryless organization, in which employees do not identify with separate departments, but instead interact with whomever they must to get the job done.[53]

Empowered Decision Making   Jobs today require constant learning, higher-order thinking, and much more worker commitment. This calls for more employee empowerment, and less of a 9-to-5 mentality. Experts like Karl Albrecht argue for turning the typical organization upside-down.[54] They say today's organization should put the customer—not the CEO—on top, to emphasize that every move the company makes must be aimed at satisfying customer needs. This in turn requires empowering the front-line employees—the front desk clerks at the hotel, the cabin attendants on the plane, and the assemblers at the factory—with the authority to respond quickly to these needs. The main purpose of managers in this "upside-down" organization is to serve the front-line employees, to see that they have what they need to do their jobs, and thus to serve the customers. They're not simply there to oversee what workers do and to control their actions.

Flatter Organizational Structures   Instead of the familiar pyramid-shaped organization with its seven or more layers of management, flat organizations with just three or four levels prevail. Many companies have already cut the management layers from a dozen to six or fewer, and therefore the number of managers.[55] As the remaining managers are left with more people to supervise, they are less able to meddle in the work of their subordinates, who thus have more autonomy.

New Bases of Management Power   In today's organizations, says management theorist Rosabeth Moss Kanter, leaders can no longer rely on their formal authority to get employees to follow them.[56] Instead, "success depends increasingly on tapping into sources of good ideas, on figuring out whose collaboration is needed to act on those ideas, and on working with both to produce results. In short, the new managerial work implies very different ways of obtaining and using power."[57] Peter Drucker put it this way: "You have to learn to manage in situations where you don't have command authority, where you are neither controlled nor controlling."[58] In other words, managers have to win the respect and commitment of their highly trained and empowered employees to get their jobs done today.

Knowledge-Based Organizations   Management expert Tom Peters says new organizations are knowledge based. Teams of highly trained and educated professionals apply their knowledge to clients' problems, in a setting in which the employees direct and discipline their own activities.[59]

This means managers must help their employees get their jobs done by training and coaching them, removing roadblocks, and getting them the resources they need: You can't simply "boss" teams of professionals. This highlights one big difference between the old and the new manager. Yesterday's manager thinks of himself or herself as a "manager" or "boss." The new manager thinks of himself or herself as a "sponsor," a "team leader," or an "internal consultant." The old-style manager makes most decisions alone; the new one invites others to join in the decision making. The old-style manager hoards information to build his or her personal power. The new manager shares information to help subordinates get their jobs done.[60]

An Emphasis on Vision and Values   Formulating a clear vision and values to which employees can commit themselves is more important than ever. Managers must communicate clear values regarding what is important and unimportant, and regarding what employees should and should not do. As GE's Welch said,

> Every organization needs values, but a lean organization needs them even more. When you strip away the support system of staffs and layers, people need to relearn their habits and expectations or else the stress will just overwhelm them. . . . Values [are] what enable people to guide themselves through that kind of change.[61]

Other experts agree. Drucker says today's organizations—staffed as they are by professionals and other employees who largely control their own behavior—require "clear, simple, common objectives that translate into particular actions." In other words, they need a clear vision of where the firm is heading.[62] Even without a lot of supervisors to guide them, employees can then be steered by the company's vision and values.

Managers are Change Agents   As GE's Welch puts it, "You've got to be on the cutting edge of change. You can't simply maintain the status quo, because somebody's always coming from another country with another product, or consumers' tastes change, or the cost structure does, or there's a technology breakthrough. If you are not fast and adaptable, you are vulnerable."[63]

Leadership Is Key   Empowered workers, service jobs, and the need to get workers thinking like owners puts a premium on the people side of managing. Understanding how to work with and through people and how to use behavioral science concepts and techniques at work will be more important than ever before.

More Companies Are Becoming E-based   Today virtually all companies—from tiny ".com" startups like hungryminds.com to giant companies like General Motors, Wal-Mart, and GE are reorganizing in a way that enables them to take advantage of the great potential of the Internet. Today, as we'll see in this book, managers are using the Internet in thousands of ways to help them to better plan, organize, lead, and control their organizations. In the sections to follow we'll use "Managing @ the Speed of Thought" boxes as well as short illustrated "Webnotes" to show how managers are using the power of the Internet to help them better manage their companies today.

SUMMARY   ■

1. An organization consists of people who have formally assigned roles and who must work together to achieve the organization's goals. Organizations needn't be just business firms.

2. Organizations cannot simply run themselves. Instead, they are run by managers. A manager is someone who plans, organizes, leads, and controls the people and the work of the organization in such a way that the organization achieves its goals.

3. Management writers traditionally refer to the manager's four basic functions of planning, organizing, leading, and controlling as the management process.

4. We can classify managers based on organizational level (top, middle, first line), position (executives, managers or directors, supervisors), and functional title (vice president of production, sales manager). All managers get their work done through people and by planning, organizing, lead-

ing, and controlling. Top managers spend more time planning and setting goals. Lower-level managers concentrate on implementing goals and getting employees to achieve them.

5. Managers play other roles too: for instance, figurehead, leader, liason. They also engage in entrepreneurial, competence-building, and renewal processes.

6. Almost everything a manager does involves interacting with and influencing people. The bottom line is that the leading, or people, side of what managers do is not just another step in the management process, but an integral part of the manager's job.

7. Managers and their organizations have to confront rapid change and intense competition today. Trends contributing to this change and unpredictability include technological innovation, globalization, deregulation, changing political systems, category killers, the new global workforce, more service-oriented jobs, and an emphasis on knowledge work.

8. Companies like ABB, Saturn, and Dell illustrate the new organization of the twenty-first century, in which responsiveness is a top priority and effective leadership is extraordinarily important.

TYING IT ALL TOGETHER ■

This section explains what managers do, and the trends (like globalization) that are forcing companies and other types of organizations to become more competitive. The fact that companies must be more competitive means that managers must organize and manage their companies to be faster and more efficient. In this text we'll see how they do that. First, in the next section, "Managing in a Global Environment," we'll look more closely at one of these trends—globalization—and its effect on how managers manage.

Skills and Study Materials

CRITICAL THINKING EXERCISES ■

1. The traditional organization is usually depicted as a pyramid-shaped hierarchy with authority and decision making flowing from the top down. As this section points out, the changing environment demands that new forms of organization be designed. Your assignment is to graphically depict some new organizational designs. Draw the shapes you think represent the boundaryless, team-focused, and process-oriented organizations that are evolving. Then write a brief narrative describing what you have drawn and what you think the implications behind your designs are.

2. In *The New New Thing: A Silicon Valley Story* (W. W. Norton & Co., 1999), Mike Lewis relates the contrasts that are likely to frame the next century. The story focuses on how two different and powerful firms are approaching their journey. Lewis argues that Jim Clark, the founder of Netscape, is the model for the future. Clark is seen as a genius "on an endless search for some unattainable solution." Clark has a talent for anarchy that well suits him at this juncture in history. In contrast, Microsoft's Bill Gates is characterized as someone who wants the future "to look exactly like the present." Lewis characterized Microsoft as a company that doesn't want to discover the new thing, but rather to tame it. Speculate on what management model you think will survive and why. Will it be the world of Jim Clark or the world of Bill Gates (assuming Lewis is right about both men)? Predict what the management process might involve by the year 2020.

E X P E R I E N T I A L   E X E R C I S E S   ■

1. The federal government sued Microsoft for its monopolistic tendencies. In fall 1999 a judge ruled that indeed Microsoft was a monopoly. There was talk of breaking up the company into three different entities. Not so long ago, the giant Microsoft was unconcerned about the regulatory role of the federal government. Then competitors as well as the government filed a number of lawsuits against it. Some analysts felt that Microsoft believed it was so large, powerful, and dominant that it would rule without interference from anyone. Neither the government nor rivals felt the same way. Now Microsoft has hired a battery of well-known and well-connected lobbyists. However, this action may be too little, too late. Is it too powerful? Is it a monopoly, and if so, is it good for the country to have such a monopoly? What if anything does the attitude of Microsoft say about its management?

2. An excellent way to find out about entrepreneurship is to talk to an entrepreneur. By asking your professor, other professors, the Small Business Administration in your region, or another small business organization such as the Small Business Chamber of Commerce, you should be able to identify an entrepreneur or entrepreneurs who have started a business in the past five years. Contact the person and conduct an informational interview. Some questions you might want to ask are: What did it take to establish the business? Did you have a business plan? Where did you get your financing? What management challenges do you face today? How did you develop your human resource policies? Also ask any other questions that specifically fit the type of business. Then prepare a page on the major points you found about entrepreneurship and be ready to present your findings in class or in a small group.

   You might want to do this project with two or three other students and divide the labor according to expertise.

   Use references like *Inc.* or *Fast Company* magazines that are devoted to entrepreneurship. These resources may help you find an entrepreneur or decide what questions you want to ask an entrepreneur.

FOUNDATIONS OF MODERN MANAGEMENT

Management existed even in antiquity. Hunters banded into tribes for protection; the Egyptians used organizations to build pyramids and control the rise and fall of the Nile; and the Romans relied on organizing to build their armies and control their empire. Management is thus a very old idea.

Some recurring themes become apparent when we view management over the ages. First, many of the concepts we take for granted today, such as dividing employees into departments, can be traced to the earliest human organizations, including those of the ancient Egyptians and Greeks. The close supervision and reliance on coercion and rules that management expert Peter Drucker called "command and control" is also a product of earlier times, in particular of the militaristic organizations of ancient Egypt and Rome.

Second, we will see that the forms organizations take and the ways managers manage have always been a product of the time. As futurist Alvin Toeffler says, in describing 19th-century management,

> Each age produces a form of organization appropriate to its own tempo. During the long epic of agricultural civilization, societies were marked by low transcience. Delays in communication and transportation slowed the rate at which information moved. The pace of individual life was comparatively slow. And organizations were seldom called upon to make what we would regard as high-speed decisions.[1]

So management is also an evolutionary process. Let us now look back to the beginning of modern management theory.

▶ CLASSICAL AND SCIENTIFIC MANAGEMENT

Management theory as we know it today is an outgrowth of the first attempts to view the management process with a new, more scientific rigor.

The Industrial Revolution

By 1750, with the advent of the Industrial Revolution, what Toeffler referred to as "the long epic of agricultural civilization" was about to end. The Industrial Revolution was a period of several decades during which machine power was increasingly substituted for human or animal labor. During these years several major trends converged. Scientific and technological discoveries, including the invention of the steam engine and the use of electricity, contributed to enormous increases in productivity and output. England, generally recognized as the epicenter of the Industrial Revolution, had a stable, constitutional government, a sensitivity to laissez-faire (hands-off) economics, and a strong spirit of self-reliance. In his book *The Wealth of Nations*, Adam Smith described the division and specialization of work—giving each worker a specialized job—as essential for efficiency and competitiveness.[2]

The Industrial Environment

For firms in the 1800s industrialization therefore meant resource accumulation and company growth. Division of work and specialization required the high volume and stability that only growth could bring. Growth led to higher profits; as sales, volume, and stability increased, efficiency went up and unit costs decreased.

But bigger operations created new problems for entrepreneurs. They needed management techniques to run their new, large-scale enterprises. Where would they learn how to manage large enterprises? These industrialists quickly adopted the structures and principles nurtured in military and religious organizations for thousands of years, such as centralized decision making, a rigid chain of command, specialized division of work, and autocratic leadership.

Frederick Winslow Taylor and Scientific Management

The race to grow and accumulate resources was particularly pronounced in the United States. The War of 1812 severed the United States from England economically and spurred the growth of domestic manufacturing operations. Technological advances included the steamboat, the cotton gin, the iron plow, the telegraph, the electric motor, and the expansion of a railroad and canal network that opened new markets for producers. In turn, these new markets provided the volume that was a basic requirement for effective division of work.

Historian Alfred Chandler pointed out that by the late 1800s many new industries were completing the resource-accumulation stage of their existence and beginning to move into what he calls a "rationalization stage."[3] The management focus shifted from growth to efficiency. As organizations became large and unwieldy, and as competition became more intense, managers needed better ways to utilize the resources they had accumulated. They sought new concepts and techniques to cut costs and boost efficiency. It was out of this environment that the classical school of management emerged.

Frederick Winslow Taylor was among the first of what historians today call the classical management writers; he developed a set of principles that became known as *scientific management*. Taylor's basic theme was that managers should study work scientifically to identify the "one best way" to get the job done. His framework for scientific management was based on four principles:

1. The "one best way." Management, through observation and "the deliberate gathering . . . of all the great mass of traditional knowledge, which in the past has been in the heads of the workmen," finds the "one best way" for performing each job.

2. Scientific selection of personnel. This principle requires "the scientific selection and then the progressive development of the workmen." Management must uncover each worker's limitation, find his or her "possibility for development," and give each worker the required training.

3. Financial incentives. Taylor knew that putting the right worker on the right job would not by itself ensure high productivity. Some plan for motivating workers to do their best and to comply with their supervisors' instructions was also required. Taylor proposed a system of financial incentives, in which each worker was paid in direct proportion to how much he or she produced, instead of according to a basic hourly wage.

4. Functional foremanship. Taylor called for a division of work between manager and worker such that managers did all planning, preparing, and inspecting, and the workers did the actual work. Specialized experts, or functional foremen, would be responsible for specific aspects of a task, such as choosing the best machine speed, determining job priorities, and inspecting the work. The

worker was to take orders from each of these foremen, depending on what part of the task was concerned.[4]

Frank and Lillian Gilbreth and Motion Study

The work of the husband-and-wife team Frank and Lillian Gilbreth also exemplifies the techniques and points of view of the scientific management approach. Born in 1868, Frank Gilbreth passed up an opportunity to attend MIT, deciding instead to enter the contracting business. He began as an apprentice bricklayer and became intrigued by the idea of improving efficiency. By carefully studying workers' motions, he developed innovations—for instance, in the way bricks were stacked, in the way they were laid, and in the number of motions used—that nearly tripled the average bricklayer's efficiency.[5]

In 1904 Frank married Lillian, who had a background in psychology, and together they began to develop principles and practices to more scientifically analyze tasks. In addition to using stopwatches, these experts developed various tools, including motion-study principles, to assist in their quest for efficiency. They concluded, for example, that

1. The two hands should begin and complete their motions at the same time.

2. The two hands should not be idle at the same time except during rest periods.

3. Motions of the arms should be made at opposite and symmetrical directions and should be made simultaneously.[6]

Therbligs, another example of the tools used by the Gilbreths, were elemental motions such as searching, grabbing, holding, and transporting. (The Gilbreths created the term *therblig* by using their last name spelled backward and transposing the *th*.) *Micromotion study* was the process of taking motion pictures of a worker doing his or her job and then running the film forward and backward at different speeds so that details of the job could be examined. Used in conjunction with timing devices, micromotion study made it possible to determine precisely how long it took to complete each component activity of a task. Performance could then be improved by modifying or eliminating one or more of these components.

Henri Fayol and the Principles of Management

The work of Henri Fayol also illustrates the classical approach to management and work behavior. Fayol had been a manager with a French iron and steel firm for 30 years before writing his book *General and Industrial Management*. In it, Fayol said that managers performed five basic functions: planning, organizing, commanding, coordinating, and controlling.

He also outlined a list of management principles he had found useful during his years as a manager. Fayol's 14 principles are summarized here and include his famous principle of *unity of command*:

1. Division of work. The worker, always on the same part, and the manager, concerned always with the same matters, acquired ability, sureness, and accuracy, which increased their output.

2. Authority and responsibility. Authority is the right to give orders and the power to exact obedience. Distinction must be made between official authority, deriving from office, and personal authority, compounded of intelligence, experience, moral worth, and ability to lead.

3. Discipline. The best means of establishing and maintaining [discipline] are good superiors at all levels; agreements as clear and fair as possible; sanctions [penalties] judiciously applied.

4. Unity of command. For any action whatsoever, an employee should receive orders from one superior only.

5. Unity of direction. There should be one head and one plan for a group of activities serving the same objective.

6. Subordination of individual interests. In a business, the interests of one employee or group of employees should not prevail over those of the concern. Means of effecting it are firmness and good example on the part of superiors and agreements as far as is possible.

7. Remuneration of personnel. Remuneration should be fair and as far as possible afford satisfaction to both personnel and the firm.

8. Centralization. The question of centralization or decentralization is a simple question of proportion; it is a matter of finding the optimum degree for the particular concern. What appropriate share of initiative may be left to intermediaries depends on the personal character of the manager, on his moral worth, on the reliability of his subordinates, and also on the conditions of the business.

9. Scalar chain. The scalar chain is the chain of superiors ranging from the ultimate authority to the lowest ranks. It is an error to depart needlessly from the line of authority, but it is an even greater one to keep to it when detriment to the business ensues.

10. Order. For social order to prevail in a concern, there must be an appointed place for every employee, and every employee must be in his or her appointed place.

11. Equity. For the personnel to be encouraged to carry out its duties with all the devotion and loyalty of which it is capable, it must be treated with kindliness, and equity results from the combination of kindness and justice. Equity excludes neither forcefulness nor sternness.

12. Stability of tenure of personnel. Time is required for an employee to get used to new work and succeed in doing it well, always assuming that he possesses the requisite abilities. If, when he has gotten used to it, or before then, he is removed, he will not have had time to render worthwhile service.

13. Initiative. Thinking out a plan and ensuring its success is one of the keenest satisfactions for an intelligent person to experience. This power of thinking out and executing is what is called initiative. It represents a great source of strength for business.

14. Esprit de corps. "Union is strength." Harmony, union among the personnel of a concern, is a great strength in that concern. Effort, then, should be made to establish it.[7]

Max Weber and Bureaucratic Organization Theory

Max Weber was a contemporary of Taylor, Fayol, and the Gilbreths. His work, first published in Germany in 1921, provides further insight into the ideals of the classical management writers. But unlike most of these writers, Weber was not a practicing manager, but an intellectual. He was born in 1864 to a well-to-do family and studied law, history, economics, and philosophy at Heidelberg University.

During the 1920s Weber correctly predicted that the growth of the large-scale organization would require a more formal set of procedures for how to administer them. At the time, managers had few principles they could apply in managing organizations. He therefore created the idea of an ideal or "pure form" of organization, which he called *bureaucracy*. This term did not refer to red tape and inefficiency—bureaucracy, for Weber, was the most efficient form of organization. Weber described bureaucracy as having certain characteristics:

1. A well-defined hierarchy of authority.
2. A clear division of work.
3. A system of rules covering the rights and duties of position incumbents.
4. A system of procedures for dealing with the work situation.
5. Impersonality of interpersonal relationships.
6. Selection for employment, and promotion based on technical competence.[8]

Summary: The Classical Approach to Management

The classical approach to management generally focused on boosting efficiency. To Taylor, Fayol, Weber, and the Gilbreths, an efficiently designed job and organization were of prime importance. These writers therefore concentrated on developing analytical tools, techniques, and principles that would enable managers to create efficient organizations. Work behavior was not unimportant to the classical writers; they simply assumed its complexities away by arguing that financial incentives would ensure motivation. As a result, intentionally or not, the classicists left the impression that workers could be treated as givens in the system, as little more than appendages to their machines. "Design the most highly specialized and efficient job you can," assumed the classicist, and "plug in the worker, who will then do your bidding if the pay is right."

► THE BEHAVIORAL SCHOOL OF MANAGEMENT

In the 1920s and 1930s, many changes swept the United States, and indeed the world. Increasing numbers of people moved from farms to cities and thus became more dependent on each other for goods and services. Factories became more mechanized, and the jobs became more specialized and interdependent.[9] Government became more deeply involved in economic matters, and a number of lawsuits were filed to break up industrial monopolies. Social movements worked at giving women the right to vote, electing senators by direct popular vote, establishing a minimum wage, and encouraging trade unions. Even the literature of the period became more anti-individualistic, as people questioned whether a philosophy based on hard work, individualism, and maximizing profits—the building blocks of the classical management era—might actually have some drawbacks.

The Hawthorne Studies

In 1927 the Hawthorne studies began at the Chicago Hawthorne Plant of the Western Electric Company. They eventually added an entirely new perspective to the management of people at work. Three main sets of studies took place, one of which became known as the relay assembly test studies. A group of workers was isolated and studied as a series of changes was made, such as modifying the length of the workday and altering the morning and afternoon rest breaks. Researchers noted with some surprise that these changes did not greatly affect performance, underscoring their growing belief that performance depended on factors other than physical conditions or rate of pay.

The relay assembly test studies led the researchers to conclude that the social situations of the workers, not just the working conditions, influenced behavior and performance at work. The researchers discovered, for instance, that in countless ways, their observations had inadvertently made the workers feel they were special. The observer had changed the workers' situation by "his personal interest in the girls and their problems. He had always been sympathetically aware of their hopes and fears. He had granted them more and more privileges."[10]

The Hawthorne Effect   These results have been codified as the Hawthorne effect. This is what happens when the scientist, in the course of an investigation, inadvertently influences the participants so that it is not the scientist's intended changes that affect the subject's behavior, but the way the scientist acts. In the relay assembly test, for instance, the researchers wanted to schedule rest periods when they would be most advantageous. They therefore called a meeting during which they showed the workers their output curves and pointed out the low and high points of the day. "When asked at what times they would like to have their rest, they unanimously voted in favor of ten o'clock in the morning and two o'clock in the afternoon." Accordingly, the investigators agreed to schedule the rests at these times. In retrospect, however, the researchers concluded that the subsequent rise in employee morale and performance was due to more than just the rest breaks; it was also due to the fact that the researchers had involved the workers in the decision.

Hawthorne's Consequences   The Hawthorne studies were a turning point in the study of management. As the research became more widely known, managers and management experts began to recognize that human behavior at work is a complex and powerful force. The human relations movement, inspired by this realization, emphasized that workers were not just givens in the system, but had needs and desires that the organization and task had to accommodate.

Environment, Increased Diversity, and Change

Historian Alfred Chandler said that after accumulating and then rationalizing resources, managers traditionally moved to a third stage, in which they attempted to better utilize their organizational resources by developing new products and new markets—by diversifying. In the United States, movement into this third stage was hampered in the 1930s by the Depression. However, excess production capacity ultimately stimulated research and development. Coupled with the technological and managerial advancements that emerged in the years surrounding World War II, this excess capacity finally shifted most U.S. industries into Chandler's diversification stage.[11]

To understand evolving management theory, it is important to recognize that this period was characterized by differentiated, complex, and rapidly changing environments. Even before World War II, many firms had embarked on extensive research and development to develop new products. For example, at GE and Westinghouse, research and development activities resulted in the manufacture of plastics as well as a variety of other products based on electronics. The automobile companies had begun to produce airplane engines, electrical equipment, and household appliances. After the war, companies in the rubber industry—such as United States Rubber and BF Goodrich, which had concentrated on tire manufacturing—

entered into systematic research and development and began to market products such as latex, plastics, and flooring.

These changes in the business environment contributed to the development of management theory in several ways. First, the increased rate of change and novelty triggered by diversification meant that managers and management theorists could no longer view organizations as closed systems operating within predictable, unchanging environments.[12] Second, efficiency was no longer a manager's main concern. It was eclipsed by the drives to diversify and then to monitor the activities of previously unrelated companies. Third, the shift toward making organizations more responsive to their environments was characterized by a trend toward *decentralization*, which in essence meant letting lower-level employees make more of their own decisions. Decentralization required a new managerial philosophy: Allowing subordinates to do more problem solving and decision making meant that managers had to rely on their employees' self-control. This change, coming as it did just after Hawthorne's results were popularized, led to a new emphasis on participative, people-oriented leadership and a more behavioral approach to management.

Douglas McGregor: Theory X and Theory Y

The work of Douglas McGregor is a good example of this new approach. According to McGregor, the classical organization (with its highly specialized jobs, centralized decision making, and top-down communications) was not just a product of the need for more efficiency. It was a reflection of certain basic assumptions about human nature.[13] These assumptions, which McGregor somewhat arbitrarily classified as *Theory X*, held that most people dislike work and responsibility and prefer to be directed; that they are motivated not by the desire to do a good job, but simply by financial incentives; and that, therefore, most people must be closely supervised, controlled, and coerced into achieving organizational objectives.

McGregor questioned the truth of this view and asked whether traditional management practices were appropriate for the tasks faced by more modern organizations. He felt that management needed new organizations and practices to deal with diversification, decentralization, and participative decision making. These new practices had to be based on a revised set of assumptions about the nature of human beings, which McGregor called *Theory Y*. Theory Y held that people could enjoy work and that an individual would exercise substantial self-control over performance if the conditions were favorable. Implicit in Theory Y is the belief that people are motivated by the desire to do a good job and by the opportunity to affiliate with their peers, rather than just by financial rewards.

Rensis Likert and the Employee-Centered Organization

What new management procedures are called for? Researcher Rensis Likert's work is an example of trends in management theory during the postwar years. Likert concluded that effective organizations differ from ineffective ones in several ways. Less effective job-centered companies focus on specialized jobs, efficiency, and close supervision of workers. More effective organizations, on the other hand, "focus their primary attention on endeavoring to build effective work groups with high performance goals."[14] As Likert noted, in these employee-centered companies

> the leadership and other processes of the organizations must be such as to insure a maximum probability that in all interactions and all relationships with the organization, each member will, in the light of his background,

values and expectations, view the experience as supportive and one which builds and maintains his sense of personal worth and importance.[15]

Chris Argyris and the Mature Individual

Chris Argyris reached similar conclusions, but approached the problem from a different perspective.[16] Argyris argued that healthy people go through a maturation process. As they approach adulthood, they move to a state of increased activity, greater independence, and stronger interests, and they pass from the subordinate position of a child to an equal or superordinate position as an adult. Gaining employees' compliance by assigning them to highly specialized jobs with no decision-making power and then closely supervising them inhibits normal maturation by encouraging workers to be dependent, passive, and subordinate. It would be better to give workers more responsibility and broader jobs.

The Behavioralist Prescriptions

Behavioral scientists such as Argyris, McGregor, and Likert soon translated their ideas into practical methodologies that became the heart of the emerging field of organizational behavior. Likert emphasized leadership style and group processes. "The low-producing managers, in keeping with the traditional practice, feel that the way to motivate and direct behavior is to exercise control through authority."[17] In contrast, "the highest-producing managers feel, generally, that this manner of functioning does not produce the best results, that the resentment created by direct exercise of authority tends to limit its effectiveness."[18] Therefore, said Likert, "widespread use of participation is one of the more important approaches employed by the high-producing managers."[19] He found that the value of participation applied to all aspects of the job and of work, "as, for example, in setting work goals and budgets, controlling costs, organizing the work, etc."[20]

McGregor had his own prescriptions. He said decentralization and pushing decision making down the company hierarchy should be the norm in order to free people from the "too-close control of conventional organization." Management should encourage job enlargement (in which the variety of tasks an employee performs is increased), so that workers' jobs are made more challenging and more interesting. Participative management (which McGregor said would give employees some voice in decisions that affect them) would similarly enhance self-control. Finally, McGregor urged using management by objectives, in which subordinates set goals with their supervisors and are measured on the accomplishment of these goals, thus avoiding the need for close day-to-day supervision.

Bridging the Eras: Chester Barnard and Herbert Simon

The work of Chester Barnard and Herbert Simon does not fit neatly into any one school of management theory. Their research actually spanned several schools and contributed to the development of an integrated theory of management.

The Zone of Indifference Chester Barnard used his experience as an executive to develop an important new management theory. He was the president of New Jersey Bell Telephone Company and, at various times, president of the United States Organization (the USO of World War II), president of the Rockefeller Foundation, and chair of the National Science Foundation.

Barnard was the first major theorist after the Hawthorne studies to emphasize the importance and variability of the individual in the workplace. He said, for example, that "an essential element of organizations is the willingness of persons to contribute their individual efforts to the cooperative system." He added that "the individual is always the basic strategic factor in organization. Regardless of his history or obligations, he must be induced to cooperate, or there can be no cooperation."

Barnard set about developing a theory of how to get workers to cooperate. How do you get the individuals to surrender their personal preferences and to go along with the authority exercised by supervisors?[21] He believed the answer could be found in what he called the person's *zone of indifference*, a range within each individual in which he or she would willingly accept orders without consciously questioning their legitimacy.[22] Barnard saw willingness to cooperate as an expression of the net satisfactions or dissatisfactions experienced or anticipated by each person. In other words, organizations had to provide sufficient inducements to broaden each employee's zone of indifference and thus increase the likelihood that orders would be obeyed.

But Barnard, in a clear break with the classicists, said that material incentives by themselves were not enough: "The unaided power of material incentives, when the minimum necessities are satisfied, in my opinion, is exceedingly limited as to most men."[23] Several other classes of incentives, including "the opportunities for distinction, prestige, [and] personal power" are also required.

Gaining Compliance   Whereas Barnard wrote from the vantage point of an executive, Herbert Simon was a scholar who had mastered organization theory, economics, natural science, and political science, and who went on to win the Nobel Prize in economics. Like Barnard, Simon viewed getting employees to do what the organization needed them to do as a major issue facing managers. He proposed two basic ways to gain such compliance, which can be paraphrased as follows:

> Decisions reached in the highest ranks of the organization hierarchy will have no effect upon the activities of operative employees unless they are communicated downward. Consideration of the process requires an examination of the ways in which the behavior of the operative employee can be influenced. These influences fall roughly into two categories:
>
> First, the manager can establish in the employee him- or herself the attitudes, habits and state of mind that lead him or her to reach the decision that is advantageous to the organization. In other words, the manager somehow gets the worker to want to do the job. Or, second, the manager can impose upon the employee decisions reached elsewhere in the organization, for instance by closely supervising everything the person does.[24]

Therefore, according to Simon, managers can ensure that employees carry out tasks in one of two ways. They can impose control by closely monitoring subordinates and insisting that they do their jobs as they have been ordered (using the classicists command and control approach). Or managers can foster employee self-control by providing better training, encouraging participative leadership, and developing commitment and loyalty. As rapid change forced employers to depend more and more on employee initiative, developing such self-control became a major theme in management writings.

▶ THE QUANTITATIVE SCHOOL

After World War II, management theorists also began to apply quantitative techniques to a wide range of problems. This movement is usually referred to as *operations research* or *management science* and has been described as "the application of scientific methods, techniques, and tools to problems involving the operations of systems so as to provide those in control of the system with optimum solutions to the problems."[25]

The Management Science Approach

Management science has three distinguishing characteristics. First, management scientists generally deal with well-defined problems that have clear and undisputable standards of effectiveness. They want to know, for instance, whether inventory costs have been too high and should be reduced by 20% or whether a specific number of items should be produced at each of a company's plants to minimize transportation costs to customers.

Second, management scientists generally deal with problems that have well-defined alternative courses of action. A company might have four different plants from which to ship products, or various levels of Product A and Product B that can be produced to maximize sales revenues. The management scientist's task is to recommend a solution. Finally, management scientists must develop a theory or model describing how the relevant factors are related. Like any scientist, management scientists must understand the problem and relationships clearly enough to formulate a mathematical model.

Historian Daniel Wren points out that operations research/management science has "direct lineal roots in scientific management."[26] Like Taylor and the Gilbreths, today's management scientists try to find optimal solutions to problems. As Taylor and his colleagues used scientific methods to find the one best way to do a job, management scientists used the scientific method to find the best solution to industrial problems. The difference in the two approaches is twofold. First, modern-day management scientists have at their disposal much more sophisticated mathematical tools and computers. Second, management science's goal is not to try to find a science of management so much as it is to use scientific analysis and tools to solve management problems.

The Systems Approach

The management science approach is closely associated with what is called the *systems approach* to management. A *system* is an entity—a hospital, city, company, or person, for instance—that has interdependent parts and a purpose. Systems approach advocates argue that viewing an organization as a system helps managers to remember that a firm's different parts, departments, or subsystems are interrelated and that all must contribute to the organization's purpose.

According to systems approach advocates such as C. West Churchman, all systems have four basic characteristics.[27] First, they operate within an environment, which is defined as those things outside of and important to the organization but largely beyond its control. For a company these include clients, competitors, unions, and governments.

Second, all systems are composed of building blocks called elements, components, or subsystems. In an organization, these basic building blocks might be departments, like those for production, finance, and sales. The subsystems may also cut across traditional departmental lines. For example, the marketing subsystem might include sales, advertising, and transportation, because each of these elements has an impact on the task of getting the product to the customer.

Third, all systems have a central purpose against which the organization's efforts and subsystems can be evaluated. For example, the optimal inventory level for a firm that serves top-of-the-line customers would probably be higher than for a firm whose customers want the best buy in town and are willing to wait for shelves to be restocked.

Fourth, focusing on the interrelatedness among the subsystems (and between the subsystems and the firm's environment) is an essential aspect of systems thinking. Interrelatedness emphasizes the fact that a manager can't change one subsystem without affecting the rest; hiring a new production manager might have repercussions in the sales and accounting departments, for instance. Similarly, managers and management theorists need to be sensitive to the way changes taking place in their environments, since they affect the organization and management of the firm.

▶ TOWARD A SITUATIONAL MANAGEMENT THEORY AND THE FUTURE

In the early 1960s, at about the same time the systems approach was popular, organizational research studies in England and the United States began to underscore the need for a situational or contingency view of management. This was one in which the appropriateness of the organization and its management principles were contingent on the rate of change in an organization's environment and technology. In one such study, Tom Burns and G. M. Stalker analyzed a number of industrial firms in England. They concluded that whether what they called a "mechanistic" or an "organic" management system was appropriate depended on the nature of the organization's environment.

Burns and Stalker argued that a *mechanistic management system* was appropriate if the company's tasks were routine and unchanging. Thus, in a textile mill they studied, it was important to have long, stable production runs that kept surprises to a minimum and thereby prevented the necessity of shutting down huge machines. In such unchanging conditions, Burns and Stalker found that a mechanistic (or classical) management approach—characterized by an emphasis on efficiency, specialized jobs, elaborate procedures for keeping behavior in line, and an insistence that everyone play by the rules—was appropriate.

On the other hand, Burns and Stalker found that the more behavioral *organic management system* was appropriate if innovative, entrepreneurial activities were important. In high-tech electronics firms, for instance, companies and their employees are constantly under pressure to come up with new devices. Burns and Stalker found that management often ran such firms with an approach that emphasized creativity rather than efficiency. These firms placed less emphasis on specialized jobs and issued fewer rules and procedures. Instead, they delegated decisions to employees who then exercised self-control in getting their jobs done.

Also in England, Joan Woodward and researchers from the Tavistock Institute analyzed a group of firms to discover the relationship between an organization and its production technology. The organic, flexible system described by Burns and Stalker again appeared to be more appropriate where dealing with unexpected, unpredictable occurrences was of paramount concern. Thus it was used in small job shops, and in large factories that were built to run continuously and in which unexpected breakdowns were a great concern. Woodward and her team found that the mechanistic, classical approach was appropriate where predictability and efficiency were paramount, such as where mass production technologies and assembly lines were utilized.[28] These findings and others like them culminated in what came to be called a situational, or contingency, approach to management theory.

On to the Future The history of management thought certainly doesn't stop with the situational theorists, as you can imagine. Writing mostly in the 1960s, what the situational theorists did was to provide a theoretical framework that allowed management writers and practitioners to focus on the relationship between the management system and the nature of the task, and in particular on how the increasingly rapid changes brought on by technological advances and globalization would have to be managed by organizations. More recently, theorists and researchers have added to our store of knowledge regarding how managers plan, organize, lead, and control their organizations under highly competitive conditions and in the face of rapid change. However, their findings are not so much a matter of history as they are a road map of things as they are today and how they will be. The following sections are built on these modern findings.

MANAGING IN A GLOBAL ENVIRONMENT

WHAT'S AHEAD?

Customers shopping in Wal-Mart's new store in Frankfurt, Germany, were in for a big surprise. For one thing, the changes Wal-Mart had made since buying the Wertkauf chain just a year before were astonishing. In remaking the stores to fit Wal-Mart's low-price, customer-friendly image, aisles had been widened, prices reduced, and "the employees are a lot more polite than they used to be," says one shopper.[1] Wal-Mart's German competitors have gotten the message: They're already working hard to remake their own stores and management systems. Meanwhile Wal-Mart, which only began "going global" a few years ago, must grapple with the challenge of managing operations that are far removed both geographically and culturally from Benton, Arkansas.

THIS SECTION FOCUSES ON THE FOLLOWING:

- Why companies expand operations abroad and discuss strategies for expanding abroad, such as exporting and licensing

- The economic, legal, political, sociocultural, and technological factors that influence a manager's decision to expand abroad

- How going global affects the business team in the global business

- How doing business internationally affects how managers plan, organize, lead, and control

The Language of International Business

Once the manager decides to do business abroad, he or she must become familiar with the basic vocabulary of international business. An **international business** is any firm that engages in international trade or investment.[2] International business also refers to those activities, such as exporting goods or transferring employees, that require the movement of resources, goods, services, and skills across national boundaries.[3] **International trade** refers to the export or import of goods or services to consumers in another country. **International management** is the performance of the management functions of planning, organizing, leading, and controlling across national borders. As Wal-Mart managers expand abroad, for instance, they necessarily engage in international management.

The multinational corporation is one type of international business. A **multinational corporation (MNC)** is an international business that is controlled by a parent corporation and owned and managed essentially by the nationals of the firm's home country. An MNC operates manufacturing and marketing facilities in two or more countries; these operations are coordinated by a parent firm, whose owners are mostly based in the firm's home country. Firms like GE and GM have long been multinational corporations. However, thousands of small firms, like KnitMedia, are now MNCs, too.

Some experts say that the MNC is slowly being displaced by a special multinational enterprise called the global (or transnational) corporation. The MNC operates in a number of countries and adjusts its products and practices to each. The **global corporation**, on the other hand, operates as if the entire world (or major regions of it) were a single entity. Global corporations sell essentially the same things in the same way everywhere. Thus a global corporation such as Sony sells a standardized Walkman around the world, with components made in or designed in different countries.[4] Ikea's furniture is much the same the world over. Coke tastes the same everywhere, and Chanel and Lanvin sell the same products around the globe. However, global companies may still reflect their national roots.[5] For example, when the German firm DeutscheBank took over a British bank, the traditionally high incentive pay of the British managers created considerable tension between them and their new, lower-paid German bosses (tension that took some time to resolve).

▶ THE MANAGER IN AN INTERNATIONAL ENVIRONMENT

Going international or, certainly global, presents the manager with new and often perplexing problems. He or she must be adept at dealing with a wide range of economic, legal, political, sociocultural, and technological factors, since the manager's plans, organization, and incentives and controls will be molded by them.

The Economic Environment

For example, managers doing business abroad need to be familiar with the economic systems of the countries in question, the level of each country's economic development, and exchange rates and economic integration.

The Economic System For one thing, countries still vary in the extent to which they adhere to a capitalistic economic system like America's. For example, consider the dilemma facing business managers in Hong Kong. In 1997 the People's Republic of China resumed governing Hong Kong. How did this affect Hong Kong's existing economic structure, and how did foreign firms react?

Hong Kong is an example of a market economy. In a pure market economy, the quantities and nature of the goods and services produced are not planned by anyone. Instead, the interaction of supply and demand in the market for goods and services determines what is produced, in what quantities, and at what prices.

At the other extreme, the People's Republic of China until recently was a pure command economy. In a command economy, central planning agencies try to determine how much is produced by which sectors of the economy, and by which plants and for whom it is produced. Countries like these usually base their yearly targets on five-year plans. They then establish specific production goals and prices for each sector of the economy (for each product or group of products) and for each manufacturing plant.

By agreement, China is to let Hong Kong keep its capitalist system for 50 years, and so far that generally seems to be going fairly smoothly. A shipping magnate, Tung Chee-hwa, was elected Hong Kong's first post-handover chief executive. However, Hong Kong's political administration is governed closely by Beijing, and Hong Kong's new legislature recently imposed limits on opposition activities and on the number of people eligible to vote. If the politicians start to pass laws that limit private ownership and free trade in any way, Hong Kong's capitalist system may be in for some rough sailing. Therefore, developing long-run management plans under such circumstances can be quite a challenge.

In a **mixed economy**, some sectors of an economy are left to private ownership and free market mechanisms, while others are largely owned by and managed by the government.[6] "Mixed" is, of course, a matter of degree. For example, France is basically a capitalist country, but is mixed to the extent that the government still owns shares of industries like telecommunications (France Telecom) and air travel (Air France).

Shifting economic systems can lead to social instability, as occurred in the newly capitalized Russia. Free-market economies require things like commercial laws, banking regulations, and an effective independent judiciary and law enforcement, without which business transactions are difficult. Without such a political and legal infrastructure in Russia, the first years of transition to a market economy there were especially turbulent for business managers: They had to cope not just with competitors, but with criminals, lax law enforcement, and the virtual control of several industries by friends of powerful politicians. Some experts warn of the possibility of similar turbulence in other developing economies including South Korea, Malaysia, and Vietnam.[7] Managers taking their firms into such areas therefore must be concerned, not just with the economic system, but with the turbulence caused as the country moves from a command economy to a capitalist one.

Economic Development Countries also differ dramatically in levels and rates of economic development. For example, some countries—the United States, Japan, Germany, France, Italy, and Canada, for instance—have large, mature, well-established economies with extensive industrial infrastructures (industry, telecommunications, transportation, and regulatory and judicial systems, for instance). Their **gross domestic product** (the market value of all goods and services that have been bought for final use during a period of time, and therefore the basic measure of a nation's economic activity) ranges from about $700 billion for Canada, to $1.0 trillion for France, $1.5 trillion for Germany, almost $3 trillion for Japan, and $7.5 trillion for the United States.[8]

However, some countries are growing much faster than others. For example, the growth rate of mature economies like those above generally averages around 4% per year. On the other hand, China, India, and Taiwan are generally growing at just over 7.5%, 5.0%, and 5.2%, respectively. Many multinationals are therefore boosting their investments in these high-growth (and thus high-potential) countries.[9]

Exchange Rates Managers engaged in international business must also juggle exchange rates. The **exchange rate** for one country's currency is the rate at which it can be exchanged for another country's currency. In July 1999, one Brazilian real was worth about $0.56 in U.S. currency. Similarly, a French franc was worth about $0.16. Exchange rates can have a big impact on a company's performance. A dramatic drop in the value of the dollar relative to the pound could have a devastating effect on a small U.S. company that suddenly found it needed 30% more dollars to build a factory in Scotland than it had planned.

Economic Integration and Free Trade The existence of "free trade" agreements among some countries is a big part of the economic environment facing managers. **Free trade** means that all trade barriers among participating countries are removed.[10] Free trade occurs when two or more countries sign an agreement to allow free flow of goods and services, unimpeded by trade barriers such as **tariffs** (special governmental taxes on imports which boost the costs of international trade). **Economic integration** occurs when two or more nations obtain the advantages of free trade by minimizing trade restrictions between them.

Economic integration occurs on several levels. In a **free trade area**, all barriers to trade among member countries are removed, so that goods and services are freely traded among member countries. A **customs union** is the next higher level of economic integration. Here members dismantle trade barriers among themselves while establishing a common trade policy with respect to nonmembers. In a **common market**, no barriers to trade exist among members, and a common external trade policy is in force; in addition, factors of production, such as labor, capital, and technology, move freely between member countries, as in Figure 1-4.

Economic integration is taking place around the world. In 1957 the European Economic Community (now called the European Union, or EU) was established by founding members France, West Germany, Italy, Belgium, the Netherlands, and Luxembourg (Figure 1-5). Their agreement, the Treaty of Rome, called for the formation of a free trade area, the gradual elimination of tariffs and other barriers to trade, and the formation of a customs union and (eventually) a common market. By 1987 the renamed European Community had added six other countries (Great Britain, Ireland, Denmark, Greece, Spain, and Portugal) and signed the Single Europe Act. This act "envisages a true common market where goods, people, and money move among the twelve EC countries with the same ease that they move between Wisconsin and Illinois."[11] Austria, Finland, and Sweden joined in 1995, and several more countries are preparing to join in the years ahead.

In Asia, the Association of Southeast Asian Nations (ASEAN) was organized in 1967 (Figure 1-6). It includes Brunei, Indonesia, Malaysia, the Philippines, Singapore, Thailand, and Vietnam. These countries are cooperating in reducing tariffs

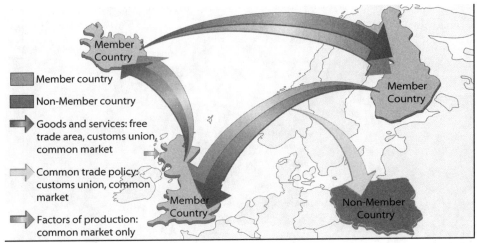

◄ **FIGURE 1-4**
Levels of Economic Integration

Member country

Non-Member country

Goods and services: free trade area, customs union, common market

Common trade policy: customs union, common market

Factors of production: common market only

and in attempting to liberalize trade, although the results at this point have been limited.[12] Asia also formed the Asia Pacific Economic Cooperation (APEC) forum, which is a loose association of 18 Pacific Rim states that aims to facilitate freer trade in its region. Members include Australia, Chile, China, Japan, Malaysia, Mexico, Singapore, and the United States.[13]

Canada, the United States, and Mexico have together reestablished a North American Free Trade Agreement (NAFTA; see Figure 1-7). NAFTA creates the world's largest free trade market, with a total output of about $6 trillion.

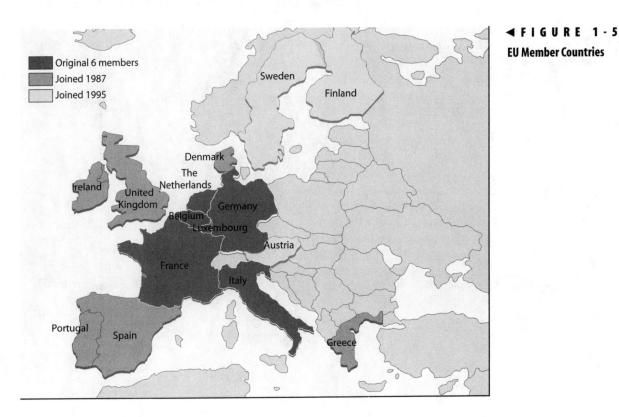

◄ **FIGURE 1-5**
EU Member Countries

Original 6 members

Joined 1987

Joined 1995

► F I G U R E   1 - 6
ASEAN Member Countries

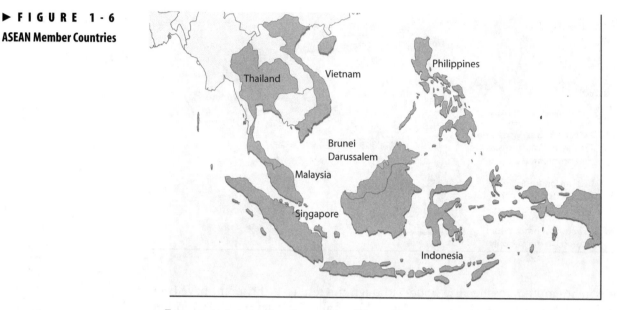

Economic integration has a big effect on company managers. For one thing, it vastly increases the level of competition. In Europe today, for instance, airlines and telecommunication firms that once had little or no outside competition face new competitors from similar firms within their trading blocs. However, it can also, of course, let more effective companies expand into new markets. Some fear that the EU's existence will lead to a "fortress Europe to which non-EU firms will find it increasingly difficult to export goods."[14] Many U.S. managers are therefore entering joint ventures with European partners, to establish local beachheads from which to sell throughout the EU.

► F I G U R E   1 - 7
NAFTA Member Countries

The Political and Legal Environment

International managers also must consider the legal and political environments of the countries in which they do business. Consider the uneven playing field between Japan and the United States, for example. A Chrysler LeBaron sells for $18,176 in the United States, but for $33,077 in Japan.[15] How could this be?

Trade Barriers   The answer is that trade barriers can dramatically distort the prices companies must charge for their products. **Trade barriers** are governmental influences usually aimed at reducing the competitiveness of imported products or services. Tariffs, the most common trade barrier, are governmental taxes levied on goods shipped internationally.[16] The exporting country collects export tariffs, the importing country collects import tariffs, and the country through which the goods are passed collects transit tariffs.

A multitude of nontariff trade barriers exist too. For example, in addition to the fact that Japan sets high automobile import tariffs, cars not made in Japan must meet a complex set of regulations and equipment modifications. Side mirrors must snap off easily if they come into contact with a pedestrian, for example. And any manufacturer selling 1,000 or fewer cars of a particular model annually must test each car individually for gas mileage and emission standards.

Some countries make direct payments to domestic producers. These are called **subsidies**, and they can make an otherwise inefficient producer more cost competitive. Other countries impose **quotas**—legal restrictions on the import of particular goods—as further barriers to trade.[17]

Political Risks   The international manager must be concerned not just with governmental influences on trade, but with political risks as well. For example, companies doing business in Peru must be vigilant against terrorist attacks. In 1999 ethnic violence in the former Yugoslavia brought economic activities for many companies exporting to that area to a standstill.[18] Similarly, racial strife in South Africa, civil unrest in Ireland, and religious attacks in Egypt and Israel make doing business in these areas more difficult than it would otherwise be, and obviously influence how managers run their businesses.

Legal Systems   There are also important differences in legal systems. Many countries adhere to a system known as common law, which is based on tradition and depends more on precedent and custom than on written statutes. England and the United States are examples of countries that use common law.

Other countries have a code law system, or a comprehensive set of written statutes. Some countries use a combination of common law and code law. For example, the United States adheres to a system of common law in many areas, but to a written Uniform Commercial Code for governing business activities.

International laws and agreements can also affect a manager's strategy, as the "Entrepreneurs in Action" box shows. International law is not so much an enforceable body of law as it is agreements embodied in treaties and other types of agreements. For example, international law governs intellectual property rights (such as whether KnitMedia's music can be reproduced in Japan without its permission).

Among other things, legal issues influence the strategy a manager uses to expand abroad.[19] For example, joint venture laws vary. In India, for instance, a foreign investor may own only up to 40% of an Indian industrial company, while in Japan up to 100% of foreign ownership is allowed.[20] Some managers go global by appointing sales agents or representatives in other countries. But in some countries that's not legally an option. In Algeria, for instance, agents are not permitted to represent foreign sellers, and in other countries agents are viewed as employees subject to those countries' employment laws.[21]

The Sociocultural Environment

Managers who travel to other countries quickly learn they must also adapt to cultural differences. In Latin America, for instance, *machismo* ("maleness") is defined as virility, zest for action, daring, competitiveness, and the will to conquer. This is translated into business life by demonstrating forcefulness, self-confidence, courage, and leadership.[22] In Japan, saving face and achieving harmony are very important. Indirect and vague communication is therefore preferred, with sentences frequently left unfinished so the other person may draw his or her own conclusions. The people of Saudi Arabia, it is said, love the spoken word and tend not to get to the point quickly. This can frustrate U.S. managers, who must be careful not to show impatience or annoyance. In France, a firm and pumping handshake may be considered uncultured; instead, a quick shake with some pressure on the grip is more appropriate.

Entrepreneurs in Action

The Global Positioning System Meets an International Roadblock

▶ When he paid Hewlett-Packard $80,000 for the remains of a canceled engineering project back in 1982, Charlie Trimble never thought the business he was starting would be involved in an international incident. What he bought—shelves of research notes, and a circuit board that could pick up a signal from the first of what would soon be a ring of 24 military satellites orbiting the globe—were the rights to commercialize what would become the global positioning system.

As most people know by now, when a global positioning system (GPS) receiver picks up satellite signals, it calculates its position based on its distance from 8 satellites. With one of these handheld systems, someone can now almost instantaneously determine his or her location to within 20 or 30 feet, anywhere on the globe. GPS receivers are now used worldwide not only by sea captains and hikers keeping track of their locations, but by naturalists tracking wild goats in the Galapagos Islands and scientists measuring movements atop Mount Everest.

There was a time, though, when it looked like GPS would never be a worldwide system (although it would have been ironic to have something called a global positioning system that couldn't be used in vast areas of the globe). The technology was developed by the United States Department of Defense, which in fact still maintains and controls the satellites. The problem was that many foreign users, both governmental and private, didn't want to be at the mercy of the U.S. government when it came to critical positioning and navigating information. The problem almost torpedoed the use of the GPS system abroad when 47 member countries of the International Telecommunications Union (including Britain, Germany, France, Italy, Japan, Korea, and Mexico), voted to take a big part of the radio spectrum used by the GPS satellites and use it for mobile phones instead. Only the direct intervention of NATO's commander at the time, General Wesley Clark, convinced the ITU that it should back off, and let the GPS system be used worldwide.

Today, it's still not all clear sailing for Charlie Trimble. The market for the GPS devices never took off the way he thought it would, and he was recently removed as CEO of the company he founded by his own Board of Directors because of disappointing sales. However, like a true entrepreneur, Trimble is still dedicated to the eventual success of GPS, especially since, having overcome cultural and political resistance from abroad, the system can now be used worldwide.

Source: Claire Tristram, "Has GPS Lost Its Way?" *Technology Review*, July–August 1999, pp. 78–75.

Cross-Cultural Challenges: An Example   Cultural differences can have very practical consequences, such as affecting how disagreements are resolved. Consider the challenge of negotiating with people abroad. A researcher at Georgetown University found that Japanese, German, and U.S. managers tended to use very different approaches when resolving workplace conflict.[23] The Japanese prefer the power approach, tending to defer to the party with the most power. Germans tend to emphasize a more legalistic, "sticking to the rules" approach. U.S. managers tend to try to take all parties' interests into account and to work out a solution that maximizes the benefits for everyone.

Such "cross-cultural differences may complicate life for expatriate managers who find themselves trying to manage conflict in a foreign cultural system."[24] For example, American managers may be shocked to learn that those from other countries aren't so interested in finding solutions that benefit everyone. They may also become upset at endlessly discussing bureaucratic regulations and practices (which Germans did significantly more than U.S. managers).

Values   Research by Geert Hofstede shows that a society's values are among the most influential of cultural differences. **Values** are basic beliefs we hold about what is good or bad, important or unimportant. Values (such as West Point's famous "duty, honor, country") are important because they shape the way we behave. Hofstede says that different societies reflect four basic values as follows:

- *Power distance.*[25] *Power distance* is the extent to which the less powerful members of institutions accept and expect that power will be distributed unequally.[26] Hofstede concluded that the institutionalization of such an inequality was higher in some countries (such as Mexico) than it was in others (such as Sweden).

- *Individualism versus collectivism.* The degree to which ties between individuals are normally loose or close is measured as individualism or collectivism. In more individualistic countries, "all members are expected to look after themselves and their immediate families."[27] Individualistic counties include Australia and the United States. In collectivist countries, people are expected to care for each other more; Indonesia and Pakistan are examples.

- *Masculinity versus femininity.* According to Hofstede, societies differ also in the extent to which they value assertiveness (which he called "masculinity") or caring ("femininity"). Japan and Austria ranked high in masculinity; Denmark, Costa Rica, and Chile ranked low.

- *Uncertainty avoidance.* Uncertainty avoidance refers to whether people in the society are uncomfortable with unstructured situations in which unknown, surprising, novel incidents occur. In other words, how comfortable are people in a society when it comes to dealing with surprises? People in some countries (such as Sweden, Israel, and Great Britain), according to Hofstede, are relatively comfortable dealing with uncertainty and surprises. People living in other countries (including Greece and Portugal) tend to be uncertainty avoiders.[28]

Differences in values manifest themselves in very real ways. In Russia, for instance, changing occupations, being unemployed, or looking for work is rare (or at least it was, until quite recently). Workers therefore try exceptionally hard to avoid being out of work: "Even an indefinite paid leave is accepted by employees hoping to return later."[29] Differences in values also manifest themselves in different working conditions. While child labor and even work produced by prisoners is much less common today, long hours and low pay are still widespread in many

Asian factories. One recent report referred to "sweatshop Barbie" in describing conditions at one Asian plant of a Mattel subcontractor.[30]

Language and Customs   The international manager must also deal with differences in language. For example, one airline's "Fly in Leather" slogan was embarrassingly translated as "Fly Naked" for the company's Latin American campaign.[31] A country's traditional manners and customs can also be important. Campbell's, for instance, learned that Japanese drink soup mainly for breakfast. A country's predominant religions, cultural orientations (such as styles of music and art), and educational processes can all influence the manner in which business should be conducted in that country. In the United States or Japan, inviting a businessperson out for an alcoholic drink is sometimes done, for instance, whereas in Saudi Arabia such an invitation might be shocking.

The Technological Environment

A country's technological environment—such as the relative ease with which technology can be transferred from one country to another—can determine a product's success abroad. **Technology transfer** is the "transfer of systematic knowledge for the manufacture of a product, for the application of a process, or for the rendering of a service, and does not extend to the mere sale or lease of goods."[32]

Successful technology transfer depends on several things. First, there must be a suitable technology to be transferred—for instance, pollution filter devices. Second, social and economic conditions must favor the transfer. Pollution-reducing technology might be economically useless in a country where pollution reduction is not a priority. Finally, technology transfer depends on the willingness and ability of the receiving party to use and adapt the technology.[33] If using the pollution control filters requires chemical engineers to whom the receiving country has no access, the technology transfer might be impossible. Similarly, opening a new plant, or franchising a process, requires an acceptable level of technical expertise on the receiving country's end. If this is absent, the expansion into this country may well fail.

▶ THE MANAGEMENT TEAM IN A GLOBAL BUSINESS

In most companies today, most managers are attached to specific functional departments or teams, such as production, marketing, finance, or human resources. Managing in a global business creates some special challenges in that regard. Managers in each function must analyze how best to manage their functions abroad, while working together with the other teams to make sure they achieve overall company goals. We'll look next at some examples.

Global Marketing

Marketing abroad is often a necessity today. As one expert says, "Even the biggest companies in the biggest countries cannot survive on their domestic markets if they are in global industries. They must be in all major markets."[34]

Wal-Mart is a good example. Between 1998 and 1999 its total company sales rose by 16%, but its international sales jumped by 26%. In just the first quarter of 1999, it opened nine international units, including three in Mexico. As of April 30, 1999, Wal-Mart's international units included stores in Argentina (13 stores), Brazil (14), Canada (154), Germany (95), Mexico (423), and Puerto Rico (15), as well as units in China and Korea.[35] About 10%—or 135,000—of Wal-Mart's employees are outside the United States. Its Web site (www.wal-mart.com) is a good example of how giants like Wal-Mart (or tiny companies, for that matter), can market their products or services globally, often without ever leaving their home countries.

Expanding sales abroad confronts the marketing manager with several challenges. For example, plans for the move must take local tastes into consideration. While it's true that for many products the tastes and preferences of consumers in different nations are beginning to converge on some global norm, the fact is that even global companies like McDonald's and the Gap (both of which tend to emphasize standardized products) need to fine-tune those products when they go abroad.[36] You won't find beef in McDonald's restaurants in India. And, you'll find several unusual products including sparkling water on sale at the McDonald's on the Champs Elysees.

Therefore, whether it's a giant firm like McDonald's or a smaller one like Knit-Media, considerable market research and analysis is required before the marketing plans for expanding overseas can be finalized. Similarly, incentive plans that work for salespeople in the United States may not work for the marketing manager's sales force in Argentina. She will also have to decide how to organize the sales effort abroad, particularly since she—while still in charge of overall company sales—will be many miles away.

Globalization of Production

Globalizing production means placing parts of a firm's production process in various locations around the globe. Thus the productions manager might place plants in France and Peru, and distribution warehouses in Germany and Brazil. One aim is to provide manufacturing and supply support for local markets abroad. Another is to take advantage of national differences in the cost and quality of production—it might be cheaper to produce certain items in Peru, for instance.

For many production managers, the overall aim today is to integrate their global operations into a unified and efficient system of manufacturing facilities around the world.[37] This can present a considerable challenge when it comes to managing the coordination of such an effort. Xerox Corporation's worldwide manufacturing system is an example. In the early 1980s, each Xerox company in each country had its own suppliers, assembly plants, and distribution channels. Each country's plant managers gave little thought to how their plans fit into Xerox's global needs. This approach became unworkable as international competition in the copier market grew more intense. Canon, Minolta, and Ricoh penetrated Xerox's U.S. and European markets with low-cost copiers.[38]

The competitive threat prompted Xerox's senior managers to coordinate their global production processes. They organized a new central purchasing group to consolidate raw materials purchases, and thereby cut worldwide manufacturing costs. They instituted a "leadership through quality" program to improve product quality, streamline and standardize manufacturing processes, and cut costs. Xerox managers also eliminated over $1 billion of inventory costs by installing a computer system that linked customer orders from one region more closely with production capabilities in other regions.

With the proper training and guidance, the production manager can develop and expand the role of his or her foreign facilities. Consider the story of the

Hewlett-Packard factory in Singapore. When originally built, its purpose was to produce simple labor-intensive components at low cost. Within several years it was upgraded to produce a complete, low-cost calculator. As the Singapore plant managers became more experienced at manufacturing complete products, they improved their ability to redesign products as well. By redesigning one calculator—the HP 41C—they cut production costs by 50%. By building on their new design capabilities, plant managers and engineers were gradually entrusted by Hewlett-Packard's U.S. headquarters with increasingly sophisticated assignments. Today, Singapore is Hewlett-Packard's global center for the design, development, and manufacture of portable printers for markets worldwide.[39]

Managing @ the Speed of Thought

Using the Internet as a Global Management Tool

Managing a global production operation is always a challenge: The distances involved are usually enormous, and it's easy for home-office managers to lose track of what's going on in the field, especially when the field is 8,000 miles away. If that happens, the benefits of efficiency sought by firms like Xerox and Hewlett-Packard in the examples above will not materialize.

Production managers today are therefore using the Internet to keep tabs on their global operations. Schlumberger Ltd. is a good example. Schlumberger, which manufactures oil-drilling equipment and electronics, has headquarters in New York and Paris. The company operates in 85 countries, and in most of them employees are in remote locations.[40] How do the company's managers maintain control over so many far-flung locations? Here's how experts describe the company's system:

> To install their own network for so few people at each remote location would have been prohibitively expensive. Using the Internet, Schlumberger engineers in Dubai (on the Persian Gulf) can check e-mail and effectively stay in close contact with management at a very low cost. In addition, the field staff is able to follow research projects as easily as can personnel within the United States. Schlumberger has found that since it converted to the Internet from its own network, its overall communications costs are down 2% despite a major increase in network and information technology infrastructure spending. The main reason for the savings is the dramatic drop in voice traffic and in overnight delivery service charges (they attach complete documents to their e-mail messages).[41] At Schlumberger, the Internet plays a central role in creating an efficient world-wide production system.

Global Staffing

Companies around the world are also tapping a vast new supply of skilled labor.[42] Thus, 3M makes tapes, chemicals, and electrical parts in Bangalore, India, and Hewlett-Packard assembles computers and designs memory boards in Guadalajara, Mexico. In Jamaica, 3,500 office workers make airline reservations, process tickets, and handle calls to toll-free numbers via satellite dishes for U.S. companies. Back in Bangalore, an educated workforce has drawn Texas Instruments and 30 more firms, including Motorola and IBM, to set up software programming offices in the area.[43]

Firms like these aren't just chasing cheap labor: They are moving plants and jobs over-seas to tap the growing pool of highly skilled employees in Latin America and Asia.

Any decision to do business abroad usually triggers global staffing issues. Setting up factories abroad requires first analyzing employment laws in the host country and establishing a recruiting office. Even a more modest expansion abroad requires a global staffing outlook. For example, sending the company's sales manager abroad for several months to close a deal means deciding how to compensate her for her expenses abroad, what to do with her house here, and how to make sure she is trained to handle the cultural demands of her foreign assignment. Developing effective staffing policies and plans and then coordinating these with production, marketing, and other functions can thus be a challenging aspect of going abroad.

▶ THE GLOBAL MANAGER

Globalization of markets, production, and labor is coinciding with the rise of the global manager. To managers like Wal-Mart's CEO David Glass, the bonds between company and country are thinning. A global manager is one who views markets and production globally and who seeks higher profits for his or her firm on a global basis.[48] He or she is also able to deal effectively with cultural differences like those in the Mexico factory example below.

Being a global manager is easier said than done. It's one thing to say that you view your markets and production globally and intend to integrate operations so as

The People Side of Managing

■ Managing in Mexico

Managers must carefully consider the people side of managing when staffing production facilities abroad.[44] For example, consider some of the following issues in setting up a factory in Mexico.

Workplace Harmony. The Mexican workplace has a low tolerance for adversarial relations. While getting along with others is important in U.S. factories, too, Mexican employers put much more emphasis on hiring employees who have a record of working cooperatively with authority. Mexican employers, according to one expert, "tend to seek workers who are agreeable, respectful, and obedient rather than innovative and independent."[45] This can lead to counterproductive behavior, even on the part of supervisors. For example, in attempting to preserve the appearance of harmony, supervisors may hide defective work rather than confront the problem or report it to a manager.

Role and Status. Mexican employees often put a relatively high emphasis on social order and on respecting one's status. In one factory in Chihuahua, Mexico, for instance, a U.S. manager wore jeans and insisted that everyone call him Jim. He assumed those around him would prefer that he reduce the visible status gap between himself and the workers. He was then amazed to learn that the local employees considered him "uncultured and boorish."[46]

Exercising Authority. Mexican employees tend to have a more rigid view of authority than do their U.S. counterparts. Therefore, attempts by U.S. managers to encourage input and feedback from employees may cause confusion. As one expert puts it:

> [Mexican] supervisors see their role as strictly following orders to the best of their ability, never questioning nor taking matters into their own hands, and this is exactly how they view the proper role of their subordinates. The Mexican supervisor's style is to supervise closely, and look for willing obedience. Opinions expressed by employees are often regarded as backtalk.[47]

to maximize profits around the world. It's quite another thing to be sitting in your office in Kansas and to actually be willing to give your customers and employees in France or India the same attention that you give to customers and employees who are in the next town. Not everyone has what it takes to be so global in outlook.

Cosmopolitan Managers

For one thing, global managers tend to be cosmopolitan in the way they view people and the world. What do we mean by "cosmopolitan?" Webster's dictionary defines cosmopolitan as "belonging to the world; not limited to just one part of the political, social, commercial or intellectual spheres; free from local, provincial, or national ideas, prejudices or attachments."[49] Global managers must be comfortable anywhere in the world, and being cosmopolitan helps them to be so.

How can you tell if you're cosmopolitan? Cosmopolitan people have a clear identity that also values others' views, a sensitivity to what is expected of them in any context in which they find themselves, and the flexibility to deal intelligently and in an unbiased way with people and situations in other cultures. International travel can certainly contribute to one's cosmopolitanism (by exposing you to people and cultures around the world). However, travel is certainly neither a prerequisite nor a guarantee that the traveler will be cosmopolitan. Yet travel is often one thing that sets such managers apart. Take the travel schedule of Ellen Knapp, chief knowledge and information officer for the accounting and consulting firm Price-waterhouseCoopers.[50] In an average month, Knapp is lucky to spend two days in the office; the rest of the time she's on the road, mostly outside the United States. One week recently, for instance, she took three red-eye (overnight) flights in six days. She uses office space wherever she may be, sticks to airlines and hotels she knows well. "My place of work is simply where I am," is how she puts it.[51]

To a great extent, cosmopolitanism reflects a person's values—the basic beliefs he or she has regarding what people should or should not do. As a result, the philosophy of the company's top managers tends to both reflect and affect how cosmopolitan its managers are, and influences its managers' willingness to take that company global. For example, an ethnocentric (home-base-oriented) management philosophy may manifest itself in an **ethnocentric** or home-market-oriented firm. A **polycentric** philosophy may translate into a company that is limited to several individual foreign markets. A **regiocentric** (or geocentric) philosophy may lead managers to create more of an integrated global production and marketing presence.

Do You Have a Global Brain?

In addition to being cosmopolitan, global managers also have what some experts call a *global brain*, which means, for instance, that they accept the fact that, at times, their home-grown ways of doing business are not always best. For example, when Volkswagen formed a partnership with Skoda, a Czech Republic car maker, it focused on training Skoda's managers in Western management techniques; however, it was wise enough to follow Skoda's suggestions about how business was conducted in its country.[52] This sort of willingness to understand that going global means choosing the best solutions from different systems and then applying them to the problems at hand is what management writers mean by having a global brain.

Again, though, being global does not mean acting like a chameleon. As one expert put it, "A company's goal shouldn't be to operate like a French company in France and a Brazilian company in Brazil. Instead, a company—whether it is multinational or local—should bring a multinational approach to each business issue."[53] Ernst and Young, a consulting firm, takes exactly that approach. It is therefore developing a global database of "best practices" that can be accessed by its consultants. As one of Ernst and Young's officers put it, "a solution that works in India may have a component that works in the UK. . . . Sharing best practices helps each office respond more rapidly"[54] (and also helps make the firm truly global).

How do managers with global brains behave? For one thing, "global thinkers have a real interest in other cultures."[55] They also tend to be more sensitive to the possibility of important contributions by other societies, and so give ideas from other nations as much credence as those from their own or other Western nations.[56] You needn't have lived or traveled extensively abroad or be multilingual to have a global brain, although such experiences can help. The important thing is that you be deeply interested in the greater world around you, make efforts to learn about other people's perspectives, and take those perspectives into consideration when you make your own decisions.[57] For a manager, the result might be, for example "applying a successful Brazilian marketing solution to a similar situation in Malaysia, or honoring the local communications hierarchy while keeping the appropriate people in your company in the loop."[58]

Would Your Company Choose You to Be an International Executive?

Of course, there's more involved in getting picked to be a global manager than liking to travel or having a global brain. What do companies look for in trying to identify international executives?

A recent study by behavioral scientists at the University of Southern California provides some answers. The researchers studied 838 lower-, middle- and senior-level managers from 6 international firms in 21 countries, focusing particularly on personal characteristics. Specifically, they studied the extent to which personal characteristics such as "sensitivity to cultural differences" could be used to distinguish between managers who had high potential as international executives and those whose potential was not so high.

Fourteen personal characteristics successfully distinguished those identified by their companies as having high potential from those identified as lower performing in 72% of the cases. To get an initial, tentative impression of how you would rate, see Table 1-3, which lists the 14 characteristics (along with sample items). For each, indicate (by placing a number in the space provided) whether you strongly agree (number 7), strongly disagree (number 1), or fall somewhere in between.

Generally speaking, the higher you score on each of these fourteen characteristics, the more likely it is you would have been identified as a high-potential international executive in this study.[59]

▶ THE PROCESS OF INTERNATIONAL MANAGEMENT

Today, almost every manager is an international manager because almost every business is involved in some way in international trade (and if that trade spans the globe, *global manager* would of course be the better term).

International management means carrying out the management functions of planning, organizing, leading, and controlling on an international scale. Doing business internationally obviously affects the way each of these functions is carried

T A B L E 1 - 3	Characteristics of More Successful International Managers	

Scale	Score	Sample Item
Sensitive to cultural differences		When working with people from other cultures, works hard to understand their perspectives.
Business knowledge		Has a solid understanding of our products and services.
Courage to take a stand		Is willing to take a stand on issues.
Brings out the best in people		Has a special talent for dealing with people.
Acts with integrity		Can be depended on to tell the truth, regardless of circumstances.
Is insightful		Is good at identifying the most important part of a complex problem or issue.
Is committed to success		Clearly demonstrates commitment to seeing the organization succeed.
Takes risks		Takes personal as well as business risks.
Uses feedback		Has changed as a result of feedback.
Is culturally adventurous		Enjoys the challenge of working in countries other than his or her own.
Seeks opportunities to learn		Takes advantage of opportunities to do new things.
Is open to criticism		Appears brittle—as if criticism might cause him or her to break.*
Seeks feedback		Pursues feedback even when others are reluctant to give it.
Is flexible		Doesn't get so invested in things that he or she cannot change when something doesn't work.
*Reverse scored.		

out. We will present several examples here, and then continue our discussion of international management in each section.

Planning Issues

Planning involves setting goals and identifying the courses of action for achieving those goals. It therefore also requires identifying opportunities and threats, and balancing these with the strengths and weaknesses of the enterprise. Planning in an international arena uses this same basic approach. However, global planning also means dealing with some unique issues.

For one thing, as we've seen, international planners must consider special political, legal, and technological issues. In Germany, for instance, Wal-Mart discovered it was illegal to advertise that it would refund to customers the difference in price if they found the same items elsewhere for less. International planners must also consider the possibility of political instability, since many countries have frequent changes of government.[60] Similarly, currency instability, competition from state-owned enterprises, and pressures from national governments (including changing trade barriers) can all throw even the best-laid plans into disarray.

Instabilities like these are not just a characteristic of developing countries. Between 1993 and 1995, Italy embarked on a sweeping privatization of its nationalized businesses. During that time, Italy sold banks and companies worth about $60 billion, including some of the country's largest telecommunications, oil and gas, and insurance companies.[61] At the same time, sweeping criminal investigations created havoc among the country's political and managerial elite. The resulting upheaval brought enormous opportunities for foreign firms doing business in Italy. But it also increased the risks by boosting both the competitiveness of the newly privatized Italian firms and the uncertainties of dealing with the country's political institutions.

Other complications arise in international planning.[62] A domestic U.S. planner faces a relatively homogeneous home market, while the international planner faces a relatively fragmented and diverse set of foreign customers and needs. For U.S. planners, data are usually available and relatively accurate and easy to collect. Internationally, collecting information—about demographics, production levels, and so on—can be a formidable task, and the actual data are often of questionable accuracy.

Organizing Issues

How do you organize an international business?[63] Figure 1-8 shows the typical options, including the traditional domestic organization, the export-oriented organization, the international organization, and the multinational organization.

These organizational structures differ in how they maintain authority over the foreign operations. In a domestic organization, each division handles its own foreign sales, which may come largely from unsolicited overseas orders. In response to increasing orders from abroad, the firm may move to an export-oriented structure. Here, one department (often called an import-export department) coordinates all international activities such as licensing, contracting, and managing foreign sales. In an international organization, the company is divided into separate domestic and international divisions. The international division focuses on production and sales overseas, while the domestic division focuses on domestic markets. Reynolds Metals, for instance, is organized into six worldwide businesses, with a U.S.-focused group and a separate international group.[64]

Finally, the firm may move to a multinational organization, in which each country where the firm does business will have its own subsidiary. The oil firm Royal Dutch Shell is organized this way. It has separate subsidiaries for Shell Switzerland and Shell U.S.A. (as well as many other countries), for instance.[65]

Globalization also complicates a firm's human resource decisions. New policies will have to include how to select, train, and compensate the managers who will be sent to foreign posts and how to deal with intercountry differences in labor laws.

Global staffing policies like these can be very important. For example, when international managers fail, they generally fail either because they can't adapt to the customs of the new country or because their families can't deal with the emotional stress that relocation entails.[66] Global companies must therefore provide training that focuses on cultural differences, on raising trainees' awareness of the impact of these cultural differences on business decisions, and on other matters like building language and adaptation skills. Explaining intercountry differences in labor laws (such as the fact that what is sexual harassment in one country might

▼ **F I G U R E   1 - 8**   **International Organizations**

As firms evolve from domestic to multinational enterprises, their increasing international operations necessitate a more globally oriented organization.

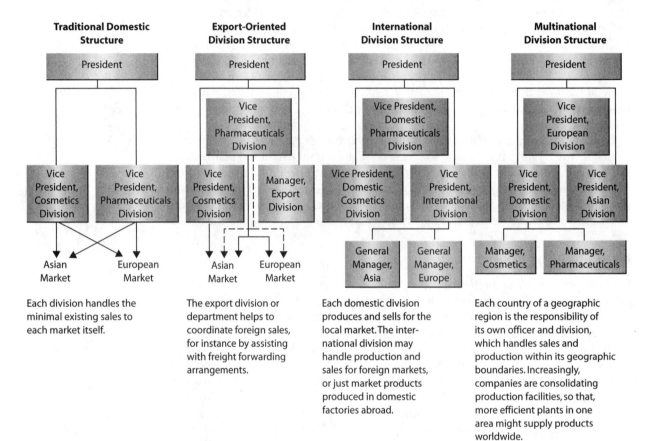

Traditional Domestic Structure	Export-Oriented Division Structure	International Division Structure	Multinational Division Structure
Each division handles the minimal existing sales to each market itself.	The export division or department helps to coordinate foreign sales, for instance by assisting with freight forwarding arrangements.	Each domestic division produces and sells for the local market. The international division may handle production and sales for foreign markets, or just market products produced in domestic factories abroad.	Each country of a geographic region is the responsibility of its own officer and division, which handles sales and production within its geographic boundaries. Increasingly, companies are consolidating production facilities, so that, more efficient plants in one area might supply products worldwide.

not be in another) is another example.[67] Yet few firms actually provide such "going abroad" training to employees.[68]

Issues in Leading the International Enterprise

Globalizing also influences the people side of managing. In Latin America, for instance, bosses are expected to be more autocratic, so participative management (in which employees are encouraged to make work-related decisions) can cause problems. At the other extreme, Japanese managers value consensus and rarely welcome the kind of take-charge leader who wants to make all the decisions personally.

In their book *Working for the Japanese*, Joseph and Suzy Fucini describe the cultural problems between the Japanese and U.S. workers that eventually caused Denny Pawley, the highest-ranking American at the Mazda Michigan plant, to leave for a new job with United Technologies Corporation:

> Pawley did not quit for the money. He left Mazda because he had become frustrated with the constraints that the company's Japanese management had placed on him. After two years and one month with Mazda, it had become

SECTION ONE **55**

obvious . . . that because he was an American he would never be given real authority at Flatrock. As he would later observe, "it started looking more and more to me [like] the real decision-making would always come out of Hiroshima, and [this] just didn't offer me the opportunity to use my broad-based management experience."[69]

Controlling Issues

For managers, maintaining control means monitoring actual performance to ensure it's consistent with the standards that were set. However, doing so can be easier said than done, especially when the thing you're trying to keep tabs on is 5,000 miles and an ocean away. In June 1999, for instance, Coca-Cola was hit by a rude surprise as country after country in Europe required Coke to take its beverages off store shelves. While Coke has perhaps the industry's highest standards for product quality and integrity, keeping an eye on what's happening at every plant can be a challenge. It turned out that chemicals had seeped into the beverages at one of Coke's European plants, and many consumers had apparently become sick as a result.

Going global also usually means the company must install effective computerized information systems so that managers can monitor and maintain control over worldwide operations. For example, for many years Kelly Services, Inc., the Troy, Michigan-headquartered staffing service, let its offices in each country operate with their own individual billing and accounts receivable systems. However, according to Tommi White, Kelly's executive vice president and chief technology officer, with the international division now representing about 25% of the company's total revenue, "we are consolidating our operations in all countries and subsidiaries under a standard [information system]. . . All our customers expect us to deliver consistent

SUMMARY   ■

1. An international business is any firm that engages in international trade or investment. Firms are globalizing for many reasons, the three most common being to expand sales, to acquire resources, and to diversify sources of sales and supplies. Other reasons for pursuing international business include reducing costs or improving quality by seeking products and services produced in foreign countries and smoothing out sales and profit swings.

2. Free trade means that all barriers to trade among countries participating in an agreement are removed. Its potential benefits have prompted many nations to enter into various levels of economic integration, ranging from a free-trade area to a common market.

3. Globalizing production means placing parts of a firm's production process in various locations around the globe. The aim is to take advantage of national differences in the cost and quality

of production and then integrate these operations in a unified system of manufacturing facilities around the world. Companies also are tapping new supplies of skilled labor in various countries. The globalization of markets, production, and labor coincides with the rise of a new type of global manager, who can function effectively anywhere in the world.

4. International managers must be adept at assessing a wide array of environmental factors. For example, managers must be familiar with the economic systems, exchange rates, and level of economic development of the countries in which they do business. They must be aware of import restrictions, political risks, and legal differences and restraints. Important cultural differences also affect the way people in various countries act and expect to be treated. Values, languages, and customs are examples of elements that distinguish people of one culture from those of another. Finally, the relative ease with which technology can be transferred from one country to another is an important consideration in conducting international business.

TYING IT ALL TOGETHER ■

The previous section explained how trends like globalization are boosting the level of competition companies face, and therefore the challenges managers face in managing their companies successfully. In the present section we turned our spotlight on managing in a global environment—what globalizing means, and specifically how going global affects what managers do and the skills they need. We saw that globalizing confronts the manager with many international management issues and challenges. The effectiveness with which he or she deals with these new issues—whether they involve planning, organizing, leading, managing human resources, controlling, or managing the people side of a firm—determines whether the decision to internationalize turns out to be a good one.

One of the main things discussed in this section is that managers must take into account a society's values and culture when dealing with people from other cultures. However, cross-cultural issues don't necessarily involve just dealing with people abroad. Particularly with today's diverse workforce, differences in values and cultures may be as pronounced in one's own office as they are when dealing with people overseas. That's one reason why, in the following section, we'll look more closely at the issue of values and ethics and how they influence what people do.

Skills and Study Materials

CRITICAL THINKING EXERCISES ■

1. At the end of the 20th century, an admiral of the U.S. Navy predicted that as the Mediterranean had been the sea of the past and the Atlantic the sea of the present, so the Pacific would be the sea of the future. What do you think he meant? Is the Pacific Rim the leading market for goods and services in the twenty-first century? Write your own version of the admiral's prediction, looking ahead to the year 3000.

2. As we look around the globe, there seems to be war or conflict on most continents. Africa continues to have tribal warfare. Poverty is rampant. Technology is somewhat rare. Disease is everywhere. In the former USSR, Russia continues to fight with its former satellite countries, while the country

itself seems to be falling apart. There is famine in the military, an inadequate food supply for regular citizens, a growing black market, and dissatisfaction from the many unemployed Russians. The European Union (EU) seems to be working on the surface, but not without conflict. The United Kingdom and France are boycotting each other's meat and other products. Not all nations have decided to join the EU; for example, Sweden has yet to join. The conflict in Bosnia involved the United States and other European nations. In Asia, Pakistan and India are at odds on a regular basis. Indonesia has been at odds with itself and the people of East Timor. Taiwan and China are at odds. The United

States is not without its problems, ranging from the need for better schools to crime. In terms of business, the United States seems to be thriving. How does the above picture affect future global investment and business opportunities? How would you prepare for these problems if expanding your business abroad?

EXPERIENTIAL EXERCISES

1. You have just taken an assignment to move to Russia. Your company is heavily invested in biotechnical farming techniques. The company is located in David, California, a community known for a heavy sense of social responsibility, progressive agricultural techniques, and a liberal political atmosphere. You have a week to prepare to go to St. Petersburg and then to Moscow. How would you begin to prepare? Would you look at political turmoil in Russia and its relationships with the former members of the USSR? Would you study the social customs? Would you take a crash course in the language? How would you prepare yourself to enter this new world of Russia? Would you interview recent immigrants from Russia? What might reading history tell you about how to conduct business meetings in Russia?

2. It is projected that by the middle of the next century, if not before, India will surpass China in population. What do you know about either of these countries? They are home to approximately two-fifths of the world population. Some of the richest and poorest people live in these two nations. Wealth is not distributed as it is in the United States. China is still a communist country, developing an entrepreneurial and capitalistic economy. India is a democratic country, ruled by religion and other ancient values. How does religion (mainly Confucianism in China and Hinduism in India) affect managerial thinking? How do you think these countries' ancient history and religions affect their respective approaches to business and the global marketplace? What types of governmental structures do they have, and how do these structures affect business? What political issues in these regions would make them potential risks for U.S. investment? With a team of four or five people, research each country's history and current situation. Look at the political, social, economic, technological, and environmental issues, concerns, and attitudes. Then write up this information in the form of a recommendation to companies that might wish to invest in either country. Be sure to note ethical and moral issues in the recommendation.

CASE 1-1
U.S. BOOKSELLER FINDS A STRONG PARTNER IN GERMAN MEDIA GIANT

When Barnes & Noble was exploring ways to become more competitive in its battle with Amazon.com, there were hundreds of U.S. companies to which it could turn. Research clearly demonstrated that the cultural differences which characterize cross-border ventures made them far more complicated than domestic ones. Yet, Barnes & Noble surprised competitors when it chose to form its Internet joint venture with the German media giant Bertelsmann. Was Barnes & Noble mistaken to look abroad for a partner?

Bertelsmann is best known among college students for its record label and music club, BMG (now both owned by Universal). At the time, BMG entertainment was second in the market with $1.9 billion in sales. The BMG music club is well known to US college students with its buy 1 get 10 free CD offers posted on campus bulletin boards nationwide. With $3.9 billion in sales and nearly 65,000 employees, Bertelsmann is much more than a CD club. Its holdings include Random House, the world's largest English-language book publisher, and Offset Paperback, a firm that manufactures nearly 40% of all the paperback books sold in the U.S. Bertelsmann had also actively pursued e-commerce on its own. By the end of the twentieth century, Bertelsmann had quietly staked out a position as the world's third largest Internet business.

To fund barnesandnoble.com, the two created a separate company and conducted an initial public offering (IPO) to raise capital. The offering raised $421 million for the new venture, after commissions and expenses, making it the largest e-commerce offering in history. Since launching its on-line business in May 1997, barnesandnoble.com has quickly become one of the world's largest e-commerce retailers. The company has successfully capitalized on the recognized brand value of the Barnes & Noble name to become the second largest on-line retailer of books.

Discussion Questions

1. What may have motivated Barnes & Noble to partner with the German firm Bertelsmann?

2. In general terms, what advantages would Barnes & Noble gain by having an international partner?

3. With all its experience in e-commerce, why wouldn't BMG just set up its own competitor to Amazon.com?

4. What are a few of the planning, organizing, leading, and controlling issues Barnes & Noble's managers faced in joining forces with Bertelsmann?

CASE 1-2
SHOULD FORD OUTSOURCE THE FINAL ASSEMBLY OF AUTOS?

As CEO of one of the world's largest auto manufacturers, Jacques Nassar has spearheaded a number of major initiatives aimed at making Ford more competitive globally. (Within the past year, for instance, Ford announced the acquisition of the Volvo car business from AB Volvo for $6.45 billion.) Ford was also in the process of considering a subtle but profound change in its strategy: the company was beginning to articulate a vision that did not include final assembly of its vehicles as a core competence. Chairman William Clay Ford, Jr., described Ford's 21st century vision as becoming "the world's leading consumer company that provides automotive products and services." Nassar was thinking of taking that vision a step further. He was considering outsourcing the final assembly of Ford cars—in other words, letting other companies actually assemble their cars.

At the same time, Ford had radically internationalized its operations. In addition to its acquisition of Volvo, Ford had acquired Aston-Martin and Jaguar. The Ford brand was already immensely popular in Europe. Fifty-five leading motoring journalists in Europe had selected Ford's new Focus as the 1999 European car of the year. However, in its manufacturing operations worldwide, Ford had continued its practice of performing the final assembly on all its autos and light trucks.

Ford had a long and proud history of manufacturing. In the early 1970s the Michigan Rouge Plant was Ford Motor Company's testament to large-scale manufacturing. Starting with iron ore and sand, the company manufactured its own steel and glass. Completed autos rolled off the assembly line, comprised almost entirely of Ford-made parts. But over the decades, the business environment in which Ford competed changed dramatically. Competition in the industry became progressively more global; auto companies actively sought parts sources and assembly operations around the globe. In the tumultuous 1980s, Ford became the best-selling car in Europe, while Nissan, Honda, and Toyota captured the U.S. market.

Throughout the 1990s, Ford continued to assemble its own cars with parts from worldwide sources. In late 1999, however, Nassar signaled a potential major change in Ford's manufacturing practices. Beginning with its plant in Northeast Brazil, Ford was considering having its equipment manufacturers and parts suppliers perform vital parts of the final assembly of its cars. Under the plan, Ford would pay only for the units produced. If the Bahia Brazil plant was successful, Ford would begin outsourcing final assembly worldwide. In essence, Ford would signal that auto assembly was not one of its core activities.

Ford would not be the first auto maker to move in this direction. DaimlerChrysler and Volkswagen have already introduced similar plans. Under Nassar's plan, a division of the Italian firm Fiat would provide management and maintenance services, as well as body assembly.

Discussion Questions

1. What motivated Ford to become a more global manufacturing operation?

2. If Ford no longer considers assembling cars as part of its core business, on what activities should management focus its attention?

3. Why would this "outsource assembly" decision likely be made only at the highest levels of the Ford organization?

4. What specific global management problems would you see Ford encountering if it decides to let other firms assemble its cars around the world?

MANAGING IN A CULTURAL AND ETHICAL ENVIRONMENT

WHAT'S AHEAD?

It was a public relations disaster of global proportions. It seems that some people were so anxious to make Salt Lake City home to the 2002 Winter Olympics that they apparently bribed several members of the Olympics selection committee to get their way. And, after further investigation, it turned out that Salt Lake City was probably not the first to boost its chances with some well-placed bribes: A number of other cities had used much the same tactics. The Olympics—often viewed as a shining example of amateur sports and international harmony—came out of this with its reputation tarnished and with some of its committee members openly accused of questionable ethics and forced to resign. For many years, people would wonder about the culture and values that the Olympics leadership had allowed to take root.

THIS SECTION FOCUSES ON THE FOLLOWING:

- The nature of ethical decisions, including what makes a decision a moral one

- The factors that influence whether specific people in specific organizations make ethical or unethical decisions

- How to create a company's culture

- The main approaches to corporate social responsibility

- Techniques managers can use to manage workforce diversity

Previously, we explained the challenges of managing in a global environment, and emphasized the problems that can arise from cross-cultural differences in values and points of view. In this section we'll turn to other environmental challenges, and focus on the subjects of culture, ethics, social responsibility, and diversity, and on why they are important.

Environmental challenges like these are interrelated. For example, globalizing forces companies to deal more effectively with diversity and particularly with a more diverse workforce. Similarly, globalizing and ethics are inseparable. Consider the international corruption index shown in Figure 1-9. The figure highlights a truism that many managers deal with every day: Bribes and unethical behavior are the price of doing business in many countries around the world. In Albania, for instance, it's been estimated that businesses pay out bribes equal to about 8% of their sales (about one-third of their potential profits) as a cost of doing business.[1] Similarly, it's been estimated that U.S. businesses in one recent year lost $15 billion in orders abroad to firms from countries that allow bribes (which are prohibited in the United States by the Foreign Corrupt Practices Act). Businesspeople hope a

▶ **F I G U R E 1 - 9**

The International Corruption Index

Source: © 1999 The Economist Newspaper Group, Inc. Reprinted with permission. Further reproduction is prohibited. www.economist.com

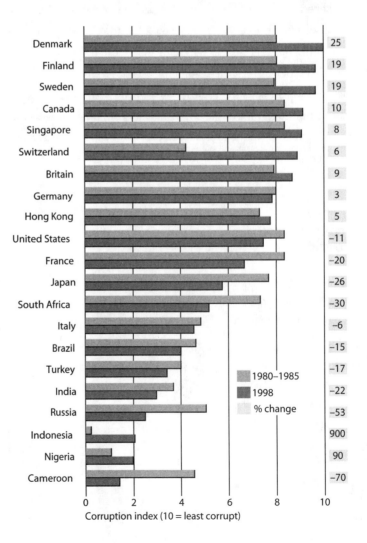

number of steps, among them an "antibribery" treaty recently signed by 34 trading nations, including those responsible for most of world trade, will reduce the incidence of corruption.

The problems facing the Olympics Committee are just one example of how an organization's value set—what we'll call in this section it's *culture*—can create a powerful environment that affects everything its employees and other stakeholders do. There are therefore few more important things a manager can do than to infuse his or her company with the right values. We'll discuss how to do that, and several related matters, in this section.

▶ WHAT DETERMINES ETHICAL BEHAVIOR AT WORK?

We all face ethical choices every day. Consider this dilemma: Your best friend sits next to you in a large college class, and can't afford to miss any more sessions since attendance counts so much in the final grade. She's just called to ask that you sign the class roll for her tomorrow, and you know that she does in fact have a serious family matter to attend to. There are 190 students in the hall, so your chances of getting caught are virtually zero. Should you help your best friend? Or would it be unethical to do so? How can you decide? What factors will influence whether you say yes or no? These are some of the questions we address here. Let's look first at the meaning of ethics.

The Meaning of Ethics

Ethics refers to "the principles of conduct governing an individual or a group,"[2] and specifically to the standards you use to decide what your conduct should be. Ethical decisions always involve normative judgments.[3] A **normative judgment** implies that "something is good or bad, right or wrong, better or worse."[4] "You are wearing a skirt and blouse" is a non-normative statement; "That's a great outfit!" is a normative one.

Ethical decisions also always involve **morality**, in other words, society's accepted ways of behavior. Moral standards differ from other types of standards in several ways.[5] They address matters of serious consequence to society's well-being, such as murder, lying, and slander. They cannot be established or changed by decisions of authoritative bodies like legislatures,[6] and they should override self-interest. Moral judgments are never situational: Something that is morally right (or wrong) in one situation is right (or wrong) in another. Moral judgments tend to trigger strong emotions. Violating moral standards may make you feel ashamed or remorseful. If you see someone else acting immorally, you may feel indignant or resentful.[7]

It would simplify things if it was always crystal clear which decisions were ethical and which were not. Unfortunately, this is not always true. Ethics—principles of conduct—are rooted in morality, so in many cases it's true that what is ethical is pretty clear. (For example, if the decision makes the person feel ashamed or remorseful, or involves a matter of serious consequence such as murder, then chances are it's pretty clear that it is probably unethical.) Yet there are many borderline situations you must consider. In Albania, for instance, it may be that bribing is so widely ingrained and viewed as a necessary evil that most people there would not view it as "wrong." The fact that "everyone is doing it" is certainly no excuse. However, the fact that a society as a whole doesn't view bribery as wrong may suggest that a local businessperson making a bribe may not be doing something that we should consider wrong, at least in terms of his or her own frame of reference.

Ethics and the Law

So there you are, trying to decide whether or not to sign your friend's name on the class roll. What will you do? Several factors influence whether specific people in specific situations make ethical or unethical decisions. The law is one. Is there a law against signing your friend's name? Well, perhaps there's just a college rule, so chances are other factors will influence your decision. Let's look at them.

First, something may be legal but not right. You can make a decision that involves ethics (such as firing an employee) based on what is legal. However, that doesn't mean the decision will be ethical, since a legal decision can be unethical (and an ethical one illegal). Firing a 38-year-old employee just before she has earned the right to her pension may be unethical, but generally it is not illegal. Charging a naïve customer an exorbitant price may be legal but unethical.

Some retailers survey their customers' buying habits by using electronic and infrared surveillance equipment.[8] Videocart, Inc., of Chicago, used infrared sensors in store ceilings to track shopping carts, and video screens on shopping carts as well. Other firms compile information from credit card purchases. These activities are not illegal at the present time. But many believe that such encroachment into a person's privacy is unethical.

Individual Standards

People bring to their jobs their own ideas of what is morally right and wrong, so the individual must shoulder most of the credit (or blame) for the ethical decisions he or she makes. Every decision we make and every action we take reflects, for better or worse, the application of our moral standards to the question at hand.

Here's an example. A national survey of CEOs of manufacturing firms was conducted to explain the CEOs' intentions to engage (or to not engage) in two questionable business practices: soliciting a competitor's technological secrets and making payments to foreign government officials to secure business. The researchers concluded that the CEOs' ethical intentions were more strongly affected by their personal predispositions than by environmental pressures or organizational characteristics.[9]

It's hard to generalize about the characteristics of ethical or unethical people, although older people—perhaps because they're more experienced—do tend to make more ethical decisions.

In one study, 421 employees were surveyed to measure the degree to which age, gender, marital status, education, dependent children, region of the country, and years in business influenced responses to ethical decisions. (Decisions included "doing personal business on company time," "not reporting others' violations of company rules and policies," and "calling in sick to take a day off for personal use.") With the exception of age, none of the variables were good predictors of whether a person would make the "right" decision. Older workers in general had stricter interpretations of ethical standards and made more ethical decisions than younger employees.

This generation gap in business ethics has also been found by other researchers.[10] One Baylor University study surveyed 2,156 individuals who were grouped by age; those ages 21–40 represented the younger group, and those age 51–70 represented the older group. As in the previous study, respondents were asked to rate the acceptability of a number of ethics-related vignettes.[11] The following are several of the 16 vignettes used in the study:

1. A company president found that a competitor had made an important scientific discovery that would sharply reduce the profits of his own company. He then hired a key employee of the competitor in an attempt to learn the details of the discovery.

2. In order to increase profits, a general manager used a production process that exceeded legal limits for environmental pollution.

3. Because of pressure from his brokerage firm, a stockbroker recommended a type of bond that he did not consider to be a good investment.

4. A small business received one-fourth of its gross revenue in the form of cash. The owner reported only one-half of the cash receipts for income-tax purposes.

5. A company paid a $350,000 "consulting" fee to an official of a foreign country. In return, the official promised assistance in obtaining a contract that should produce a $10 million profit for the contracting company.

In virtually every case, the older group viewed the ethically questionable decision as more unacceptable than did the younger group. Of course, such findings don't suggest that all older employees are ethical, or that all younger ones are unethical. But they do raise the question of whether the younger employees' relative lack of experience leaves them more open to making "wrong" decisions. One danger is that most people view themselves as being more ethical than others. In other words, most people tend to have a distorted view of how ethical they really are.[12]

How to Foster Ethics at Work

After a review of the ethics programs at eleven major firms, one study concluded that fostering ethics at work involved five main steps:

1. *Emphasize top management's commitment.* "To achieve results, the chief executive officer and those around the CEO need to be openly and strongly committed to ethical conduct, and give constant leadership in tending and renewing the values of the organization."[13]

2. *Publish a "code."* Firms with effective ethics programs set forth principles of conduct for the whole organization in the form of written documents.[14]

3. *Establish compliance mechanisms.* For example, pay attention to values and ethics in recruiting and hiring; emphasize corporate ethics in training; institute communications programs to inform and motivate employees; and audit to ensure compliance.[15]

4. *Involve personnel at all levels.* For example, use roundtable discussions among small groups of employees regarding corporate ethics and surveys of employee attitudes regarding the state of ethics in the firm.[16]

5. *Measure results.* All eleven firms used surveys or audits to monitor compliance with ethical standards.[17] The results of audits should then be discussed among board members and employees.[18]

▶ CREATING THE RIGHT CULTURE

You know from your own experience that it's not just what you say that's important; it's what you do. A father can talk about being ethical till he's blue in the face, but if his children see him always cutting ethical corners—bringing home "free" office supplies from where he works, or bragging about buying stocks based on "inside" information, for instance—his children may learn that "being unethical is really ok."

The same is true in organizations. Whether it's in regard to ethics or some other matter, the manager—and especially the top manager—creates a culture by what he or she says and does, and the employees then take their signals from that behavior and from that culture.

What Is Organizational Culture?

Organizational culture can be defined as the characteristic traditions and values employees share. Values (such as "be honest," "be thrifty," and "don't be bureaucratic") are basic beliefs about what you should or shouldn't do and what is or is not important. Values guide and channel behavior; leading and influencing people and molding their ethical behavior therefore depends in part on influencing the values they use as behavioral guides.

Let's take a closer look at what organizational culture means. To do that, think for a moment about what comes to mind when you hear the word *culture* applied to a country. In France, China, or the United States, you'd probably think of at least three things. Culture means, first, the *physical aspects* of the society, things like art, music, and theater. Culture also means the *values* citizens share—for instance, the emphasis on "equality" and fraternity in France, or on democracy and hard work in the United States, and the assumptions—such as "people can govern themselves"— that the values stem from. By culture you'd also probably mean the characteristic way the people of that country *behave*—the patience of the people in England, or the emphasis on fine food and art among the people of France.

We can use this country culture analogy to get a better understanding of the components of organizational culture. **Cultural artifacts** are the obvious signs and symbols of corporate culture, such as written rules, office layouts, organizational structure, and dress codes.[19] Organizational culture also includes the company's **patterns of behavior**, such as ceremonial events, written and spoken comments, and actual employee behaviors. For example, the firm's managers and employees may engage in behaviors such as hiding information, politicking, or expressing honest concern when a colleague requires assistance.

In turn, these cultural signs and behaviors are a product of **values and beliefs**, such as "the customer is always right" or "don't be bureaucratic." These guiding standards—these values and beliefs—lay out what ought to be, as distinct from what is.[20] If management's *stated* values and beliefs differ from what the managers actually value and believe, this will show up in their behavior. For example, Fred Smith, founder and chairman of FedEx, says that many firms *say* they believe in respecting their employees and putting their people first.[21] But in a lot of these firms it's not what the managers say, but the way they behave—insisting on time clocks, routinely downsizing, and so on—that makes it clear what their values really are.

Organizational culture is important to ethics because a firm's culture reflects its shared values, and these in turn help guide and channel employees' behavior. At Sears, for instance, the service advisers and mechanics apparently had little to go by in making decisions other than the "boost sales"–oriented incentive plan and quotas top management had put in place. There was not a strong set of shared values throughout the company that said, for instance, "potentially unethical sales practices will not be tolerated," and "the most important thing is to provide our customers with top-quality services that they really need."

The Managers' Influence

Managers play a major role in creating and sustaining a firm's culture, through the actions they take and the comments they make. Following are some specific ways in which managers can shape their organization's culture.

Clarify Expectations   First, make it clear what your expectations are with respect to the values you want subordinates to follow. For example, investment banking firm Goldman Sachs has long been guided by a set of written principles, such as "our client's interests always come first," and "we take great pride in the professional quality of our work."

Publishing a formal core values statement is thus a logical first step in creating a culture. For example, the core values credo of Johnson & Johnson reads: "We believe our first responsibility is to the doctors, nurses and patients, to mothers and fathers and all others who use our products and services. In meeting their needs everything we do must be of high quality.[22]

A firm's values should then guide the company's behavior. When Johnson & Johnson faced the poisoned Tylenol capsules crisis several years ago, the management knew from the credo what it had to do: Be responsible to patients, mothers, and so on, emphasize high quality, and be good citizens.[23]

Use Signs and Symbols   Remember that it's not just what the manager says but what he or she does that subordinates will pick up on. At Sears, for instance, it was important that top managers not just pay lip service to the importance of top-quality ethical service. After problems arose, they also tried to engage in practices that symbolized those values. For example, they eliminated the service quotas and the commission incentive plan for service advisers. And they instituted unannounced shopping audits. Yet, given the problem's apparent reoccurrence in 1999, the steps they took may have been insufficient.

Many believe that the symbolism—what the manager says and does and the signals he or she sends—ultimately does the most to create and sustain the company's culture. At Saturn Corporation—known for its culture of quality, teamwork, and respect for the individual—one of the firm's top managers said this about company culture:

> Creating a value system that encourages the kind of behavior you want is not enough. The challenge is then to engage in those practices that symbolize those values [and] tell people what is really O.K. to do and what not [to do]. Actions, in other words, speak much more loudly than words.[24]

Signs and symbols, stories, and rites and ceremonies are concrete examples of such actions.

Signs and symbols are used throughout strong-culture firms to create and sustain the company's culture. At Ben & Jerry's, the "joy gang" is a concrete symbol of the firm's values (charity, fun, and goodwill toward fellow workers). The joy gang is a voluntary group that meets once or twice a week to create new ways to inject fun into what the Ben & Jerry's people do, often by giving out "joy grants," which are "five hundred quick, easy, no-strings attached dollars for long-term improvements to your work area."[25] Sam Walton's hula dance on Wall Street (after Wal-Mart met its goals) is another example of a culture-building symbol.

Stories illustrating important company values are also widely used to reinforce the firm's culture. Thus, at Procter & Gamble there are many stories about relatively trivial decisions going all the way to the top of the company.[26] IBM has similar stories, such as how IBM salespeople took dramatic steps (like driving all night through storms) to get parts to customers.

Rites and ceremonies can also symbolize the firm's values and help convert employees to them. At JC Penney (where loyalty and tradition are values), new management employees are inducted at ritualistic conferences into the "Penney Partnership." Here they commit to the firm's ideology as embodied in its statement of core values. Each inductee solemnly swears allegiance to these values and then receives his or her "H.C.S.C. lapel pin." These letters symbolize JC Penney's core values of honor, confidence, service, and cooperation.

The following "People Side of Managing" box provides an example of culture in action.

The People Side of Managing

■ Corporate Culture at Procter & Gamble

Procter & Gamble's culture reflects what one management theorist has called the firm's legendary emphasis on "thoroughness, market-testing, and ethical behavior," values that are transmitted to new employees through selection, socialization, and training processes.[27]

The basic elements of Procter & Gamble's strong corporate culture go back to the founders, William Procter and James Gamble. They started P&G in Cincinnati in 1837 to produce relatively inexpensive household products that were technically superior to those of the competition, quickly consumed, and an integral part of their customers' lifestyle.[28] Their intention was to "foster growth in an orderly manner, to reflect the standards set by the founders, and to plan and prepare for the future."[29]

This philosophy was translated into several core P&G values. The emphasis on orderly growth manifests itself in "tremendous conformity."[30] A new recruit soon learns to say *we* instead of *I*.[31] This conformity bolsters thoroughness and a methodical approach. Its result, according to one past chair, is a "consistency of principles and policy that gives us direction, thoroughness, and self-discipline."[32]

Procter & Gamble's culture manifests itself in and is sustained by various management practices. College graduates are recruited and placed in highly competitive situations. Those who can't learn the system are quickly weeded out; the remainder enjoy the benefits of promotion from within. As a result, no one reaches middle management without 5 to 10 years of close scrutiny and training. This in turn creates what one researcher called "a homogeneous leadership group with an enormous amount of common experience and strong set of shared assumptions."[33]

New recruits may assume major responsibility for projects almost immediately, but the authority for most big decisions is made far up the chain of command, usually by committees of managers. Nearly everything must be approved through a written memo process. Stories abound that reinforce this process; one describes the decision about the color of the Folger's coffee lid, supposedly made by the CEO after four years of extensive market testing.[34]

Internal competition is fostered by the brand management system: Brands compete for internal resources, have their own advertising and marketing, and act as independent cost centers. The extensive use of memos, the continual rechecking of each other's work, and the rigid timeline for promotions also contribute to (and reflect) P&G's strong culture and emphasis on thoroughness.

► MANAGERS AND SOCIAL RESPONSIBILITY

Corporate **social responsibility** refers to the extent to which companies should and do channel resources toward improving one or more segments of society other than the firm's own stockholders. Socially responsible behavior might include creating jobs for minorities, controlling pollution, or supporting educational facilities or cultural events.

As you know from reading and watching the news, social responsibility issues comprise a major part of the environmental forces with which managers must cope. Hardly a day goes by without news reports about companies grappling with problems like oil spills, pollution control, or manufacturing products in sweatshops. As you can see from these examples, social responsibility is also largely an ethical issue, since it involves questions of what is morally right or wrong with regard to the firm's responsibilities. As you will see, though, there is less unanimity regarding what is right or wrong in this area than there is with respect to traditional ethical issues such as bribery, stealing, and corporate dishonesty. Many perfectly ethical people strongly believe that a company's only social responsibility is to its shareholders.

Being Socially Responsible Today

The Asia Monitor Resource Center Hidden on a small street in Hong Kong's Kowloon area is the tiny headquarters of the Asia Monitor Resource Center, whose job is to monitor working conditions in mainland China. Its reports often shock huge U.S. firms like Disney, and help to illustrate what socially responsible behavior means today. Its aim is to uncover and publicize unacceptable working conditions in plants producing products for global firms. It hopes to thereby improve working conditions for manufacturing workers in mainland China.

What sorts of unethical practices does the center report? Its Disney report alleges that some main-land Chinese employed by Disney contractors were working up to 16 hours a day, seven days a week, and paid little or no overtime. Another report, on China's toy industry, describes what some have called "sweatshop Barbie" assembly lines, because of abuses including long work hours and heavy fines for workers.

Companies with brands especially vulnerable to such criticism have been among the first to react in a socially responsible way. In fact, the plants of contractors for firms like Disney and Mattel are now reportedly among some the most progressive in mainland China.[35] Both Disney and Mattel have codes of conduct, and Disney has carried out tens of thousands of inspections of its contractors' plants to make sure they comply. Disney even cut off one of its noncomplying factories. Mattel emphasizes that it has received the certificate of workplace standards that Asia Monitor itself calls for.

Ben & Jerry's Managers must make up their own minds regarding where on the social responsibility scale their firm should lie. For Ben & Jerry's ice cream company, the decision was never in doubt. Founders Ben Cohen and Jerry Greenfield started a company that had, as part of its mission,

> To operate the company in a way that actively recognizes the central role that business plays in the structure of a society by initiating innovative ways to improve the quality of life of a broad community: local, national and international.[36]

How does Ben & Jerry's put its socially responsible mission into practice? The firm has "green teams" responsible for assessing environmental impact and for developing and implementing programs to reduce any negative impact. The firm donates (at its board's discretion) 7.5% of its pretax earnings to the Ben & Jerry's Foundation, a nonprofit institution established by personal contributions from founders Cohen and Greenfield. And, in explaining Ben & Jerry's choice of suppliers, Ben Cohen says:

> Wild Maine Blueberry is another step in how we are defining what caring capitalism is all about. Our goal is to integrate a concern for the community in every business decision we make. We are trying to develop a system that improves the quality of life through socially conscious purchasing of our ingredients. For example, the brownies in Chocolate Fudge Brownie benefit the employment of underskilled persons.[37]

To Whom Should the Corporation Be Responsible?

Mattel's run-in with the Asia Monitor Resource Center helps to crystallize the dilemma that lies at the heart of social responsibility: To whom should a company be socially responsible? Improving workers' living standards in China is certainly a laudable and socially responsible goal. But would it not be more socially responsible, others ask, for the company to concentrate on boosting its profits, so that its stockholder-owners and their families would gain?

Managerial Capitalism The classic view of social responsibility is that a corporation's primary purpose is to maximize profits for its stockholders. Today, this view is most notably associated with economist and Nobel laureate Milton Friedman, who said,

> The view has been gaining widespread acceptance that corporate officials and labor leaders have a "social responsibility" that goes beyond the interest of their stockholders or their members. This view shows a fundamental misconception of the character and nature of the free economy. In such an economy, there is one and only one social responsibility of business—to use its resources and engage in activities designed to increase its profits so long as it stays within the rules of the game, which is to say, engages in open and free competition, without deception and fraud. . . . Few trends could so thoroughly undermine the very foundation of our free society as the acceptance by corporate officials of a social responsibility other than to make as much money for their stockholders as possible.[38]

Friedman's position is built on two main arguments.[39] First, stockholders are owners of the corporation and so the corporate profits belong to them and to them alone. Second, stockholders deserve their profits because these profits derive from a voluntary contract among the various corporate stakeholders—the community receives tax money, suppliers are paid, employees earn wages, and so on. Everyone gets their due, and additional social responsibility is not needed.

Stakeholder Theory An opposing view is that business has a social responsibility to serve all the corporate stakeholders affected by its business decisions. A **corporate stakeholder** is "any group which is vital to the survival and success of the corporation."[40] As in Figure 1-10, six stakeholder groups are traditionally identified: stockholders (owners), employees, customers, suppliers, managers, and the local community (although conceivably others could be identified as well).[41] To stakeholder

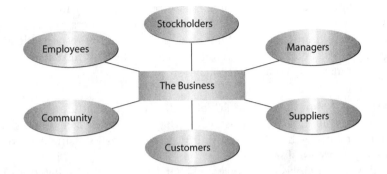

▶ **FIGURE 1-10**

A Corporation's Major Stakeholders

One view of social responsibility is that a firm must consider and serve all the stakeholders that may be affected by its business decisions.

advocates, being socially responsible means more than just maximizing profits; being up front with employees is important too.

Whereas Friedman's corporation focuses on maximizing profits, stakeholder theory holds that[42]

> the corporation should be managed for the benefit of [all] its stakeholders: its customers, suppliers, owners, employees, and local communities. The rights of these groups must be ensured, and, further, the groups must participate, in some sense, in decisions that substantially affect their welfare.[43]

The Moral Minimum Between the extremes of Friedman's capitalism and stakeholder theory is an intermediate position known as the **moral minimum**. Advocates agree that the purpose of the corporation is to maximize profits, but subject to the requirement that it must do so in conformity with the moral minimum,[44] meaning that the firm should be free to strive for profits so long as it commits no harm. By this view, a business would certainly have a social responsibility not to produce exploding cigarette lighters or operate chemical plants that poison the environment. However, it is unlikely that the social responsibilities of the business would extend to donating profits to charity or educating the poor, for instance.

It would be a mistake to assume that this brief discussion of managerial capitalism, stakeholder theory, and the moral minimum adequately summarizes the complicated field of corporate responsibility. For example, "the moral minimum" is certainly not the only intermediate position between managerial capitalism and stakeholder theory. Indeed, many find the idea that maximizing profits is acceptable, as long as the company adheres to the moral minimum of committing no harm, is itself unacceptable. Similarly, while many definitely do view managerial capitalism as a worthy goal, many others would tell managers that in reality ignoring the interests of non-owner stakeholders—ignoring the needs of the community in which the corporation has facilities, for instance—is bound to be counterproductive. The bottom line is that when it comes to being socially responsible there are a range of options a manager can pursue. How he or she decides to deal with these issues should reflect an intelligent and informed decision, one built around a strong sense of what is right and wrong.

How to Improve Social Responsiveness

The question of how to improve a company's social responsiveness isn't easy to answer because, as we've seen, there's no agreement on what being socially responsible means. Some companies take a proactive approach: They make being socially responsible the core of almost all their decisions. Other companies seem to pay as little attention to being socially responsible as they can. Others (such as Disney and Mattel) fall somewhere in the middle: They pursue socially responsible aims after being gently reminded to do so. Being proactively socially responsible is not the only option pursued by companies today.

Corporate Social Monitoring: The Social Audit   Given a commitment to being socially responsible, how can firms ensure that they are in fact responsive? Some firms monitor how well they measure up to their aims by using a rating system called a **corporate social audit**.[45]

The Sullivan Principles for Corporate Labor and Community Relations in South Africa was one of the first such rating systems.[46] The Reverend Leon Sullivan was an African-American minister and GM board of directors member. For several years during the 1970s he had tried to pressure the firm to withdraw from South Africa, whose multiracial population was divided by government-sanctioned racist policies, known as *apartheid*.

As part of that effort, Sullivan formulated the code that came to be named for him, the purpose of which was "to guide U.S. business in its social and moral agenda in South Africa."[47] The code provided for measurable standards by which U.S. companies operating in South Africa could be audited, including nonsegregation of the races in all eating, comfort, and work facilities, and "equal pay for all employees doing equal or comparable work for the same period of time."[48] In the 1990s he proposed a new code for companies returning to South Africa after *apartheid* had ended stressing the protection of equal rights and the promotion of education and job training.

Whistle-Blowing   Many firms have a reputation for actively discouraging **whistle-blowing**, the activities of employees who try to report organizational wrong-doing. Yet many arguments can be made for actually *encouraging* whistle-blowers. In a firm that adheres to the moral minimum view, for instance, whistle-blowers can help the company avoid doing harm. As one writer put it, whistle-blowers "represent one of the least expensive and most efficient sources of feedback about mistakes the firm may be making."[49] Other firms find the "benefit of muffling whistle-blowers is illusory."[50] Once the damage has been done—whether it is asbestos hurting workers or a chemical plant making hundreds of people ill—the cost of making the damage right can be enormous.[51]

Boosting Performance by Managing Diversity

As mentioned above, managing diversity means maximizing diversity's potential advantages while minimizing its potential barriers. In practice, doing so includes both legally mandated and voluntary management actions.

There are, of course, many legally mandated actions employers must take to minimize workplace discrimination. For example, employers should avoid discriminatory employment advertising (such as "young man wanted for sales position"), and prohibit sexual harassment. Yet, while actions like these can reduce the more blatant barriers, blending a diverse workforce into a close-knit community also requires other steps, as Figure 1-11 shows. Based on his research, one diversity expert concludes that five sets of activities are at the heart of a managing diversity program, as follows:

▼ **F I G U R E   1 - 1 1**   **Activities Required to Better Manage Diversity**

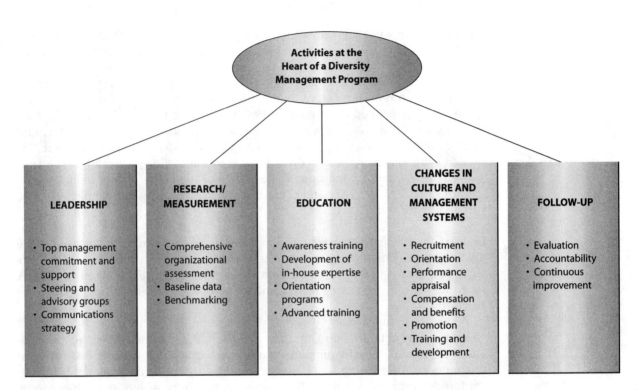

Source: Reprinted with permission of the publisher. From *Cultural Diversity in Organizations: Theory, Research and Practice*, copyright © 1993 by Taylor Cox Jr. Berrett-Koehler Publishers, Inc., San Francisco, CA. All rights reserved.

Provide Strong Leadership   Companies with exemplary reputations are typically led by chief executives who champion diversity's cause. Leadership in this case means taking a strong personal stand on the need for change; becoming a role model for the behaviors required for the change; and providing the mental energy and financial and other support needed to implement actual changes, for instance in hiring practices. It can also mean writing a statement that defines what you mean by diversity and how diversity is linked to your business.[52]

Research: Assess Your Situation   The company must assess its current situation with respect to diversity management. This might include using surveys to measure current employee attitudes and perceptions toward different cultural groups in the company and about relationships between the groups.

Provide Diversity Training and Education   One expert says "the most commonly utilized starting point for . . . managing diversity is some type of employee education program."[53] Employers typically use several types of programs, most often a one- to three-day workshop aimed at increasing awareness and sensitivity to diversity issues.

What might such a seminar cover? Suggestions include involve a diverse group of employees in the process, and ask them: What does diversity mean to you? Why do you have those perceptions of diversity? What does it mean to our organization? How can we develop an inclusive and positive definition of diversity that will be understood and accepted by everyone?[54] Since disagreements may arise, it's usually best that meetings like this be managed by professional facilitators.

Change Culture and Management Systems Education programs should be combined with other steps aimed at changing the organization's culture and management systems. For example, the performance appraisal procedure might be changed so that supervisors are appraised based partly on their success in minimizing intergroup conflicts. Many companies also institute mentoring programs. **Mentoring** is defined as "a relationship between a younger adult and an older, more experienced adult in which the mentor provides support, guidance, and counseling to enhance the protégé's success at work and in other arenas of life."[55]

Mentoring can contribute to diversity management efforts: After all, why attract a diverse workforce and then simply leave the new people to sink or swim? A good mentor provides the advice and counsel required to deal with challenges at work, particularly for those who may be new to the workforce.[56]

Evaluate the Diversity Program The evaluation stage is aimed at measuring the diversity management program's results. For example, do the surveys now indicate an improvement in employee attitudes toward diversity? How many employees have entered into mentoring relationships, and do these relationships appear to be successful?

What effects do diversity programs have on employee attitudes and points of view? Do they actually boost mutual understanding? Many peoples' first experience with formal diversity programs is in college, so schools' experiences with such programs can be informative. A study conducted by the former presidents of Harvard and Princeton was recently reported in the *Harvard Business Review*: Some results are presented in Figure 1-12.[57]

The findings suggest that diversity has generally had a positive impact on university education and on student attitudes. For example, the study found "a strong and growing belief in the value of enrolling a diverse student body," and "[a] belief among graduates that college had contributed much to their ability to work well and get along with members of other races."[58] At least in college, in other words, programs aimed at encouraging and managing diversity seem to be having the desired effects.

▶ **FIGURE 1-12**

The Impact of Diversity on Education

Source: Reprinted by permission of *Harvard Business Review*. An exhibit from "A Report Card on Diversity," January–February 1999, Copyright © 1999 by the President and Fellows of Harvard College. All rights reserved.

What College Diversity Management Survey Data Show

- a strong and growing belief among graduates in the value of enrolling a diverse student body;

- the affirmation by 79% of white graduates that race-sensitive admissions policies at their alma mater should either be retained or strengthened;

- almost exactly the same level of support for diversity by white matriculants who had been turned down by their first-choice school (and who might therefore be expected to resent race-sensitive admissions policies);

- a significant degree of social interaction between the races during college;

- the belief among graduates that college had contributed much to their ability to work well and get along with members of other races.

SUMMARY ■

1. Managers face ethical choices every day. Ethics refers to the principles of conduct governing an individual or a group. Ethical decisions always include both normative and moral judgments.

2. Being legal and being ethical are not necessarily the same thing. A decision can be legal but still unethical, or ethical but still illegal.

3. Several factors influence whether specific people in specific organizations make ethical or unethical decisions. The individual making the decision must ultimately shoulder most of the credit (or blame) for any ethical decision he or she makes.

4. Organizational culture may be defined as the characteristic traditions, norms, and values that employees share. Values are basic beliefs about what you should or shouldn't do and what is and is not important.

5. Several things contribute to creating and sustaining the corporate culture. One is a formal core values statement. Leaders also play a role in creating and sustaining culture. One of a leader's most important functions is to influence the culture and shared values of his or her organization. Managers also use signs and symbols, stories, and rites and ceremonies to create and sustain their companies' cultures.

6. Social responsibility is largely an ethical issue, since it involves questions of what is morally right or wrong with regard to the firm's responsibilities. People differ in answering the question, To whom should the corporation be responsible? Some say solely to stockholders, and some say to all stakeholders. Some take an intermediate position: They agree that the purpose of the corporation is to maximize profits, but subject to the requirement that it must do so in conformity with the moral minimum.

7. As the workforce becomes more diverse, it becomes more important to manage diversity so that the benefits of diversity outweigh any potential drawbacks. Potential barriers to managing diversity include stereotyping, prejudice, and tokenism. Managing diversity involves taking steps such as providing strong leadership, assessing the situation, providing training and education, changing the culture and systems, and evaluating the program.

TYING IT ALL TOGETHER ■

Organizations and their employees get things done within an environment that is continually shifting. Outside forces such as globalization, deregulation, and technological change create a competitive environment, within which managers must do their jobs. Within the company too there's an "environment," consisting of its values, ethics, and culture.

Now, having looked at the things that surround and influence what managers do, we can turn to a detailed discussion of what managers do and how they do it—in others words, to the management process topics of planning, organizing, leading, and controlling.

Skills and Study Materials

CRITICAL THINKING EXERCISES   ■

1. You work for a medical genetics research firm as a marketing person. You love the job. The location is great, the hours are good, and work is challenging and flexible. You receive a much higher salary than you ever anticipated. You hear via the rumor mill that the company's elite medical team has cloned the first human, the CEO. It was such a total success that you have heard that they may clone every employee so that they can use the clones to harvest body parts as the original people age or become ill. You are not sure you believe in cloning. You joined the firm for reasons of its moral and ethical reputation. You feel that the image presented to you was one of research and development of life-saving drugs and innovative medical procedures. The thought of cloning was never on your mind, but now it must be. What would you do? What are the ethical and cultural issues involved? Do you think that managers in Japan, Sweden, Chile, or France would manage the discovery differently? Why? Do you think cloning will become even a more controversial ethical and moral issue in the future as cloning becomes part of the medical decision making model?

2. A key to ethical perception is realizing that all people bring different views, experiences, and other relevant influences to decisions. This is particularly true in U.S. society. Read the following narratives about perception, and relate them to ethical decision making examples in the workplace.

   First narrative, by Taoist writer Lieh-tse: A man noticed that his axe was missing. Then he saw the neighbor's son pass by. The boy looked like a thief, walked like a thief, behaved like a thief. Later that day, the man found his axe where he had left it the day before. The next time he saw the neighbor's son, the boy looked, walked and behaved like an honest, ordinary boy.[59]

   Second narrative, by Taoist writer Chuang-tse: An archer competing for a clay vessel shoots effortlessly, his skill and concentration unimpeded. If the prize is changed to a brass ornament, his hands begin to shake. If it is changed to gold, he squints as if he were going blind. His abilities do not deteriorate, but his belief in them does, as he allows the supposed value of an external reward to cloud his vision.[60]

EXPERIENTIAL EXERCISES   ■

1. In teams of four or five class members, research and then write about the ethical philosophies and attitudes toward business in the following nations: Russia, India, Egypt, Israel, the Congo, Norway, Saudi Arabia, and Australia. Compare and contrast their respective approaches to ethics and corporate social responsibility. Explain why there are differences.

2. You were taking a month's holiday in Europe. In your first week there, you became very ill with a recurring ailment for which you have been treated with limited success in the United States. In fact, it is a chronic condition that is inhibiting your ability to advance your career. The doctors who treated you in Europe have given you some medication that is legal there but has not been approved by the U.S. Food and Drug Administration. You feel better than you have in years. Because the European drug restrictions allow this drug to be purchased across the counter without a prescription, you are able to buy a year's supply. However, you know that it is listed as an illegal drug in the United States and you must pass through customs. What would you do? What are the ethical and moral dilemmas facing you? Is there any action you can take as an individual to change the situation? If your decision is to smuggle the drug in and you are successful, what will you do in a year?

CASE 1-3
ALLSTATE PLANS TO RESTRUCTURE— CUTTING 4,000 JOBS

Like many companies, Allstate faces pressure to be both cost competitive and provide new services to its customers. It also faces pressure for continuous improvement in its financial performance from its shareholders. Assuming that for Allstate to survive and prosper it needs to respond to both customers and shareholders, what responsibilities does it have toward another important group of stakeholders, its employees?

Here is the situation. In November 1999 the Allstate Corporation announced a series of strategic initiatives to expand its selling and service capabilities, buy back company shares to raise its stock price, and cut expenses by reducing the workforce. As part of its restructuring, Allstate would transfer its existing captive agency program to a single exclusive agency independent contractor program, thus markedly reducing the need for agency support staff. In its press release on this initiative, Allstate management also announced it would eliminate 4,000 current non-agent positions by the end of 2000, or approximately 10 percent of the company's non-agent workforce.

Said Allstate CEO Edward Liddy, "Now, many of our customers and potential customers are telling us they want our products to be easier to buy, easier to service and more competitively priced. We will combine the power of our agency distribution system with the growth potential of direct selling and electronic commerce. . . . This unique combination is without parallel in the industry and will make Allstate the most customer-focused company in the marketplace."

Proponents of this type of restructuring might argue that Allstate is simply taking the steps needed to be competitive. They might even say that if Allstate did not cut jobs to create the cash flow needed to fund new competitive initiatives, it might ultimately fail as a business, putting all 54,000 of its employees at risk.

Yet Allstate's program raises concerns. One analyst noted that by encouraging customers to purchase insurance products directly from the Internet, Allstate could threaten the commissions of its more than 15,000 agents. The announcement of cost cutting came one day after Allstate announced it would meet its regular quarterly dividend of $0.15 per share. The company has raised its dividend annually since 1993.

Discussion Questions:

1. Is reducing the number of employees in a company in and of itself unethical? Why or why not?

2. If you decided it was generally ethical, what would the company have to do to make the employee dismissals unethical?

3. What responsibilities does a company like Allstate have toward its employees?

4. Is there a moral dimension to the question of marketing Allstate insurance via the Internet?

SECTION TWO

PLANNING AND SETTING OBJECTIVES

WHAT'S AHEAD?

While most people assume Wal-Mart's people-friendly stores and great selection account for the firm's success, some planning experts believe it's actually the firm's data warehouse. What's a data warehouse? It's a computerized repository of information. Wal-Mart's data warehouse collects information on things like sales, inventory, products in transit, and product returns from Wal-Mart's 3,000 stores. Wal-Mart managers can monitor this information to see what's actually "occurring on the ground", analyze trends, understand customers, and more effectively manage inventory. For example (as we'll see later in this section), the data warehouse enables Wal-Mart managers to make uncannily accurate forecasts about how much of what products will be sold (based on past experience). It therefore helps the company, and vendors like Warner-Lambert, develop amazingly accurate and realistic manufacturing plans, and is a good example of how leading-edge managers plan today.[1]

THIS SECTION FOCUSES ON THE FOLLOWING:

- Planning

- The five steps in the planning process

- The formulation of effective objectives

- A hierarchy of objectives

- Executive action plans

Planning is often called the "first among equals" of the four management functions (planning, organizing, leading, and controlling), since it establishes the goals that are (or should be) the basis of all these functions. The people you hire, the incentives you use, and the controls you institute all relate to what you want to achieve and to the plans and goals you set. (Conversely, the way your plans are implemented—the final results—will be no better than the people you have doing the work and how they do it.) In this section we'll focus on planning and on the techniques for setting goals and objectives. Then, we'll turn to the crucial subject of strategic planning, in other words to setting the long-term, companywide plans for your enterprise.

▶ THE NATURE AND PURPOSE OF PLANNING

Why Plan?

Plans, as Wal-Mart knows well, are methods formulated for achieving a desired result. All plans specify goals (such as "boost sales by 10%") and courses of action (such as "hire a new salesperson and boost advertising expenditures by 20%"). Plans should specify, at a minimum, what you will do, how you will do it, and by when you'll get it done.[2] **Planning**, therefore, is "the process of establishing objectives and courses of action, prior to taking action."[3] **Goals**, or **objectives**, are specific results you want to achieve. Wal-Mart's data warehouse helps its managers forecast what its customers will buy, and therefore to plan to have that merchandise in their stores when it is needed. In this section we'll look at the nature of planning, and then turn to the methods managers use to forecast the future.

As you can see from these descriptions, planning and decision making are closely intertwined. Planning means choosing your objectives and the courses of action that will get you there. In other words, when you make a plan, you're really deciding ahead of time what you or your company are going to do in the future. A plan is thus a group of premade decisions that will allow you to achieve a future goal.

So if you're planning a trip to Paris, your plan might include the following decisions: the date you leave; how you get to the airport; your airline and flight; the airport of arrival; how you'll get into Paris; your hotel; and (of course) a fairly detailed itinerary (or plan) for each day you're in Paris. You could just wing it, and many people do. If you don't decide ahead of time how you're getting to or from the airport, or what you'll be doing on each of your days in Paris, what will happen? Perhaps nothing. More likely, though, you'll find yourself having to make a lot of last-minute decisions under stressful conditions. Instead of arranging ahead of time to have a friend take you to the airport, you may be scrambling at the last minute to find a cab. Instead of researching and pricing your options ahead of time, you may find yourself at Orly Airport, tired, and faced with a bewildering variety of buses and cabs, including some high-priced "gypsy" cabs. And instead of deciding ahead of time in the comfort of your home (and with all your guidebooks) what you'll do each day, you may kill two hours or more each day deciding what to do and finding out what is open, or drifting aimlessly through the Paris streets (which is not necessarily all bad, of course). Done right, planning also forces you to get in touch with what's actually happening "on the ground"—for instance, to check to see if the Louvre is closed the day you arrive because it's a national holiday. Your Paris plans thus will be quite useful, and your trip a lot more pleasant than it might be without a plan.

The point, again, is that planning gives you the luxury of deciding ahead of time what you're going to do. You don't have to plan, but if you don't, you're going to find yourself scrambling, probably under less-than-hospitable conditions, to make those decisions on the run. And this can lead to lots of errors.

Here's another example. If you are like most readers of this text, you're probably reading it as part of a management course. And why are you taking this course? Chances are the course is part of your program of studies. This program (it is hoped) is planned. It identifies your goal (say, getting a degree in business in two years), and it identifies how you will get that degree, by specifying the courses you'll need to graduate. Your plans may not end with earning the degree (although for many students, just doing so while working may be hassle enough for now). You may also have a broader goal, a vision of where you're headed in life. If you do, then your degree may be just one step in a longer-term plan. For example, suppose you dream of running your own management consulting firm by the time you are 35. Now (you ask yourself), "What do I have to do to achieve this goal?" The answer may be to work for a nationally known consulting firm, thus building up your experience and your reputation in the field. So here is your plan: Take this course to get the degree, get the degree to get the consulting job, and then work hard as a consultant to achieve your dream.

What Planning Accomplishes

In discussing the trip to Paris, we mentioned one big benefit of planning: You get to make your decisions ahead of time, in the comfort of your home (or office), and with the luxury of having the time to do research and weigh your options. There are a few other benefits of planning.

Planning provides direction and a sense of purpose. "If you don't know where you're going, any path will get you there," Alice is told as she stumbles into Wonderland. The same is true for all your endeavors: In the career example above, knowing ahead of time your goal is to have your own consulting firm provides a sense of direction and purpose for all the career decisions you have to make, such as what to major in and what experience you'll need along the way. This helps you avoid piecemeal decision making: It's a lot easier to decide what to major in and what courses to take when you've got a clear career objective.

The same is true in management: A plan provides a unifying framework against which decisions can be measured. For example, R. R. Donnelley & Sons Company is in the business of printing documents and other materials for a broad range of clients including investment bankers. Indeed, the company today is a leading content manager and printer of books, magazines, and catalogs, and is one of the world's largest manager, storer, and distributor of books in electronic form.[4] Donnelley's planning led its managers to anticipate a demand caused by the globalization of its customers. The company therefore invested heavily in advanced technology and a worldwide network. Now, with the help of satellites, R. R. Donnelley can print a securities prospectus simultaneously in locations around the globe.[5]

It would have been wasteful for R. R. Donnelley to spend its investment dollars building ever-bigger printing factories in the United States. The globalization of its customers demanded—and technological advances made possible—that it be capable of transmitting and creating documents via satellite around the globe. Its plan for doing so helped ensure that the firm channeled all its resources toward those desired results, thus avoiding activities—such as building unneeded domestic printing plants—that were inconsistent with the firm's overall direction.

Management theorist Peter Drucker says that planning can also help identify potential opportunities and threats and at least reduce long-term risks.[6] For example,

R. R. Donnelley's planning process helped identify the opportunity for satellite-based global printing.

Planning facilitates control. Control means ensuring that activities conform to plans; it is a three-step process in which standards are set, performance is measured against these standards, and deviations are identified and corrected. Planning is the first step in this cycle—specifying what is to be achieved. Thus, a company's plan may specify that its profits will double within five years. This goal can then be a standard against which the manager's performance is measured, compared, and controlled.

Types of Plans

While all plans specify goals and the courses of action chosen for reaching them, the plans themselves can come in all shapes and sizes, and each makes sense under different circumstances. For example, plans differ in format, or the way they are expressed. **Descriptive plans**, like the career plan above, state in words what is to be achieved and how. Plans stated in financial terms are called **budgets**. **Graphic plans** show what is to be achieved and how in charts.

Plans also differ in the spans of time they cover. Top management usually engages in long-term (5- to 10-year) strategic planning. A **strategic plan**—such as Wal-Mart's plan to expand abroad and apply its leading-edge planning methods globally—specifies the business or businesses the firm will be in and the major steps it must take to get there. Middle managers typically focus on developing shorter-term tactical plans (of up to five years' duration). **Tactical plans** (also sometimes called **functional plans**) show how top management's plans are to be carried out at the departmental level. First-line managers focus on shorter-term **operational plans**, or detailed day-to-day planning. These might show, for instance, exactly which workers are to be assigned to which machines or exactly how many units will be produced on a given day.

Andrew Carnegie, an early-20th-century multimillionaire, supposedly once happily paid $10,000 (a royal sum at the time) for a remarkably simple day-to-day operational planning system, one that millions of people use to this day. "I will show you a way to plan your day," a planning expert supposedly told Carnegie, "and if you like my idea, you'll pay me $10,000 for it." The idea—which may seem obvious today—was to write a daily to-do list. "Each night before you go to bed," the advisor told Carnegie, "list in priority order the things you need to get done the following day. Then, when tomorrow comes, methodically cross off each task as you do it." Carnegie was reportedly so impressed with how it boosted his efficiency that he paid the adviser the very next day.

Some plans are made to be used once, and others over and over. For example, some plans are **programs** established to lay out in an orderly fashion all the steps in a major one-time project. In contrast, **standing plans** are made to be used repeatedly, as the need arises.[7] Policies, procedures, and rules are examples of standing plans. **Policies** usually set broad guidelines. For example, it might be the policy at Saks Fifth Avenue that "we sell only high-fashion apparel and top-of-the-line jewelry." **Procedures** specify what to do if a specific situation arises. For example, "Before refunding the customer's purchase price, the salesperson should carefully inspect the garment and then obtain approval for the refund from the floor manager." Finally, a **rule** is a highly specific guide to action. For example, "Under no condition will the purchase price be refunded after 30 days." Standing plans like procedures or rules are usually written so that the standing plan's purpose is clear.

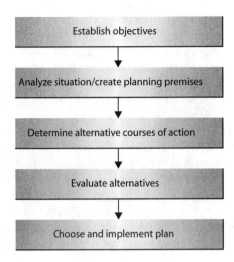

▶ THE MANAGEMENT PLANNING PROCESS

There is nothing mysterious about the planning process, since, as we said, planning is something we all do every day, often without even knowing it. For example, what planning process would you follow to choose a career? Here are the basic steps you would probably take: (1) set a tentative career goal, such as "to work as a management consultant"; (2) analyze the situation to assess your skills and to determine the future prospects for management consulting; (3) determine what your alternative courses of action are for getting there—in other words the paths you'll follow (college major, summer experiences, etc.) to reach your goal of management consultant; (4) evaluate them; and finally (5) choose your plan, and write it down (including a budget to show the money you'll need and where it will come from). This process is summarized in Figure 2-1.

You may notice that the planning process parallels the decision-making process; this makes sense, since developing plans involves deciding today what you'll do tomorrow. Both involve establishing objectives on criteria, developing and analyzing alternatives based on information you obtain, evaluating the alternatives, and then making a choice.

The planning process is basically the same when managers plan for their companies, but there are two added complications. First, there's usually a *hierarchical aspect* to management planning: Top management approves a long-term plan first; then each department creates its own budgets and other plans to show how it will contribute to the company's long-term plan.

Second—and especially in big companies—the planning process may be quite formal and involve much interaction and give-and-take between departments and a group we might call "corporate central." In other words, in many firms plans are bounced back and forth between the departments and a centralized planning staff, whose main purpose is to review and help define the plans of each department.

▶ HOW TO SET OBJECTIVES

There is one thing on which every manager can expect to be appraised: the extent to which he or she achieves his or her unit's goals or objectives. Whether it's a work team or a giant enterprise, the manager in charge is expected to move the unit ahead, and this means visualizing where the unit must go and helping get there. Organizations exist to achieve some purpose, and if they fail to move forward and achieve their aims, to that extent they have failed. As Peter Drucker put it, "There has to be something to point to and say, we have not worked in vain."[8]

Effectively setting goals is important for other reasons. Objectives (or goals— we'll use the terms interchangeably) are the targets toward which plans are aimed, and the anchor around which the hierarchy of goals is constructed. Goals can also aid motivation. Employees—individually and in teams—focus their efforts on achieving concrete goals with which they agree, and usually perform better with goals than without them. In fact, when performance is inadequate, it is often not because the person or team is loafing, but because the individual or team doesn't know what the goals are.

All managers today require a good working knowledge of how to set goals or objectives. We'll look first at the various types of objectives, and then at how to set and express them.

Types of Objectives

The range of activities for which goals or objectives may be set is virtually limitless. In a classic analysis, Peter Drucker listed eight areas in which objectives should be set:

1. Market standing
2. Innovation
3. Productivity
4. Physical and financial resources
5. Profitability
6. Managerial performance and development
7. Worker performance and attitude
8. Public responsibility[9]

One planning expert listed more than a dozen other areas in which objectives may be set, including the following:

1. Market penetration
2. Future human competencies
3. Revenue/sales
4. Employee development
5. New product/service department
6. New/expanded market development
7. Program/project management
8. Technology
9. Research and development
10. Customer relations/satisfaction
11. Cost control/management
12. Quality control/assurance

13. Productivity

14. Process improvement

15. Production capability/capacity

16. Cross-functional integration

17. Supplier development/relations

18. Unit structure (reorganization)[10]

It is clear from these lists that profit maximization alone is not a good enough guide. It is true that in economic theory and in practice managers aim to maximize profits (although other goals, including social responsibility, are crucial too). However, managers also need specific objectives in areas like market penetration and customer service if they are to have any hope of boosting profits. (At the same time, top management must also take care that the goals are complete. People put their efforts where they know they count, so if you measure only market penetration or revenue, profits may be ignored.)

Using Management by Objectives

Management by objectives (MBO) is a technique used by many firms to assist in the process of setting organizationwide objectives as well as goals for subsidiary units and their employees. Supervisor and subordinate jointly set goals for the latter and periodically assess progress toward those goals. A manager may engage in a modest MBO program by setting goals with his or her subordinates and periodically providing feedback. However, the term *MBO* almost always refers to a comprehensive organizationwide program for setting goals, one usually reserved for managerial and professional employees. One advantage of this technique (in terms of the goal-setting studies just reviewed) is that, implemented properly, it can lead to specific, measurable, and participatively set objectives.

The MBO process generally consists of five steps:

1. *Set organization goals.* Top management sets strategic goals for the company.

2. *Set department goals.* Department heads and their superiors jointly set supporting goals for their departments.

3. *Discuss department goals.* Department heads present department goals and ask all subordinates to develop their own individual goals.

4. *Set individual goals.* Goals are set for each subordinate, and a timetable is assigned for accomplishing those goals.

5. *Give feedback.* The supervisor and subordinate meet periodically to review the subordinate's performance and to monitor and analyze progress toward his or her goals.[11]

Managers can do several things to make an MBO program successful. They can state goals in measurable terms, be specific, and make sure each person's goals are challenging but attainable. Goals should also be reviewed and updated periodically, and be flexible enough to be changed if conditions warrant.[12]

Again, however, an effective MBO program requires more than just setting goals. The main purpose is integrating the goals of the individual, of the unit in which the individual works, and of the company as a whole. In fact, to Drucker, the creator of MBO, the method was always more a philosophy than a rigid sequence of steps. As he said, "the goals of each manager's job must be defined by the contribution he or she has to make to the success of the larger unit of which they are part." MBO therefore basically gives managers a road map for how to link the goals at each level and across the firm's departments, and to thereby create the company's hierarchy of goals.

▶ DEVELOPING PLANNING PREMISES

Good plans—whether for a career, a trip to Paris, or an expansion by Wal-Mart into Europe—are built on **premises**, assumptions we make about the future. Managers use several techniques to produce the premises on which they build their plans. These include forecasting, marketing research, and competitive intelligence.

Sales Forecasting Techniques

IBM's strategy in the new century—for instance to make all its products more Internet-compatible—reflects the assumptions it made regarding demand for its traditional products like mainframe computers. **Forecast** means to estimate or calculate in advance or to predict.[13] In business, forecasting often starts with predicting the direction and magnitude of the company's sales.

There are two broad classes of sales forecasting methods: quantitative and qualitative. **Quantitative forecasting** methods use statistical methods to examine data and find underlying patterns and relationships. **Qualitative forecasting** methods emphasize human judgment.

Quantitative Methods   Quantitative methods like time-series methods and causal models forecast by assuming that past relationships will continue into the future. A **time series** is a set of observations taken at specific times, usually at equal intervals. Examples of time series are the yearly or monthly gross domestic product of the United States over several years, a department store's total monthly sales receipts, and the daily closing prices of a share of stock.[14]

If you plot time-series data on a graph for several periods, you may note various patterns. For example, if you were to plot monthly sales of Rheem air conditioning units, you would find seasonal increases in late spring and summer, and reduced sales in the winter months. For some types of time series, there may also be an irregular pattern, such as a sudden blip in the graph that reflects unexplained variations in the data. The basic purpose of all time-series forecasting methods is to remove irregular and seasonal patterns so that management can identify fundamental trends.

Managers often need to understand the causal relationship between two variables, such as their company's sales and an indicator of economic activity, like disposable income. **Causal methods** develop a projection based on the mathematical relationship between a company factor and those variables that management believes influence or explain the company factor.[15] The basic premise of causal models is that a particular factor—such as company sales of television sets—is directly influenced by some other, more predictable, factor or factors—such as the number of people unemployed in a state or the level of disposable income in the United States.[16] **Causal forecasting** thus estimates the company factor (such as sales) based on other factors (such as advertising expenditures or level of unemployment). Statistical techniques such as correlation analysis (which shows how closely the variables are related) are generally used to develop the necessary relationships.

Companies like Wal-Mart use sophisticated technology to forecast sales; the "Managing @ the Speed of Thought" box provides an example.

Managing @ the Speed of Thought

■ Demand Forecasting at Wal-Mart

When it comes to retailing, Wal-Mart is larger than its three closest competitors combined, and that's not just because it buys its merchandise inexpensively. Wal-Mart has what is probably the most sophisticated information technology system in all of retailing, and it uses that system's power to give its customers what they want, while squeezing every bit of extraneous cost from its products.

Wal-Mart's data warehouse (introduced in the section opener) is a good example of how Wal-Mart does this. Recall that the data warehouse collects information on things like sales, inventory, products in transit, and product returns from Wal-Mart's 3,000 stores. These data are then analyzed to help Wal-Mart's managers analyze trends, understand customers, and more effectively manage inventory. How is this information used? As one example, Wal-Mart is implementing a new demand-forecasting system. Its data warehousing tracks the sale by store of 100,000 Wal-Mart products. This powerful system lets Wal-Mart managers examine the sales of individual items for individual stores, and also creates seasonal profiles for each item. Armed with this information, managers can more accurately plan what items will be needed for each store and when.

Wal-Mart is also teaming with vendors like Warner-Lambert to create an Internet-based collaborative forecasting and replenishment (CFAR) system. Wal-Mart collects data (on things like sales by product and by store, and seasonal trends) for its sales of Warner-Lambert products. Managers at Wal-Mart and Warner-Lambert then collaborate to develop forecasts for sales by store for Warner-Lambert products, such as Listerine. Once Warner-Lambert and Wal-Mart planners decide on mutually acceptable figures, a purchase plan is finalized and sent to Warner-Lambert's manufacturing planning system. So far, CFAR has helped cut the supply cycle time for Listerine from 12 weeks to 6, and that means less inventory, lower costs, and better buys for Wal-Mart customers.[17]

Qualitative Forecasting Methods   Time series and causal forecasting have three big limitations: They are virtually useless when data are scarce, such as for a new product with no sales history; they assume that historical trends will continue into the future.[18] They also tend to disregard unforeseeable, unexpected occurrences. Yet it is exactly these unexpected occurrences that often have the most profound effects on companies.

Qualitative forecasting techniques emphasize and are based on human judgment. They gather, in as logical, unbiased, and systematic a way as possible, all the information and human judgment that can be brought to bear on the factors being forecast.[19] Don't underestimate the value of qualitative forecasting methods. It's true that in developing adequate plans hard data and numbers are usually very important. However, it's also true that if you want plans to be realistic, there's usually no substitute for an intelligent human analysis of the situation and its possible consequences for the company.

The **jury of executive opinion** is one such qualitative forecasting technique. It involves asking a jury of key executives to forecast sales for, say, the next year. Generally, each executive is given data on forecasted economic levels and anticipated changes. Each jury member then makes an independent forecast. Differences are reconciled by the president or during a meeting of the executives. In an enhancement of this approach, experts from various departments gather to make the forecast.

The **sales force estimation** method is similar to the jury of executive opinion technique, but it gathers the opinions of the sales force regarding what they think sales will be in the forthcoming period. Each salesperson estimates his or her next year's sales, usually by product and customer. Sales managers then review each estimate, compare it with the previous year's data, and discuss changes with each salesperson. The separate estimates are then combined into a single sales forecast for the firm.

Marketing Research

Tools like causal models and sales force estimation can help managers explore the future to develop more accurate planning premises. However, there are times when, to formulate plans, managers want to know not just what may happen in the future, but what customers are thinking right now. **Marketing research** refers to the procedures used to develop and analyze customer-related information that helps managers make decisions.[20]

Marketing researchers depend on two main types of information. One source is **secondary data**, or information that has been collected or published already. Good sources of secondary data include the Internet, libraries, trade associations, company files and sales reports, and commercial data, for instance from companies such as A. C. Nielsen. **Primary data** refer to information specifically collected to solve a current problem. Primary data sources include mail and personal surveys, in-depth and focus-group interviews, and personal observation (watching the reactions of customers who walk into a store).[21]

Competitive Intelligence

Developing useful plans often requires knowing as much as possible about what competitors are doing or are planning to do. **Competitive intelligence** (CI) is a systematic way to obtain and analyze public information about competitors. Although this sounds (and is) a lot like legalized spying, it's become much more popular over the past few years. According to one report, the number of large companies with CI groups has tripled since 1988, to about 1000.[22]

Competitive intelligence (CI) practitioners use a variety of techniques to find out what clients' competitors are doing. These include keeping track of existing and new competitors by having specialists visit their facilities, and hiring their workers and questioning their suppliers and customers. CI firms also do sophisticated Internet searches to dig up all available information about competitors, as well as more mundane searches like reading stock analysts' reports on the competitors' prospects. Several private CI consulting firms, including Kroll Associates, have built successful businesses using prosecutors, business analysts, and former FBI and Drug Enforcement Agency employees to ferret out the sorts of information one might want before entering into an alliance with another company or before deciding to get into a given business.

As Table 2-1 illustrates, CI consultants provide a range of information. For example, a firm can help client companies learn more about competitors' strengths and vulnerabilities, product strategies, investment strategies, financial capabilities, and

T A B L E   2 - 1

Competitive Intelligence: Kroll's Business Intelligence and Analysis Services and Capabilities

CI Can Address Four Critical Management Concerns

COMPETITION: Learning enough about competitors to devise proactive and reactive strategies, including competitors' strengths and vulnerabilities, product strategies, investment strategies, financial capabilities, operational issues, and anti-competitive behavior.

BUSINESS RELATIONSHIPS AND TRANSACTIONS: Evaluating the capabilities, weaknesses, and reputation of potential or existing joint venture partners, strategic alliances, acquisitions, distributors, licensees/licensors, critical suppliers/vendors, and project finance participants.

ENTRY INTO NEW MARKETS: Developing entry strategies into new geographic and/or product markets, including identifying players in an industry, analyzing industry structure and trends, assessing local business practices, and ascertaining entry barriers, government regulation, and political risk.

SALES OPPORTUNITIES: Maximizing opportunities to win contracts, develop major new customers, or maintain existing ones, including identifying purchasing decision makers and critical factors, determining current suppliers, understanding the competition, and assessing the status of bids.

By Providing Intelligence Like This on Companies, Industries, and Countries

Operations: Nature of business, sales, locations, headcount.
Financial: Ownership, assets, financing, profitability.

Management: Organization structure, decision makers, integrity/reputation, management style, history as partner, political connections.
Marketing/Customers: Market position, major accounts, pricing, distribution, sales force, advertising.

Manufacturing: Plant and equipment, capacity, utilization, sourcing materials/components, shifts, labor costs, unions.
Technology: New products and processes, research and development practices, technological assessment.

Strategic Directions: Business priorities, diversification, geographic strategy, horizontal/vertical integration, strategic relationships.
Legal: Lawsuits, judgments, potential liabilities, environmental exposure.

current or prior behavior. Other CI services include evaluating the capabilities, weaknesses, and reputation of potential or existing joint-venture partners; identifying the major players in a new market or industry the firm is thinking of entering; and helping planners boost sales opportunities, for instance by identifying the decision makers who actually do the purchasing and the critical factors they look for in vendors.

Managers using CI must beware of slipping into activities that are ethically or legally wrong. Reading brokers' reports on a competitor or finding information about it on the Internet would be viewed as legitimate by almost everyone. However, when CI practitioners dig through the target's trash on public property to search for memos or hire former employees to pick their brains, ethical alarms should start ringing.

Some CI investigators may cross the line. For example, in a recent court case involving a large American chemical firm, former news reporters allegedly worked as investigators on behalf of one of the parties, posing as journalists to try to unearth confidential information about the firm. Another former reporter was allegedly offered a $25,000 bonus to get any national newspaper to publish a negative article about the company.[23]

Entrepreneurs In Action

Planning Under the Gun

▶When Gary Steele joined Internet startup Netiva, the company looked like a sure bet. It had big-name venture-capital backers, and a product, the Netiva Internet application system, which let larger companies build databases, using the Java programming language.

Steele soon discovered, though, that most of the company's plans were based on some erroneous assumptions. Its software was designed for the customer to run and maintain, but that meant Netiva's technical people had to get deeply involved up front in selling the software, and the deals were taking too long to complete. The original business plan also assumed that customers would develop multiple applications based on Netiva's software (and thereby have to pay multiple license fees); that wasn't happening, so Netiva was doing a lot of work for just the one-time license fee of $25,000.

Steele quickly concluded that the company was doomed unless drastic measures were taken. Forty per-

cent of the employees were laid off the next week. Working mostly on his own, Steele produced an eight-point plan of action, laying out what the company had to do in the following six weeks. Several weeks later he and four members of his executive team held 75 fact-finding meetings with executives at medium- and large-sized firms to get the information they required about what customers wanted and thus what Netiva's plans should be. ServicePort was one new product to come out of these meetings; it is basically a Web portal for consulting firms to enable their employees (who are often out of town) to conveniently plug in to their companies' databases and share things like client reports.

Now called Portera, the company has 70 employees, and Steele has raised more money, thanks in large part to his ability to almost single-handedly develop his company's new plan.[24]

▶ PLANNERS IN ACTION

So far in this section we've explained the planning process and some techniques for setting goals and predicting the future. In this final section we turn to a discussion of how planners actually plan, in other words to illustrations of planners and planning departments in action.

Who Does the Planning?

Who does the planning depends a lot on the size of the firm. The basic process—set goals, develop background information such as forecasts, develop and evaluate alternatives, and finalize the plan—is pretty standard. However, in a small business the entrepreneur (such as Gary Steele in the following "Enterpreneurs in Action" box) will likely do most of the planning himself or herself, perhaps informally bouncing around ideas with a few employees or using business planning software. In larger firms there's usually a central corporate planning group (some call it corporate central) whose role it is to work with top management and each division to continually challenge and refine the company's plans.

Over the past few years, most large companies have made dramatic changes in the way they do their planning. For example, most large companies like General Electric have moved from centralized to decentralized planning.[25] Today, in other words, the people doing the actual planning in big firms like GE are generally not specialists housed in large, centralized headquarters departments. Instead, the actual planning is carried out by product and divisional managers, often aided by small headquarters advisory groups. Pushing planning down from centralized departments to product managers reflects the fact that the latter are usually in the best position to sense changes in customer, competitive, and technological trends and react to them.

In practice, many entrepreneurs and managers turn to packaged planning software when it comes to developing and creating their business plans. Used in this context, the phrase "business plan" means a comprehensive plan—often prepared for prospective funding sources—for all aspects of the business for the next two to three years. Such a plan traditionally begins with a brief overview called an executive summary and then covers topics such as company summary, products or services, market analysis, strategy and implementation, and financial plan.

The basic idea of such a plan is usually to give the bank or other funding source a clear picture of your business, the industry and the competition, what you intend to accomplish, and how you will use your new funds. The following "Entrepreneurs in Action" box presents one planning package.

What Planners Do

Most large companies still have small central planning departments, and these planners still play a crucial role. For example, the corporate-central planning departments of multinational firms like GE engage in several basic planning activities:[26]

- *Act as "information central."* They compile and monitor all planning-related data such as data on divisions' progress toward meeting planned financial targets, and competitor intelligence.

- *Conduct competitor and market research.* They help the divisions analyze global competition, for instance, by identifying major global competitors.

- *Develop forecasts.* They develop forecasts that are applicable companywide.

- *Provide consulting services.* They help divisions conduct industry analyses and provide divisional planners with training in the techniques they could or should be using.

- *Create a common language.* They devise corporationwide planning reports and forms so that the divisions' plans are comparable in the information they provide.

- *Communicate companywide objectives.* They communicate companywide objectives to divisional managers, who then formulate plans for achieving their assigned objectives.

Planning in Action

The idea that planning is done by lower-level managers rather than a planning department is in fact somewhat misleading, since the actual process in larger firms involves much give and take. Based on input from product and divisional managers and other sources, top management sets an overall strategic direction for the firm. The resulting objectives then become the targets for which the product and divisional managers formulate specific tactical and operational plans. Strategic planning and direction setting are still mostly done by top managers, usually with their planning unit's assistance. However, more of the premising, alternatives-generating, and product-planning input goes up the hierarchy than in previous years.

GE's recent planning activities provide a "big company" example. In 1998–1999, three themes guided organizationwide planning at GE: globalization, product—services, and "six-sigma quality" (what GE calls its quality improvement–cost minimization process.) These basic themes, or "growth initiatives," provided the guidelines for the top managers of various divisions (such as Aerospace, GE Capital, and NBC). For example, with Asia in economic crisis in 1998, several of GE's divisions moved fast to take advantage of extraordinary global opportunities in Japan. GE's Edison Life quickly became a force in the Japanese insurance industry, acquiring over $6 billion of Japanese insurance assets.

Companywide, GE also wants to move to providing more high-value, information technology–based productivity services. Several GE divisions have therefore invested hundreds of millions of dollars to allow them to provide services to upgrade the competitiveness and profitability of customers as wide-ranging as utilities, hospitals, railroads, and airlines. Finally, the first of GE's six-sigma–guided products are now coming to market from various GE divisions. One, the LightSpeed scanner, dramatically reduces (from 3 minutes to 17 seconds) the time a trauma patient must spend being scanned to diagnose an illness such as a pulmonary embolism.[27]

Planning in action, in other words, is really an interplay between headquarters and divisions, particularly in large, multibusiness firms. In a typical company, top management and the board might formulate a few guiding themes at the start of the year. The divisions might then complete reviews of their businesses in April, and forward these to corporate planning. In June the board might adopt a set of planning assumptions and guidelines prepared by the corporate planning department. At the same time, central planning might be preparing various financial forecasts, again based in part on projections from the divisions.

In July the board reviews and sets the firm's financial objectives, and in early August these goals are sent to each business unit. The units then use these financial targets (as well as other guidelines, like GE's three growth initiatives) to prepare their own plans. These are submitted for approval in January. Once adopted, the plans are monitored by central planning, perhaps via quarterly reports from the operating units. After the broad divisional plans are approved, the divisions and their departments develop their shorter-term tactical plans.

There's No One Best Way

Planning can sometimes be more trouble than it's worth. Even on something as simple as a trip to Paris, for instance, blind devotion to the plan could cause you to miss a great opportunity that pops up at the last minute. In a company, such inflexibility can be even more dangerous. For example, department stores like JC Penney would be foolish to ignore the possibility of Internet catalog sales just because the word *Internet* didn't appear in their long-term plans two or three years ago.

A recent *Harvard Business Review* article explains some other ways misguided planning can destroy a company's value. An extensive and time-consuming planning process can be a waste of time and money unless top management and its planning group can coax divisional managers to do things differently than they would have done on their own. Yet, "at many companies, business unit plans get through the process largely unscathed." The result is that a lot of time and money has been spent for very little gain.

The opposite is also true: If they're not careful, top managers and central planning may insist on counterproductive changes in the division managers' plans. Top managers, after all, can spend only a fraction of their time understanding the details of each of the many separate businesses of the company, so "the potential for misguided advice is high, especially in diversified companies."[28]

Problems like these don't have to happen. One way to avoid them, says one expert, is to remember that a planning process that works for one company won't necessarily work for another. A good planning process, he contends:

> is not a generic process but one in which both analytic techniques and organizational processes are carefully tailored to the needs of the businesses as well as to skills, insight, and experiences of senior corporate managers. A mature electrical-products business, for example, has different planning needs than a fast growing entertainment business or a highly cyclical chemicals business.[29]

What this means is that each company must develop a planning process that's right for it, starting with what it wants its planning process to achieve. The planning process at Granada, a British conglomerate that has businesses in television programming and broadcasting, hotels, catering, and appliances, emphasizes *not* relying on comparing or benchmarking its financial results to those of the industry. When you do that, "you lock yourself into low ambitions" the CEO says.[30] Granada's planning process is therefore built around challenging business managers to find ways to achieve huge leaps in their divisions' sales and profitability. "Planning is about raising ambitions and helping businesses get more creative in their search for ways to increase profits."[31]

On the other hand, Dow Chemical Corporation's planning process is aimed at finding small, incremental improvements in processing costs—such as a 2% savings in maintenance costs—because in the slow-growing chemicals industry costs are very important. The whole planning process at Dow is therefore very formal, analytical, comparative, and numbers oriented. The point, says one planning expert, is that managers must define what they want to achieve from their planning before establishing a planning process.

SUMMARY ■

1. Plans are methods formulated for achieving desired results. Planning is the process of establishing objectives and courses of actions prior to taking action. Plans differ in format, timetable, and frequency.

2. The management-planning process consists of a logical sequence of five steps: establish objectives; conduct situation analysis; determine alternative courses of action; evaluate alternatives; and choose and implement the plan. In practice, this produces a planning hierarchy because top management's goals become the targets for which subsidiary units must formulate derivative plans.

3. Every manager can expect to be appraised on the extent to which he or she achieves assigned objectives, which makes setting objectives an essential management skill. The areas for which objectives can be set are virtually limitless, ranging from market standing to innovation and profitability.

4. Among the techniques for developing planning premises are forecasting, marketing research, and competitive intelligence. Forecasting techniques include quantitative methods such as time-series analysis and causal methods. Qualitative forecasting methods such as sales-force estimation and jury of executive opinion emphasize human judgment.

5. Most companies have moved from centralized to decentralized planning in the past few years, in part to place the planning responsibility with the product and divisional managers who are probably in the best position to understand their customers' needs and competitors'

activities. However, central planning units in larger companies, though dramatically downsized, still carry out important planning-related activities such as competitor and market research, communicating companywide objectives, and providing planning-related consulting services to the divisions.

TYING IT ALL TOGETHER   ■

As we've seen, planning and decision making are closely intertwined. Planning means choosing, ahead of time, your objectives and the courses of action that will get you there. So your plan is actually a set of prior decisions.

This section focuses on the overall planning process and goals, and on the hierarchical nature of corporate planning. We saw that all of a company's plans tend to revolve around and service top management's longer-term strategic plan.

Skills and Study Materials

CRITICAL THINKING EXERCISES   ■

1. Consider an ancient country with a long tradition of religious philosophy, an ethic of hard work, and strong warrior instincts. Imagine this country emerging into the world marketplace almost overnight, a country with over 1.2 billion consumers. Many of its citizens have a per capita income of only $500, but economists estimate that as many as 200 million middle-class consumers have disposable income to spend on a variety of products. There are believed to be at least one million millionaires in this socialistic-capitalistic country.

   This country has had most-favored-nation trade status since 1980. However, because it does not allow freedom of emigration as called for by a 1974 U.S. amendment, it must have its trade privileges reauthorized by the president every year. Many U.S. citizens are concerned with the civil and intellectual rights of the people of this country, which has imposed government sanctions on demonstrators and has a history of human-rights violations. Bilateral trade between the United States and this country recently reached $57 billion. U.S. investment rose from $358 million in 1990 to $25 billion in 1996.

   The country, of course, is the world's largest: China. There is great potential and opportunity for business here. However, there are also threats. Using the concepts presented in this section, explain how you would go about developing a plan for doing business in China for the next five years.

2. The Internet is increasingly a part of our lives. We can bank with it; shop for groceries, cars, and homes; go to college; be our own travel agents; research topics; talk with others in chat rooms; and use it for a host of other uses. The long-term implications of the Internet are amazing. The Internet can provide a much more flexible and convenient lifestyle for many. But there are potential downsides. What happens to all the jobs that are displaced by technology? For example, many of us have not been into a bank for years because we use ATMs. Now we can bank over the Internet from home. We can pay bills. We can shop and have goods delivered. Critical questions arise in terms of the planning and setting of objectives for companies, individuals, and society. What will happen to displaced workers? Will there be enough jobs for everyone? What about those who are not technologically literate or do not own a computer? What about the cost of the Internet for those who cannot afford to use the service? Explain how you would use the concepts and techniques in this section to write an essay titled "The Impact on Society of the Internet."

CASE 2-1
KMART'S HIGH HOPES

Kmart president and CEO Floyd Hall believes his company will ultimately be identified as one of the top five retailers in the country—in any area. Could Hall's vision for Kmart be translated into meaningful objectives, or is it too ambitious for the merchandising firm? Hall feels there is sufficient room for growth in the discount retailing industry for the next five years. Given the strength of Kmart's brands, its savvy store managers, and competitive pricing, Hall envisions customers coming back to Kmart.

As part of Kmart's objective to be one of the top five retailers, the company is expanding its physical presence in the market. In October 1999 Kmart Corporation announced that it expects to expand or open 400 new stores over the next five years, half of them supercenters. In 2000, Kmart opened more than 70 new stores in key metropolitan markets across the country. All this expansion comes from a company that can already boast that 80% of the U.S. population is within a 15-minute drive of one of its 2,153 Kmart, Big Kmart, or Super Kmart stores.

One of Kmart's successful tactics for meeting its sales objectives involves merchandising. Kmart promotes heavily to get customers into its stores, and then merchandizes to them when they are there. Kmart uses a wide range of tactics to get customers into the stores. For example, Kmart has nearly 1,560 pharmacies, making it the third largest pharmacy chain in the United States. While customers are waiting for their prescriptions, they are likely to browse one of the artfully crafted display areas. Kmart is also the world's largest photo processor. More than 25 million rolls of film per year are brought to Kmart stores to be developed. The end result is that specialty traffic means increased sales for Kmart's branded lines. Kmart's Jaclyn Smith clothing line, for example, is the fourth most popular sportswear line in America, with sales of more than 30 million pieces.

Hall feels that Kmart must develop an identity to which the customer can relate. Hall has Kmart pursuing a differentiation strategy by further developing the company's own labels, especially the Martha Stewart line. Kmart also offers the Penske auto products line, Sesame Street, Thom McAn, and others. In this way it hopes to differentiate itself from competitors like Wal-Mart, and to underscore that Kmart has items and brands that others do not.

In addition to its in-store merchandising, the company is also pursuing more innovative promotional channels. Kmart has developed sophisticated database marketing capabilities. With this information technology, Kmart can track 2 billion transactions annually from more than 85 million households. One use of this data is to reach customers through targeted direct mail. The database may also help Kmart in a move to Internet marketing.

In addition to its Super Kmart offering, the company plans to renovate more than 160 smaller stores to its new small-store prototype. Kmart has successfully positioned itself as the largest discount retailer in urban markets, which is one of the ways that Kmart differentiates itself from rival Wal-Mart.

Outside analysts feel that one of Kmart's greatest strengths is its current management team. Most feel this team can carry Kmart to a bright future. Kmart's target, however, is constantly moving. While Kmart may be meeting its current sales objectives, its competitors are also developing new products and promotional strategies.

Some feel that continued growth at Super Kmart may be tied to an alliance with a food retailer, which could provide Kmart with some important benefits. For example, such an alliance would allow Kmart to focus on its traditional general merchandise, an area where Kmart has more expertise and more profit than in groceries.

Discussion Questions

1. What evidence can you see that Kmart's growth is the result of management's plans rather than just chance?

2. How do you think Kmart's departmental plans link together to help it achieve its objectives?

3. Can Kmart become one of the top five retailers, as Hall envisions? Why or why not?

STRATEGIC MANAGEMENT

WHAT'S AHEAD?

To Microsoft Corporation, the phrase "The network is the computer" is anything but benign. Every company needs to know who it will compete with and where and how it will compete—in other words, to have a strategy. For years Microsoft's strategy was to produce operating systems for desktop computers. But the growing success of Sun Microsystems's new strategy may well change all that. Under CEO Scott McNealy, Sun is focusing on using its Java Internet-based software to enable anyone anywhere to tap into an almost limitless range of computer applications via the Internet, even if their computers are fairly primitive. Already, through alliances with companies like AOL and Netscape, Sun is making its new strategy a reality. But if the network is the computer, who's going to need all those expensive Microsoft operating systems? Microsoft must therefore move fast to reorient how it defines its core business and how it intends to compete with the likes of Sun, while dealing with many lawsuits accusing it of anti-competitive practices.

THIS SECTION FOCUSES ON THE FOLLOWING:

- The steps in the strategic management process
- The three main types of strategies
- Three strategy-development tools

Planning means setting objectives and deciding on the courses of action for achieving them. We also saw that plans are usually hierarchical, since the firm's long-term strategic plan provides the framework within which its other plans must fit. So defining your occupational business (or strategy) as "management consultant" will lead you to make short-term plans—regarding which college to attend and which courses to take, for instance—which are vastly different than they would be if you had decided to be a dentist. In business management too, says management guru Peter Drucker, top management's primary task is thinking through the mission of the business—that is, asking the question "What is our business and what should it be?" This leads to the setting of objectives, the development of strategies and plans, and the making of today's decisions for tomorrow's results.[1]

In this section, we therefore turn to strategic planning and management. Planning and strategic planning have much in common: Both involve assessing your situation today and predicting the future; both involve setting objectives; and both involve crafting courses of action to get you from where you are today to where you want to be tomorrow.

But we'll see in this section that strategic planning is also in a class of its own. Tom Peters, another management guru, reportedly once offered $100 to the first manager who could demonstrate that he or she had created a successful strategy from a planning process.[2] His point is that a highly-structured planning process may actually produce worse—not better—strategic plans.

Why? Because, unlike shorter-term plans (What courses should I take this term?), strategic planning (What occupation is best for me after I graduate?) requires looking far ahead and using insight and creativity to make sense of a great many imponderables. (For your personal strategic plan, these might include Will I be a good consultant? Will I enjoy that career? and Will there be enough jobs to make being a consultant worth my while?). As two experts put it, "Planning processes are not designed to accommodate the messy process of generating insights and molding them into a winning strategy."[3] So, do not be misled into believing that strategic planning is (or could ever be) entirely mechanical: Insight and creativity always play a very big role.

▶ THE STRATEGIC MANAGEMENT PROCESS

How do firms like Sun Microsystems know what strategy they should pursue to stay competitive? **Strategic management** is the process of identifying and pursuing the organization's mission by aligning the organization's internal capabilities with the external demands of its environment.[4] As Figure 2-2 shows, the strategic management process consists of five tasks: defining the business and developing a vision and mission; translating the mission into specific goals; crafting a strategy to achieve the goals; implementing and executing the strategy; and evaluating performance, reviewing the situation, and making adjustments.

Let's look at each step in turn.

Step 1: Define the Business and Its Mission[5]

Strategic management starts with answering the question What business should we be in? This is tricky because two companies can be in the same industry but answer that question in very different ways. For example, Ferrari and Toyota both make cars. However, Ferrari specializes in high-performance cars, and its competitive

► FIGURE 2-2

The Five Strategic
Management Steps

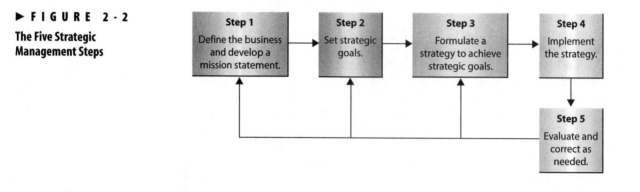

advantage is built on craftsmanship and high-speed performance. Toyota produces a range of automobiles, and many of its own supplies and parts; its competitive advantage is built on cost-efficient production and a strong dealer network.

Wal-Mart and Kmart are also in the same industry. Wal-Mart, however, distinguished itself from Kmart by at first concentrating its stores in small southern towns, and by building a state-of-the-art satellite-based distribution system. Kmart opened stores throughout the country (where it had to compete with a great many other discounters, often for expensive, big-city properties). Kmart also based its competitive advantage on its size, which it (erroneously) assumed would provide it with the economies of scale necessary to keep costs below those of competitors.

Answering the question, What business should we be in? may require both a vision statement and a mission statement (although the two are often the same). The company's **vision** is a "general statement of its intended direction that evokes emotional feelings in organization members."[6] As Warren Bennis and Bert Manus say:

> To choose a direction, a leader must first have developed a mental image of a possible and desirable future state for the organization. This image, which we call a vision, may be as vague as a dream or as precise as a goal or mission statement. The critical point is that a vision articulates a view of a realistic, credible, attractive future for the organization, a condition that is better in some important ways than what now exists.[7]

For example, Rupert Murdock (chairman of News Corporation, which owns the Fox network and many newspapers and satellite TV operations) has a vision of an integrated global news-gathering, entertainment, and multimedia firm. Bill Gates had a vision of a software company serving the needs of the microcomputer industry.

Thanks to the Internet, even young entrepreneurs with the right vision and the skills to implement it can be enormously successful, almost overnight. Take Jeffrey Arnold, the CEO of WebMD. Jeff had a crystal-clear vision of a Web site supplying everything a consumer might want to know about medical-related issues, and today the startup he founded in late 1999 is valued at over $3.5 billion. That kind of success took more than luck and a clear vision, of course. He was also able to put in place all the elements of his strategy, for instance by getting Microsoft to invest over $250 million in WebMD, and getting CNN to make it a partner on its own Web site.[8]

The firm's **mission statement** operationalizes the top manager's vision. A mission statement "broadly outlines the organization's future course and serves to communicate 'who we are, what we do, and where we're headed.'"[9] Some examples are presented in Figure 2-3.

APEX ELEVATOR

To provide a high reliability, error-free method for moving people and products up, down, and sideways within a building.

UNITED TELEPHONE CORPORATION OF DADE

To provide information services in local-exchange and exchange-access markets within its franchised area, as well as cellular phone and paging services.

JOSEPHSON DRUG COMPANY, INC.

To provide people with longer lives and higher-quality lives by applying research efforts to develop new or improved drugs and health-care products.

GRAY COMPUTER, INC.

To transform how educators work by providing innovative and easy-to-use multimedia-based computer systems.

◀ **FIGURE 2-3**

Examples of Mission Statements

Mission statements usually crystallize the purpose of the company.

Step 2: Translate the Mission into Strategic Goals

The next strategic management task is to translate top management's vision and mission into operational strategic goals. For example, strategic goals for Citicorp include building shareholder value through sustained growth in earnings per share; continuing its commitment to building customer-oriented business worldwide; maintaining superior rates of return; building a strong balance sheet; and balancing the business by customer, product, and geography.[10]

Step 3: Formulate a Strategy to Achieve the Strategic Goals

A **strategy** is a course of action that explains how the enterprise will move from the business it is in now to the business it wants to be in (as stated in its mission), given its opportunities and threats and its internal strengths and weaknesses. For example, Wal-Mart decided to pursue the strategic goal of moving from being a relatively small, southern-based chain of retail discount stores to becoming the national leader in low-cost merchandise. One of Wal-Mart's strategies was to reduce distribution costs and minimize inventory and delivery times through a satellite-based distribution system.

Step 4: Implement the Strategy

Strategy implementation means translating the strategy into actions and results. Doing so requires drawing on all management functions: planning, organizing, leading, and controlling. For instance, employees need to be hired and motivated, and budgets need to be formulated so progress toward strategic goals can be measured. (That's one reason it's called the strategic *management* process.)

Step 5: Evaluate Performance

Finally, **strategic control**—the process of assessing progress toward strategic goals and taking corrective action as needed—keeps the company's strategy up to date. Strategic control should also ensure that all parts and members of the company are contributing in a useful way toward the strategy's implementation.

Managing strategy is thus an ongoing process. Competitors introduce new products, technological innovations make production processes obsolete, and societal

► F I G U R E 2 - 4

Relationships Among Strategies in Multiple-Business Firms

Companies typically formulate three types of strategies: Corporate strategies, business-level/competitive strategies, and functional strategies.

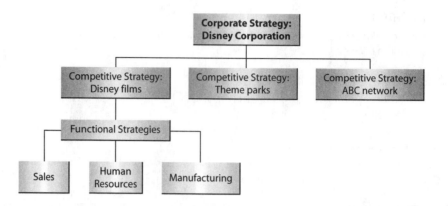

trends reduce demand for some products or services while boosting demand for others. Managers must therefore be alert to opportunities and threats that might require modifying or totally redoing their strategies.

Strategic Planning

Strategic planning is the process of identifying the business of the firm today and the business it wants for the future, and then identifying the course of action it will pursue, given its opportunities, threats, strengths, and weaknesses. It specifies who the firm will compete with and how it will compete with them.

Strategic planning is part of the overall strategic management process. As illustrated in Figure 2-2, it represents the first three of the strategic management tasks: defining the business and developing a mission, translating the mission into strategic goals, and crafting a strategy or course of action to move the organization from where it is today to where it wants to be.

We'll look more closely at how to develop and implement strategic plans later in this section. First, we'll look at the types of strategies a firm might pursue.

► TYPES OF STRATEGIES

There are three main types of strategies, as summarized in Figure 2-4. Many companies consist of a portfolio of several businesses. For instance, Disney includes movies, theme parks, and the ABC TV network. These companies need a **corporate-level strategy**, which identifies the portfolio of businesses that comprise the corporation and the ways in which these businesses fit together.

Each of these businesses then has its own business-level or **competitive strategy**. This strategy identifies how to build and strengthen the company's long-term competitive position in the marketplace.[11] It identifies, for instance, how Microsoft will compete with AOL/Netscape.

Each business is in turn composed of departments, such as manufacturing, marketing, and HR. **Functional strategies** identify the basic courses of action each functional department will pursue to contribute to attaining the business's competitive goals. We'll look at each type of strategy in turn.

Corporate-Level Strategies

Every company must choose the number of businesses in which it will compete and the relationships that will exist among those businesses. These decisions are driven by the firm's corporate-level strategy, which identifies the portfolio of businesses that will comprise the company. Companies can pursue one or more of the following corporate strategies when deciding what businesses to be in and how these businesses should relate to each other.

Concentration   A concentration/single business strategy means the company focuses on one product or product line, usually in one market. Organizations that have successfully pursued single business strategies include McDonald's, KFC, and WD-40 Company. The main advantage of a concentration strategy is that the company can focus on the one business it knows well, allowing it to do that one thing better than competitors (Thus Gerber stresses that "baby foods are our only business"). The main disadvantage is the risk inherent in putting all one's eggs into one basket. Concentrators must always be on the lookout for signs of decline. McDonald's, after years of concentrating in the hamburger franchise business, tried unsuccessfully to diversify into franchising children's play areas in covered shopping malls. Harley Davidson, on the other hand, successfully diversified into clothing, restaurants, and finance from motorcycles.

Concentrating in a single line of business need not mean the firm won't try to grow. Indeed, some traditional concentrators like the Coca-Cola Company have achieved very high growth rates through concentration.

Four strategies can contribute to growth.[12] Single-business companies can grow through **market penetration**. This means taking steps to boost sales of present products by more aggressively selling and marketing into the firm's current markets. **Geographic expansion** is another alternative. The *Wall Street Journal* has achieved above-average growth rates while concentrating on its traditional business by aggressively expanding into new geographic markets, domestic and overseas. Growth can also be achieved through **product development**, which means developing improved products for current markets. **Horizontal integration**, acquiring ownership or control of competitors in the same or similar markets with the same or similar products, is another option. For example, the Humana hospital chain has grown rapidly while remaining a concentrator by acquiring hundreds of hospitals.

Vertical Integration   Instead of staying in one business, a firm can expand into other businesses through a vertical integration strategy. **Vertical integration** means owning or controlling the inputs to the firm's processes and/or the channels through which products or services are distributed. (The former is backward integration, and the latter is forward integration.) Thus, Ford owns Libby-Owens glass, which supplies it with windshields; major oil companies like Shell not only drill and produce their own oil, but also sell it through company-controlled outlets.

Diversification   **Diversification** means a strategy of expanding into related or unrelated products or market segments.[13] Diversifying helps to move the organization into other businesses or industries, or perhaps just into new product lines. In any case, it helps the firm avoid the problem of having all its eggs in one basket by spreading risk among several products or markets. However, diversification adds a new risk: It forces the company and its managers to split their attention and resources among several products or markets instead of one. To that extent, diversification may undermine the firm's ability to compete successfully in its chosen markets.

Several forms of diversification are widely used. **Related diversification** means diversifying into other industries in such a way that a firm's lines of business still possess some kind of fit.[14] When women's-wear maker Donna Karan expanded into men's clothing, that was related diversification. Campbell's Soup purchased

Pepperidge Farm Cookies because it felt that Pepperidge Farm's customer base and channels of distribution were a good fit.

Conglomerate diversification, in contrast, means diversifying into products or markets that are *not* related to the firm's present businesses or to one another. For example, Getty Oil diversified into pay television, and several years ago Mobil Oil Company purchased (and then sold) the Montgomery Ward retail chain.

Status Quo Strategies   Unlike other growth-oriented strategies, a stability or status-quo strategy says "the organization is satisfied with its rate of growth and product scope." Operationally, this means it will retain its present strategy and, at the corporate level, continue focusing on its present products and markets, at least for now. Status quo is one corporate strategy pursued by the lubricant company that makes WD-40, which rarely advertises or aggressively pursues increased market share.

Investment Reduction Strategies   Investment reduction and defensive strategies are generally corrective actions required due to overexpansion, ill-conceived diversification, or some other financial emergency. They are taken to reduce the company's investments in one or more of its lines of business. For example, Levi Strauss, suffering a dramatic loss of market share, recently closed many of its U.S. clothing plants.

There are several ways to reduce investment. **Retrenchment** means the reduction of activity or operations. IBM engaged in a massive retrenchment effort, dramatically reducing (downsizing) the number of its employees and closing many facilities. **Divestment** means selling or liquidating individual businesses. (Divestment usually denotes the sale of a viable business, while liquidation denotes the sale or abandonment of a nonviable one.)

Strategic Alliances and Joint Ventures   Sometimes the firm's corporate strategy involves forming a partnership with another company, rather than growing internally. In such cases, strategic alliances and joint ventures are corporate strategic options.

Both terms generally refer to a formal agreement between two or more separate companies, the purpose of which is to enable the organizations to benefit from complementary strengths. For example, a small, cash-poor Florida-based company with a patented industrial pollution control filter might form a joint venture with a subsidiary of a major European oil firm. In this case, the joint venture might be a separate corporation based in Europe to which each partner contributes funds and other resources. The oil firm gets access to a product that could revolutionize its distilling facilities; the filter company gets access to the oil firm's vast European marketing network.[15]

The Virtual Corporation   For many firms encountering rapid change, the ultimate strategic alliance is the **virtual corporation**, "a temporary network of independent companies—suppliers, customers, even erstwhile rivals—linked by information technology to share skills, costs, and access to one another's markets."[16] Virtual corporations don't have headquarters staffs, organization charts, or the organizational trappings that we associate with traditional corporations. In fact, virtual corporations are not corporations at all, in the traditional sense of common ownership or a chain of command. Instead, they are networks of companies, each of which lends the virtual corporation/network its special expertise. Information technology (computer information systems, fax machines, electronic mail, and so on) then helps the virtual corporation's often far-flung company constituents stay in touch and quickly carry out their contributions.[17] When a virtual corporation is managed correctly, the individual contributors aren't just impersonal suppliers or marketers. Instead, successful virtual corporation relationships are built on trust and on a sense of "co-destiny." This means that the fate of each partner and of the virtual corporation's whole enterprise is dependent on each partner doing its share.[18]

Virtual corporations abound today. For example, AT&T called on Japan's Marubeni Trading Company to help it link up with Matsushita Electronic Industrial Company when it wanted to speed production of its Safari notebook computer (which was designed by Henry Dreyfuss Associates).[19] And when start-up company TelePad came up with an idea for a handheld, pen-based computer, a virtual corporation was its answer for breathing life into the idea: An industrial design firm in Palo Alto, California, designed the product; Intel brought in engineers to help with some engineering details; several firms helped develop software for the product; and a battery maker collaborated with TelePad to produce the power supply.[20] (Unfortunately, the idea didn't click, and TelePad went out of business).

The Internet, not surprisingly, is spawning a multitude of virtual operations. For example, the Web site eLance (www.elance.com) lets freelance consultants, graphic designers, and anyone else who wants to sell business services to businesses compete for work with one another by posting information on their skills and fees.[21] Denver-based graphic designer Serena Rodriguez now gets about 10% of her business through that site, and works, virtually—long distance, and without seeing them or being a formal part of their company—with firms like pharmaceuticals manufacturer Merck. Getting a big project often means recruiting other free agents to join your virtual team. For example, says Web designer Andrew Keeler, "I work with lots of people here in San Francisco whom I've never even met . . . It happens so fast, and it's all done by e-mail."[22]

Competitive Strategies

Whether a company decides to concentrate on a single business or to diversify into several different ones, it should develop a competitive strategy for each business. Strategic planning expert Michael Porter defines competitive strategy as a plan to establish a profitable and sustainable competitive position against the forces that determine industry competition.[23] The competitive strategy specifies how the company will compete; for instance, based on low cost or high quality. Porter says three basic or generic competitive strategic options are possible: cost leadership, differentiation, and focus.

Cost Leadership   Just about every company tries to hold down costs. In this way, a company can price its products and services competitively. **Cost leadership** as a competitive strategy goes beyond this. A business that pursues this strategy is aiming to become *the* low-cost leader in an industry. The unique characteristic is the emphasis on obtaining absolute cost advantages from any and all possible sources. Wal-Mart is a typical industry cost leader. Its distribution costs are minimized through a satellite-based warehousing system, the stores themselves are plain, and Wal-Mart negotiates the lowest prices from suppliers.

Pursuing a cost leadership strategy requires a tricky balance between pursuing lower costs and maintaining acceptable quality. Southwest Airlines, for instance, keeps its cost per passenger mile below those of most other major airlines while still providing service as good as or better than that of its competitors.

Differentiation   In a **differentiation strategy**, a firm seeks to be unique in its industry along some dimensions that are valued by buyers.[24] In other words, it picks one or more attributes of the product or service that its buyers perceive as important, and then positions itself to meet those needs.

In practice, the dimensions along which you can differentiate range from the "product image" offered by cosmetics firms, to concrete differences such as the product durability emphasized by Caterpillar. Volvo stresses safety, Apple Computer stresses usability, and Mercedes-Benz emphasizes quality. Firms can usually charge a premium price if they successfully stake out their claim to being different in some important way.

Focus Differentiators like Volvo and low-cost leaders like Wal-Mart generally aim their business at all or most potential buyers. A business pursuing a **focus strategy** selects a market segment and builds its competitive strategy on serving the customers in its market niche better or more cheaply than its competitors.

The basic question in choosing whether to pursue a focus competitive strategy is this: By focusing on a narrow market, can we provide our target customers with a product or service better or more cheaply than our generalist competitors?

Examples of focusers abound. Pea in the Pod, a chain of maternity stores, focuses on selling stylish clothes to pregnant working women. By specializing in "working woman maternity clothes," the company is able to provide a much wider range of such clothes to its target customers than can generalist competitors like Macy's or JCPenney.

The Five Forces Model To formulate a competitive strategy, the manager should understand the competitive forces that together determine how intense the industry's rivalries are and how to best compete. Based on that analysis, the company must find a sustainable **competitive advantage**, that is, a basis on which to identify a relative superiority over competitors. Strategy expert Michael Porter argues that how a company competes—its competitive strategy—depends on the intensity of the competition in its industry. Years ago when competition was not so keen in the auto industry, GM was not so concerned with competing on cost and quality.

Competitive intensity, says Porter, reflects five competitive forces, as shown in Figure 2-5. The task is to analyze them so that management can decide how best to compete in that industry.[25] We'll look at each of the five forces in turn.

Threat of Entry Intensity of industry competition depends first on the threat of new entrants. For instance, the competitive landscape for Encyclopaedia Britannica changed when Microsoft introduced Encarta.

In general, the more easily new competitors can enter the business, the more intense the competition. However, several things can make it harder for new competitors to enter an industry. For example, it's not easy to enter the auto industry because of the high investment required for plant and equipment. Making it more expensive for customers to switch to a competitor is another entry barrier: For instance, after a travel agent signs up for the American Airlines computerized reservation system, it's expensive for that agent to switch to the Delta system.

Rivalry Among Existing Competitors Rivalry among existing competitors manifests itself in tactics like price competition, advertising battles, and increased customer service.[26]

The rivalry in some industries is more intense and warlike than in others. For example, for many years the rivalry among law firms and CPA firms could be characterized as cordial. Recently, it has turned quite cutthroat. This in turn has motivated many law firms to emphasize efficiency, to offer special pricing plans to clients, and to merge.

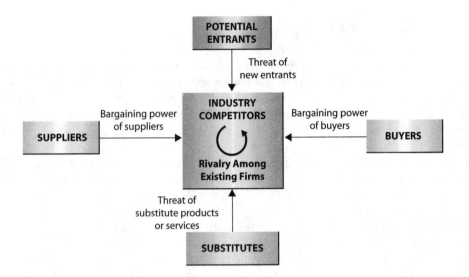

◀ FIGURE 2-5

Forces Driving Industry Competition

Source: Reprinted with the permission of The Free Press, a division of Simon & Schuster from *Competitive Strategy: Techniques for Analyzing Industries and Competitors* by Michael E. Porter. Copyright © 1980 by The Free Press.

Pressure from Substitute Products Intensity of competition also depends on substitute products. For example, frozen yogurt is a substitute for ice cream, and synthetics are a substitute for cotton.

Substitute products perform the same or similar functions. The more substitute products, then, in effect, the more competitive the industry. To the extent that few substitutes are available (as would be the case with certain patented drugs), rivalry is reduced and the industry is more attractive and less cutthroat.

Bargaining Power of Buyers The buyers' power is another competitive factor. For example, a buyer group is powerful if it purchases large volumes relative to the seller's sales; Toyota has a lot of clout with its suppliers, for instance. Similarly, when the products purchased are standard or undifferentiated (such as apparel elastic), and when buyers face few switching costs or earn low profits, then buyers' bargaining power over suppliers tends to be enhanced.

Bargaining Power of Suppliers Suppliers can also influence an industry's competitive intensity and attractiveness, for instance by threatening to raise prices or reduce quality.

Suppliers tend to have greater bargaining power when they are dominated by a few firms and are more concentrated. When few substitute products are available, when the buying industry is not an important customer of the supplier group, and when the supplier's product is an important input to the buyer's business, the supplier's power rises. In its lawsuit, for example, the U.S. government claimed that Microsoft exerted tremendous power as the only Windows supplier.

Analyzing an industry using the five forces model helps a company choose competitive strategy options. For example, where rivalry among existing competitors is very intense or there is a threat of new entrants, boosting product differentiation is a sensible option. That's one reason law firms now try to stress their differences and why image-oriented advertising is important to cosmetics firms. Boosting switching costs (as American Airlines did when it convinced thousands of travel agents to use its SABRE computerized reservation system) can also reduce rivals' (or new entrants') ability to compete, even when the product or service itself is fairly undifferentiated. Building competitive barriers is in "Entrepreneurs in Action."

Functional Strategies

At some point, each business's competitive strategy (low-cost leader, differentiator, or focuser) is translated into supporting functional strategies that each of its departments must pursue. Note that in some very large firms like GE, similar businesses are first grouped into strategic business units for control purposes. A **strategic business unit** (SBU) is an organizational entity that contains several related businesses. A firm's forest products SBU, for instance, might include separate fine papers, newsprint, and pulp businesses.

A functional strategy is the basic course or courses of action each department will follow in enabling the business to accomplish its strategic goals. Wal-Mart competes as the industry's low-cost leader. To implement this competitive strategy, it formulated departmental functional strategies that made sense for moving Wal-Mart toward its desired position. For example, the distribution department pursued a strategy (satellite-based warehousing) that ultimately drove down distribution costs to a minimum; the company's land development department found locations that fit the firm's customer profile and kept construction costs to a minimum; and the merchandise buyers found sources capable of providing good-quality merchandise at the lowest possible prices. Functional strategies can't be formulated intelligently unless the business has a clear direction in terms of the competitive strategy it wants to pursue. Then its functional strategies must fit its competitive strategy.

Entrepreneurs In Action

MovieFone Builds Entry Barriers

▶The success of Russ Leatherman and his colleagues at MovieFone illustrates how a smart entrepreneurial company put these competitive strategy ideas into practice. In 1989 Leatherman dreamed up the idea for an interactive telephone movie guide he called MovieFone. Callers in many cities get complete up-to-the-minute listings of theater offerings and show times in their area and can even purchase tickets over the phone. Leatherman's task, once his firm was launched, was to build barriers to keep potential competitors like Ticketmaster at bay.

To build these competitive barriers, MovieFone managers sought the following:

1. *Exclusivity*. MovieFone acquired highly desirable phone numbers in each of its area codes, such as 777-FILM, and registered these as trademarks. The numbers are easy for callers to remember, differentiating MovieFone and keeping competitors out.

2. *Focus*. By focusing on movie listings instead of branching out into other markets such as theaters or sporting events, MovieFone has become the industry expert when it comes to supplying listings and tickets. It knows its customers' profiles and has mastered the hardware, software, and logistics required to obtain, compile, and deliver listings and tickets better than anyone else.

3. *Expert systems*. MovieFone has developed what it calls *expert systems*, comprising special hardware, software, and electronic "will-call windows" in which customers can automatically pick up tickets. These systems further differentiate MovieFone and create substantial barriers to any new competitors that might be considering entering the market.

4. *Strategic alliances*. Many of the electronic will-call windows are placed in movie theaters, with which MovieFone has formed strategic alliances for this purpose. The alliances provide an additional source of income for the theaters and strengthen MovieFone's relationship with them.[27]

Today, MovieFone is growing fast. Moviegoers can reach it not just by phone, but on the Internet, too.

► CREATING STRATEGIC PLANS

Strategic plans like that of Sun's Scott McNealy (the network is the computer) usually don't just appear overnight. Instead, considerable thought goes into creating good plans, since a mistake—in terms of choosing the wrong way to compete—can be deadly. In this section we'll look more closely at how to create a strategic plan.

The Strategic Planning Process

"Define the business's mission," "set strategic goals," and "formulate a strategy to achieve those goals" are basic steps in strategic planning (see Figure 2-2). But strategic planning in practice is more complicated: Most managers don't formulate strategic missions or goals without first scanning the firms environment to see what competitors are doing. And once the strategy is in place, subsidiary plans to support the goals must be crafted.

Strategic planning therefore usually starts with identifying the driving forces in a firm's environment. These include the economic, demographic, technological, and competitive forces that shape a company's strategy.

There are several tools you can use to identify and assess these forces, but remember that it's important to avoid being too mechanical in your approach: you don't want to miss important forces. Encouraging insight and creativity is therefore necessary. Brainstorming can be a useful tool at this first stage. One strategy expert suggests having the top management team spend several hours brainstorming all the possible forces that might influence the firm. They must be sure to avoid criticizing or disposing of any until its potential usefulness and impact have been thoroughly aired.[28] Only then can the managers move on to actually formulating a strategy. Here again, brainstorming is useful for generating strategic options.

It's hard to overestimate the importance of this strategy formulation stage. A recent *Fortune* article emphasizes how the 17 companies that topped the *Fortune* 1000 in shareholder return did so in large part based on brilliant strategies. For example: "While many of its competitors in the biotech industry let the disease lead them to the science, Amgen stays ahead by taking the opposite approach. It develops its drugs by identifying areas of promising research that may lead to breakthrough products."[29] "Worldcom saw there was more than one way to be a telephone company. By offering customers not only long distance but also local and Internet services, it broke out of the pack and became a powerhouse in the U.S. telecommunications industry."[30] Here's another example: "Seeing opportunity and a market made up of mom-and-pop hardware stores, Home Depot launched a national chain of mega stores. Economies of scale let the giant retailer offer better prices, selection, and service to the home-improvement crowd."[31] For a view of the Internet's effect on strategy, see the accompanying "Managing @ the Speed of Thought" box.

Managing @ the Speed of Thought
■ Strategy for the Internet

Strategies can't be crafted today without considering how information technology (IT) and the Internet could and should affect the company's strategy.

This is nothing new. For example, Wal-Mart has grown fast thanks to its satellite-based warehouse and distribution system. UPS, the world's largest air and ground package distribution company, has maintained its competitive edge in large part due to the $1 billion invested on an annual basis in information technology. UPS drivers use handheld computers to capture customers' signatures, along with pickup, delivery, and time card information, and automatically transmit this information to headquarters via a cellular telephone network. For companies like these and thousands more, IT lies at the heart of their strategies.

But it's likely that the Internet's effect on companies' strategies will be even more profound. On-line companies like Amazon.com are perhaps the most obvious examples here. Consider how the strategies of traditional booksellers like Barnes & Noble and countless smaller ones have had to change in reaction to Amazon.com. Barnes & Noble has had to create its own on-line bookstore. Many smaller booksellers have had to reconsider whether they even want to or can remain in business, given the new competitive landscape. And in January 2000, AOL and Time Warner announced that they would combine. Their new strategy would involve using Time Warner's cable access and content along with AOL's system to reach hundreds of millions of customers.

And it's not just information businesses that must adapt to the Internet.[32] Two experts argue that even businesses not widely considered information businesses are or will be highly dependent on the Net. For example, GE's divisions used to purchase their supplies from suppliers with which they had long and established relationships. Today, GE has created special on-line purchasing Web sites, and any supplier can bid on the GE orders. That drives down GE's purchasing costs and gives it a new competitive advantage; meanwhile, its former suppliers must adapt their strategies to make themselves a lot more Web friendly.[33] GE's divisions have also been told to create Internet businesses that would replace their traditional brick and mortar businesses.

Finally, once the firm's mission and strategy are in place, the manager must of course create subsidiary plans for actually implementing the strategy. This brings the strategic planner back to the hierarchical planning process. Specific strategy-related goals are formulated and assigned to the company's managers, who in turn are responsible for crafting plans to ensure that those goals are achieved.

When the Future Is More Predictable

You are the president of Delta Airlines and need a strategy to deal with the possible entrance of a low-cost, no-frills airline into one of your major markets. What strategies might you pursue? Options include introducing a low-cost Delta service, surrendering the low-cost niche to the new entrant, or competing more aggressively on price and service to drive the entrant out of the market.[34]

The question is, What kind of information would you need to make your decision? Generally, you need the sorts of information provided by traditional planning tools. For example, you'll need market research on the size of the different markets, on the likely responses of customers in each market segment to different combinations of pricing and service, and information about the new entrant's competitive objectives. There are also traditional strategic planning tools you might use, including SWOT analysis, environmental scanning, benchmarking, and portfolio analysis.

SWOT Analysis   SWOT analysis is used to list and consolidate information regarding a firm's internal strengths and weaknesses and external opportunities and threats. As illustrated in Figure 2-6, potential strengths might include adequate financial resources, economies of scale, and proprietary technology. Potential internal weaknesses include lack of strategic direction, obsolete facilities, and lack of managerial depth and talent.

Formulating strategic plans is partly a process of identifying strategic actions that will balance these strengths and weaknesses with the company's external

POTENTIAL STRENGTHS	POTENTIAL WEAKNESSES
• Market leadership	• Large inventories
• Strong research and development	• Excess capacity for market
• High-quality products	• Management turnover
• Cost advantages	• Weak market image
• Patents	• Lack of management depth
POTENTIAL OPPORTUNITIES	**POTENTIAL THREATS**
• New overseas markets	• Market saturation
• Falling trade barriers	• Threat of takeover
• Competitors failing	• Low-cost foreign competition
• Diversification	• Slower market growth
• Economy rebounding	• Growing government regulation

◀ **FIGURE 2-6**

Examples of a Company's Strengths, Weaknesses, Opportunities, and Threats

opportunities and threats. Opportunities might include the possibility of serving additional customers (market penetration), the chance to enter new markets or segments (market development), or falling trade barriers in attractive foreign markets. Threats might include the likely entry of new lower-cost foreign competitors, rising sales of substitute products, and slowing market growth. Delta's managers would consider all these facts, summarize them on the four quadrants of a SWOT chart, and use this information to help develop a corporate strategy, and then a competitive strategy.

Environmental Scanning   All companies operate in an external environment. The **external environment** of an organization is the set of forces with which that organization interacts.[35] These forces include all the things—like economic trends, regulatory policies and laws, and competitors' actions—that influence the company. **Environmental scanning** means obtaining and compiling information about the environmental forces that might be relevant to the company's strategic planners.

Six key areas of the company's environment are usually scanned to identify opportunities or threats. A form like that in Figure 2-7 can be used for this:

1. *Economic trends*. These are factors related to the level of economic activity and to the flow of money, goods and services. For example, there has been a trend for people living in Asia to hoard more of their money in gold and gold items. What opportunities and threats would such a trend imply for bankers or for companies in the business of selling gold items?

2. *Competition trends*. These are the factors that involve actions taken or possibly taken by current and potential competitors. For example, Microsoft's move into Internet browsers helped push Netscape into the waiting arms of AOL, which acquired it.

3. *Political trends*. These are factors related to dealings with local, national, and foreign governments. For example, cigarette manufacturers like R. J. Reynolds must monitor trends in the regulation of cigarette smoking around the globe.

4. *Technological trends*. These factors relate to the development of new or existing technology, including electronics, machines, tools, and processes. Several years ago, Microsoft's Bill Gates noticed that the Internet's explosive growth provided both opportunities and threats to his company. The threat lay in the possibility that computer users might come to rely on the Internet itself for computer processing and thus need less sophisticated personal computers and Microsoft programs (the Sun Microsystems "the network is the computer"

threat). The opportunity lay in the possibility of linking more and more Microsoft programs directly to the Internet, thus making Microsoft the gateway to the Internet. (Microsoft chose to include browsers in its Windows operating systems, triggering a federal antitrust charge against the firm.)

5. *Social trends*. These are factors that affect and reflect the way people live, including what they value. In the United States, for instance, the proportion of Hispanic people is rising quickly. What impact might this have on major advertising companies?

▶ **FIGURE 2-7**

Worksheet for Environmental Scanning

Economic Trends
(such as recession, inflation, employment, monetary policies)

_____

_____

_____

_____

Competitive Trends
(such as competitors' strategic changes, market/customer trends, entry/exit of competitors, new products from competitors)

_____

_____

_____

_____

Political Trends
(such as national/local election results, special interest groups, legislation, regulation/deregulation)

_____

_____

_____

_____

Technological Trends
(such as introduction of new production/distribution technologies, rate of product obsolescence, trends in availability of supplies and raw materials)

_____

_____

_____

_____

Social Trends
(such as demographic trends, mobility, education, evolving values)

_____

_____

_____

_____

Geographic Trends
(such as opening/closing of new markets, factors effecting current plant/office facilities location decisions)

_____

_____

_____

6. *Geographic trends*. This includes factors related to climate, natural resources, and so forth. In Florida, for instance, an apparent long-term cooling trend has reduced the growing area for oranges, so that "Florida oranges" now increasingly come from South America.

Scanning can be done in several ways. For example, employees can be assigned to watch particular areas (economic, social), perhaps by scouring publications like the *New York Times* and the *Wall Street Journal*, as well as the Internet, consultants' reports, information services, and industry newsletters. Other firms use consultants called *environmental scanners*, who read and abstract a wide variety of publications to search for environmental changes that could affect the firm. You can also set up Internet news services to continuously and automatically screen thousands of news stories and provide precisely the types of stories in which you're interested.

Benchmarking   Sometimes a company must develop its strengths to become a better competitor. **Benchmarking** is the process through which a company learns how to become the best in some area by carefully analyzing the practices of other companies that already excel in that area (best-practices companies). The basic benchmarking process typically follows several guidelines:[36]

1. Focus on a specific problem and define it carefully. Such a problem might be, What order-fulfillment processes do best-practices companies use in the mail-order business? L.L. Bean is often analysed by other firms, since it's viewed as a best-practice company for the way it expeditiously handles customers' questions and fulfills orders.

2. Use the employees who will actually implement those changes to identify the best-practices companies and to conduct on-site studies. Having the employees who will actually implement the best practices do the study helps ensure their commitment to the required changes.

3. Studying best practices is a two-way street, so be willing to share information with others.

4. Avoid sensitive issues such as pricing, and don't look for new product information.

5. Keep information you receive confidential.

Portfolio Analysis   In developing their corporate strategies, most firms (like Pepsi) end up with several businesses in their "portfolio" (such as Colas and Frito-Lay in Pepsi's case). How do you decide which businesses to keep in (or drop from) a portfolio? Several portfolio analysis tools are used to help managers decide.

The BCG Matrix, developed by the Boston Consulting Group (BCG), helps to identify the relative attractiveness of each of a firm's businesses. As shown in Figure 2-8, it does this by comparing growth rate and relative competitive position (market share) for each of the company's businesses. Each business is usually placed in a matrix as in Figure 2-8. Once all businesses have been placed on the matrix, it's easier to decide which to keep or drop. **Stars** are businesses in high-growth industries in which the company has a high relative market share. For example, Intel's microprocessor business (microprocessors are the heart of computers such as IBM's Pentium-driven PCs) has a high growth rate and Intel has a relatively high market share. Star businesses usually require large infusions of cash to sustain growth. However, they generally have such a strong market position that much of the needed cash can be generated from sales and profits.

▶ **F I G U R E 2 - 8**

BCG Matrix

After the position of each of the company's businesses is plotted, a decision can be made regarding which businesses will be cash sources and which will be cash users.

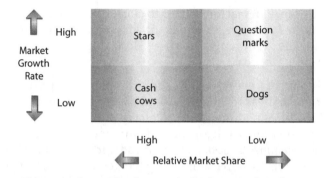

Question marks are businesses in high-growth industries, but with low market shares. These business units face a dilemma: They are in attractive high-growth industries, but they have such low market shares that they lack the clout to fend off larger competitors. A company must either divert cash from its other businesses to boost the question mark's market share or get out of the business.

Cash cows are businesses in low-growth industries that enjoy high relative market shares. Their being in a low-growth, unattractive industry argues against making large cash infusions into these businesses. However, their high market share generally allows them to generate high sales and profits for years, even without much new investment. Cash cows can thus be good cash generators for the company's question mark businesses.

Finally, **dogs** are low-market-share businesses in low-growth, unattractive industries. Having a low market share puts the business in jeopardy relative to its larger competitors. As a result, dogs can quickly become "cash traps," absorbing cash to support a hopeless and unattractive situation. They are usually sold to raise cash for stars and question marks.

The People Side of Managing

■ **It's the People That Make the Strategy Work**

While strategic tools like scenario planning are important in strategic planning, as a practical matter the people side of managing is crucial, too. One nationwide survey of 9,144 employees illustrates this. The results showed that the vast majority (83%) of surveyed employees understood their employers' goals and their own job responsibilities (87%), both important factors in getting employees to cooperate in carrying out the firm's strategies. Yet fewer than half of the employees (43%) said they were given the skills and training and information they needed to achieve their goals.[37] The problem, of course, is that having a strategy that's widely known and accepted is of little use if the employees don't have the ability to implement it.

Smart companies know that, and are doing something about it. In companies like Motorola, Saturn, and 3M, employees average between 40 and 80 hours per year of training. And many, including The Lane Group, practice "open-book management," which means keeping all employees continuously informed about the company's financial and other situations so that the employees are, in a real sense, treated like partners.

In other words, the CEOs of most successful companies today understand that even creating a brilliant strategy is a job that's only half done. As Herb Kelleher, CEO of Southwest Airlines once put it, his company's ability to keep costs down (for instance, by turning aircraft around in half the time it takes competitors) is not the result of special equipment or methods. Instead, it's the work of a group of highly motivated managers and employees who believe in Southwest's low-cost strategy, and who have the skills and wherewithal to implement it.

How Entrepreneurs Actually Craft Strategies

Entrepreneurs often take a short cut when it comes to actually creating a strategy for their firms. Interviews with the founders of 100 of the fastest-growing private companies in the United States and research on 100 other thriving ventures showed that entrepreneurs use three general guidelines in formulating strategies:[38]

1. *Screen out losers quickly*. Successful entrepreneurs know how to quickly discard ideas for new products and services that have a low potential. Their decision-making tends to emphasize judgment and intuition, rather than lots of data.

2. *Minimize the resources devoted to researching ideas*. With limited resources, entrepreneurs can obviously do only as much planning and analysis as are absolutely necessary. They then make subjective judgment calls, sometimes based on very limited data. Indeed, about 20% of entrepreneurs got the ideas for their businesses by replicating or modifying an idea encountered in their previous employment. Apparel designer Ralph Lauren reportedly got the kernel of his idea for classic men's and women's wear when he began his career as a salesperson with Brooks Brothers.

   About 20% got their ideas serendipitously—building a temporary job into a business, developing a family member's idea, or "thought up during honeymoon in Italy," for instance.

3. *Don't wait for all the answers, and be ready to change course*. Large companies often use a fairly ponderous planning process. Plans are carefully drawn up; a hierarchy of goals is assigned; and duties are allocated to actually get the work done. Entrepreneurs often "don't know all the answers before they act." In fact, many entrepreneurs change the traditional motto "Ready, aim, fire" to "Ready, fire, aim." They try a product or service based on the most preliminary market data and then quickly drop or modify the product if it doesn't click with customers.

SUMMARY   ■

1. A primary task of top management is to think through the mission of the business and ask, What is our business, and what should it be? Strategic management is the process of identifying and pursuing the organization's mission by aligning internal capacity with the external demands of the environment.

2. There are five steps in the strategy management process: define the business and develop a mission; translate the mission into strategic objectives; formulate a strategy to achieve the strategic objectives; implement the strategy; and evaluate performance and initiate corrective adjustments as required. Strategic planning includes the first three steps of this process.

3. There are three main types of strategies. The corporate-level strategy identifies the portfolio of businesses that in total will comprise the corporation and the ways in which these businesses will relate; the competitive strategy identifies how to build and strengthen the business's long-term competitive position in the marketplace; and functional strategies identify the basic courses of action that each department will pursue to contribute to the attainment of its goals.

4. Each type of strategy contains specific standard or generic strategies. Generic corporate strategies include concentration, market penetration, geographic expansion, product development, horizontal integration, vertical integration, and diversification, as well as status quo and retrenchment strategies.

5. Generic competitive strategies include being a low-cost leader, differentiator, or focuser. For-mulating a specific competitive strategy then requires understanding the competitive forces that determine how intense the competitive rivalries are and how best to compete. The five forces model helps managers understand the five big forces of competitive pressure in an industry: threat of entry, intensity of rivalry among existing competitors, pressure from substi-tute products, bargaining power of buyers, and bargaining power of suppliers.

6. Creating strategic plans involves: identifying environmental forces, formulating a plan, and cre-ating implementation plans. Useful techniques include SWOT analysis, environmental scan-ning, benchmarking, portfolio analysis, and scenario planning.

7. Implementing the organization's strategy involves several activities, among them achieving strategic fit, leveraging the company's core competencies, and effectively leading the change process.

TYING IT ALL TOGETHER ■

Creating a plan is just the first step in the strategic planning process; like any plan, it must then be carried out. In practice, for instance, implementation requires achieving strategic fit—in other words, crafting functional plans so that all the firm's activities, from maintenance to sales to finance, contribute in a coordinated way to what the company wants to achieve. In practice, implementation also requires that work assignments be made; authority delegated to carry them out; employees hired, trained, and motivated; and final results compared to the plan and adjusted if required (in other words, controlled). Therefore, implementing the company's plans ultimately depends on how good a job the manager does with the remaining management functions of organizing, leading, and controlling.

Skills and Study Materials

CRITICAL THINKING EXERCISES ■

1. You have just been appointed to a strategic planning committee for Apple Computer. You know that in the late 1990s the company had been having a difficult time with its strategies. Do some research on the history of Apple. (Both *Fortune* and *Business Week* have many articles on Apple.) Using this information, apply the ideas, concepts, and approaches discussed in this section to develop a strategic plan for Apple.

2. You are a strategic planner for GM. In the late 1990s you saw the merger of DaimlerChrysler. By fall 1999 the Ger-mans had taken greater control of the company and put some Chrysler people off the board of directors, and you saw the somewhat early departure of the Chrysler CEO. Rumor has it that the cultures of the two companies did not completely "merge." Now there is a rumor that Ford and Toyota are thinking of merging. What would you rec-ommend that GM do? Using the concepts presented in the section, analyze the situation and make recommenda-tions to the GM board.

EXPERIENTIAL EXERCISES

1. With three to four other students in the class, form a strategic management group for your college or university. In a 2-hour time period, identify what "business" your college or university is in, where it is in terms of implementing a strategy, and where it needs to be strategically headed. Prior to meeting to develop your plan, look at what your college or university has developed in the way of a strategic plan by interviewing some administrators, faculty members, and students about their knowledge of the strategic plan. From the information gathered, prepare some strategic alternatives for the other students to discuss in a class brainstorming session.

2. You are the newest member of the design team for a major toy manufacturer. You just saw a show on the A&E channel that identified the most popular toys of the last century. The top five were, in ascending order, Playdoh, Lionel trains, Barbie, the Crayon, and the Yo-Yo. Your job is to design a new toy that could be the top toy of the twenty-first century. In a team of four to five students, do a strategic analysis for the purpose of developing such a toy, and propose a toy.

SECTION THREE

THE FUNDAMENTALS OF ORGANIZING

WHAT'S AHEAD?

Howard Schultz, head of Starbucks Corporation[1] knows that with more than 2,200 Starbucks stores in the U.S., organizing the company is no easy task. There must be training departments to turn college students into café managers (who know, for example, that every espresso must be pulled within 23 seconds or be thrown away); departments to sell coffee to United Airlines and supermarkets; and a way to manage stores as remote as the Philippines and Beijing. How to organize is, therefore, not an academic issue to Howard Schultz.

THIS SECTION FOCUSES ON THE FOLLOWING

- Organization

- The basic alternatives for organizing departments

- What is meant by decentralization by providing two real-life examples

►FROM PLANNING TO ORGANIZING

Starbuck's Howard Schultz is discovering that planning and organizing are inseparable. When his firm was small, its strategy focused on offering high-quality coffee drinks through small, specialized neighborhood coffee houses. This strategy in turn suggested the main jobs for which Schultz had to hire lieutenants—for example store management, purchasing, and finance and accounting. Departments then grew up around these jobs.

As Schultz's strategy evolved to include geographic expansion across the United States and abroad, his organization also had to evolve. Regional store management divisions were established to oversee the stores in each region. Today, with Starbucks coffee also sold to airlines, bookstores, and supermarkets, the company's structure is evolving again, with new departments organized to sell to and service the needs of these new markets. What Schultz is discovering, in other words, is that the organization is determined by the plan: strategy determines structure.

We All Have Things to Organize

The planning–organizing link applies, whether it's General Motors, or Starbucks, or a small start-up business. Let's go back to the management task we addressed earlier—your assignment as summer tour master. What's your organization's strategic mission? To plan, organize, and execute a successful trip to France. What job assignments will that require? One way to organize is to break the job into the main functions that must be performed. So we put Rosa in charge of airline scheduling, Ned in charge of hotels, and Ruth in charge of city sites.

How might your organization change if your strategic mission were different? Suppose next year your friends promote you (you lucky thing): You are now in charge of simultaneously planning several trips—to England, to Sweden, and to the south of France. Your organization's strategic mission has therefore changed, too; it is now to plan, organize, and execute three successful trips, and to do so more or less simultaneously. How would you organize now? Perhaps by putting each of last year's trusted lieutenants in charge of a country (say, Rosa—England, Ned—Sweden, and Ruth—South of France). You'd then have a sort of "regional" organization, and each lieutenant might in turn hire trusted friends to arrange for airline tickets, hotels, and sites to see. Again, the tasks to be done, and thus how you organize, have flowed logically out of your plan.

What Is Organizing?

Organizing means arranging the activities in such a way that they systematically contribute to enterprise goals. An organization consists of people whose specialized tasks are coordinated to contribute to the organization's goals.

The usual way of depicting an organization is with an **organization chart**. It shows the structure of the organization; specifically, the title of each manager's position and, by means of connecting lines, who is accountable to whom and who is in charge of what area. The organization chart also shows the **chain of command** (sometimes called the *scalar chain* or the *line of authority*) between the top of the organization and the lowest positions in the chart. The chain of command represents the path a directive should take in traveling from the president to employees at the bottom of the organization chart or from employees at the bottom to the top of the organization chart.

In a corporation, the stockholders generally elect a board of directors to represent their interests, so the board, strictly speaking, is at the top of the chain of command. The board's main functions are to choose the top executives, to approve strategies and long-term plans, and to monitor performance to make sure that the stockholders' interests are protected. The board then delegates (we discuss delegation in more detail below) to the CEO the authority to actually run the company—to develop plans, to hire subordinate managers, and to enter into agreements. This is how an organization chart and chain of command evolve.

One thing the organization chart does not show is the **informal organization**—the informal, habitual contacts, communications, and ways of doing things that employees develop. Thus, a salesperson might develop the habit of calling a plant production supervisor to check on the status of an order. The salesperson might find this quicker than adhering to the chain of command, which would entail having the sales manager check with the plant manager, who in turn would check with the supervisor.

In fact, there's more informality in most organization charts than most managers would probably like to admit. An executive, hoping to amuse his audience, opened his speech with the following story:

A young and enthusiastic lion, straight out of lion school, was hired by a circus. After his first day on the job, the lion, by now famished, was surprised to be served not a huge plate of meat, but a bunch of bananas. The lion stormed over to the ringmaster and said "I'm the lion, what are you doing feeding me bananas?" "Well, the problem is," the ringmaster said, "our senior lion is still around, so you're down on the organization chart as a monkey."

The moral of the story is, an organization chart is not always what it seems. For example, the president's assistant may be "only" a secretary, but as the president's gatekeeper may wield enormous authority. The computer systems manager may be so crucial to the company that even the president and other senior executives routinely defer to her decisions. And sometimes a young lion gets hired thinking he is going to be the president, only to find out that the president remains as chairman of the board and effectively second-guesses and undercuts almost everything the president does. You have to learn to exercise some healthy skepticism when reviewing a company's organization chart.

The rest of this section is organized around four main topics. The first two focus on what you might call the "horizontal" aspects of organizing—namely, creating departments and then coordination among departments. The final two sections focus on the "vertical" aspects of organizing—namely, delegating or pushing authority down from the top to the bottom of the chain of command, and comparing companies with many levels (and therefore a tall chain of command) with companies that have fewer levels (and therefore a flatter chain of command).

▶ CREATING DEPARTMENTS

Every enterprise—including your summer tour organization—must carry out various activities to accomplish its goals. In a company, these activities might include manufacturing, selling, and accounting. In a city, they might include fire, police, and health protection. In a hospital, they might include nursing, medical services, and radiology. **Departmentalization** is the process through which an enterprise's activities are grouped together and assigned to managers; it is the organizationwide division of work. Departments—logical groupings of activities—are often called divisions, units, or sections.

The basic question is, Around what activities should you organize departments? Should you organize people around functions such as airline scheduling and hotels, or around places such as England and the south of France? In a company, should departments be organized for sales and manufacturing? Or should there be separate departments for industrial and retail customers, each of which then has its own sales and manufacturing units? As we'll see, many options are available.

Creating Departments Around Functions

Functional departmentalization means grouping activities around basic functions like manufacturing, sales, and finance. Figure 3-1 shows the organizational structures for STM (your summer tour organization) and for the ABC car company. At ABC each department is organized around a different business function—sales, finance, and production. Here the production director reports to the president and manages ABC's production plants. The directors carry out the sales, finance, and production functions.

Service businesses like STM can be built around business functions too—scheduling, reservations, and sightseeing destinations. And the basic business functions around which banks are often departmentalized include operations, control, and loans. In a university, the business functions might include academic affairs, business affairs, and student affairs.

There are other types of functions, too. For example, organizing around managerial functions means putting supervisors in charge of departments like planning, control, and administration. Departmentalization based on technological functions means grouping activities such as plating, welding, or assembling. The basic idea of any functional departmentalization is to group activities around the core functions the enterprise must carry out.

▶ **FIGURE 3-1**

Functional Departmentalization

This chart shows *functional* organizations, with departments for basic functions like finance, sales, and production.

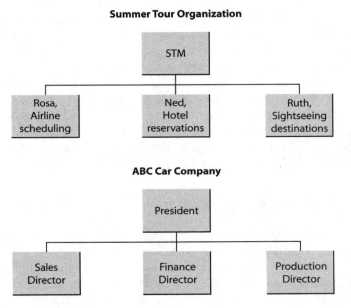

FUNCTIONAL ORGANIZATIONS

Summer Tour Organization

STM

Rosa, Airline scheduling

Ned, Hotel reservations

Ruth, Sightseeing destinations

ABC Car Company

President

Sales Director

Finance Director

Production Director

Advantages   Organizing departments around functions has several advantages:

1. It is simple, straightforward, and logical; it makes sense to build departments around the basic functions in which the enterprise must engage.

2. Functional organizations usually have single departments for areas like sales, production, and finance that serve all the company's products, rather than duplicate facilities for each product. Because the volume in these departments is relatively high, the firm typically gets increased returns to scale—in other words, employees become more proficient from doing the same job over and over again, and the company can afford larger plants and more efficient equipment. Functional organizations are therefore often associated with efficiency.

3. The managers' duties in each of the functional departments tend to be more specialized (a manager may specialize in finance or production, for instance); the enterprise therefore needs fewer general managers—those with the breadth of experience to administer several functions at once. This can simplify both recruiting and training.

4. Functional department managers also tend to receive information on only part of the big picture of the company—on that which concerns their own specialized functions. This can make it easier for top management to exercise control over the department managers' activities.

Disadvantages   Functional organizations also have disadvantages:

1. Responsibility for the enterprise's overall performance rests on the shoulders of one person, usually the president. He or she may be the only one in a position to coordinate the work of the functional departments, each of which is only one element in producing and supplying the company's product or service. This may not be a serious problem when the firm is small or does not work with a lot of products. But as size and diversity of products increase, the job of coordinating, say, production, sales, and finance for many different products may prove too great for one person; the enterprise could lose its responsiveness.

2. Also, the tendency for functional departments to result in specialized managers (finance experts, production experts, and so forth) makes it more difficult to develop managers with the breadth of experience required for general management jobs like president.

Creating Departments Around Products

With product departmentalization, departments are organized for each of the company's products or services, or for each family of products. Department heads in this type of organization are responsible for both creating and marketing a product, a family of products, or a service. Figure 3-2 shows the organization charts for the Summer Tour Organization and for a product-related company, Bright Star Pharmaceuticals. In Bright Star, a president heads North Atlantic operations. Three product divisions report to this person: one for drugs and pharmaceuticals, one for personal care products, and one for stationery products. Each of these three product divisions then has its own staff for activities such as production and sales.

Arranging departments around products in this way is sometimes called **divisionalization**. Divisionalization exists *when the firm's major departments are organized so that each can manage all the activities needed to develop, manufacture, and sell*

▼ **F I G U R E   3 - 2**   **Product Departmentalization**

In product departmentalizations like these, separate departments or divisions are set up for services—tour management—or products—drugs, pharmaceuticals, personal care, and stationery.

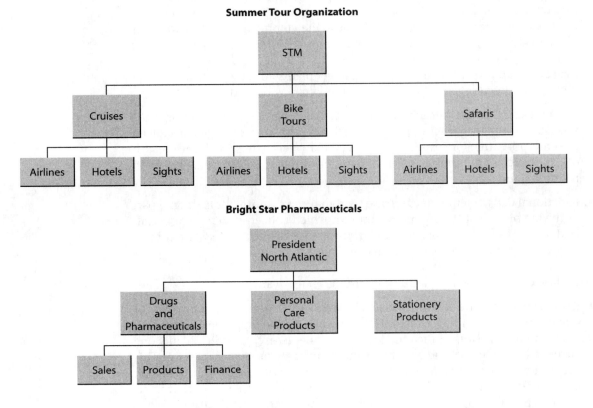

a particular product, product line, or service. The head of such a division usually has functional departments—say, for production, sales, and personnel—reporting to him or her. As a result, each of these product divisions is *self-contained.* In other words, each controls all or most of the resources required to create, produce, and supply its product or products.

Advantages   Divisionalization can be advantageous in several ways.

1. A single manager is charged with overseeing all the functions required to produce and market each product. Each product division can therefore focus its resources on being more sensitive and responsive to the needs of its particular product or product line. (The manager in charge of the North American personal care group in Figure 3-2, for example, has his or her own research, manufacturing, and sales departments. As a result, the division can usually respond quickly when a competitor brings out a new and innovative product.) The manager need not rely on research, manufacturing, or sales managers who are not within his or her own division. Divisionalization is thus appropriate where quick decisions and flexibility (rather than efficiency) are paramount.

2. Performance is more easily judged. If a division is doing well (or not doing well), it is clear who is responsible because one person is managing the whole division.

3. Being put in charge of "the whole ball game" can help motivate the manager to perform better.

4. Self-contained divisions can also be good training grounds for an enterprise's executives because they are exposed to a wider range of problems, from production and sales to personnel and finance.

5. Finally, divisionalization helps shift some of the management burden from top management to division executives. Imagine if the North American president had to coordinate the tasks of designing, producing, and marketing each of the company's many products. The diversity of problems he or she would face would be enormous. Therefore, virtually all very large companies, as well as many small ones with diverse products and customers, have divisionalized.[2]

That helps explain why Bill Harris, then executive vice president of software company Intuit, praised the company's divisional structure:

Two years ago, it was becoming clear that the bigger we got, the more being organized by functions was a liability. . . . The executive team had become a real bottleneck. We needed a new structure [and decided] to bust the organization apart. [Our new CEO] created eight business units, each with its own general manager and customer mission. The basic goal was to flatten the organization and fragment the decision-making process. Each business unit would be the size that Intuit had been a few years ago, and each would focus on one core product or market.

The effects of the reorganization have been dramatic. The new organization forces Intuit's top managers to give more decision-making authority to the individual business units. The executive team used to make or approve most product-related decisions. Now these decisions are left to the business units, and within these units they are usually left to the individual product teams. Intuit has become more responsive and effective at managing change.[3]

Disadvantages Organizing around divisions can also produce disadvantages, such as the following:

1. Divisions breed an expensive duplication of effort. The fact that each product-oriented unit is self-contained implies that there are several production plants instead of one, several sales forces instead of one, and so on. Related to this, the company's customers may become annoyed at being visited by many salespeople representing different divisions.

2. Divisionalization may also diminish top management's control. As at Intuit, the division heads often have great autonomy because they are in charge of all phases of producing and marketing their products. Top management therefore tends to have less control over day-to-day activities. A division might run up excessive expenses before top management discovers there is a problem. In fact, striking a balance between providing each division head with enough autonomy to run the division and maintaining top management control is crucial.

3. Divisionalization also requires more managers with general management abilities. Each product division is, in a sense, a miniature company, with its own production plant, sales force, personnel department, and so forth. Divisional managers therefore

cannot just be sales, production, or personnel specialists. Companies with divisional structures and strong executive development programs tend to be prime hunting grounds for executive recruiters. GE is often listed as the place where recruiters look first when trying to find CEOs for other companies.

Creating Departments Around Customers

Customer departmentalization is similar to product departmentalization, except that here departments are organized to serve the needs of specific customers. Figure 3-3, for instance, shows the organization chart for the Grayson Steel Company. Notice how the company's main divisions are organized to serve the needs of particular customers, such as metals and chemicals customers, packaging systems customers, aerospace and industrial customers, and the international group.

Advantages and Disadvantages   Organizing around customers has several advantages. As in product departmentalization, a manager is charged with giving continuous, undivided attention to a customer or group of customers. This can result in faster, more satisfactory service to each of the company's customers, particularly when their needs are substantially different.

As in product departmentalization, the main disadvantage is duplication of effort. The company may have several production plants instead of one, and several sales managers, each serving the needs of his or her own customers, instead of one. This can reduce overall corporate efficiency.

Creating Departments Around Marketing Channels

With **marketing-channel departmentalization**, top-level departments are organized around each of the firm's marketing channels (instead of products, services, or customers). A **marketing channel** is the conduit (wholesaler, drugstore, grocery, or the like) through which a manufacturer distributes its products to its ultimate customers.

Marketing-channel departmentalization is illustrated in Figure 3-4. As you can see, it is similar to customer departmentalization, but there are several differences. In customer departmentalization, each customer-oriented department is usually responsible for both manufacturing and selling its own product to its own customers. In marketing-channel departmentalization, the same product (such as Ivory soap) is typically marketed through two or more channels. Usually one department is chosen to manufacture the product for all the other marketing-channel departments.

Organizing around marketing channels assumes that each marketing channel's unique needs must be catered to. For example, Revlon may sell through both department stores and discount drugstores. Yet the demands of these two channels

▶ **FIGURE 3-3**

Customer Departmentalization, Grayson Steel Company

With customer departmentalization, separate departments are organized around customers such as aerospace and metals and chemicals customers.

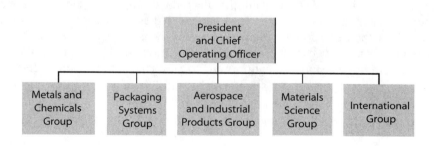

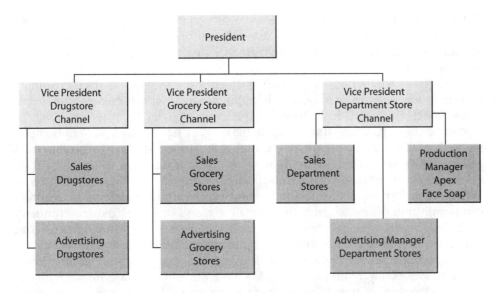

◀ **FIGURE 3-4**

Marketing Channel Departmentalization

With marketing channels, the main departments are organized to focus on particular marketing channels such as drugstores and grocery stores.

Note: Only the department-store channel produces the soap, and each channel may sell to the same ultimate consumers.

are quite different: The department store may want Revlon to supply specially trained salespeople to run concessions in its stores. The discount druggist may just want quick delivery and minimal inventory. Putting a manager and department in charge of each channel can help ensure these diverse needs are met quickly and satisfactorily. As in product and customer departmentalization, the resulting duplication—in this case, of sales forces—is the main disadvantage.

Creating Departments Around Geographic Areas

Finally, as when you put Rosa in charge of England, Ned in charge of Sweden, and Ruth in charge of the south of France, you can organize departments around geographic regions. With geographic, or territorial, departmentalization, separate departments are organized for each of the territories in which the enterprise does business. Territorial geographic departments are usually examples of divisional departmentalization: Each area tends to be self-contained, perhaps with its own production, sales, and personnel activities.

Advantages and Disadvantages   The main advantage of territorial departmentalization is that one self-contained department focuses on the needs of its particular buyers—in this case, those in its geographic area. This can lead to speedier, more responsive, and better service. A department store chain like JCPenney might organize territorially to cater to the tastes and needs of customers in each area. Like product, customer, and marketing-channel departmentalization, territorial departmentalization is advantageous insofar as it ensures quick, responsive reaction to the needs of the company's clients.

Also like the other types of departmentalization, however, territorial departmentalization may create duplication of effort. And again, with these types of divisions, the company needs to hire and train managers capable of managing several functions (like production, sales, and personnel).

An Example: Heinz   To some extent, organizing geographically was a product of a time when it was difficult to communicate across borders, particularly international borders. Taking the pulse of consumer needs and monitoring operations in a far-flung global operation is no easy task. As a result, many companies departmentalized globally, so that local managers could run their regional or country businesses as more or less autonomous companies. Two trends are making the geographic organization less practical today.

First, global competition is becoming much more intense, so it's increasingly important for a company to be able to apply product improvements it obtains in one locale to another. If H. J. Heinz in Japan, for instance, discovers a new way to formulate one of its soups, it will want to make sure that the improvement is implemented in all the company's markets, including Europe and the United States. A geographic organization—with its relatively compartmentalized country divisions—may hamper such cross-fertilization.

Second, information technology is reducing the impediments to cross-border communication. Video conferencing, e-mail, fax, and computerized monitoring of operations means that an executive in one region—say, the United States—can now easily keep his or her fingers on the pulse of operations around the world.

Many companies are therefore switching from a geographic to a product organization. For example, Heinz's new CEO, William Johnson, said he will end the company's system of managing by country or region.[4] Instead, the company will manage by products or categories, so that managers in the United States can work with managers in Europe, Asia, and other regions to implement the best ideas from one region in other regions as well.

Procter & Gamble recently said it was taking the same approach. Its new organization eliminates its old four business units based on regions of the world, and puts profit responsibility in the hands of seven executives who will report directly to new CEO, Durk Jager. Each executive will globally manage product units such as baby care, beauty, and fabric and home care. The company said the reorganization will speed decision making and send products to market faster.[5]

Managing @ the Speed of Thought
■ Using the Internet for Global Communications

Companies like Heinz can use the Internet in many ways to improve global communications. Videoconferencing is one of them. For the cost of a local telephone call, companies now have global, face-to-face communications that help eliminate the barriers distance formerly placed in the way of such face-to-face talk.[6]

CU-SeeMe is one of the systems companies use to hold multiparty videoconference meetings over the Internet. This system uses a "reflector" program, which sends simultaneous transmissions to every participant. While the system is used primarily for "talking head" meetings (each participant appears on the screen in a 4-inch box), it provides an inexpensive and effective way to hold long-distance meetings.

The World Bank, which is headquartered in Washington, DC, is an example of how one organization uses CU-SeeMe. With offices or partners in 180 countries, the World Bank has an urgent need to communicate quickly and efficiently across borders. It uses CU-SeeMe to conduct small meetings and virtual seminars. While the images may be small and the video may not always be very smooth, the system's low cost and ease of use makes it easy for the World Bank and other organizations and companies to communicate instantly and face to face around the globe. It therefore reduces the need to depend so heavily on a global organization structure.

Creating Matrix Organizations

A **matrix organization**, also known as matrix management, is an organization in which one form of departmentalization is superimposed on another.[7] In one example, illustrated in Figure 3-5, product departments are superimposed on a functional departmentalization. This company's automotive products division is functionally organized, with departments for functions like production, engineering, and personnel. Superimposed over this functional departmentalization are three product groups—for the Ford project, the Chrysler project, and the GM project. Each of these product groups has its own product manager, or project leader. One or more employees from each functional department (like production and engineering) is temporarily assigned to each project.

▼ **FIGURE 3-5**   **Matrix Organization Departmentalization**

With a matrix organization, a project structure is often superimposed over a functional organization.

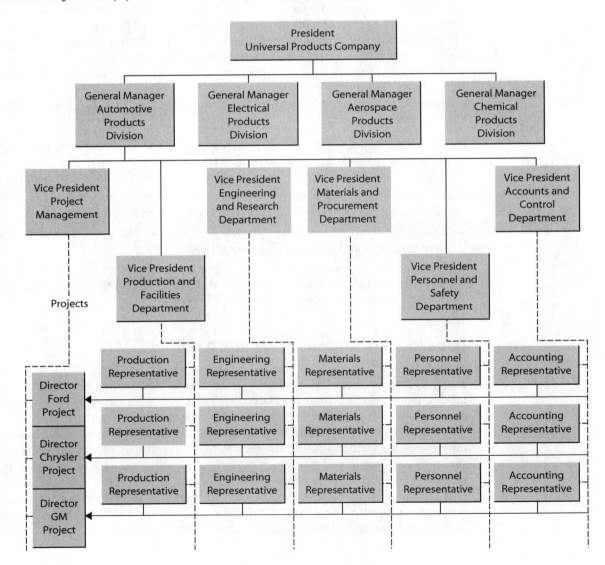

Combining customer and geographic organizations is another common matrix approach.[8] For example, a bank may be organized geographically, with separate officers in charge of operations in each of several countries. At the same time, the bank has a customer structure superimposed over this geographic organization. Project heads for major bank customers such as IBM lead teams comprised of bank employees from each country who concentrate on the local and worldwide financial interests of IBM. Bank employees in each country may report to both their country managers and their project managers. Some matrix organizations are more formal than others. Sometimes temporary project managers are assigned to provide coordination across functional departments for some project or customer. Other firms sometimes add a semipermanent administrative structure (including, for instance, project employee appraisal forms) to help build the project teams' authority.[9]

Matrix organizations have proved successful in a wide range of companies, including Citicorp, TRW Systems, NASA and many of its subcontractors, UNICEF, and various accounting, law, and security firms.[10]

Advantages and Disadvantages Matrix departmentalization can help give bigger companies some of the advantages of smaller ones. For example, a self-contained project group can devote undivided attention to the needs of its own project, product, or customer, yet the entire organization need not be permanently organized around what may turn out to be temporary projects. Another advantage is that management avoids having to establish duplicate functional departments for each project.

However, matrix organizations can also trigger problems that, although avoidable, are potentially serious.

- *Power struggles and conflicts.* Since authority tends to be more ambiguous and up for grabs in matrix organizations, struggles between managers who head the functional and project groups may be more common than in traditional organizations.

- *Lost time.* Matrix organizations tend to result in more intragroup meetings, which can make people feel decision making takes too long.

- *Excessive overhead.* Matrix organizations may tend to raise costs because hiring more managers and secretaries raises overhead.

- *Confusion.* Dual reporting lines can cause confusion, and are appropriate only "for complex tasks and uncertain environments" where ambiguity is a reasonable price to pay for dealing with rapid change.[11]

Departmentalization in Practice: A Hybrid

Most enterprises use several forms of departmentalization: They are hybrids. For example, top management might decide to establish functional departments for production, sales, and finance. They then break the sales department into geographic areas, with separate sales managers for the north, east, south, and west.

An example of this type of hybrid is presented in Figure 3-6, which shows a large multinational organization. Within the United States, this is basically a divisional structure, with separate departments organized around business systems, programming systems, and so forth. However, this firm also uses territorial departmentalization, with separate officers in charge of Asia, the United States, and the Middle East. As is often the case with divisional structures, the headquarters itself is organized around managerial functions (general counsel, finance and planning, and law, for instance).

The People Side of Managing

■ **Implementing Matrix Management at Texas Instruments**

As you may imagine, the people side of managing holds the key to effectively implementing a matrix organization. This is illustrated by a recent reorganization in the Materials & Controls division (M&C) of Texas Instruments Corp.[12]

Texas Instruments M&C is headquartered in the Netherlands, and specializes in the design of low-cost, high-quality, customer-specific sensors, controls, and materials. As the industry's product life cycle—the time required to design, introduce, and then redesign or replace a product—became shorter, the company decided it needed to develop new products faster. At the time, M&C had a functional organization, with separate departments for design, engineering, manufacturing, purchasing, and quality engineering. After participating in a training course on project management, the division's management and staff became enthusiastic about organizing around projects, but decided doing so would require instituting a matrix management structure.

In the division's "balanced matrix" organization, "the project managers and functional managers share roughly equal authority and responsibility for the project."[13] Project managers were appointed and project teams installed, so that team members reported to both a project manager and their existing functional managers. This new structure "required the teams and their managers not only formally but also actively to commit themselves to a project."[14]

Yet getting that kind of commitment in the face of the ambiguities created by dual reporting lines is often easier said than done, and relies heavily on the people side of managing. For example, some project managers who were initially appointed reportedly lacked the skills, time, or commitment to perform the job and had to be replaced. M&C's managers soon discovered that having project teams which didn't have a strong team culture was undermining the effectiveness of the teams. Implementing the matrix structures therefore led management to introduce activities aimed at team building, such as pre-project motivation exercises.

Even this wasn't enough. The teams seemed to divide into two factions, one focusing on manufacturing employees, and one on design engineers. Meetings were organized to promote interaction, but, as the researcher notes, promoting interaction is one thing, and collaboration is another. Ultimately, Texas Instruments M&C got its matrix structure to work right, but doing so required enormous attention to the people side of managing.

Hybrid Organization: An Example   Rosenbluth International is a fast-growing 1,000-office global travel agency, but the way it is organized is based on what CEO Hal Rosenbluth learned on a cattle farm.

Standing on a field in rural North Dakota several years ago, Rosenbluth made a discovery: "The family farm is the most efficient type of unit I've ever run across, because everybody on the farm has to be fully functional and multifaceted." He decided to look for an organizational design that would embody that approach to getting everyone fully involved in helping to run the company. He knew doing so would help his managers.

His company is a good example of how smart managers blend several organizational styles to build fast-moving, successful firms. Rosenbluth broke his company into more than 100 geographic units, each functioning like a farm, serving specific regions and clients. Corporate headquarters became more like what Rosenbluth calls "farm towns," where "stores" like human resources and accounting are centralized so all the farms can use them. Its computerized Global Distribution Network links each of its travel agents to the company's minicomputers in Philadelphia. There, centralized data on clients help ensure that the work of all the offices is coordinated to serve the needs of Rosenbluth clients.[15]

▼ F I G U R E   3 - 6   A Hybrid Organization

Particularly in large organizations, several types of departmentalization are typically combined, in this case functional, product, and geographic.

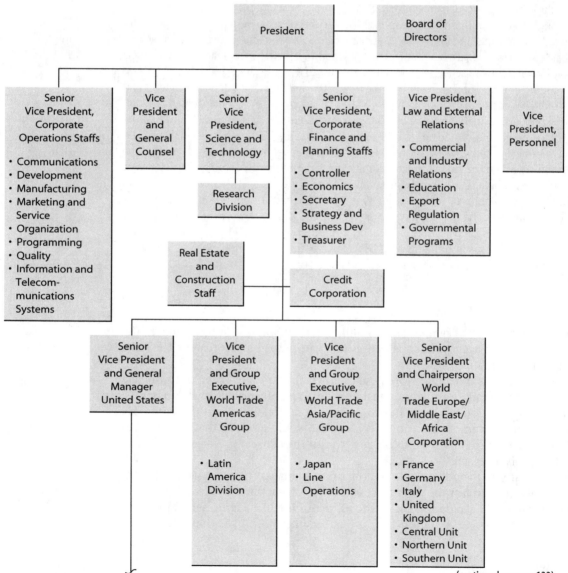

(continued on page 133)

SUMMARY ■

1. Organizing is the arranging of an enterprise's activities in such a way that they systematically contribute to the enterprise's goals. An organization consists of people whose specialized tasks are coordinated to contribute to the organization's goals.

2. Departmentalization is the process through which an enterprise's activities are grouped together and assigned to managers. Departments can be grouped around functions, products, customer groups, marketing channels, or geographic areas.

3. A matrix organization, or matrix management, is defined as an organization in which one or more forms of departmentalization are superimposed on an existing one. In practice, most enterprises are hybrids and use several forms of departmentalization.

▼ FIGURE 3 - 6 *continued*

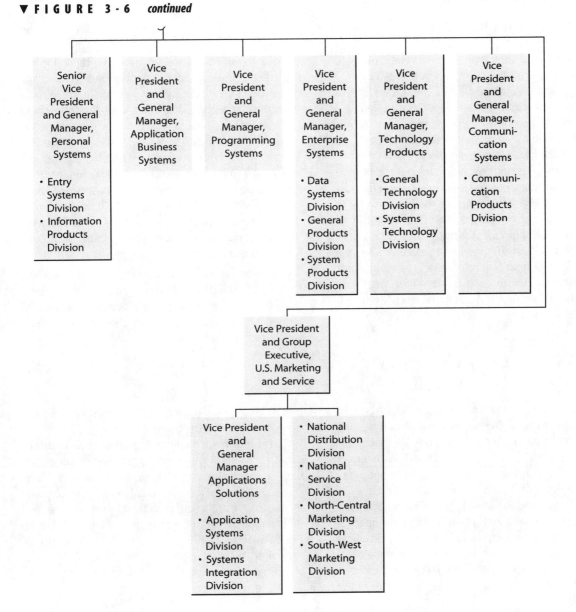

TYING IT ALL TOGETHER ■

Planning helps to determine what tasks must be done, and therefore the activities around which you should organize. For example, a plan to expand to Europe may mean organizing new departments for European sales and manufacturing. In this section we covered the fundamentals of organizing, in particular setting up departments, providing coordination, and delegating authority down the chain of command. In today's fast-changing world, new ways of organizing are required if a firm is to be able to respond quickly enough to competitive and technological changes.

Skills and Study Materials

CRITICAL THINKING EXERCISES ■

1. Organizations and how managers structure them to accommodate a changing set of circumstances is increasingly important to company survival. New organizational models are required. In less turbulent times, the bureaucracy with its top-down control and hierarchically arranged roles and authority was relatively efficient and effective. With the advent of the global economy, constantly changing technology, and immense competitive pressures, most managers are looking for a way to more efficiently and effectively structure the flow of work in their organizations. One of the most frequently touted means is the use of groups or teams. Warren Bennis's and Patricia Ward Biederman's *Organizing Genius: The Secrets of Creative Collaboration* (Addison-Wesley, 1997), explores the workings of famous collaborations from what they call "Troupe Disney" to The Manhattan Project. Their thesis is "None of us is as smart as all of us." They come to a number of interesting conclusions, including the following: Greatness starts with superb people; great groups and great leaders create each other; every great group has a strong leader; leaders of great groups love talent and know where to find it; and great groups see themselves as winning underdogs and always have an enemy. To survive in the next millennium, we can speculate that all our brainpower and creativity will be needed. Given the structures discussed in the section and the information about needing teams-based organizations in *Organizing Genius*, design a new structure for a company in the following industries: retail sales, the aerospace industry, hospitals, auto manufacturing, and construction.

2. Think about the university or college you are attending. How is it organized? Could it be organized more efficiently, using the concepts discussed in this section? How would you reorganize the university to be more effective and efficient for all stakeholders?

EXPERIENTIAL EXERCISES ■

1. Imagine that you are attending a college that is about to transform its structure. The environment around the university is changing. The senior faculty decides that a new structure is required to accommodate the changing demands of students and society. They vote to decentralize their power as the sole decision makers on issues of personnel and curriculum matters, as well as other organizational policies. The new structure is fluid, and amoebae-like. There is no all-powerful head. There is still a dean and administrators, but they are only advisory to some committees and have only a partial vote on some important matters. The dean and administrators still take care of the overall running of the college, but they must include input from all members of the college.

The college holds meetings four times a year to gather, debate, and decide important matters. Anyone connected or once connected to the college, such as alumni, is welcome to attend the meetings and has one vote on policy matters. Each current college student, faculty member, and staff member has one vote on matters of importance. Matters discussed may include merging with another part of the university or changing the name of the college or the college's mission.

At the first meeting, three committees are elected. One is the Policy Committee, which deals with major policy issues. Anyone may be elected to this committee, such as students or faculty members. The second committee is the Personnel Committee, whose members are elected by representative groups (e.g., the students elect their representatives). This committee makes tenure decisions and other decisions of importance to the college. The third committee is the Academic Affairs Committee, which is voluntary and usually consists of faculty and students. This committee deals with curricular matters and course offerings.

With this approach to structure in mind, redesign your college's organization chart around these structural principles. Be sure to consider the environment the college is in, the type of student body that usually attends the university, and the mission of the university or college or school or department. Also think about the problems that might arise, why change might be difficult, and where resistance might come from.

2. By the time the office opens at 8:45 A.M., the line of people waiting to do business at the Registry of Motor Vehicles (RMV) in Watertown, Massachusetts, will be 25 deep. By mid-day, especially if it is near the end of the month, the line may extend around the building. Inside, motorists wait in slow-moving rows before poorly marked windows to get a driver's license or to register an automobile. When someone gets to the head of the line, he or she is often told by the clerk that it is the wrong line. The customers grumble impatiently. The clerks act harried and sometimes speak rudely.

Not far away, people also wait in line at a McDonald's fast-food restaurant. There are several lines; each is short and moves quickly. The menu is clearly displayed on attractive signs. The workers behind the counter are invariably polite. If someone's order cannot be filled immediately, he or she is asked to step aside for a moment while the food is prepared, and then is brought back to the head of the line to receive the order. The atmosphere is friendly and good natured. The room is immaculately clean.

What might the RMV learn from McDonald's? What are some of the issues and problems in redesigning the RMV to be more like McDonald's? What concepts discussed in the section might help the RMV and maybe even improve McDonald's?

Source: James Q. Wilson, *Bureaucracy* (New York: Basic Books. 1989), p. 112.

DESIGNING ORGANIZATIONS TO MANAGE CHANGE

WHAT'S AHEAD?

Technical and Computer Graphics Company (TCG) is at the forefront of information technology. It makes high-tech communication devices, such as handheld data terminals (like those used by UPS) and electronic data interchange systems. You probably could not find a company whose competitive and technological terrain is changing as fast or unexpectedly as TCG's. To succeed in such a fast-changing environment, TCG has to make sure it's organized for speed. In TCG's case, this means what the company calls a cellular organization. TCG is actually composed of 13 small, more-or-less autonomous and self-reliant firms (or cells), each interacting with the others and with partners and customers outside the company.

THIS SECTION FOCUSES ON THE FOLLOWING:

- Traditional ways managers redesign organizations to make them more responsive

- How to organize and lead team-based organizations

- Network-based and boundaryless organizations

- The horizontal corporation

- The factors affecting how organizations are designed and structured

Companies from giants like IBM to relatively small ones like TCG, are creating new means of organizing their operations: They hope these will help them better respond to today's fast-moving competition, and thus to manage change. However, those are just the basic elements and language of how to organize. Now we turn to organizing to manage change, and specifically to the new ways companies are organizing to better respond to competitive, technological, and political pressures.

▶BUILDING TEAM-BASED STRUCTURES

Increasingly, steps like delayering, reassigning support staff, and establishing mini-units are not enough. Managers have sought additional ways to streamline how decisions are made. New structural approaches are therefore being tried. Specifically, managers are using teams, networks, and "boundaryless" structures to redesign their organizations so as to better manage change. We'll look at these in this and the next few sections.

The Building Blocks of Team-Based Organizations[1]

Many firms today, for example, organize activities around self-contained and self-managing work teams. A **team** is a group of people who work together and share a common work objective.[2]

For example, at the GE jet engine plant in Durham, North Carolina, over 170 employees work with only one manager—the plant manager—and are organized into small, self-managing teams.[3] At Johnsonville Foods in Wisconsin, the CEO organized most of the firm's activities around self-managing, 12-person work teams. At Johnsonville, work teams are responsible for running and maintaining the firm's packaging equipment. But unlike in traditional management structures, such teams are empowered to manage themselves and make fast, on-the-spot decisions. For example, the duties of a typical Johnsonville work team include:

- Recruit, hire, evaluate, and fire (if necessary)
- Handle quality control, inspections, subsequent troubleshooting, and problem solving
- Develop and monitor quantitative standards for productivity and quality
- Suggest and develop prototypes of possible new products and packaging[4]

At Chesebrough-Ponds USA, a functional organization was replaced with a structure built around self-directed teams that now run the plant's four production areas. Hourly employees make employee assignments, schedule overtime, establish production times and changeovers, and even handle cost control, requisitions, and work orders. They are also solely responsible for quality control under the plant's Continuous Quality Improvement Challenge, a program in which employees can post suggestions or challenges to improve quality. Team member Sherry Emerson summed up employee sentiments: "The empowerment is exciting. If we see something that will affect the quality to customers, we have the freedom to stop a process. They [management] trust us." And the results have been extraordinary. Quality acceptance is 99.25%. Annual manufacturing costs are down $10.6 million; work-in-process inventory has been reduced 86%; and total inventory is down 65%.[5]

As these examples suggest, team-based organizations are different from the traditional departmentalized and hierarchical organizations. Companies were traditionally organized with individuals, functions, or departments as the basic work units or elements. This is evident in the typical organization chart, which might show separate boxes for each functional department, and perhaps even separate tasks for individual workers at the bottom of the chart.

In team-based organizations, the team is the basic work unit or element. Employees work together as a team, and do much of the planning, decision making, and implementing required to get their assigned jobs done, while being responsible for things like receiving materials, installing parts, and dealing with vendors who ship defective parts. Or, instead of simply organizing around traditional publishing functions like production, editorial, and sales, some publishers create more of a team-based organization; they create, for each book in process, a multidisciplined and self-managing team whose members work together to develop, produce, and market the book.

If you've ever worked on a team (say, to present a project at school), you know that such an approach can have many advantages. Everyone's attention tends to be focused on the team's goal; everyone tends to the more committed to achieving that goal; and everyone generally tends to be more willing to pitch in and get the job done. And since these teams tend to be small and don't have the traditional departmental barriers separating its members, communication and interaction tends to be open and free-flowing. At least, that's the theory. In practice, smoothly functioning team-based organizations don't arise spontaneously; instead, they depend on the presence of several supporting mechanisms, to which we now turn.

Designing Organizations to Support Teams[6]

Managers can't create team-based organizations without providing the supporting mechanisms that will allow the teams to flourish. At least five support mechanisms are required to enable work teams to do their jobs: The firm must have the right philosophy, structure, systems, policies, and employee skills (Figure 3-7).

- *Organizational philosophy.* The philosophy underlying a team-based organization is obviously different in several ways from the philosophy in companies that are organized traditionally. In facilities like GE/Durham and Johnsonville, the workers are basically responsible for supervising themselves and for making sure that their work is getting done and getting done properly. There's no supervisor looking over their shoulders.

  To establish a team-based organization, management therefore can't just pay lip service to the idea that employees should be involved and trusted. For example, organizing around self-managing teams and then showing employees you don't trust them by having supervisors second-guessing everything they do is counterproductive.

  Committing to the right organizational philosophy is thus the first step managers have to take before setting out to create a team-based organization. What people believe and value tends to guide what they do, and if top management doesn't really buy into the philosophy of employee involvement and trust, it's liable to institute practices that end up undermining the entire team effort. Successful team-based organizations are run by managers committed to a philosophy and core values emphasizing high employee involvement and trust.

- *Organizational structure.* In team-based organizations, teams are the basic work units. Firms are characterized by flat structures with few supervisors, and delegation of much decision-making authority to the work teams. In turn, the work

▼ **F I G U R E   3 - 7**   **Designing Organizations to Manage Teams**

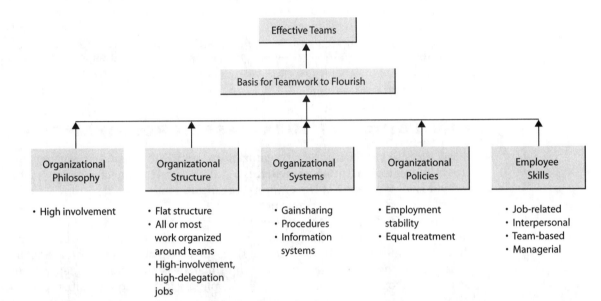

Source: Adapted from James H. Shonk, *Team-based Organizations*, (Homewood, IL: Irwin, 1997 p.36)

teams in firms like GE/Durham carry out supervisory tasks ranging from scheduling overtime to actually doing the work.

- *Organizational systems.* Every company depends in part on standard operating systems to make sure that everything goes smoothly. These systems range from performance appraisal and financial rewards to the systems used to gather marketing data and to keep track of sales and production levels.

  Instituting team-friendly support systems is another building block of team-based structures. For example, team-based companies often use a performance appraisal system called "360-degree appraisals," since systems like these are based on feedback from all the worker's teammates, not just the facility's managers. Similarly, financial incentives tend to be paid to the team as a whole rather than to individual employees.

- *Organizational policies.* We've also seen that every company uses organizational policies (such as "the customer is always right" and "we only use fresh ingredients") as standard guidelines regarding how the work of the organization is to be accomplished. Policies like these can play an important role in supporting the company's team effort. For example, organizing around self-managing teams means building close-knit, stable teams of highly trained employees, and it hardly pays to do so if employees are fired every time revenue dips.

  Team-based organizations therefore tend to emphasize employment stability. At Toyota's Camry facility in Lexington, Kentucky, for instance, slack demand might mean that more employees spend time being trained to develop new skills rather than being laid off. Similarly, rigid policies such as "any employee coming to work more than 12 minutes late will not be allowed on the premises" would be counterproductive in a team-based organization, since here the teams themselves usually have the responsibility to supervise their own team member-employees.

- *Employee skills.* Work teams typically have wide-ranging responsibilities (such as scheduling their own time, hiring team members, and managing their own quality). It's therefore essential that all team members have a wide range of skills, including (1) the skills to actually do the job (such as welding); (2) the interpersonal skills to work in a healthy manner with and in the team (listening, communicating, and so on); (3) team skills (such as problem solving and running decision-making meetings); and (4) management skills (including planning, leading, and controlling).

▶ BUILDING NETWORK-BASED ORGANIZATIONS

Many firms today superimpose "organizational networks" over their existing structures. An **organizational network** is a system of interconnected or cooperating individuals.[7] We'll look at three: formal organizational networks, informal organizational networks, and electronic networks.

Whether formal, informal, or electronic, the network enhances the likelihood that the work of even far-flung units can be accomplished promptly and in a coordinated manner, especially if quick decisions must be made. All organizational networks share the same core idea: They link managers from various departments, levels, and geographic areas into a multidisciplinary team whose members communicate across normal organizational boundaries.

Formal Networks

A **formal organizational network** has been defined as

> A recognized group of managers assembled by the CEO and the senior executive team.... The members are drawn from across the company's functions, business units, and geography, and from different levels of the hierarchy. The number of managers involved almost never exceeds 100 and can be fewer than 25—even in global companies with tens of thousands of employees.[8] The cross-functional nature of formal networks is illustrated in Figure 3-8. Note the number of organizational levels and departments represented by the black boxes.

Formal networks differ from teams or cross-functional task forces in three ways.[9] First, unlike most task forces, networks are *not temporary*. In fact, each manger's continuing experience in the network helps build the shared understanding among members and explains the network's effectiveness. Second, unlike most teams and task forces, networks *take the initiative* in finding and solving problems. In other words, they do not just solve the specific problems they are given. Third, the existence of the formal network changes—or should change—the nature of top management's job. With the networks in place, CEOs "no longer define their jobs as making all substantive operating decisions on their own.[10] Instead, although CEOs still make many decisions, the network can handle more of the interunit coordination the CEO might otherwise have to do, leaving him or her more time for strategic planning.

A formal network is used at the railroad firm Conrail. Here, 19 middle managers from various departments and levels constitute the firm's operating committee, which is actually a formal network, and thereby influence most of the firm's key operating decisions. They meet for several hours on Monday mornings to review and decide on tactical issues (delivery schedules and prices, for instance) and work on longer-term issues such as five-year business plans.[11] But, as a formal network, they are also expected to communicate continuously during the week to monitor operations activities across their departments.

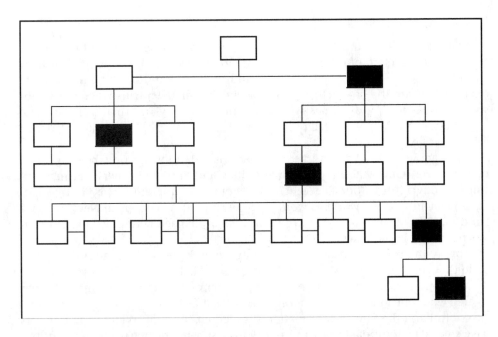

◄ **FIGURE 3-8**

How Networks Reshape Organizations

The members of a formal network may be selected from various departments and organizational levels.

Source: Reprinted by permission of *Harvard Business Review.* From "How Networks Reshape Organizations—For Results," by Ram Charan, September–October 1991. Copyright © 1991 by the President and Fellows of Harvard College; all rights reserved.

The vacuum cleaner company Electrolux provides another example. When Leif Johansson took over an Electrolux division that stretched from Norway to Italy, he inherited a daunting task. Electrolux's line included 20 products, numerous acquired companies, and more than 200 plants in many countries. Each presented unique market positions, capabilities, plant capacity, and competitive situations. Johansson saw that his strategy had to be to create strengths across functional and geographic borders if he was to derive maximum economies of scale from the multiproduct, multiplant, multinational operation.

Local managers convinced him that abandoning local brands would jeopardize existing distribution channels and customer loyalty. How could he derive the benefits of Electrolux's multicountry scale while maintaining local brand autonomy? His solution was to create a formal network composed of managers from various countries. The network structure helped keep operations flexible and responsive. Local managers still had wide authority to design and market local brands. But the formal network helps provide the overall multinational and multiproduct coordination in areas like production and inventory management that helped Electrolux obtain economies of scale.[12]

While our focus here is mostly on internal formal organizational networks, such formal networks are also increasingly important in international trade. For example, in telecommunications, the Global One joint venture, led by Sprint, Deutsche Telecom, and France Telecom, is managed by a formal network serving 65 countries and functioning as one company to serve the global telecommunications needs of corporations.[13] In fact, it's been estimated that by the year 2000, more than 20,000 such strategic alliances were in place and operating around the world. Other examples include the major strategic alliances in the airline business, such as the Star Alliance, which includes United, Lufthansa, SAS, Varig, and others. As with internal formal organizational networks, strategic alliances are also managed by formal networks: a recognized group of managers—in this case, in each of the various alliance member companies—is appointed to achieve the day-to-day and strategic coordination required to make the strategic alliance a success.

Informal Networks

Networks needn't be formal, and indeed many firms, particularly multinationals, encourage the growth of informal networks. "Here," as one expert put it, "Creating confidence in the work of colleagues around the world and building up personal relationships are the key factors."[14] **Informal organizational networks** consist of cooperating individuals who are connected only informally. They share information and help solve each other's problems based on personal knowledge of each other's expertise.

There are several ways to nurture the personal relationships on which informal networks are built. Multinationals like Philips and Shell build personal relationships through international executive development programs. They bring managers from around the world to work together in training centers in New York and London. Other firms, like GE, have international management development centers near their home cities.

Moving managers from facility to facility around the world is another way to build these informal networks. Some firms, such as Shell, transfer employees around the world in great numbers. In one case, for instance: "[International mobility] has created what one might call a 'nervous system' that facilitates both corporate strategic control and the flow of information throughout the firm. Widespread transfers have created an informal information network, a superior degree of communication, and mutual understanding between headquarters and subsidiaries and between subsidiaries themselves, as well as a stronger identification with the corporate culture, without compromising the local subsidiary cultures."[15]

Management development programs like these help build informal networks in several ways. The socializing that takes place builds personal relationships among managers. Such personal relationships then facilitate global networking and communications. So if a new Shell Latin America sales manager needs to get in to see a new client, she might call a Shell Zurich manager she knows who has a contact at the client firm.

Electronic Networks

The rise of the Internet and of collaborative computing networking software lets companies make better use of existing formal and informal networks and, indeed, encourages all employees throughout the firm to network. Collaborative computing software includes packages such as Lotus Notes that help employees "get together" and make decisions, even at great distances.

Electronic networking—networking through e-mail and the use of collaborative computing software like Lotus Notes—helps manage businesses today. PricewaterhouseCooper's 18,000 accountants stay in touch thanks to **electronic bulletin boards**. Thus a Dublin employee with a question about dairy plant accounting might have her question answered by a networked colleague half a world away.[16] Group decision support systems allow employees—even those in different countries—to brainstorm ideas and work together on projects.[17]

Indeed, collaborative packages like Lotus Notes are changing how companies are managed and organized.[18] For example, a product called IP Team 3.0 includes new decision-building tools that automate and document the making of engineering decisions. One of its key features is that it integrates suppliers and contractors into the product development cycle. It thus lets a geographically dispersed group from the company and its suppliers work together to develop a product, and then automates

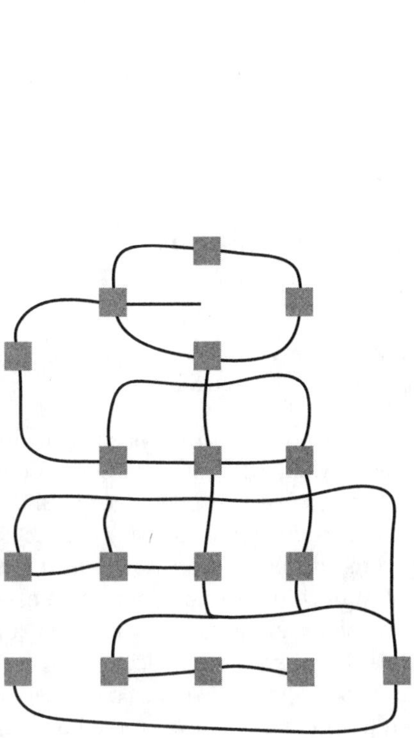

◀ **FIGURE 3-9**

Hyperarchy

Source: Reprinted by permission of the Harvard Business Review. An exhibit from "Strategy and the New Economics of Information" by Philip B. Evans and Thomas S. Wurster, September–October 1997, Copyright © 1997 by the President and Fellows of Harvard College; all rights reserved.

the bidding procedure.[19] Another collaborative groupware product called OneSpace allows several design teams "to collaborate over the Internet and across fire walls in real-time by working directly on the 3 D solid model. . . ."[20] When it comes to using the Internet for networking business processes, the UK-based British Telecommunications PLC (BT) provides a good illustration of "managing@the speed of thought." BT has developed an Intranet—an internal network based on Internet technologies—which is used by over 60,000 employees, customers, and suppliers. For example, the Intranet is used for BT's project proposal submission process and helps everyone involved to instantaneously submit, review, and track the status of each project.[21] The system uses a simple security/authentication system to ensure that only involved parties have access to the project data. But by linking everyone together via the Internet, all those involved in a project (both within and outside BT) are able to monitor and manage their project, thanks to Internet-based networking.

Products like these do more than expedite the company's design process or automate its purchasing. By linking employees, customers, suppliers, and partners electronically (often over the Internet), they enable companies to create what amount to electronic networked organizations. Here communications and relationships ignore traditional departmental boundaries, and even the traditional boundaries separating the company from its customers and suppliers largely cease to exist. In fact, companies today use the Internet, intranets, and similar links between themselves and customers and suppliers to communicate in what two experts call **hyperarchies**. Figure 3-9 illustrates the effect of such networking. In a hyperarchy, the network is so complete that basically everyone can communicate with anyone else, and is encouraged to do so. As these experts put it: "Hyperarchy challenges all hierarchies, whether of logic or of power, with the possibility (or the threat) of random access and information symmetry."[22] Everyone, in other words, from first-line employees on up can communicate digitally with everyone else. The result is an organization where communications aren't restricted by the organization chart or the chain of command—a sort of digital boundaryless organization, as we'll see in a moment.

Managing @ the Speed of Thought
■ Knowledge Management

To Microsoft's Bill Gates, making sure that employees can communicate is a good example of knowledge management. Here's how he puts it:

> Knowledge management is nothing more than managing information flow, getting the right information to the people who need it so they can act on it quickly. . . .And, knowledge management is a means, not an end. The end is to increase institutional intelligence, or corporate IQ. In today's dynamic markets a company needs a high corporate IQ to succeed. By corporate IQ I don't mean simply having a lot of smart people at your company—although it helps to start with smart people. Corporate IQ is a measure of how easily your company can share information broadly and of how well people within the organization can build on each other's ideas. . . . The workers in a company with a high corporate IQ collaborate effectively so that all of the key people on a project are well-informed and energized. The ultimate goal is to have a team develop the best ideas from throughout an organization and then act with the same unity of purpose and focus that a single, well-motivated person would bring to bear on the situation.[23]

► BOUNDARYLESS ORGANIZATIONS

"Old-style" organizations have boundaries. Vertically, the chain of command implies clearly defined authority boundaries: The president gives orders to the vice president, who gives orders to the managers, and so on down the line. There are also clearly delineated horizontal or departmental boundaries. Most companies are separated into what some call "smokestacks." The production department has its own responsibilities, the sales department has its own, and so on. If the company happens to be divisionalized, the work of each division is self-contained and each division often proceeds on the assumption that it can (and should) do its job with little or no interaction with other divisions.[24]

We've seen that such boundary-filled organizations once served a useful purpose. Jobs were specialized, lines of communication were well defined, and the slow-arriving problems could be solved in a relatively mechanical, step-by-step manner by an organization in which all knew exactly where they stood. For most firms, things are different today. Rapid change demands a more responsive organization: First-line employees may need quick responses from managers two levels up, or someone in the U.S. division may need a quick response from someone in Europe. As a result, yesterday's neat organizational boundaries need to be pierced, as they are with teams and formal and informal networks. As two experts summarized it: "Companies are replacing vertical hierarchies with horizontal networks; linking together traditional functions through interfunctional teams; and forming strategic alliances with suppliers, customers, and even competitors."[25] In so doing, they are creating boundaryless organizations.

A **boundaryless organization** is one in which the widespread use of teams, networks, and similar structural mechanisms means that the "walls" which typically separate organizational functions and hierarchical levels are reduced and made more permeable.[26] Taken to the extreme, the boundaryless company is one in which not only internal organizational boundaries are stripped away, but also those between the company and its suppliers and customers.

Piercing Organizational Boundaries

In practice, four specific boundaries must be pierced if the company is to take full advantage of teams and networks: the authority boundary, the task boundary, the political boundary, and the identity boundary.[27] A summary of these four boundaries and the managerial tensions and feelings that must be addressed in order to pierce them is shown in Figure 3-10.

The Authority Boundary   In every company, superiors and subordinates—even those in self-managing teams or formal networks—always meet at an **authority boundary**. Therein lies the problem: To achieve the responsiveness required of a team-based or network structure, just issuing and following orders "is no longer good enough."[28] For example, a manager in a formal network who happened to be a vice president would inhibit the network's effectiveness if she demanded the right to give orders based solely on the fact that she was the highest-ranking person in the network. Doing so would undermine the collaboration and the reliance on experts that are two advantages of teams and networks.

Piercing the authority boundary thus requires three things. Bosses must learn how to lead while remaining open to criticism. They must be willing to accept "orders" from lower-ranking employees who happen to be experts on the problems at hand. And "subordinates" must be trained and encouraged to follow but still challenge superiors if necessary.

The Task Boundary   Creating a boundaryless organization also requires managing the **task boundary**. This means changing the way employees feel about who does what when employees from different departments work on a task. Managing the task boundary means training and encouraging employees to rid themselves of the

	KEY QUESTIONS	TENSIONS DEVELOPING DUE TO THIS BOUNDARY
Authority Boundary	"Who is in charge of what?" ➡	How to lead but remain open to criticism. How to follow but still challenge superiors.
Task Boundary	"Who does what?" ➡	How to depend on others you don't control. How to specialize yet understand other people's jobs.
Political Boundary	"What's in it for us?" ➡	How to defend one's interests without undermining the organization. How to differentiate between win–win and win–lose situations.
Identity Boundary	"Who is—and isn't—'us'?" ➡	How to feel pride without devaluing others. How to remain loyal without undermining outsiders.

◀ **F I G U R E   3 - 1 0**

The Four Organizational Boundaries That Matter

In setting up a boundaryless organization, four boundaries must be overcome, but doing so means dealing with the resulting tensions.

Source: Reprinted by permission of *Harvard Business Review.* "The Four Organizational Boundaries that Matter," from "The New Boundaries of the 'Boundaryless' Company," by Larry Hirschorn and Thomas Gilmore, May–June 1992. Copyright © 1992 by the President and Fellows of Harvard College. All rights reserved.

"It's not my job" attitude that typically compartmentalizes one employee's area from another's:

> Indeed, their own performance may depend on what their colleagues do. So, while focusing primarily on their own task, they must also take a lively interest in the challenges and problems facing others who contribute in different ways to the final product or service.[29]

The Political Boundary   Differences in political agendas often separate employees as well. For example, manufacturing typically has a strong interest in smoothing out the demand for its products and in making the firm's products as easy to produce as possible. Sales, on the other hand, has an equally legitimate interest in maximizing sales (even if it means taking in a lot of custom or last-minute rush orders). The result of such opposing agendas in a traditional organization can be a conflict at the departments' **political boundary**.

Members of each special-interest group in a boundaryless firm may still ask "What's in it for us?" when a decision must be made. But they have to be encouraged to take a more collegial, consensus-oriented approach, to defend their interests without undermining the best interests of the team, network, or organization.

The Identity Boundary   Everyone identifies with several groups. For example, a General Motors accountant might identify with her colleagues in the accounting profession, with her co-workers in the GM accounting department, and perhaps with GM itself, to name a few. The **identity boundary** means that we tend to identify with groups with which we have shared experiences and with which we believe we share fundamental values.

Unfortunately, such identification tends to foster an "us" versus "them" mentality. The problem at the identity boundary arises because people tend to trust those with whom they identify but distrust others. Attitudes like these can undermine the free-flowing cooperation that responsive networked or team-based organizations require.

There are several ways to pierce the identity boundary. One is to train and socialize all the firm's employees so they come to identify first with the company and its goals and ways of doing things: "The company comes first" becomes their motto. Another is to emphasize that while team spirit may be laudable, employees must avoid "devaluing the potential contribution of other groups."[30]

IBM's research facilities provide an illustration of how the boundaryless process works in practice.[31] IBM has eight labs worldwide, employing about 3,000 researchers. While the labs' results are obviously brilliant—they generated $1.3 billion in licensing revenues in one recent year—it's not just the discoveries but how they're developed and implemented that makes IBM's R&D effort truly unique.

As in many organizations, the usual way of doing things tends to be much different in the research group than on the development side. As IBM's senior vice president for research puts it: "The development side is highly disciplined, with a lot of checkpoints, tests, and milestones." On the other hand, "The research side is the exact opposite; it's much more freewheeling." A big reason for IBM's success in commercializing its discoveries has been it's ability to eliminate barriers between the research and development groups. While they're separate departments, their efforts are more like that of a joint venture group. In other words, by reducing the barriers created by the authority, task, political, and identity boundaries, IBM has been able to blend the work of two very different departments into a concerted team-like effort.

SUMMARY   ■

1. Some managers find that to manage change, responsive organizational structures are advisable. Team-based organizations built around self-managing teams are an example. Here the team is the basic work unit, and teams do much of the planning, decision making, and implementing required to get their assigned jobs done.

2. Many firms superimpose organizational networks over existing structures. A network is a system of interconnected or cooperating individuals. It can be formal or informal, and it can be electronically based. The basic idea is to link managers from various departments, levels, and geographic areas so they form a multidisciplinary team whose members communicate across normal organizational boundaries.

3. Taken to its logical conclusion, a networked organization results in a boundaryless organization in which managers have taken the steps required to pierce the organizational boundaries that often inhibit networked communications and decision making. These are the authority boundary, the task boundary, the identity boundary, and the political boundary.

4. The horizontal corporation is a structure organized around basic processes such as new-product development, sales fulfillment, and customer support. Everyone works together in multidisciplinary teams, with each team assigned to perform one or more of the processes.

5. Federal organizations are organizations in which power is distributed between a central unit and a number of a constituent units, but the central unit's authority is intentionally limited; virtual organizations and cellular organizations are two examples. A virtual organization is a collection of independent enterprises tied together by contracts and other means, such as partial ownership arrangements. In a cellular organization, small independent companies are the basic building blocks, and while each is self-sufficient, they all contribute to each other's and to the parent firm's success.

TYING IT ALL TOGETHER   ■

After plans are made, managers have to organize the work to be done. Previously, we focused on the fundamentals of organizing, including departmentalization (by function or product, for instance), coordination, and delegation. In this section we turned to designing organizations to manage change, and to structures such as boundaryless and cellular organizations.

 However, designing the organization and organization chart is only part of the overall job of creating an organization: Having a box that says "Finance Department" doesn't really tell you very much about what the employees in that department actually do on a day-to-day basis. Nor is an organization chart of much use without employees to fill its positions.

CASE 3-1
W. L. GORE & ASSOCIATES: STRUCTURING FOR CONTINUOUS CHANGE

Would you offer someone a high-salary position without knowing what job they would have? W. L. Gore & Associates does. It is one of the many unusual practices that have helped Gore, makers of the waterproof fabric GORE-TEX®, to be repeatedly named to the *Fortune* list of 100 Best Companies to Work for in America, most recently ranking as the 11th best firm. While only 40 years old, Gore has amassed revenues in excess of $1 billion and operates in 45 countries, while employing only 6,100 people.

 Gore operates a high-tech company in a market (textiles) that is traditionally low-tech. As a high-tech company, Gore must be prepared to change rapidly when the market changes. To do this, Gore's structure and processes are distinguished by three unique characteristics: sponsors rather than bosses, a "lattice" organization, and the "waterline principle."

Gore sees the way it organizes and works as one of the things that sets it apart from its competitors. Gore militates against bureaucracy: it sees hierarchies as the enemies of innovation. Gore hires "associates" (not *employees*) into general work areas. When hired, these employees don't have specific job titles or positions. With the help of their Gore *sponsors* (*bosses*), associates select and commit to projects that seem to match their skills and interests. One of the sponsors' jobs is to help associates find a place in Gore that will offer personal fulfillment and maximize their contribution to the enterprise. Gore does not assign managers. In the company's view, leaders are people who have followers. If the organization is left on its own, leaders will emerge naturally, by demonstrating the character, knowledge, and skills that attract followers. To become a leader at Gore, you need to perform in a way that attracts followers.

This self-selecting process leads to what Gore calls the *lattice organization*. In the lattice, there are no chains of command; decision making is delegated to the point where the decision must be made. It is assumed that employees are sufficiently concerned about the good of the organization to make good decisions on behalf of the organization. Gore's lattice has no preestablished channels of communication. New associates are coached by their sponsors to communicate directly with each other. Associates work in multidisciplinary teams and are accountable to each other. The goal of this innovative structure is to unleash the creative potential of all of the associates, thus allowing Gore to become a truly innovative company.

The last commitment, the *waterline principle*, is cited by many as a key to Gore's successful ability to adapt. The company is viewed as a ship. Holes above the waterline are unattractive and even uncomfortable, but not deadly. Holes below the waterline would sink the ship. If you are a Gore associate and you see an action or event that could hit Gore below the waterline, then it is your individual responsibility to do something, even if the event or action happens outside your department or area. Failing to act on a waterline

issue would earn you a severe reprimand from your peers, the other associates. After all, it is the role of every employee to protect the ship. With these principles firmly in place, Gore has been able to be remarkably flexible, to change constantly to meet the needs of current and future clients.

The results of Gore's structure and processes have been impressive. Its world-renowned fluoropolymer technology has allowed it to extend the product line far beyond the well-known GORE-TEX® brand. The same technology has allowed the company to produce Glide®, a nonstick dental floss, and Elixir®, a corrosion-resistant guitar string. Lesser known but equally impressive products, including next-generation materials for printed circuit boards and fiber optics, and new methods to detect and control environmental pollution, are marketed in the industrial sector. Gore has also been recognized for its work in advancing the science of regenerating tissue destroyed by injuries.

The Company's founder, Bill Gore, originally articulated the Company's unique structure and culture. To Gore, the company would be successful only if it could create an environment that was naturally conducive to the highest levels of innovation and productivity. Gore envisioned associates making a commitment to four basic principles: fairness to each other and everyone they came in contact with; freedom to encourage, help, and allow other associates to grow in knowledge, skill, and scope of responsibility; the ability to make one's own commitments and keep them; and consultation with other associates before undertaking actions that could affect the reputation of the company by hitting it "below the waterline."

Discussion Questions

1. In what ways is Gore's lattice structure similar to the structures discussed in this section?

2. In what ways does Gore's lattice structure make it better suited to change?

3. Gore asserts that its structure makes it more innovative. Could a traditionally structured company be as innovative as W. L. Gore & Associates? How?

4. What difficulties might you encounter if you tried to apply Gore's structural principles to an existing company?

STAFFING THE ORGANIZATION

WHAT'S AHEAD?

When it comes to leading-edge, fast-changing companies, it's hard to think of one more on the edge than Cisco Systems. Cisco is the worldwide leader in Internet networking, and it supplies the network solutions that let people transfer information over the Internet. With offices in more than 115 countries worldwide and growing at hyper-speed, Cisco has a constant need to hire the best of the best employees. To keep growing fast in this high-tech field, Cisco needs a constant supply of new top candidates, and outstanding training and HR programs to assimilate and motivate them.

Cisco has some of the most sophisticated HR programs anywhere. And as you'd expect from the world's Internet networking leader, much of its recruiting and initial screening takes place via the Internet.[1]

THIS SECTION FOCUSES ON THE FOLLOWING:

- Why human resource management is crucial today

- Methods to recruit a pool of good candidates

- Testing in selecting new employees

- The main steps in conducting an employment interview

- Important employee selection techniques

Having a box in an organization chart that says "Finance Department" doesn't really tell you much about what the employees in that department actually have to do, or what kinds of people should be hired for these positions. In this section we focused on organizing, including organizational fundamentals (like how to departmentalize and achieve coordination). Now we turn to staffing, and in particular to developing job descriptions and to the methods managers use to recruit and select the employees who will actually fill job slots.

Staffing, personnel, or (as it is generally known today) **Human Resource Management** (HRM) is the management function devoted to acquiring and training the organization's employees, and then appraising and paying them. This section emphasizes those staffing functions that relate most directly to organizing (such as recruiting and selecting employees). Toward the end of the section we'll briefly cover appraisal and compensation. Once a company is organized and staffed, its employees are ready to be motivated and led. These are the topics we'll turn to in the next part of the text.

All managers are, in a sense, personnel managers, because they all get involved in activities like recruiting, interviewing, selecting, and training. But most large firms also have Human Resource (HR) departments with their own human resource managers.

▶ HUMAN RESOURCE MANAGEMENT AS A STRATEGIC PARTNER

Intense global competition means that companies today need competent and committed employees more than they ever have before. To be more competitive, companies must now rely on things like self-managing work teams and empowering employees. In turn, organizing like this boosts the need for motivated and self-directed employees: You can't very well have self-managing work teams if the employees don't have the skills or attitudes to manage themselves.

Many experts describe this situation by saying that employees have become for most companies, their main competitive advantage or "competitive edge." For example, the reason Southwest Airlines can be so efficient is that its employees are all driven to make their company succeed. But if employees are a competitive advantage, then selecting, training, and managing them should be an important part of the company's strategic planning process. This in turn has led to the emergence of strategic human resource management.

Strategic human resource management has been defined as "the linking of HRM with strategic goals and objectives in order to improve business performance and develop organizational cultures that foster innovation and flexibility."[2] Strategic HR means accepting the fact that human resource management plays an important role in *formulating* company strategies, as well as in *executing* those strategies through its activities like recruiting, selecting, and training personnel.

HR's Role in Formulating Strategy

HR management can play a crucial role in helping companies formulate their strategies. For example, HR management is in a good position to supply competitive intelligence that the firm's top managers need to know. Details regarding incentive plans being used by competitors, opinion surveys from employees that elicit information about customer complaints, and information about pending legislation like labor laws or mandatory health insurance are examples.

HR also supplies information regarding the company's internal strengths and weaknesses. IBM's decision to buy Lotus was prompted in part by IBM's conclusion that its own human resources were inadequate to enable the firm to reposition itself as an industry leader in networking systems, or at least to do so quickly enough.

HR's Role in Executing Strategy

HR also can play a big role in executing the company's strategy. For example, FedEx's competitive strategy is to differentiate itself from its competitors by offering superior customer service and guaranteed on-time delivery. Since basically the same technologies are available to UPS, DHL, and FedEx's other competitors, it is FedEx's workforce that gives it a crucial competitive advantage. The firm's HR processes and its ability to create a highly committed, competent, and customer-oriented workforce are crucial to FedEx's ability to execute its strategy. FedEx has therefore implemented many leading-edge HR practices, including extensive incentive plans and a grievance process that goes all the way to the FedEx president.

▶ PERSONNEL PLANNING AND RECRUITING

Once the firm's organization is in place, its positions must be filled. For most companies, the heart of the human resource management system (as illustrated in Figure 3-11) is a sequence of steps in which employees are recruited, screened, and finally trained to do their jobs. This is also referred to as the manager's **staffing** function, the function that involves actually filling the firm's open organizational positions. In most companies, this process begins by looking at the organization chart and then deciding specifically what each job entails and who (both in and out of the company) might be available to fill it. It begins, in other words, with analyzing the company's personnel requirements and then recruiting applicants to fill them.

▼ **FIGURE 3-11**   **Steps in the Recruitment and Selection (staffing) Process**

The recruitment and selection process is a series of hurdles aimed at selecting the best candidate for the job.

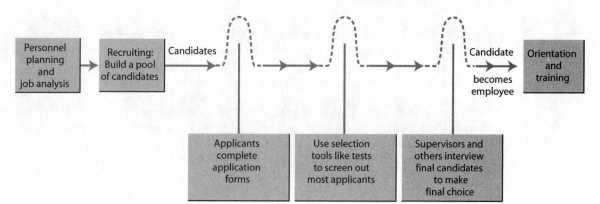

Job Analysis and Personnel Planning

Developing an organization chart creates jobs to be filled. **Job analysis** is the procedure used to determine the duties of the jobs and the kinds of people (in terms of skills and experience) who should be hired for them.[3] These data are then used to develop a **job description,** or a list of duties showing what the job entails, and **job specifications,** a list of the skills and aptitudes sought in people hired for the job. A job description like the one in Figure 3-12 identifies the job, provides a brief job summary, and then lists specific responsibilities and duties.

Managers often use a **job analysis questionnaire** to determine a job's duties and responsibilities. This generally requires employees to provide detailed information on what they do, such as briefly stating their main duties in their own words, describing the conditions under which they work, and listing any permits or licenses required to perform duties assigned to their positions. Supervisors and/or specialists from the company's HR department may then review this information, question the employees, and decide exactly what each job does—or should—entail.

Job analysis is part of personnel planning. **Personnel planning** is the process of determining the organization's personnel needs, as well as the methods to be used to fill those needs. If Sears decides to create a new department to handle Internet retail sales, it will need to do personnel planning. This will involve developing job descriptions and specifications to determine what sorts of people it will need to staff the new department. And its personnel plans should lay out where those new employees will come from (from within or from outside the current Sears employee pool), and how they should be trained and developed to function effectively.

Thanks to computers, personnel planning is becoming increasingly sophisticated. Many firms maintain data banks containing information on hundreds of traits (like special skills, product knowledge, work experience, training courses, relocation limitations, and career interests) for each of their employees. Such systems can make it much easier to identify promotable current employees and their training needs.[4]

The availability of so much employee data can obviously make it easier to plan for and fill positions in big companies. However, it also intensifies the need to protect the privacy of the data that are stored in the firm's computers.

Managing @ the Speed of Thought

■ **JobDescription.com**

There was a time, not too long ago, when producing job descriptions meant spending hours going through job description manuals. Today, it's possible to produce the job description you need almost instantaneously by using an Internet-based job description service.

JobDescription.com is one example. When the manager clicks on the site, he or she begins (for a fee) by choosing a job title from the 3,700 jobs listed in the JobDescription.com library. Then the manager follows the prompts to provide the requested information and/or customize the samples provided by JobDescription.com for each of the job description's sections (such as summary, duties and responsibilities, job information, and supervisory responsibilities).

The description in Figure 3-12—in this case for a marketing manager—provides an example. As you can see, the description is quite complete and includes such essential elements as summary, duties, and the human qualifications for the job.

▼ **FIGURE 3-12**   Sample Job Description

OLEC CORP.
Job Description

Job Title:	Marketing Manager
Department:	Marketing
Reports To:	President
FLSA Status:	Non Exempt
Prepared By:	Micheal George
Prepared Date:	April 1, 2000
Approved By:	Ian Alexander
Approved Date:	April 15, 2000

SUMMARY

Plans, directs, and coordinates the marketing of the organization's products and/or services by performing the following duties personally or through subordinate supervisors.

ESSENTIAL DUTIES AND RESPONSIBILITIES include the following. Other duties may be assigned.

Establishes marketing goals to ensure share of market and profitability of products and/or services.

Develops and executes marketing plans and programs, both short and long range, to ensure the profit growth and expansion of company products and/or services.

Researches, analyzes, and monitors financial, technological, and demographic factors so that market opportunities may be capitalized on and the effects of competitive activity may be minimized.

Plans and oversees the organization's advertising and promotion activities including print, electronic, and direct mail outlets.

Communicates with outside advertising agencies on ongoing campaigns.

Works with writers and artists and oversees copywriting, design, layout, pasteup, and production of promotional materials.

Develops and recommends pricing strategy for the organization which will result in the greatest share of the market over the long run.

Achieves satisfactory profit/loss ratio and share of market performance in relation to pre-set standards and to general and specific trends within the industry and the economy.

Ensures effective control of marketing results and that corrective action takes place to be certain that the achievement of marketing objectives are within designated budgets.

Evaluates market reactions to advertising programs, merchandising policy, and product packaging and formulation to ensure the timely adjustment of marketing strategy and plans to meet changing market and competitive conditions.

Recommends changes in basic structure and organization of marketing group to ensure the effective fulfillment of objectives assigned to it and provide the flexibility to move swiftly in relation to marketing problems and opportunities.

Conducts marketing surveys on current and new product concepts.

Prepares marketing activity reports.

SUPERVISORY RESPONSIBILITIES

Manages three subordinate supervisors who supervise a total of five employees in the Marketing Department. Is responsible for the overall direction, coordination, and evaluation of this unit. Also directly supervises two non-supervisory employees. Carries out supervisory responsibilities in accordance with the organization's policies and applicable laws. Responsibilities include interviewing, hiring, and training employees; planning, assigning, and directing work; appraising performance; rewarding and disciplining employees; addressing complaints and resolving problems.

QUALIFICATIONS

To perform this job successfully, an individual must be able to perform each essential duty satisfactorily. The requirements listed below are representative of the knowledge, skill, and/or ability required. Reasonable accommodations may be made to enable individuals with disabilities to perform the essential functions.

EDUCATION and/or EXPERIENCE

Master's degree (M.A.) or equivalent; or four to ten years related experience and/or training; or equivalent combination of education and experience.

LANGUAGE SKILLS

Ability to read, analyze, and interpret common scientific and technical journals, financial reports, and legal documents. Ability to respond to common inquiries or complaints from customers, regulatory agencies, or members of the business community. Ability to write speeches and articles for publication that conform to prescribed style and format. Ability to effectively present information to top management, public groups, and/or boards of directors.

MATHEMATICAL SKILLS

Ability to apply advanced mathematical concepts such as exponents, logarithms, quadratic equations, and permutations. Ability to apply mathematical operations to such tasks as frequency distribution, determination of test reliability and validity, analysis of variance, correlation techniques, sampling theory, and factor analysis.

REASONING ABILITY

Ability to define problems, collect data, establish facts, and draw valid conclusions. Ability to interpret an extensive variety of technical instructions in mathematical or diagram form.

Employee Recruiting

Once you know what jobs must be filled, **recruiting**—attracting a pool of viable job applicants—becomes very important. If you have only two candidates for two openings, you may have little choice but to hire them. But if many applicants appear, you can use techniques like interviews and tests to hire the best.

Effective recruiting is especially important today, for several reasons. First, the U.S. unemployment rate has been declining for several years, which has led some experts to refer to the current recruiting situation as one of "evaporated employee sources."[5] Many also believe that today's Generation X employees (those born between 1963 and 1977) are less inclined to build long-term employment relationships than were their predecessors.[6] High average turnover rates for some occupations is another problem; the average annual turnover rate for high-tech employees is 14.5%, according to one recent study.[7]

Current Employees While *recruiting* often brings to mind employment agencies and classified ads, current employees are often the largest source of recruits. Filling open positions with inside candidates has both pros and cons. On the plus side, employees see that competence is rewarded and morale and performance may thus be enhanced. Inside candidates are also known quantities in terms of performance and skills, and may already be committed to the company and its goals.

On the other hand, current employees who apply for jobs and don't get them may become demoralized. Inbreeding is another drawback: When an entire management team has been brought up through the ranks, there may be a tendency to maintain the status quo when innovation and a new direction are needed. Some companies (like Delta Airlines) have thus recently gone outside to hire their CEOs.

Promotion from within generally requires job posting.[8] **Job posting** means publicizing the open job to employees (often by literally posting it on bulletin boards and Intranets) and listing the job's attributes, like qualifications, supervisor, working schedule, and pay rate. Some union contracts require job posting to ensure that union members get first choice of new and better positions. Job posting can be a good practice, even in nonunion firms, if it facilitates the transfer and promotion of qualified inside candidates.[9]

Advertising As you know from the many help-wanted ads that appear in your local newspaper, advertising is a major way to attract applicants. The main issue here is selecting the best advertising medium, be it the local paper, the *Wall Street Journal*, or a technical journal.

The medium chosen depends on the type of job and on how wide a net the company believes it has to use. The local newspaper is usually best for blue-collar help, clerical employees, and lower-level management employees. For specialists, employers often advertise in trade and professional journals like *American Psychologist*, *Sales Management*, and *Chemical Engineering*. Executive jobs are often advertised in the *Wall Street Journal*.

Employment Agencies An employment agency is an intermediary whose business is to match applicants with positions. There are three types of agencies: (1) those operated by federal, state, or local governments; (2) those associated with not-for-profit organizations; and (3) those that are privately owned.

Public employment agencies exist in every state and are often referred to as *job service* or *unemployment service agencies*. Agencies like these are a major free source of hourly blue-collar and clerical workers and are increasingly establishing themselves as agents for professional and managerial-level applicants as well.

Other employment agencies are associated with not-for-profit organizations. For example, most professional and technical societies have units to help members find jobs.

Private agencies charge a fee for each applicant they place. These fees are usually set by state law and are posted in the agencies' offices. Whether the employer or the candidate pays the fee is mostly determined by market conditions. The trend in the past few years has been toward "fee paid" jobs, in which the employer pays the fees. These agencies are important sources of clerical, white-collar, and managerial personnel.

Temporary Help Agencies   Many employers today supplement their permanent employee base by hiring **contingent** (or **temporary**) **workers**, often through special agencies. The contingent workforce is big and growing, recently accounting for about 20% of all new jobs created in the United States. It is broadly defined as workers who don't have permanent jobs.[10]

Contingent staffing owes its growing popularity to several things. First, corporate downsizing seems to be driving up the number of temp workers firms employ. For example, while DuPont cut its workforce by 47,000 in recent years, it also estimates that about 14,000 workers returned in some temporary capacity, or as vendors or contractors.[11] Employers have always used temps to fill in for the days or weeks that permanent employees were out sick or on vacation. Today's desire for ever-higher productivity also contributes to temp workers' growing popularity. In general, as one expert puts it, "Productivity is measured in terms of output per hour paid for." "If employees are paid only when they're working, as contingent workers are, overall productivity increases."[12]

Executive Recruiters   **Executive recruiters** (also ominously called *headhunters*) are agencies retained by employers to look for top management talent, usually in the $70,000 and up category.

These firms have many business contacts, and are adept at contacting qualified candidates who are employed and not actively looking to change jobs. They can also keep a client firm's name confidential until late in the search process. The recruiter saves management time by doing the work of advertising for the position and screening what could turn out to be hundreds of applicants. The process usually starts with the recruiter meeting with the client to formulate a description of the position to be filled and the sort of person required to fill it. The recruiter then uses various methods to identify candidates, interview these people, and present a short list to the client for final screening.

Top firms used to take up to seven months to complete a search, with much of that time spent shuffling between headhunters and researchers who dig up the initial long list of candidates.[13] This often takes too long in today's fast-moving environment. Most search firms are therefore creating Internet-linked computerized databases, the aim of which, according to one senior recruiter, is "to create a long list [of candidates] by pushing a button."[14] Recruiter Korn/Ferry launched a new Internet service called Futurestep to draw more managerial applicants into its files; in turn, it has teamed up with the *Wall Street Journal*, which runs a career Web site of its own.[15] The "Entrepreneurs in Action" box shows how Melba Duncan built a search firm from scratch—and how she chooses great candidates.

Referrals and Walk-ins   Particularly for hourly workers, walk-ins—people who apply directly at the office—are a major source of applicants. Encouraging walk-in applicants may be as simple as posting a handwritten help-wanted sign in a window. Some organizations encourage walk-in applicants by mounting employee referral campaigns. Announcements of openings and requests for referrals are made in the company's newsletter or posted on bulletin boards and Intranets.

Employee referral programs are increasingly popular. Of the firms responding to one survey, 40% said they use an employee referral system and hire about 15% of their employees through such referrals. A cash award for referring hired candidates is the most common incentive. The cost per hire, however, was uniformly low; average per-hire expenses were only $388, far below the cost of an employment service.[16] Recruiting high-tech employees is especially amenable to such programs. In fact, some experts contend that the most effective recruiting method is to encourage existing employees to refer qualified friends and colleagues.[17]

College Recruiting   College recruiting—sending employers' representatives to college campuses to pre-screen applicants and create an applicant pool from that college's graduating class—is an important source of management trainees, promotable candidates, and professional and technical employees. One study of 251 staffing professionals concluded, for instance, that about 38% of all externally filled jobs requiring a college degree were filled by new college graduates.[18] What do recruiters look for in new college grads? Traits assessed include motivation, communication skills, education, appearance, and attitude.[19]

Entrepreneurs In Action

Duncan Group, Inc.

"One day," as Melba J. Duncan recalls, "I woke up, and I knew: This is a business!"[20] After years as an administrative assistant to CEOs at companies like Wall Street's Lehman Brothers, Duncan decided to strike out on her own. She correctly believed that top-ranked administrative/executive assistants were an overlooked region of the retained-search industry. Today her company successfully places administrative assistants who command salaries ranging from $55,000 to $130,000 per year, not counting bonuses and benefits, with clients including IBM, Home Depot, Bankers Trust, and the Boston Consulting group.

With years as a top assistant herself, Duncan combines a complete understanding of what the job calls for with a comprehensive system for selecting great candidates. For Duncan, it all starts with recruiting: She knows that to send three great finalists to a client, she'll need to start with a pool of 100. Her recruiters therefore work the phones "like air-traffic controllers," and review their files and their network of contacts. An initial screening cuts the original candidate pool to about 50; these complete a 15-page questionnaire, after which the pool is further cut to about 15.[21]

The screening doesn't stop there. Those 15 then go through a four-hour testing and profiling process that helps highlight their written and oral communication and clerical skills, and their management aptitude and personality. A clinical psychologist spends two days per week in Duncan's office, interviewing candidates and compiling profiles. Clients usually get their first three solid prospects within five days of the official opening of the search, along with a complete file on each candidate's background and work history. Duncan's favorite questions for applicants are summarized below.[22]

Duncan's Five Fave Questions for Applicants

At the Duncan Group candidates are asked to complete a 15-page questionnaire. It's jammed with mind-benders such as "What does service mean to you?" and "What places, people, ideas, or things arouse your curiosity?" The questionnaire doesn't change, but the questions Duncan is inspired to ask during face-to-face interviews always do. Here are her current favorites, culled from the questionnaire and the interviews:

1. Describe your worst boss and best boss.
("I'm partly thinking about discretion," says Duncan. "How much are you telling me that I shouldn't know?")

2. What would a previous employer have to say about you? ("For perspective on flexibility, judgment, and maturity.")

3. What are some of the qualities that enable you to perform successfully in a support role? ("People are more important than technology in this job; of course you need both, but does the answer reveal a technician?")

4. Given the opportunity, what new activities would you try? ("Are you curious, outgoing, strong, confident? Whiners aren't good.")

5. Please write a brief paragraph on the subject of your own choosing. You may want to focus on your life, your family, your aspirations, your goals, or your achievements.
("There's nothing as important as having people's best interests at heart; I want to guide them into the right position and this answer will help me do that. I want to know they have a sense of direction. I want to know what they care about. Also, attention to detail: please, no typos!")

Source: Reprinted with permission of Inc. Magazine, from "First Aide," by Nancy Austin, September 1999, copyright © 1999; permission conveyed through Copyright Clearance Center, Inc.

Many college students get their jobs through college internships; it's estimated that today almost three-quarters of all college students take part in an internship before they graduate, compared to 1 in 36 in 1980, for instance.[23]

Internships can be win–win situations for both students and employers. For students, it may mean being able to hone business skills, check out potential employers, and learn more about their likes (and dislikes) when it comes to choosing careers. And employers, of course, can use interns to make useful contributions while they're being evaluated as possible full-time employees.

Managing @ the Speed of Thought

■ Recruiting on the Internet

A growing number of employers recruit via the Internet. In one survey, 32% of the 203 respondents said they were using the Internet as a primary recruitment source.[24]

Many Internet job-placement and recruiting sources are available today (Figures 3-13 and 3-14). For example, the personnel journal *Workforce* has a Web site (www.workforceonline.com/postajob/) with links to various sites, including "best Internet recruiter," general recruitment Web sites, college recruitment Web sites, and specific industry recruitment Web sites. It also lets you place your own help-wanted ad on-line at the *Workforce* Web site. Yahoo (employment.yahoo.com/) is another site where you can place and access employment classified ads.

Employers are using Internet recruiting in various ways. One Boston-based recruiting firm posts job descriptions on its Web page.[25] NEC Electronics, Inc., Unisys Corp., and LSI Logicorp have all used Internet-based "cyber fairs" to recruit applicants.[26] A Minneapolis-based computer firm uses the Internet to search for temporary workers with extensive knowledge of Microsoft Excel.[27] And Cisco Systems, Inc., (as noted earlier) has a Web site with an employment opportunities page. It offers links to such things as hot jobs (job descriptions for hard-to-fill positions), Cisco culture (a look at Cisco work life), Cisco College (internships and mentoring program information), and jobs (job listings).[28]

Getting résumés and listings via the Web is only part of the Web's possibilities. At Peoplesoft Company, for instance, applications sent via the Web or fax are automatically deposited into a database (those submitted on paper are first scanned into a computer). When a hiring manager selects an applicant for interview, the system automatically phones the applicant and asks him or her to select an interview time by punching buttons on a touch-tone phone. After the call, the database system notifies the interviewers of the appointment, and sends a reminder on the day of the interview—all without human interaction.[29] Now that's managing @ the speed of thought!

▼ **FIGURE 3-13**

Employment Services on a Company's Web Site

Progressive Corp. is just one of many firms that posts a recruiting page on its Web site. Such pages often include a means for job applicants to e-mail their resumes and research what it would be like to work at the firm.

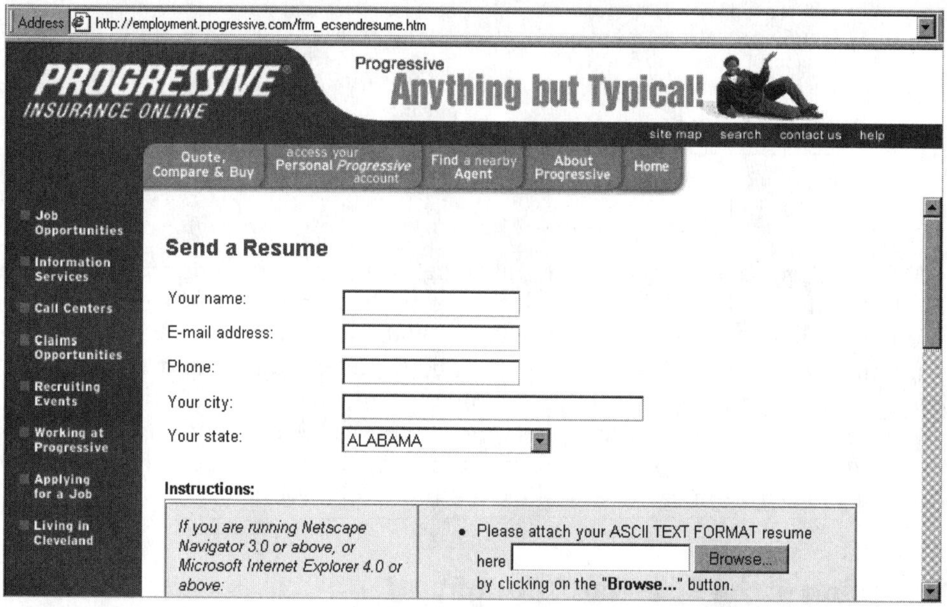

Recruiting a More Diverse Workforce Recruiting a diverse workforce is not just socially responsible; it's a necessity, given the rapid growth in the number of minority and female candidates. This means taking special steps to recruit older workers, minorities, and women.

There are many things an employer can do to assist it in these efforts. Because some minority applicants may not meet the educational or experience standards for a job, many firms offer remedial training in basic arithmetic and writing.[30] Diversity data banks or nonspecialized minority-focused recruiting publications are another option. For example, Hispan Data provides recruiters at companies like McDonald's access to a computerized data bank; it costs a candidate $5 to be included.[31] Checking with your own minority employees can also be useful: About 32% of job seekers of Hispanic origin cited "check with friends or relatives" as a strategy when looking for jobs.[32]

▼ **FIGURE 3-14**

Many Web site services permit employers to post their open positions, in this case for a fee.

Address	C:\TEMP\hrcc52.htm

JOBS Direct Placement

Welcome to JOBS Direct Placement. As an employer, you can use this online service to post your job openings in a database which currently receives **over 450,000 queries every day.**

If you are a new advertiser interested in posting your employment opportunities on CareerMosaic's JOBS Database, please register on the new advertiser form. Once we receive your form, a representative from JOBS Direct Placement will contact you, via email, to give you an ID number, verify your submission, and arrange for payment. If you have previously posted jobs directly through this section of CareerMosaic and have been assigned an ID number, go directly to the registered advertiser form. A representative from JOBS Direct Placement will contact you, via email, to confirm your job posting.

You may also request additional information regarding advertising on CareerMosaic.
Questions? Call us at our toll free number: 1-888-339-8989.

Here are some guidelines to help get your job into immediate circulation:

- Each job record is **$160.**
- Each job record should contain **one job title** and **one job description.**
- Job records run in our database for 30 days. They expire automatically.
- Make sure to complete **all** fields.
- You may include information about your company in the job description field.
- Make sure the job description is comprehensive. The more information you provide for the job seeker, the better the chance it will be found by the right people. You have plenty of room -- up to 16,000 characters...or about 40 paragraphs.
- The description should also include **clear response instructions**.
- Please indicate your preferred payment method (**credit card** or **invoice**) for each job.

Employers are also implementing various "welfare-to-work" programs for attracting and assimilating former welfare recipients. In 1996 President Clinton signed the Personal Responsibility and Welfare Reconciliation Act of 1996. The act required 25% of people receiving welfare assistance to be either working or involved in a work-training program by September 30, 1997, with the percentage rising each year to 50% by September 30, 2002.[33]

The key to a welfare-to-work program's success seems to be the employer's "pre-training" assimilation and socialization program, during which participants receive counseling and basic skills training.[34] Marriott International has hired 600 welfare recipients under its Pathways to Independence program. The heart of the program is a six-week preemployment training program teaching work and "life skills designed to rebuild workers' self-esteem and instill positive attitudes about work."[35]

▶ ORIENTATION AND TRAINING

Once employees have been recruited, screened, and selected for the company's open positions, they must be prepared to do their jobs; this is the purpose of orientation and training.

Orienting Employees

Employee **orientation** means providing new employees with basic information on things like work rules and vacation policies. In many companies, employees receive a handbook that contains such information. Orientation aims to: familiarize the new employee with the company and his or her co-workers; provide information about working conditions (coffee breaks, overtime policy, and so on); explain how to get on the payroll, how to obtain identification cards, and what the working hours are; and generally reduce the jitters often associated with starting a new job.

This initial orientation is usually followed by a **training program** aimed at ensuring that the new employee has the basic knowledge and skills required to perform the job. Traditional techniques include on-the-job training, lectures, and, increasingly, other methods—using CD-ROMs and the Internet, for example.[36]

Companies like Starbucks invest a great deal of time and money in training employees (indeed, large U.S. companies alone spent over $62 billion training their employees in one recent year).[37] "Brewing the perfect cup" is one of five classes that all Starbucks "partners" (as employees are called) complete during their first six weeks with the company.[38] What are some of the things they learn? Milk must be steamed at temperatures of at least 150°F; orders are "called out," such as "triple-tall nonfat mocha"; and coffee never sits on the hot plate for more than 20 minutes. Starbucks understands that designing an organization and job descriptions is futile unless the carefully selected employees are also well trained.

Training Techniques

Training techniques have been around for many years, and you've probably experienced some of them yourself. For example, **on-the-job training (OJT)** means having a person learn a job by actually performing it. Virtually every employee, from mailroom clerk to company president, gets some OJT when he or she joins a firm. In many companies, OJT is the only type of training available. It usually involves assigning new employees to experienced workers or supervisors, who then do the actual training.[39]

On the other hand, many training techniques are fairly new, and are based on computers and/or telecommunications. For example, companies are now using *teletraining*, through which a trainer in a central location teaches groups of employees at remote locations via television hookups.[40] AMP Incorporated, which makes electrical and electronic connection devices, uses satellites to train its engineers and technicians at 165 sites in the United States and 27 other countries. To reduce costs for one training program, AMP supplied the program content. PBS affiliate WITF of Harrisburg, Pennsylvania, supplied the equipment and expertise required to broadcast the training program to five AMP facilities in North America.[41] Macy's, the New York–based retailer, recently established the Macy's Satellite Network, in part to provide training to the firm's 59,000 employees around the country.[42]

Training on the Internet is already a reality, and many firms are using the Internet to offer at least some of their programs. For example, Silicon Graphics transferred many of its training materials to CD-ROMs. However, since not every desktop computer had a CD-ROM player, many employees couldn't access the training program. Silicon Graphics is therefore replacing the CD-ROM method with distribution of training materials via its Intranet. "Now employees can access the programs whenever they want. Distribution costs are zero, and if the company wants to make a change to the program, it can do so at a central location."[43]

As a result of such benefits, technology-based learning is booming. Management Recruiters International (MRI) uses the firm's desktop ConferView system to train hundreds of employees—each in their individual offices—simultaneously.[44] Instead of sending new rental sales agents to week-long classroom-based training courses, Value Rent-a-Car now provides them with interactive, multimedia-based training programs utilizing CD-ROMs. These help agents learn the car rental process by walking them through various procedures, such as how to operate the rental computer system.[45]

SUMMARY ■

1. Human resources management is the management function devoted to acquiring, training, appraising, and compensating employees. As workers become more fully empowered, the HR function has grown in importance.

2. Staffing—filling a firm's open positions—starts with job analysis and personnel planning. Recruiting—including the use of internal sources, advertising, employment agencies, recruiters, referrals, college recruiting, and recruiting a more diverse workforce—is then used to create a pool of applicants.

3. With a pool of applicants, the employer can turn to screening and selecting, using one or more techniques—including application blanks, interviews, tests, and reference checks—to assess and investigate an applicant's aptitudes, interests, and background.

4. Once employees have been recruited, screened, and selected, they must be prepared to do their jobs; this is the role of employee orientation and training. Orientation means providing new employees with basic information about the employer; training ensures that the new employee has the basic knowledge required to perform the job satisfactorily.

5. Once they've been on the job for some time, employees are appraised.

TYING IT ALL TOGETHER ■

After planning what's to be done, managers must create an organization. We covered planning and now in this part of the text we have focused on how to design an organization and an organization chart. Of course, an organization—be it GE, GM, or Duncan Group, Inc.—is more than just a chart of reporting relationships and positions. It's the people who make the organization, so in this section we focused on the staffing methods managers use to recruit, select, and train employees to fill the organization's positions. Once the organization is staffed with competent and well-trained individuals, the manager's job is still not complete: Employees must then be inspired, motivated, and led, the topics to which we turn in the next part of this text.

Skills and Study Materials

CRITICAL THINKING EXERCISES ■

1. The United States is a heterogeneous nation. In states like California there is a rich mixture of natives and immigrants from other states as well as from many ancient and emerging nations. Please read the following final thoughts from Ronald Takaki's book on human diversity and the United States, *A Different Mirror* (Boston: Little, Brown & Company, 1993, p. 428) from a human resources management context. Then write a brief analysis of what the quote means for managing human resources in the 21st century:

    As Americans, we originally came from many different shores, and our diversity has been the center of the making of America. While our stories contain the memories of different communities, together they inscribe a larger narrative. Filled with what Walt Whitman celebrated as the "varied carols" of America, our history generously gives all of us our "mystic chords of memory." Throughout our past of oppressions and struggles for equality, Americans of different races and ethnicities have been "singing with open mouths their strong melodious songs" in the textile mills of Lowell, the cotton fields of Mississippi, on the Indian reservations of South Dakota, the railroad tracks high in the Sierras of California, in the garment factories of the Lower East Side, the canefields of Hawaii, and a thousand other places across the country. Our denied history "bursts with telling." As we hear America singing, we find ourselves invited to bring our rich cultural diversity on deck, to accept ourselves. "Of every hue and caste am I," sang Whitman. "I resist any thing better than my own diversity."

2. As quoted in John Aram's *Presumed Superior*, affirmative action has different meanings to different people. One observer comments on the double meaning of affirmative action as a means of institutional change: "If civil rights is defined as quotas, it's a losing hand. If it's defined as protection against discrimination and efforts to promote opportunity, then it will remain a mainstream value in American life." John Aram points out, "The dilemma is that progress on civil rights both restricts and opens opportunity. No single, definitive moral premise exists."[46]

   What do you think Aram is trying to say? What aspects of HR can be related to his comments? What are your thoughts and feelings about civil rights and affirmative action as they affect organizational management and jobs?

3. In 1999 the state of California had a population of 34 million, including 51% White, 30% Hispanic, 11% Asian, 7% African American and 0.6% Native American. In 10 years these figures will shift. Total population will be 39.5 million. The population will then include 45% White, 35% Hispanic, 13% Asian, 6% African American, and 0.6% Native American. By 2019 the population is projected to be 45 million. It is projected that the demographics will have changed to 40% White, 39% Hispanics, 14% Asian, 6% African Americans, and 0.6% Native American.[47] Please think about HR management in California using these three decades of demographics. What are the implications for California? What are the challenges for HR managers? What are the social, political, and cultural challenges to be faced? Will other parts of the country, such as Florida, Texas, New York, and other states, have similar types of demographics? If so, what are the implications for HR managers around the nation?

EXPERIENTIAL EXERCISES

1. *Fast Company*'s September 1999 issue is all about the future. It is titled "21 Rules for the 21st Century." Among the articles is "2004: A Personal Odyssey." The article begins with the following questions: "What are *your* expectations five years from now? As the 21st Century arrives, are you feeling confident about your career and sure of your future? Or does the prospect of ever-more-powerful technology and never-ending change leave you wishing you could return to the simpler days of the Old Economy?" The *Fast Company* Roper Starch worldwide survey found the answers to these questions and more. First think where you will be in 2004 and where you want to be. Then go to *Fast Company* in the library or on the Internet and look at the survey and read the article. When you get to the questions, answer them yourself prior to looking at the survey results. Then compare your responses with those of others who took the survey. You may wish to discuss these issues in small groups in class or as a class.

2. You are the HR director for Manugistics, Inc., a Maryland-based, highly successful software company employing 600 people. Your HR department has 12 employees, representing all areas of human resources. In less than a decade, your company has made a major domestic acquisition and a global acquisition, added new employees, sold a

product line, and seen two of the founders leave. How has it managed to remain competitive?

   It has "institutionalized change" through its three "elements of excellence": (1) We treat others as we would like to be treated, (2) partnership with our clients results in superior products, and (3) team success is more important than personal glory.[48]

   Your department has developed a wide variety of flexible options for employees; for example, 50% of your staff are women with flexible schedules, and 30 to 40% of your employees telecommute.

   In March 1997 the company announced a joint venture with Information Resources Inc. (IRI), based in Chicago. The companies will collaborate on the development of an innovative product that integrates point-of-sale data and supply-chain planning, with 20 IRI employees from offices in Chicago, Atlanta, and Waltham, Massachusetts, joining the Manugistics workforce.

   Your task as the HR director is to develop an orientation and training program for this joint venture. Also, go to www.manugistics.com and click on the various pages offered. Then determine where the company has gone, where it may be going, and why HR management is important in its efforts.

CASE 3-2
MONSTER.COM—CAN A FIRM
OUTSOURCE ITS RECRUITING?

Most Americans became familiar with Monster.com when it ran the first of its famous advertisements during the Super Bowl in 1999. Monster.com challenged millions of Super Bowl viewers to take stock of their careers with a "when I grow up" spot. The ad features children musing about what they want to be when they grow up. Each child describes a particularly distasteful aspect of a job: "I want to file all day," or "I want to claw my way up to middle management." The spots have been immensely successful in building a brand identity for Monster.com, the online recruitment leader. MediaMetrix, a company that tracks Internet usage, ranks Monster.com as the most utilized Internet job site, boasting more than 2.6 million unique visitors. Since Monster.com reaches so many potential candidates, why should an employer undertake its own candidate search? Why shouldn't firms just outsource their recruiting efforts to a company like Monster.com?

Behind the successful image campaign at Monster.com is a well-organized corporate entity. The company is a subsidiary of TMP Worldwide, the world's largest yellow pages advertising agency and a highly respected provider of direct marketing services. TMP has more than 6,100 employees in 25 countries. The Monster.com subsidiary, a natural extension of TMP's advertising business, is drawing 2.6 million unique visits per month to its job-search Web site. Independent research has estimated Monster.com's share of the Web job search market at over 40%.

One of the most attractive features for employers is Monster.com's ability to attract high-tech employees. Only candidates with a computer, browser, and access to the Internet are likely to use the forum. There are other benefits as well. The Internet can provide instantaneous information, allowing firms to post last-minute openings. A firm can also provide links to its own Web site, offering a prospective employee far more information than is available in a print ad. Monster.com also offers résumé-screening, routing, and searching services. Currently, Monster.com has over a million résumés from active job seekers in its database.

It is common for companies to outsource areas that are not part of their core competence or in areas where they have difficulty in being competitive. Given that Monster.com already has more than a million résumés in its database and the ability to instantly post jobs, should a company give most of its recruiting to Monster.com?

Discussion Questions

1. What competition does Monster.com have in its industry?

2. What strengths does Monster.com bring to recruiting that a hiring company itself might not have?

3. In what ways is Monster.com similar to a personnel agency? Different?

4. What limitations might Monster.com have that might encourage a firm to use other recruiting sources?

SECTION FOUR

BEING A LEADER

WHAT'S AHEAD?

Barbara Hyder learned, and fast, that being CEO of a new .com company was different from being a leader in a big, traditional company like Mary Kay Cosmetics.[1] Hyder had been international regional president at Mary Kay before becoming CEO of gloss.com, an on-line beauty startup. How is a .com company different? For one thing, she's now making decisions with her management team on Internet time. For example, when they saw the airwaves clogged with .com ads in December 1999, they made a split-second decision to cancel their ads and instead launch a full $20 million campaign in February 2000. Her new mantra is "You have to act quickly; speed is of the essence."[2]

Hyder's experience says a lot about what leadership is, and how it's different than it was a few years ago. Leaders have always had to say "Here's where we're going to go," and then motivate, cajole, and influence their people to move in that direction. One of the differences today, as we'll see, is that there's a bigger element of consensus-building and teamwork in what leaders do.

THIS SECTION FOCUSES ON THE FOLLOWING:

- The foundations of leadership

- A vision for an organization

- The various leadership styles

- The specific actions one can take to be a better leader

Once your organization is staffed with competent employees, these employees must be inspired, motivated, and led. In this part of the text, we'll therefore turn to leadership.

▶ WHAT DO LEADERS DO?

Planning an ad campaign, organizing a management team, and making decisions on when to launch your site is only part of what successful managers like Barbara Hyder do. After plans are set and the organization is in place, nothing is going to happen unless the leader's teammates and subordinates want to move in the direction that's been set. Making sure that happens is a big part of what leaders do.

Leadership is generally defined as influencing others to work willingly toward achieving objectives. As we'll see in this section, leadership therefore means crystallizing a direction for subordinates, and then tapping into all the authority, charisma, and traits the leader can muster to make the subordinates want to follow the leader in achieving the leader's goals. In the last two parts of this text we've covered the management functions of planning and organizing. Now we turn to the concepts and skills involved with actually influencing the organization's employees to implement the company's plans. We turn to leadership.

Leaders Fill Many Roles

There's a lot more to being a leader than just the contents of this leadership section. That's why although we refer to it as "Leading," it also covers topics like motivation, groups, conflict, and change.[3] Leaders simultaneously fill many roles, interacting with and motivating subordinates, leading groups whose members are interacting and in which conflicts might arise, and being part of a group reporting to the leader's own boss. The knowledge contained in this section is therefore only part of what leaders must know. "Being a Leader" will get you started; to really get on the road to being a leader, you'll need to learn more about:

Motivating Employees Today. Individual differences (for example, in aptitudes and skills) that help to account for why people do what they do, and several theories that help to explain how leaders motivate employees.

Communicating in Today's Organizations. The barriers that can undermine effective communications, and what a manager has to know about communicating to be an effective leader.

Managing Groups and Teams. What leaders can do to create more cohesive teams, and the group dynamics leaders should take into account in supervising their own teams.

Managing Organizational and Cultural Change. Theories and techniques leaders can use to implement changes required to improve an organizational situation.

Don't be overwhelmed by the number of leadership and behavioral science concepts and skills discussed here. Instead, think of each as a tool in your leadership toolbox, each useful in its way and under the right conditions.

Leaders Think Like Leaders

How do leaders like Barbara Hyder go about deciding whether the situation calls for applying motivation, communications, team building, organizational change,

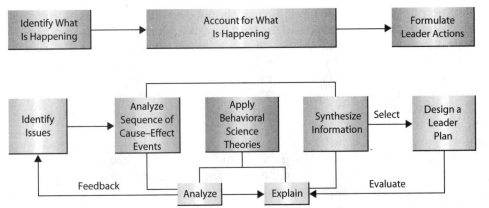

◀ **FIGURE 4-1**

How to Think Like a Leader

Source: Adapted from Jeffrey A. McNally, Stephen J. Gerra, and R. Craig Bollis, "Teaching Leadership at the U.S. Military Academy at West Point." *Journal of Applied Behavioral Science*, 32:2, p. 178, copyright © 1996 by Sage Publications. Reprinted by permission of Sage Publications.

or some other type of concept or skills? Often, by using a decision process similar to that in the three-step framework shown in Figure 4-1: step back and look at the leadership situation you're facing, and then (1) identify what's happening, (2) account for what's happening, and (3) decide on the actions you'll take.[4] Let's look at a specific example.

Identify What Is Happening Gus runs a large engineering company in Tampa. He's a genius at what he does, and as a result his company now has about 200 people working for it, including 80 engineers. They've got a recurrent problem though, one that just repeated itself yet again last week. An engineering team will work on a project, send off a proposal, but if the client doesn't like the design or demands time-consuming changes, the project team will often just shelve the project. In other words, they stick the whole project folder on the shelf, go back to working on some other deal, and avoid mentioning anything about the matter to Gus. As you might imagine, Gus is often seen storming around the office yelling "Why didn't you tell me we didn't get that deal, why didn't you tell me we didn't get that deal?" Obviously, what's happening here is that for some reason, Gus's engineers refuse to give him bad news.

Account for What Is Happening In management, as in other human endeavors, things are not always as they seem. For years, Gus has simply assumed that his engineers are a little irresponsible and that accounts for their walking away from these jobs without a word to him. However, now he's not so sure. He's been reading up on leadership skills for the past few weeks, and now understands there's a lot more than meets the eye when it comes to explaining what people do. Part of being an effective leader, he knows, is understanding how things like motivation, communications, and teamwork can influence what employees do. And he knows that the main purpose of "accounting for what is happening" is to use behavioral science theories and concepts like these to account for why the situations you identified (like the engineers refusing to divulge bad news) are occurring.

Accounting for what is happening in a situation means asking yourself which theory or theories best explain what you see happening, by linking a leadership or other behavioral concept or theory to the issue. In other words, you identify a cause–effect relationship between what has occurred and why. For example, "The engineers here refuse to divulge bad news because they are punished when they do by having Gus yell at them." The *effect* here is the refusal to divulge bad news; the behavioral *cause*— in this case a motivational one—is the fact that they are "punished" when they do.

To account for what is happening you should view the situation as a coherent whole, while at the same time looking for a logical sequence of events. You have to try to identify the root cause of the situation. For example, are the engineers just poorly trained? Are they simply irresponsible? Or are they just reacting to Gus's habit of responding quickly and harshly to any negative news?

In accounting for what is happening, you may find that more than one of the leadership or behavioral science concepts covered in this and the next few sections applies. In this case, for instance, the engineers may be irresponsible. Or, Gus may have inadvertently created a blame-oriented atmosphere in which his employees know they'll get dumped on when they bring him negative news.

Don't be put off because there may be more than one theory or concept you could use to account for the problem. You may combine several, or choose the one you'll take action on first.

Decide on Leadership Actions   After you have identified and accounted for what is happening, the next step is to decide on the actions that will remedy the situation. Doing so requires applying all the knowledge you gain in this and our other sections, such as how to motivate employees and how to resolve and manage intergroup conflict.

What actions would you take to help resolve Gus's problem? Gus's assessment of the situation is that he's been too tough and quick to react when people bring him bad news. Good possibilities for action include:

- Getting some counseling.

- Having a meeting with the engineers to explain that things are going to be different.

- Personally working with the engineers to improve a project when the client says it must be redone.

The Building Blocks of Being a Leader

There is no generally accepted theory describing how leaders effectively lead organizations. However, Figure 4-2 provides a useful model for organizing your thoughts. We'll use it to organize this section. Leaders with the power and personal traits to be effective in a leadership situation can lead by taking four sets of actions: Think like a leader; provide a vision; use the right leadership style; and apply organizational behavior skills such as motivating. We've discussed thinking like a leader; now let's turn to providing a vision.

How Leaders Provide a Vision

Fortune magazine recently published an issue with a picture of Apple Computer's Steve Jobs on the cover, with the caption "Stevie Wonder!"[5] Why the nickname "Stevie Wonder?" Because in the two or three years he'd been Apple's acting president, the company's financial situation moved from a loss of $600 million to profits of $100 million. Because in the same period the company's stock price jumped from $20 a share to about $100. And because Apple was able to develop and bring to market the brand-new iMac computer, a computer that was so popular and easy to use it was flying off the shelves.

Much of Job's success at Apple these last few years has of course resulted from the fact that he's been extraordinarily effective as a manager. He developed the right plans (including introducing the iMac computer). He reorganized the

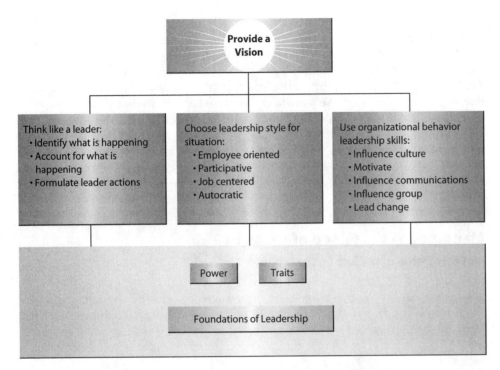

◄ **F I G U R E 4 - 2**

The Building Blocks of Being a Leader

Note: Leaders with the power and personal traits required to be effective can provide leadership by engaging in four sets of activities: Provide a vision, think like a leader, use the right leadership style, and then use the OB leadership skills explained in later sections.

Source: Adapted from an idea presented in Shelley Kirkpatrick and Edwin A. Luke, "Leadership: Do Traits Matter?" *Academy of Management Executive*, May 1991, pp. 47–60.

company and hired the right people. And he carefully monitored and maintained control over each of the company's major new products. As the *Fortune* article put it, "No detail was too trivial to escape his scrutiny as he passed final judgment on the look and feel—or what he calls the fit and finish—of a series of ambitious Apple software products and Internet initiatives."[6]

While his management skills undoubtedly had a lot to do with the company's recent success, it was also his visionary leadership that helped make Apple what it is today. He brought to Apple a vision of a company that would produce computers that were extraordinarily easy to use, computers with the most user-friendly interfaces on the market. And with that vision as a guide he was able to motivate Apple's thousands of engineers and employees to work tirelessly to develop the sorts of iMac-type products that would deliver on Job's vision.

As Apple's employees can tell you, there's more to a good, clear vision than a target or plan. The right vision can be so inherently exciting that employees will pursue it with an almost religious fervor. Great leaders like Steve Jobs know that the best kind of motivation is often self-motivation, the kind that drives people to do what they do because they truly believe in doing it. A clear, exciting, and well-communicated vision can help ensure just that kind of self-motivation, by giving employees a target they truly believe in to shoot for.

Today, with the iMac's success guaranteed, Jobs has set Apple off on a new mission: to marry the iMac and the Internet with an easy-to-use new operating system and free Web services for everything from your photos to your homepage. If it works, as *Fortune* says, "Microsoft, AOL, and others will be playing catch-up with a company left for dead two years ago."[7]

The type of direction the leader must set depends on the job that has to be done. Sometimes what's required is a *vision*, a general statement of the organization's intended direction that evokes positive emotional feelings in organization members. Jobs's vision is an example.

Communicating a vision like Jobs's is especially important in today's fast-changing environment, where business conditions are "volatile and carry in them the seeds of rapid and potentially hostile change."[8] Here, "the faster the chief executive officer can conceive a future vision where new products are positioned within emerging product markets the greater is the ability of the firm to control its destiny and affirm a sense of direction."[9] Indeed, CEOs like Barbara Hyder often have to do that at Internet speed.

In turn, the firm's mission statement defines and operationalizes the top manager's vision. A mission statement "broadly outlines the organization's future course and serves to communicate 'who we are, what we do, and where we're headed.'"[10] Mission statements like Apex Elevator's ("Our mission is to provide any customer a means of moving people and things up, down, and sideward over short distances.")

Managing @ the Speed of Thought

■ Chris Sinton puts Cisco on the Internet

Leadership—influencing others to move in a desired direction—doesn't necessarily mean being "the person in charge" and supervising hundreds (or even dozens) of subordinates. Sometimes, exerting leadership just means championing a new idea, and having the vision and then the drive and the courage, conviction, and self-confidence to convince others to work with you to implement that vision.

Chris Sinton at Cisco Systems is a case in point. Just a few years ago, Sinton may have been "one of the lowest-tech people at Cisco," but he did know his customers. For example, he knew they hated wasting time phoning and faxing in orders and having to call only when the Cisco salespeople were available to take those orders. And, while he may have been low-tech, he could already see—way back in 1995—that more and more people were using the Internet to place orders for various products from other companies.

At that time, Cisco Systems, although it was the leading firm in providing the various types of electronics that made the Internet work, sold virtually none of its own products via the Internet. But Sinton had a vision, and that was to have Cisco Systems set up Web sites so that customers could, at any time of the day, place orders via the Internet and check the status of those orders, all without ever speaking directly to a salesperson. Sinton first presented his vision to several marketing people two levels above him, and on that basis was given 15 minutes to present his idea at a meeting of senior executives. He urged the company to turn to e-commerce as a way of doing business, and to let customers purchase not only small items like Cisco Systems promotional T-shirts, but also technical support services and even $1.5 million electronic routers.

Today Cisco, along with pioneers like Dell, "is proving that business to business selling is e-commerce's killer app."[11] By 1999 Cisco was actually selling 80% of its products and services through the Web, thanks to the leadership of people like Sinton.

Where is Sinton today? He is "Managing @ The Speed of Thought" and overseeing the business-to-business e-commerce operation that was his brainchild. As he says, "I just knew the Net could be our business, that it could be a portal to our company."[12] The visionary proposal he wrote to the top executives at Cisco regarding the future of e-commerce is now preserved in the Smithsonian Institution archives.

Sometimes, therefore, you don't have to be leading your own subordinates to be leading other people. In championing a move to e-commerce, Sinton was able to get his bosses and the top executives at Cisco to become excited about his vision. Having done that, he was able to convince them to let him organize the resources that would enable Cisco to become a world leader in business-to-business e-commerce.

are meant to communicate the purpose of the company. If the leader's job is narrower in scale, the task might simply require that he or she provide objectives, which are specific results he or she wants the group to achieve.

▶ THE FOUNDATIONS AND TRAITS OF LEADERSHIP

Whether it is Steve Jobs, Chris Sinton, Barbara Hyder, or the manager at your local dry cleaner, leading is difficult if the leaders don't have "the right stuff." This point has been illustrated clearly by two psychologists, Shelley Kirkpatrick and Edwin Locke. They say that personal traits and power comprise the foundations of leadership—in other words, these are two prerequisites you need before you can lead.[13]

The Leader's Traits

Are people like Hyder and Jobs successful as leaders in part because they have the right personality traits for the job?[14] Identifying what those traits might be is the aim of the **trait theory** of leadership.

The Trait Theory   The idea that leaders are characterized by certain traits was initially inspired by a "great man" concept of leadership. This concept held that people like Steve Jobs, Microsoft's Bill Gates, and Hewlett-Packard's Carly Fiorina are great leaders because they were born with certain definable personality traits. Early researchers believed that if they studied the personality and intelligence of great leaders, they would sooner or later stumble on the combination of traits that made these people outstanding.

Most of the early research was inconclusive. Some studies asked leaders to describe their leadership traits. Most administered personality inventories to the leaders to assess the traits these people had. In any case, specific traits were related to effectiveness in some situations, but none was found to be consistently related in a variety of different studies and situations. However, recent research "has made it clear that successful leaders are not like other people. The evidence indicates that there are certain core traits which significantly contribute to business leaders' success."[15] Six traits on which leaders differ from nonleaders include drive, the desire to lead, honesty and integrity, self-confidence, cognitive ability, and knowledge of the business. Let's see why each of these matters:

Leaders have drive. They are action-oriented people with a relatively high desire for achievement. They get satisfaction from successfully completing challenging tasks. Leaders are more ambitious than nonleaders. They have high energy because "working long, intense work weeks (and many weekends for many years) requires an individual to have physical, mental, and emotional vitality."[16] Leaders are also tenacious and better at overcoming obstacles than are nonleaders.[17]

Leaders want to lead. Leaders are motivated to influence others. They prefer to be in a leadership rather than a subordinate role, and they willingly shoulder the mantle of authority.

A leader has honesty and integrity. Here's another way to state this: If your followers can't trust you, why should they follow you? Studies have found that leaders are generally rated more trustworthy and reliable in carrying out responsibilities than are followers.[18]

A leader has self-confidence. As two experts summarize, "Self-confidence plays an important role in decision-making and in gaining others' trust. Obviously, if the leader is not sure of what decision to make, or expresses a high degree of doubt, then the followers are less likely to trust the leader and be committed to the vision."[19]

A leader has cognitive ability. By definition, a leader is the one who must pick the right direction and then put into place the mechanisms required to get there. Leaders therefore tend to have more cognitive ability than nonleaders, and a leader's intelligence and subordinates' perception of his or her intelligence are generally highly rated leadership traits.[20]

The leader knows the business. Effective leaders are extremely knowledgeable about the company and the industry; their information helps them make informed decisions and understand the implications of those decisions.[21] There are exceptions: Louis Gertsner, Jr., became IBM chair with no computer experience, and he has excelled at the job. However, these exceptions make the rule: Gerstner has high cognitive ability and quickly immersed himself in absorbing the details of IBM's business. (And he also has a degree in engineering!)

The People Side of Managing

■ Emotional Intelligence

The idea that great leaders have the right stuff is so seductive that the list of leadership traits is always growing. One of the most interesting lines of trait research focuses on what some experts call "emotional intelligence."[22] According to Daniel Goleman, author of *Working with Emotional Intelligence*, traits like intelligence and technical knowledge matter, but only as "threshold capabilities":

> [T]hey are the entry-level requirements for executive positions. But my research, along with other recent studies, clearly shows that emotional intelligence is the *sine qua non* of leadership. Without it, a person can have the best training in the world, an incisive, analytical mind, and an endless supply of smart ideas, but he [or she] still won't make a great leader.[23]

What is emotional intelligence? Basically, a bundle of people-oriented personality traits which, taken together, reflect a person's emotional maturity, empathy, and social skills. The five component traits of emotional intelligence at work (some of which, like motivation, consistently appear in earlier trait lists as well) are summarized in Figure 4-3. They include self-awareness, self-regulation, motivation, empathy, and social skill. For example, says Goleman, "if there is one trait that virtually all the effective leaders have, it is motivation. They're driven to achieve beyond expectations—their own and everyone else's."[24]

▼ **FIGURE 4-3**

The Five Components of Emotional Intelligence at Work

Source: Reprinted by permission of the Harvard Business Review. An exhibit from "What Makes a Leader," by Daniel Goleman, November–December 1998. Copyright © 1998 by the President and Fellows of Harvard College. All rights reserved.

	Definition	**Hallmarks**
Self-Awareness	the ability to recognize and understand your moods, emotions, and drives, as well as their effect on others.	self-confidence realistic self-assessment self-deprecating sense of humor
Self-Regulation	the ability to control or redirect disruptive impulses and moods the propensity to suspend judgement—to think before acting	trustworthiness and integrity comfort with ambiguity openness to change
Motivation	a passion to work for reasons that go beyond money or status a propensity to pursue goals with energy and persistence	strong drive to achieve optimism, even in the face of failure organizational commitment
Empathy	the ability to understand the emotional makeup of other people skill in treating people according to their emotional reactions	expertise in building and retaining talent cross-cultural sensitivity service to clients and customers
Social Skill	proficiency in managing relationships and building networks an ability to find common ground and build rapport	effectiveness in leading change persuasiveness expertise in building and leading teams

Power

Perhaps you've had the unfortunate experience of being told you are in charge of something, only to find that your subordinates ignore you when you try to assert your authority and give them orders. Such an experience underscores an important fact of leadership: A leader without power is really not a leader at all, since he or she has zero chance of influencing anyone to do anything. Understanding the sources of leadership power is therefore important: It's a second foundation of leadership.

A leader's power and authority derive from several sources. A leader's authority most commonly stems, first, from the *position* to which he or she is appointed. In other words, positions like sales manager or president have formal authority attached to them. As a leader you also have power based on your authority to *reward* employees who do well or coerce or *punish* those who don't do well. As head of, say, the research lab you may also have *expert* power, and be such an authority in your area that your followers do what you ask because of their respect for your expertise. And perhaps you possess *referent* power based on your personal magnetism, so your followers will follow you just because of your charisma.

Notice that whatever your source of power, it must be legitimate if you are to call yourself a leader. A mugger on the street may have a gun and the power to threaten your life, but not qualify as a leader, because leading means influencing people to work *willingly* toward achieving your objectives. That is not to say that a little fear can't be a good thing, at least occasionally. The most famous comment on fear was made in the 16th century by the Italian writer Niccolò Machiavelli, in his book *The Prince*:

> One ought to be both feared and loved, but as it is difficult for the two to go together, it is much safer to be feared than loved . . . for love is held by a chain of obligation which, men being selfish, is broken whenever it serves their purpose; but fear is maintained by a dread of punishment which never fails.

However, while there's more than a germ of truth in what Machiavelli said, there's a danger in relying on fear. A shrewd executive named Chester Barnard wrote in his classic work *The Functions of the Executive* that managers are essentially powerless unless their followers grant them the authority to lead.[25] The reality of leading is that you have to muster all the legitimate power you can get, and that often includes convincing your followers that you have earned the right to lead them.

The issue of power and fear is especially tricky in today's downsized, flattened, and empowered organizations. Increasingly, as we've seen, the tendency is to delegate authority and organize around horizontal, self-managing teams in which the employees themselves have the information and skills they need to control their own activities. Influencing people to get their jobs done by relying too heavily on your own formal authority or even on fear is therefore probably a much less effective tactic today than it would have been even a few years ago.

The idea that the "command and control" approach is increasingly unwieldy is not just theoretical. No less an expert on power than General Peter Schoomaker, commander in chief of the U.S. Special Operations Command (which includes the Army's Delta Force, the Green Berets, the Rangers, and the Navy Seals) argues that the traditional military way of issuing orders that are then obeyed unquestioningly is often an outmoded, inaccurate, and dangerous model for leadership today.[26] That's because the armies (and companies) that win today will be those that marshal "creative solutions in ambiguous circumstances"—diffusing ethnic tensions, delivering humanitarian aid, rescuing U.S. civilians trapped in an overseas uprising. And, in such circumstances, Schoomaker says, "everybody's got to know how to be a leader."[27]

Power and the right traits are not enough to make someone a successful leader—they are only a foundation, a precondition. If you have the traits and you have the power, then you have the *potential* to be a leader.[28] As Kirkpatrick and Locke put it, "Traits only endow people with the potential for leadership. To actualize this potential, additional factors are necessary."[29] Specifically, say Kirkpatrick and Locke, the leader must provide a vision (as explained above) and then engage in the behaviors required to get his or her people to implement that vision. Let's therefore turn to leadership style and how leaders behave.

▶ HOW LEADERS ACT LIKE LEADERS

Leadership researchers have formulated several theories to explain how a leader's style or behavior is related to his or her effectiveness. The basic assumption underlying most of these theories is that leaders perform two major functions—accomplishing the task and satisfying the needs of group members. Generally speaking, the functions of a task-oriented leader are to clarify what jobs need to be done and to force people to focus on their jobs. The social or people-oriented role of a leader is to reduce tension, make the job more pleasant, boost morale, and crystallize and defend the values, attitudes, and beliefs of the group. Most experts believe that the task and people dimensions of leader behavior are not mutually exclusive. In other words, most leaders exhibit degrees of both simultaneously.[30]

A number of specific leadership styles are associated with these basic task and people dimensions. In the remainder of this section we'll describe some of the most popular styles.

Structuring and Considerate Styles

Initiating structure and *consideration* have been two of the most frequently used descriptions of leader behavior. They developed out of a research project, originally focused on manufacturing facilities, and launched many years ago at Ohio State University.[31] A survey called the Leader Behavior Description Questionnaire (LBDQ) was developed and was further refined by subsequent researchers.[32] The two leadership factors it measures—consideration and initiating structure—have become synonymous with what experts call The Ohio State Dimensions of Leadership:

Consideration. Leader behavior indicative of mutual trust, friendship, support, respect, and warmth.

Initiating structure. Leader behavior by which the person organizes the work to be done and defines relationships or roles, the channels of communication, and ways of getting jobs done.

The research results unfortunately tend to be somewhat inconclusive. With respect to employee satisfaction, the findings led researcher Gary Yukl to conclude that "in most situations, considerate leaders will have more satisfied subordinates."[33] But the effects of such considerate leadership on employee performance are inconsistent. However, it's obviously foolish to underestimate the importance of being considerate—at least as a rule. Some outstanding leaders, such as Herb Kelleher of Southwest Airlines, take great pains to emphasize the importance of being considerate of one's employees. As he says, "I've tried to create a culture of caring for people in the totality of their lives, not just at work. . . . You have to recognize that people are still most important. How you treat them determines how they treat people on the outside."[34]

Yet leaders also have to remember to avoid what some leadership experts call the "country club" style: all consideration, and no focus on the work.[35] Showing respect for employees, providing support, and generally being considerate of their material and psychological needs are certainly important. But setting goals and getting things done is the name of the game. The leader's support must therefore generally be balanced with an expectation that employees are there to get their jobs done—on initiating structure, in other words.

Yet the effects of initiating structure are inconsistent with respect to performance and satisfaction. In one representative study, structuring activities by the leader and employee grievance rates were directly related: The more structuring the leader was, the more grievances were field. However, where the leader was also very considerate, leader structure and grievances were *not* related.[36] How can we explain such inconclusive findings? Part of the explanation—as we'll see in a moment—is that the style that is right for one situation might be wrong for another. Another part of the explanation, as mentioned above, is that a balance of these two styles generally works best.

Participative and Autocratic Styles

These two styles also stem from the basic "people" and "task" leader dimensions. Faced with the need to make a decision, the autocratic leader solves the problem and makes the decision alone, using the information available at the time.[37] At the other extreme, the participative leader shares the problem with subordinates as a group, and together they generate and evaluate alternatives and attempt to reach consensus on a solution.[38]

We know that encouraging employees to get involved in developing and implementing decisions affecting their jobs can have positive benefits. For example, employees who participate in setting goals tend to set higher goals than the supervisor would normally have assigned.[39] We've also seen that participation brings more points of view to bear and can improve the chances that participants will "buy into" the final decision. On the other hand, there are obviously some situations (like a sinking ship) in which being participative is inappropriate. The tricky part is deciding when to be participative and when not to be.

The University of Michigan Studies

At about the same time that researchers at Ohio State were developing their LBDQ, a similar program was beginning at the University of Michigan. Two sets of leadership styles—production-centered and employee-centered, and close and general—emerged from the Michigan studies.

First, Rensis Likert and his associates at Michigan identified two leadership styles. **Employee-oriented leaders** focus on the individuality and personality needs of their employees and emphasize building good interpersonal relationships. **Job-centered leaders** focus on production and the job's technical aspects. Based on his review of the research results, Likert concludes:

> Supervisors with the best record of performance focus their primary attention on the human aspects of their subordinates' problems and on endeavoring to build effective work groups with high performance goals.[40]

Other University of Michigan researchers conducted studies on what they called close and general leadership styles. **Close supervision**, according to these researchers, is at "one end of a continuum that describes the degree to which a supervisor specifies the roles of subordinates and checks up to see that they comply with these specifications."[41] The **laissez-faire leader** who follows a completely hands-off policy with subordinates is at the other extreme, while a **general leader** is somewhere in the middle of the continuum.

The research findings here are much clearer with respect to how close and general leaders affect employee morale than they are with respect to employee performance. Generally speaking, people do not like being closely supervised or having someone constantly checking up on them and telling them what to do. Close supervision is therefore usually associated with lower employee morale.[42] However, no consistent relationship emerged between closeness of supervision and employee performance.

Transformational Leadership Behavior

A number of years ago James McGregor Burns wrote a book called *Leadership*, which had a major impact on the course of leadership theory.[43] Burns argues that leadership can be viewed as a transactional or a transformational process.[44] Leader behaviors like initiating structure and consideration, he suggests, are essentially based on *quid pro quo* transactions.

Specifically, **transactional behaviors** are "largely oriented toward accomplishing the tasks at hand and at maintaining good relations with those working with the leader [by exchanging promises of rewards for performance]."[45] The key here is that transactional behaviors tend to focus more on accomplishing tasks, and perhaps on doing so by somehow adapting the leader's style and behavior to the follower's expectations.

In today's fast-changing business environment, Burns argues, it's often not transactional behavior, but **transformational leadership** that's needed to manage change: "Transformational leadership refers to the process of influencing major changes in the attitudes and assumptions of organization members and building commitment for the organization's mission, objectives and strategies."[46] Transformational leaders are those who bring about "change, innovation, and entrepreneurship."[47] They are responsible for leading a corporate transformation that "recognizes the need for revitalization, creates a new vision, and institutionalizes change."[48]

What Do Transformational Leaders Do?   Transformational leaders do several things. They encourage—and obtain—performance beyond expectations by formulating visions and then inspiring subordinates to pursue them. In so doing, transformational leaders cultivate employee acceptance and commitment to those visions.[49] They "attempt to raise the needs of followers and promote dramatic changes in individuals, groups, and organizations."[50]

Transformational leaders like Steve Jobs do this by articulating a realistic vision of the future that can be shared, by stimulating subordinates intellectually, and by paying attention to the differences among subordinates. Transformational leaders also provide a plan for attaining their vision and engage in **framing**, which means giving subordinates the big picture ("produce a super-easy-to-use iMac computer and user interface") so they can relate their individual activities to the work as a whole.[51]

From the vantage point of their followers, transformational leaders come across as charismatic, inspirational, considerate, and stimulating.[52]

- *Transformational leaders are charismatic.* Employees often idolize and develop strong emotional attachments to them.
- *Transformational leaders are inspirational.* "The leader passionately communicates a future idealistic organization that can be shared. The leader uses visionary explanations to depict what the employee work group can accomplish."[53] Employees are then motivated to achieve these organizational aims.
- *Transformational leaders are considerate.* Transformational leaders treat employees as individuals and stress developing them in a way that encourages the employees to become all they can be.

- *Transformational leaders use intellectual stimulation.* They "encourage employees to approach old and familiar problems in new ways."[54] This enables employees to question their own beliefs and use creative ways to solve problems by themselves.

Examples of statements used to assess these four characteristics are

1. *Charisma.* "I am ready to trust him or her to overcome any obstacle."
2. *Individualized consideration.* "Treats me as an individual rather than just as a member of the group."
3. *Intellectual stimulation.* "Shows me how to think about problems in new ways."
4. *Inspirational leadership.* "Provides vision of what lies ahead."[55]

Studies of Transformational Leaders Transformational leadership has been studied in many settings.[56] In one study, researchers found that high-performing managers in an express delivery firm used significantly more transformational leader behaviors than did less successful managers in the firm.[57] Another study found that successful champions of technological change used more transformational leader behaviors than did less successful champions.[58]

Other studies suggest that transformational leadership tends to be more closely associated with leader effectiveness and employee satisfaction than are transactional styles of leadership such as general or laissez-faire leadership.[59] It therefore seems clear that a transformational leadership style can be very effective, especially in situations that require managing dramatic change.

Are There Gender Differences in Leadership Styles?

Although the number of women in management jobs has risen to almost 40%, barely 2% of top management jobs are held by women.[60] Women like Carly Fiorina and Barbara Hyder remain the exception. Most women managers are having trouble breaking into the top ranks. Research evidence suggests on the whole that this disparity is caused not by some inherent inability of women to lead, but by institutional biases known as "the glass ceiling" and persistent, if inaccurate, stereotypes. In other words, while there *are* a few differences in the way men and women lead, they do not account for the slow career progress of most women managers. We can summarize some of the more relevant research findings as follows.

Persistence of Inaccurate Stereotypes Women's promotions tend to be hampered first by inaccurate stereotypes. Managers tend to identify "masculine" (competitive) characteristics as managerial and "feminine" (cooperative and communicative) characteristics as nonmanagerial.[61] Women tend to be seen as less capable of being effective managers; men are viewed as better leaders. Another stereotype is that women managers tend to fall apart under pressure, respond impulsively, and have difficulty managing their emotions.[62] Such stereotypes usually don't hold up under the scrutiny of the researchers' microscope.

Leader Behaviors Studies suggest few measurable differences in the leader behaviors women and men managers use on the job. Women managers were found to be somewhat more achievement-oriented, and men managers more candid with co-workers.[63] In another study the only gender differences found were that women were more understanding than men.[64] Women and men who score high on the need for power (the need to influence other people) tend to behave more like each other than like people with lower power needs.[65]

Performance   How are women managers rated in terms of performance when compared with men? On the job and in joblike work simulations, women managers perform similarly to men. In actual organizational settings, "women and men in similar positions receive similar ratings."[66] In a special simulation called an assessment center, in which managers must perform realistic leadership tasks (such as leading problem-solving groups and making decisions), men and women managers perform similarly. Only in several off-the-job laboratory studies have men scored higher in performance.[67]

A Gender Advantage   Interestingly, one often-noticed and scientifically supported difference between men and women leaders may actually prove to be a boon to women managers. Women often score higher on measures of patience, relationship development, social sensitivity, and communication. And these may be precisely the skills that managers will need to manage diversity and the empowered members of self-managing teams.[68]

▶ SITUATIONAL THEORIES OF LEADERSHIP

One fact of corporate life is that very often a leader who was eminently qualified and successful in one situation turns out to be much less successful in another. For example, when Steve Jobs returned to Apple, he replaced the former CEO, Gus Amelio. Amelio had spent years as the successful CEO of a high-tech Silicon Valley firm, but lasted less than two years at Apple, where the company's fortunes continued to decline under his administration. Douglas Ivester was the chief operating officer for Coca-Cola Co. for many years, an effective number-two person to the company's CEO, Robert Gouizeta. When Gouizeta passed away the board unanimously chose Ivester to become CEO. Yet he lasted barely nine months before stepping down and being replaced.

It seems that successful leadership in one situation doesn't necessarily guarantee success in another. That fact has driven many experts to try to figure out how to fit the leader and his or her style to the situation. In general, we can say that their research provides some insights into the factors that determine the situational nature of leadership. However, it seems that considerably more research will be required before we have a theory that accurately predicts the conditions under which some leaders succeed while others fail. Let's turn to a synopsis of some of the more widely known approaches to studying the situational aspects of leadership.

Fiedler's Contingency Theory of Leadership

Working at the University of Illinois, psychologist Fred Fiedler originally sought to determine whether a leader who was lenient in evaluating associates was more likely or less likely to have a high-producing group than a leader who was demanding and discriminating.[69] At the core of this research is the least preferred co-worker (LPC) scale. Those who describe their least preferred co-worker favorably (pleasant, smart, and so on) are scored as "high LPC" and considered more people-oriented. "Low LPCs" describe least preferred co-workers unfavorably and are less people-oriented and more task-oriented.

According to Fiedler's theory, three situational factors combine to determine whether the high-LPC or the low-LPC style is appropriate:

1. *Position power.* The degree to which the position itself enables the leader to get group members to comply with and accept his or her decisions and leadership

2. *Task structure.* How routine and predictable the work group's task is
3. *Leader–member relations.* The extent to which the leader gets along with workers and the extent to which they have confidence in and are loyal to him or her

Fiedler initially concluded that the appropriateness of the leadership style "is contingent upon the favorableness of the group-task situation."[70] Basically, he argued that where the situation is either favorable or unfavorable to the leader (where leader–member relationships, task structure, and leader position power all are either very high or very low), a more task-oriented, low-LPC leader is appropriate. In the middle range, where these factors are more mixed and the task is not as clear-cut, a more people-oriented, high-LPC leader is appropriate. Many subsequent research findings cast doubt on the validity of Fiedler's conclusions, and the usefulness of the theory, including its more recent variants, remains in dispute.[71,72]

Path–Goal Leadership Theory

Path–goal leadership theory is based on the expectancy theory of motivation. Expectancy theory states that whether a person will be motivated depends on two things: whether the person believes he or she has the ability to accomplish a task, and his or her desire to do so. Leadership expert Robert J. House developed path–goal leadership theory. He says that in keeping with expectancy motivation theory, leaders should increase the personal rewards subordinates receive for attaining goals, and make the path to these goals easier to follow by reducing roadblocks and pitfalls.

Under this theory, the style a leader uses therefore depends on the situation. For example, if subordinates lack confidence in their ability to do the job, they may need more consideration and support. Or, if it's a situation in which subordinates are unclear about what to do or how to do it, the leader should provide structure (in terms of instructions, for instance) as required.[73] Path–goal leadership theory in general has received little support, in part, perhaps, because of the difficulty of quantifying concepts such as "path."[74]

Leader–Member Exchange Theory

Although a leader may have one prevailing style, you have probably noticed that most leaders don't treat all subordinates the same way. The **leader–member exchange (LMX) theory** says that leaders may use different styles with different members of the same work group.[75,76]

This theory suggests that leaders tend to divide their subordinates into an "in" group and an "out" group (you can imagine who gets the better treatment). What determines whether you're part of a leader's in or out group? The leader's decision is often made with very little real information, although perceived leader–member similarities—gender, age, or attitudes, for instance—are usually important.[77]

A study helps illustrate what makes a follower (or member) fall into a leader's in group or out group.[78] Completed questionnaires were obtained from 84 full-time registered nurses and 12 supervisors in 12 work groups at a large hospital in the southern United States. Of the supervisors (leaders), 83% were women, with an average age of 39 years; the nurses (followers) were mostly women (88.1%), with an average age of 36 years. Various things were measured, including the strength and quality of leader–member relationships or exchanges (friendliness between leader and member, rewards given to members, and so on).

The quality of leader–member exchanges (relationships) was found to be positively related to a leader's perceptions of two things: similarity of leader–follower attitudes and follower extroversion. For example, leaders were asked to assess the similarity between themselves and their followers in terms of attitudes toward six items: family, money, career strategies, goals in life, education, and overall perspective. Perhaps not surprisingly, leaders were more favorably inclined toward followers with whom they felt they shared similar attitudes. Followers were also asked to complete questionnaires that enabled the researchers to label them as introverted or extroverted. The extroverted nurses were more likely to have high-quality leader–member exchanges than were the introverts, presumably because they were more outgoing and sociable in general.

Findings like these suggest at least two practical implications. First, because members of the in group can be expected to perform better than those in the out group, leaders should strive to make the in group more inclusive. For followers, the findings emphasize the obvious importance of being in your leader's in group, and underscore the value of emphasizing similarities rather than differences in attitude—in politics, for instance—between you and your boss.

The Situational Leadership Model

Other behavioral scientists have developed what they call a *situational leadership model* to describe how the leader should adapt his or her style to the task; their model is presented in Figure 4-4.[79] They identify four leadership styles:

- The *delegating* leader lets the members of the group decide what to do themselves.
- The *participating* leader asks the members of the group what to do, but makes the final decisions himself or herself.
- The *selling* leader makes the decision himself or herself, but explains the reasons.
- The *telling* leader makes the decision himself or herself, and tells the group what to do.

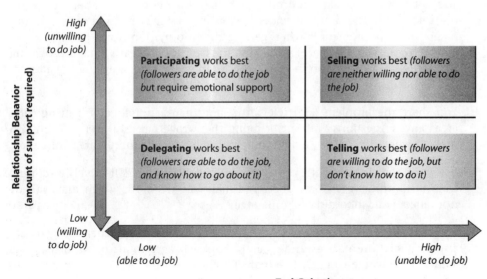

◄ FIGURE 4-4

Situational Leadership Model

Source: Jerald Greenberg. *Managing Behaviour in Organizations: Science in Service* (Upper Saddle River, NJ: Prentice Hall, 1996). Reprinted by permission.

According to the situational leadership model, each style is appropriate in a specific situation:

- Delegating works best where followers are willing to do the job and know how to go about doing it.

- Participating works best when followers are able to do the job but are unwilling and so require emotional support.

- Selling works best where followers are neither willing nor able to do the job.

- Telling works best where followers are willing to do the job, but don't know how to do it.

The Vroom-Jago-Yetton Model

Finally, leadership experts Victor Vroom, Arthur Jago, and Philip Yetton have developed a model that lets a leader analyze a situation and decide whether it is right for participation. Being participative, they point out, is usually not an either/or decision, since there are different degrees of participation. These are summarized in Figure 4-5, which presents a continuum of five possible management decision styles. At one extreme is Style I, no participation. Here the leader solves the problem and makes the decision himself or herself. Style V, total participation, is at the other extreme: Here the leader shares the problem with subordinates, and together they reach an agreement. You can see that between these two extremes are Style II, minimum participation; Style III, more participation; and Style IV, still more participation.

In their model, the appropriate degree of participation depends on several attributes of the situation that can be quantified by asking a sequence of diagnostic questions. A typical diagnostic question is, "Do I have sufficient information to make a

▶ **FIGURE 4-5**

**Five Types of Management
Decision Styles**

I. You solve the problem or make the decision yourself, using information available to you at that time.

II. You obtain the necessary information from your subordinates, then decide on the solution to the problem yourself. You may or may not tell your subordinates what the problem is when getting the information from them. The role played by your subordinates in making the decision is clearly one of providing the necessary information to you, rather than generating or evaluating alternative solutions.

III. You share the problem with relevant subordinates individually, getting their ideas and suggestions without bringing them together as a group. Then you make the decision, which may or may not reflect your subordinates' influence.

IV. You share the problem with your subordinates as a group, collectively obtaining their ideas and suggestions. Then you make the decision, which may or may not reflect your subordinates' influence.

V. You share a problem with your subordinates as a group. Together you generate and evaluate alternatives and attempt to reach agreement (consensus) on a solution. Your role is much like that of a chairperson. You do not try to influence the group to adopt "your" solution, and you are willing to accept and implement any solution that has the support of the entire group.

high-quality decision?" Another is, "Is acceptance of the decision by subordinates critical to implementation?" By answering a series of questions like these, a leader, say these experts, can determine whether—and to what extent—to let subordinates participate in making the decision.

▶ BECOMING A LEADER

Being a leader means taking the steps required to boost your effectiveness at filling the leader's role. No formula can guarantee that you can be a leader. However, based on the research presented in this section, there are some powerful actions you can take to improve the chances that in a leadership situation you will be a leader. These can be summarized as follows.

Start to Think Like a Leader

It is important to think like a leader, so that you can bring to bear everything you know about leadership and human behavior rather than just react with a knee-jerk response. First, apply the three-step model: Identify what is happening, account for what is happening by bringing to bear all your knowledge of leadership and behavioral theory and concepts, and formulate a response.

Remember that behavioral science knowledge about leading is not limited to just the material contained in this section; you need to be able to apply knowledge from the subsequent sections on motivation, groups, conflict, and change and fit it into your assessment of the situation as you account for what is happening and decide how to influence your followers to deal with the situation. Don't be overwhelmed by the number of theories and concepts that might apply; think of them as tools in your leadership toolbox. There may be—and probably is—more than one way to solve the problem.

Develop Your Judgment

Possessing the traits of leadership gives someone the potential to be a leader. Your ability to be a leader can thus be improved by enhancing your existing leadership traits. Some traits are easier to enhance than others, but all of them can be modified. For example, judgment is important because people will not long follow a leader who makes too many bad decisions. We saw that several steps can improve your decision-making ability:

- *Correctly define the problem.* Remember: Don't install new elevators when mirrors will do!

- *Increase your knowledge.* The more you know about the problem and the more facts you can marshall, the more likely it is that your confidence in your decision will not be misplaced.

- *Free your judgment of bias.* A number of cognitive or decision-making biases can distort a manager's judgment. Reducing or eliminating biases like stereotyping from your judgment process is, therefore, a crucial step toward making better decisions.

- *Be creative.* Creativity plays a big role in making better decisions. The ability to develop novel responses—creativity—is essential for decision-making activities like developing new alternatives and correctly defining the problem.

- *Use your intuition.* Many behavioral scientists argue that a preoccupation with analyzing problems rationally and logically can actually backfire by blocking someone from using his or her intuition.

- *Don't overstress the finality of your decision.* Remember that very few decisions are forever; there is more give in more decisions than we realize. Even major, strategic decisions can often be reversed or modified as situations warrant.

- *Make sure the timing is right.* Most people's decisions are affected by their passing moods. Managerial decision makers should therefore take their emotions into account before making important decisions. Sometimes it's best just to sleep on the decisions.

Develop Your Other Leadership Traits

Good judgment is just one of the leadership traits you can enhance. Leaders also exhibit self-confidence. Although developing self-confidence may be a lifelong process, you can enhance it in several ways. One is to focus more on those situations in which you are more self-confident to begin with, such as those in which you are an expert. A stamp collector might exhibit more self-confidence as president of his or her stamp club than in coaching a baseball team, for instance. You can act like a leader by exhibiting self-confidence—by making decisions and sticking with them, and by acting somewhat reserved.

Your knowledge of the business is probably the easiest trait to modify; immerse yourself in the details of your new job and learn as much about the business as you can, as fast as you can. (Figure 4-6 provides a quick test of your leadership readiness).

Start to Build Your Power Base

Remember that a powerless leader is not a leader at all. You can strengthen the foundation of your leadership by enhancing your authority and power. One way to do this is to start acting like a leader. Cracking jokes may get some laughs, but most leaders act at least somewhat reserved to maintain their power base. How much power do you have? Managers with more power generally have:

Reward power if they can:
1. Increase pay levels.
2. Influence getting a raise.
3. Provide specific benefits.
4. Influence getting a promotion.

Coercive power if they can:
5. Give undesirable work assignments.
6. Make work difficult.
7. Make things unpleasant.
8. Influence getting a promotion.

Legitimate power if they can:
9. Make others feel they have commitments to meet.
10. Make others feel they should satisfy job requirements.
11. Give the feeling that others have responsibilities to fulfill.
12. Make others recognize that they have tasks to accomplish.

The following self-assessment exercise can give you a feel for your readiness and inclination to assume a leadership role.

INSTRUCTIONS. Indicate the extent to which you agree with each of the following statements, using the following scale: (1) disagree strongly; (2) disagree; (3) neutral; (4) agree; (5) agree strongly.

1. It is enjoyable having people count on me for ideas and suggestions.	1	2	3	4	5
2. It would be accurate to say that I have inspired other people.	1	2	3	4	5
3. It's a good practice to ask people provocative questions about their work.	1	2	3	4	5
4. It's easy for me to compliment others.	1	2	3	4	5
5. I like to cheer people up even when my own spirits are down.	1	2	3	4	5
6. What my team accomplishes is more important than my personal glory.	1	2	3	4	5
7. Many people imitate my ideas.	1	2	3	4	5
8. Building team spirit is important to me.	1	2	3	4	5
9. I would enjoy coaching other members of the team.	1	2	3	4	5
10. It is important to me to recognize others for their accomplishments.	1	2	3	4	5
11. I would enjoy entertaining visitors to my firm even if it interfered with my completing a report.	1	2	3	4	5
12. It would be fun for me to represent my team at gatherings outside our department.	1	2	3	4	5
13. The problems of my teammates are my problems too.	1	2	3	4	5
14. Resolving conflict is an activity I enjoy.	1	2	3	4	5
15. I would cooperate with another unit in the organization even if I disagreed with the position taken by its members.	1	2	3	4	5
16. I am an idea generator on the job.	1	2	3	4	5
17. It's fun for me to bargain whenever I have the opportunity.	1	2	3	4	5
18. Team members listen to me when I speak.	1	2	3	4	5
19. People have asked me to assume the leadership of an activity several times in my life.	1	2	3	4	5
20. I've always been a convincing person.	1	2	3	4	5

Total score: ___

SCORING AND INTERPRETATION. Calculate your total score by adding the numbers circled. A tentative interpretation of the scoring is as follows:

=	90–100	high readiness for the leadership role
=	60–89	moderate readiness for the leadership role
=	40–59	some uneasiness with the leadership role
=	39 or less	low readiness for the leadership role

If you are already a successful leader and you scored low on this questionnaire, ignore your score. If you scored surprisingly low and you are not yet a leader or are currently performing poorly as a leader, study the statements carefully. Consider changing your attitude or your behavior so that you can legitimately answer more of the statements with a 4 or a 5.

◀ **FIGURE 4-6**

Are you Ready to Be a Leader?

Source: Andrew DuBrin, *Leadership: Research Findings, Priorities, and Skills.* Copyright © 1995 by Houghton Mifflin Company. Reprinted with permission.

Expert power if they can:

13. Give good technical suggestions.

14. Share considerable experience and/or training.

15. Provide sound job-related advice.

16. Provide needed technical knowledge.

Referent power if they can:

17. Make employees feel valued.

18. Make employees feel that I approve of them.

19. Make employees feel personally accepted.

20. Make employees feel important.

Help Others Share Your Vision

Leading means influencing people to work enthusiastically toward an objective. Ensure that your subordinates know and understand the vision, mission, or objective and that you have clarified their assignments. Remember how successful Steve Jobs has been at Apple. As leadership expert John Kotter puts it, "great leaders are all good at getting relevant partners aligned with, buying into, believing in" the direction they have set.

Adapt Your Style and Actions to the Situation

No one leadership style is appropriate for every situation in which you find yourself. Remember that the art of being a leader lies in your being able to identify the leadership-related issues and then being able to determine whether one or more leadership theories and concepts can be applied, and if so, how.

Use Your Other Management Skills to Help You Lead

Research suggests that various management actions can actually function as substitutes for the leadership you may otherwise have to provide.[80] Here are two examples.

Choose the Right Followers   If you select and train your followers well, there may be less reason for you to have to exercise leadership on a daily basis. The greater your subordinates' ability, the more their experience, the better their training, and the more professional their behavior, the less direct supervision they will need. Some followers are inherently more effective than others: Choose followers who are cooperative, flexible, and trustworthy and who have initiative and are good at solving problems.[81]

Organize the Task Properly   You may also be able to modify organizational factors to reduce the need for day-to-day leadership. Jobs for which the performance standards are clear, or for which there is plenty of built-in feedback, may require less leadership.[82] Similarly, employees engaged in work that is intrinsically satisfying (work they love to do) require less leadership.[83] Cohesive work groups with positive norms also require less leadership (as do, by definition, self-managing teams).

SUMMARY ■

1. Leadership means influencing others to work willingly toward achieving objectives. Being a leader requires more than having a command of leadership theories: It also means managing organizational culture; motivating employees; managing groups, teams, and conflict; and facilitating organizational change.

2. Thinking like a leader means reviewing a leadership situation and identifying what is happening, accounting for what is happening (in terms of leadership and other behavioral science theories and concepts), and formulating leader actions.

3. The leader must provide a direction that followers can work toward. This direction may be a statement of vision, mission, or objectives, depending largely on what the leader wants to achieve and the level at which he or she is acting.

4. To be a leader one must also have the potential to be a leader. Having the right stuff (in terms of personality traits) is the second foundation component. Some traits on which leaders differ from nonleaders include drive, the desire to lead, honesty and integrity, self-confidence, cognitive ability, and knowledge of the business.

5. Legitimate power and authority are elements in the foundation of leadership, because a leader without power is not a leader at all. Sources of leader power include position, rewards, coercion, expertise, and referent power or personal magnetism.

6. Leadership style or behaviors include structuring and considerate styles; participative and autocratic styles; employee-centered and production-centered styles; close and general styles; and transformational behavior.

7. Although there are some differences in the way men and women lead, they do not account for the slower career progress of most women managers. Institutional biases such as the glass ceiling and persistent, inaccurate, stereotypes are contributing factors.

8. Situational leadership theories like those of Fiedler and House and the leader–member exchange theory underscore the importance of fitting the style to the situation.

TYING IT ALL TOGETHER ■

Developing a plan and creating an organization is only part of the task a manager faces. Companies and other organizations are composed of people, and it's the manager's job to inspire, lead, and motivate these people to carry out the company's or the department's mission. In this section we looked at what it takes to be a leader, in particular the traits and styles of effective leaders, and how to think like a leader and size up leadership situations. As you know from your own experience, one of the leader's biggest tasks involves actually motivating subordinates.

Skills and Study Materials

CRITICAL THINKING EXERCISES ■

1. The November 22, 1999, issue of *Fortune* is devoted to the 20th century. In tracing the concept of leadership, *Fortune* divides leadership by decade. In the 1900s it was moguls such as J. P. Morgan. In the 1910s it was the government as regulator, such as breaking up of Standard Oil. By the 1920s celebrities such as Charles Lindbergh attained the sort of media-driven prominence. The union worker led the 1930s. In the 1940s the United States led the rebuilding of

Europe. In the 1950s it was the man in the gray flannel suit (think *Father Knows Best*). By the 1960s the conglomerator symbolized the times. Women emerged as leaders in the 1970s. In the 1980s the MBA consultant was the leader. In the decade of the 1990s the e-leaders, cyber chiefs such as Jeff Bezos of Amazon.com, reinvented old business models for a wired world. Think about what leadership will be like in 2000, 2010, 2020, 2030, 2040, and 2050. Base your thinking on what the section presents combined with the ideas from *Fortune*.

2. As a group, compare and contrast the perspectives on leadership presented below.[83] What concepts from the section would help you in understanding their various perspectives? Which style do you like best and why?

Leaders can't succeed if they care more about how people feel than how they perform. So focus on output, not attitude. Employees who get results should be taken at face value. Sincerity and competence rarely share a soul. Reward the latter and forget the former.

Marilyn Moats Kennedy, Managing Partner, Career Strategies,
Wilmette, Illinois

I find it amusing, frustrating, and often, quite appalling, how few business leaders recognize that people should share in the economic value they create. At LifeUSA, our employees have options on 2 million shares of company stock. It seems like common sense to us. So why is it still so uncommon in most companies?

Sharing the wealth with everyone creates a vested interest for everyone to succeed. It's also a powerful mechanism for accountability. And it encourages people to innovate and provide unbeatable service.

Nobody wins unless everybody wins.

Maggie Hughes, COO, LifeUSA Holdings, Inc.,
Minneapolis, Minnesota

CEOs are always searching for vision, and I'm no different. But I've come to appreciate the value of bifocals—the kind that let me move from a close up view of Merix to one farther away, and then back again. I try to wear my corporate bifocals regularly, alternating my view so I can get a better look at where we are as an organization and where we are going in the future.

Sometimes what you see depends on how you look.

Debi Coleman, Chair and CEO, Merix Corporation,
Forest Grove, Oregon

EXPERIENTIAL EXERCISES

1. Leaders come in all sizes, shapes, genders, and races. Your task is to research five of the following people and then write a brief analysis of what made them leaders. After you have completed that portion of the task, explain what you think an "ideal" leader is and identify someone you think fits that profile best. Write no more than two pages of analysis.

   The leaders are George W. Bush, presidential candidate; Andrew Young, politician; Former first lady Hillary Clinton; Bill Clinton, U.S. president; Mao Zedong, late communist leader of China; Rosa Parks, civil rights leader; Madeline Albright, secretary of state; Bill Gates of Microsoft; Louis Gerstner, CEO of IBM; Helmut Kohl, former chancellor of Germany; and Michael Jordan, former professional basketball star.

2. The November 22, 1999, *Fortune* lists the following men as the four finalists for businessman of the century, in order of time: Henry Ford, founder of Ford Motor Company; Alfred P. Sloan Jr., architect of the modern corporation and CEO of General Motors; Thomas J. Watson Jr., leader of IBM; and Bill Gates, of Microsoft. Which do you think the magazine selected, and why? Do some research on each. Then rank-order the four based on your research. After you have completed the ranking, look at *Fortune* and compare your analysis and theirs.

3. In *The New Global Leaders* (Jossey-Bass, 1999) authors Manfried F. R. Kets de Vries and Elizabeth Florent-Treacy select Richard Branson (United Kingdom) of Virgin Airlines, Percy Barnevik (Sweden) of ASEA Brown Boveri (ABB—engineering), and David Simon (United Kingdom) of British Petroleum as the models for global leadership. Research each of these companies on the Internet or go to the library and find *The New Global Leaders*. Then write a comparative analysis of these individuals' leadership styles and why they are seen as models for the global marketplace.

CASE 4-1
TURNING AROUND THE
U.S.S. BENFOLD

While "leadership" may seem a little theoretical in some situations, that's certainly not the case when it comes to the U.S. Navy. When you're the captain of the ship, the lives of all the people on that ship are in your hands. Leadership style can have a corrosive effect on sailors' morale and on their—and the ship's—performance.

For the past few years, in fact, the U.S. military has been in what one officer calls "deep trouble." Commander Mike Abrashoff says: "People aren't joining. More people are leaving. The attrition rates are going through the roof. In the Navy, 33 percent of those who join never complete their first tour of duty. Combat readiness is declining."[84]

Given those trends, Commander Abrashoff's experience in instituting a new leadership initiative when he took over as captain of the *U.S.S. Benfold* is all the more remarkable. In the two years he was leading the ship, the *Benfold* retention rate went from about 25% to 100% in most of the ship's top job categories. Attrition went from more than 18% to less than 1%, and mission-degrading casualties dropped from 75 to 24. During his final 12 months in command, the ship even ran on 75% of its operating budget, and returned millions of dollars to the Navy. How did he do it?

To a large extent, this turnaround in attitudes was a consequence of a remarkably simple initiative on Abrashoff's part: he brought a new leadership style to the *U.S.S. Benfold* when he took command. Abrashoff says that when he took over, he decided right away that before he could fix the problems on the ship, he had to find out what those problems were. He started his command by interviewing every crew member individually. He'd start each interview with several questions, such as "Where are you from?" "Why did you join the Navy?" "What are your goals in the Navy?" "What are your goals in life?" Then he asked three more questions:

"What do you like most about the *Benfold*?" "What do you like least?" "What things would you change if you could?"

As Abrashoff puts it, "The minute I started these interviews, our performance took off like a rocket. Whenever I got an outstanding idea from a sailor—and about 70% of the ideas that I got were, in fact, outstanding—I would implement that idea right on the spot."[85] He used the public address system to tell the rest of the crew what the new idea was, which sailor the idea came from, and that he was implementing it immediately and needed their support in doing so.

Mike Abrashoff says that whenever he needed a reminder about what leadership was all about, he took out an index card he kept in his wallet. On the card were the eight leadership traits he always used as personal guidelines: A leader is trusted. A leader takes the initiative. A leader uses good judgment. A leader speaks with authority. A leader strengthens others. A leader is optimistic and enthusiastic. A leader never compromises his absolutes. A leader leads by example.[86]

Questions

1. How does Commander Abrashoff's leadership style compare with the leadership styles described in this section? Do you think his leadership initiative would have been as useful in a company as it was on the *U.S.S. Benfold*? Why or why not?

2. What does Abrashoff's experience on the *U.S.S. Benfold* say to you about how leaders should behave? Why?

3. Abrashoff's index card contains eight leadership traits. How do these eight traits compare with the foundations of leadership covered in this section? In what ways are they similar? Different?

4. In addressing the problems on the *U.S.S. Benfold*, did Abrashoff "think like a leader"? In what way?

CASE 4-2
CAN A MANAGER'S LEADERSHIP
STYLE WORK IN MORE THAN ONE
SITUATION?

Many analysts would consider leading a manufacturing turnaround the most difficult of all leadership situations. Turnarounds usually require a tough-minded and transformational leader who can make very difficult decisions quickly. Morale can often be difficult in this type of situation as the firm may have been losing money, and radical cost-cutting is often the first move the leader must make. Ana-

lysts might prescribe a very different style for the manager of an entrepreneurial start-up or a not-for-profit service provider. Can one leader be successful in this wide range of settings? Consider the case of Vince Naimoli.

Naimoli is currently the managing general partner and CEO of the Tampa Bay Devil Rays baseball organization. It is not his first leadership role. Naimoli has also served in a variety of challenging high-level corporate management situations, including several turnarounds. Will the leadership skills Naimoli developed in industry serve him well in his new career?

As a young man, Naimoli earned a degree in engineering from Notre Dame and an MBA from Fairleigh Dickinson University. He began his career at Continental Group. Over a 12-year period, he progressed through various management positions, eventually becoming a vice president and general manager of Continental Can Company. As general manager of that division, Naimoli had responsibility for over $800 million in sales, the operation of 52 plants, and more than 11,000 employees.

Naimoli then joined Anchor Hocking Corporation as a vice president in the firm's packaging division, which was a money-loser for its parent corporation. Sensing opportunity, in 1983 Naimoli led a group of managers in the purchase of Anchor Glass Container Corporation. The investors named him chairman, president, and CEO. Within a year, the company went from losing over $12 million to making a modest profit. Under his leadership, the company pursued a series of productivity enhancements and acquisitions. Profitability increased and the company grew. By 1986, Naimoli was in a position to take Anchor Glass public again.

By 1987 *Forbes* ranked Anchor Glass as having the third highest return on assets in the nation. In 1989, when Naimoli sold the company, Anchor had revenues in excess of $1 billion and was highly profitable.

After selling Anchor Glass, Naimoli created Anchor Industries International, Inc. (AII), an investment and consulting firm specializing in corporate turnarounds. His new company would acquire companies and appoint Naimoli president and CEO. Through AII and other ventures, Naimoli became CEO of Harding Services, and president and CEO of various portfolio companies, including Electrolux Corporation. Over the next few years, Naimoli successfully orchestrated turnarounds of Doehler-Jarvis, Inc., Ladish Co., Inc., and Harvard Industries. At Harvard Industries, Naimoli became a director one month after the company's bankruptcy reorganization. One year later, the company reported over $7 million in earnings. For his work as chairman, president, and CEO of AII, Naimoli was named 1995 Florida Entrepreneur of the Year in the turnaround category. During his tenure at AII, Naimoli was successful in leading the effort to bring major league baseball to Tampa.

While most leaders would be satisfied with success in one field, Naimoli has triumphed in manufacturing and service environments in many industries. He has also found time to stay active in a leadership role in the community. He has served as chairman of the College of Business, Advisory Board at Notre Dame and chairman of the Board of Trustees of the University of Tampa. He is or has been a director of more than 24 public and private entities and corporations and has received many honors for his corporate, civic, and charitable activity. In 1999 The Northwood University Board of Trustees presented Naimoli with its prestigious Outstanding Business Leader Award.

Discussion Questions

1. Based on what you read in this section, list the leadership traits and styles you think Naimoli brings to a leadership situation that make him so successful.

2. To what extent do you feel Naimoli needed to change his leadership style as he moved from turnaround specialist to entrepreneur?

3. To what extent does Naimoli seem to show transformational leadership characteristics? Why?

THE LEADER'S ROLE IN ORGANIZATIONAL AND CULTURAL CHANGE

WHAT'S AHEAD?

Just about everyone in the U.S. has a Kodak camera, but by the late 1990s, Kodak's annual operating earnings had fallen by 25%, and sales were stagnant. Faced with what were now insurmountable cost pressures, CEO George Fisher turned to downsizing. He replaced the head of his consumer products division, fired more than 200 high-level executives, and laid plans to eliminate up to 20,000 more jobs. By 1999 profits were on the rise, and Kodak had just introduced, in partnership with AOL, a new Internet-based service called "You've Got Pictures," a process for sharing pictures over the Internet[1]. Slowly but surely, Fisher's transformation of Kodak from a sluggish giant to a lean, mean Internet-oriented fighting machine was taking shape. During 2000, he handed the reins to another CEO.

THIS SECTION FOCUSES ON THE FOLLOWING:

- Techniques for overcoming individual, interpersonal, and intergroup conflicts

Organizational and cultural changes usually don't take place spontaneously. Instead, they're triggered by problems and opportunities, and then driven by leaders like Gary Steele and Steve Jobs. And the "leader" doesn't necessarily mean just the CEO or top executive. While the person leading the change is often the CEO (like Kodak's Fisher), the leader may also be an office manager, or perhaps a champion who assumes the role of cajoling, inspiring, and negotiating a new product successfully through the firm until it's produced. Such leaders—called **change advocates**, or champions—also play a major role in any organizational change.

We've looked so far at the nature of organizational change and at an 8-step process for leading change. Now we'll look more closely at what change leaders actually do.

The Leader's Role in Strategic Change

Nowhere is the role of leadership more obvious or more important than in the sorts of organizationwide strategic changes implemented at firms like Kodak, Apple, and Netiva. A careful analysis of leaders in firms like these suggests three crucial change leader functions: charismatic, instrumental, and missionary leadership.[2]

Charismatic Leadership   David Nadler and Michael Tushman say that leading a successful change requires charismatic leaders who possess "a special quality that enables the leader to mobilize and sustain activity within an organization."[3] **Charismatic leadership** consist of three behaviors: envisioning, energizing, and enabling. As summarized in Figure 4-7, the charismatic leader is an envisioning leader who is capable of articulating a compelling vision, setting high expectations, and being a model of behaviors that are consistent with that compelling vision. He or she is also an energizing leader who can demonstrate personal excitement, express personal confidence, and seek, find, and use success among his or her colleagues. Finally, charismatic leaders are enabling leaders who are able to express

▶ **F I G U R E   4 - 7**

Charismatic Leadership Behaviors

Charismatic change leadership plays a major role in driving through a change. Its components are envisioning, energizing, and enabling leadership.

Source: Copyright © 1990, by The Regents of the University of California. Reprinted from the *California Management Review*, Vol. 32. No. 2. By permission of The Regents.

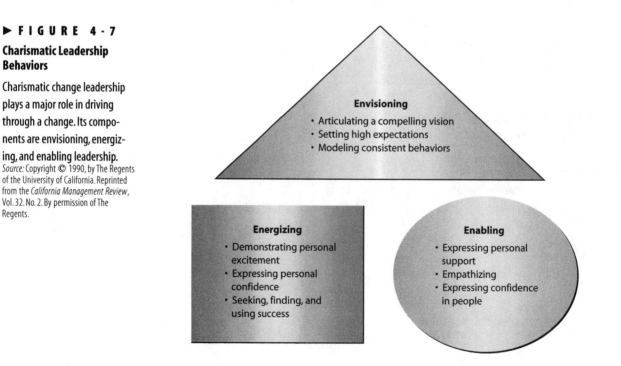

personal support, empathy, and confidence in people and thereby inspire them to undertake the required changes.

Instrumental Leadership   Charismatic leadership alone doesn't explain the sort of success that executives like Louis Gerstner had in turning IBM around. Effective leaders of change must also "build competent teams, clarify required behavior, build in measurements, and administer rewards and punishments so that individuals perceive that behavior consistent with the change is essential for them in achieving their own goals." Nadler and Tushman call this the change leader's **instrumental leadership** role: it's the managerial aspect of change leadership that puts the instruments in place through which the employees can accomplish their new tasks. For example, leaders must ensure that the necessary structure is in place to carry out the change. They must invest in building teams, creating new organizational structures, setting goals, establishing standards, and defining roles and responsibilities.[4]

Missionary Leadership   Few leaders can turn an organization around by themselves; instead, as we've seen, they must enlist the aid of others. They must then depend on this new coalition to spread the top manager's vision; this is **missionary leadership**.

In practice, successful leaders communicate their visions to three groups: their own senior teams, senior management, and leadership throughout the organization. They generally look first for opportunities to extend and institutionalize their vision for the firm to the group of individuals who comprise their own senior team. (This, in part, is why CEOs seeking to implement major changes often seek and hire subordinates whose values and visions are consistent with theirs. For example, Gerstner quickly hired several new senior vice presidents for finance, HR management, and several other functions within months of assuming the reins at IBM.) Then, senior managers just below the top executive team are encouraged to buy into the vision and become missionaries for the change.

Finally, the vision and details of the change need to be "sold" throughout the organization. This means creating cadres of employees who are capable of helping to lead the change and are eager to do so. Ford does this with its teaching programs, by annually training hundreds of employees—not just managers, but engineers, chemists, and others throughout the firm. In this way, Ford provides employees with the values and skills they will need to make their units consistent with Nasser's vision of a lean, competitive, agile organization.

Influencing Organizational Culture

Leaders who effectively transform their organizations recognize the important role that organizational culture always plays in such a process. Organizational culture is defined as the characteristic traditions, norms, and values that employees share. Values and norms (such as "be honest," "be thrifty," and "don't be bureaucratic") are basic beliefs about what you should or shouldn't do, and what is or is not important.

Norms and values guide and channel all our behavior, and so successfully changing an organization (for instance, changing it from "bureaucratic" and "stick to the chain of command" to "let's be responsive and get the job done") requires a new set of values—a new culture—as well. As reengineering advocate John Champy has said, reducing hierarchy and bureaucracy is not just a matter of rearranging the furniture: these are cultural matters.

The People Side of Managing
■ **Training Leaders to Lead Change**

Can leaders be trained to be better leaders of change? The answer, based on one recent study, is yes.

Much of what change leaders do—being charismatic, exercising instrumental leadership, and being missionaries, for instance—is part of what being a transformational leader is all about. We've seen that transformational leaders can be influential in shaping organizational change. Transformational leaders tend to be charismatic, stimulating, inspirational, and to treat employees as individuals.[5]

But can a person be trained to be more transformational? The results of one study suggest that the answer is a definite yes.[6] The study took place at one of the five largest banks in Canada. The managers of the 20 branches in one region were randomly assigned to receive transformational leadership training or not to receive it. The training group ended up with 5 male and 4 female managers; the no-training group had 6 male and 5 female managers.

The first part of the two-part training program consisted of a one-day training session that familiarized participants with the meaning of transformational leadership and explained and illustrated how it might be implemented in the managers' branches. The second part consisted of several one-on-one "booster" sessions. Here a trainer met individually with each of the managers to go over the latter's leadership style and to develop personal action plans for the manager to become more of a goal-oriented, transformational leader.

The results of this study clearly indicate that managers can be trained to be transformational leaders. For example, the subordinates of the managers who received the training subsequently perceived their managers as higher on intellectual stimulation, charisma, and individual consideration than did subordinates of managers in the no-training group.

You know from your own experience that changing someone's values involves a lot more than just talk. Parents might tell their children repeatedly to eat only healthy foods, but if the children see their parents saying one thing and doing another, chances are the parents' actions—not simply what the parents say—will mold their children's eating habits.

Much the same is true when it comes to creating or changing a company's culture. When he decided to transform Kodak, for instance, Fisher knew he had to do more than talk. Top executives who weren't performing were replaced; new incentive plans were instituted; and new, more results-oriented appraisal systems were introduced. The net effect was to send a strong signal to employees throughout the firm that the values of being efficient, effective, and responsive were a lot more important today then they'd been the week before.

Creating and Sustaining the Right Corporate Culture   There are a lot of things a leader can do to create and sustain the required corporate culture. In many firms, for instance, publishing a formal core values statement is a logical first step in creating a culture. For example the core values credo of Johnson & Johnson starts with "We believe our first responsibility is to the doctors, nurses, and patients, to mothers and all others who use our products and services. In meeting their needs, everything we do must be of high quality."

Of course the leaders' own words and actions are important, too. For example, the foundations of Wal-Mart's values can be traced to the late Sam Walton's personal values of "hard work, honesty, neighborliness, and thrift." Under Walton's leadership, the firm developed an almost religious zeal for doing things efficiently, and hard work became a requirement for getting promoted.

Your management practices also send a strong signal about what you do and do not think is important. For example, at Toyota, where quality and teamwork are essential, much of the training process focuses on how to work in teams and how to solve quality problems. Similarly, one of the first things Gerstner did when he took over at IBM was to institute a bonus-based approach to paying employees that emphasized performance much more heavily than did the company's old compensation plan.

Signs, symbols, stories, rites, and ceremonies are important, too. In fact many believe that symbolism—what the manager says and does and the signals he or she sends—ultimately does the most to create and sustain the company's culture. At Ben & Jerry's, for instance, signs and symbols are used throughout to create and sustain the company's culture. The joy gang, for example, is a concrete symbol of the firm's values, which emphasize charity, fun, and goodwill toward fellow workers. And at JCPenney, where loyalty and tradition are values, new management employees are inducted at ritualistic conferences into the "Penney partnership," where they commit to the firm's ideology as embodied in its statement of core values of honor, confidence, service, and cooperation.

How to Change a Company's Culture   Imagine you are swept into the CEO's position in a company long known for its culture of backbiting, bureaucratic behavior, and disdain for clients: What steps would you take to change the company's culture? Management expert Edgar Schein has proposed a sort of shorthand list of mechanisms leaders can use to establish, embed, and reinforce organizational culture.[7] Schein advocates five "primary embedding mechanisms":

1. *Make it clear to your employees what you pay attention to, measure, and control.* For example, you can direct the attention of your employees toward controlling costs or serving customers if those are the values you want to emphasize.

2. *React appropriately to critical incidents and organizational crises.* For example, if you want to emphasize the value that "we're all in this together," don't react to declining profits by laying off operating employees and middle managers while leaving your top managers intact.

3. *Deliberately role model, teach, and coach the values you want to emphasize.* For example, Wal-Mart founder Walton truly embodied the values "hard work, honesty, neighborliness, and thrift" that he wanted all Wal-Mart employees to follow. Although he was one of the richest men in the world, he drove a pickup truck, a preference he explained by saying, "If I drove a Rolls Royce, what would I do with my dog?"

4. *Communicate your priorities by the way you allocate rewards and status.* Leaders communicate their priorities by the way they link pay raises and promotions (or the lack thereof) to particular behaviors. For example, when the top management at General Foods decided several years ago to reorient its strategy from cost control to diversification and sales growth, it revised the compensation system to link bonuses to sales volume (rather than just to increased earnings) and to new-product development.

T A B L E   4 - 1

Mechanisms for Embedding and Reinforcing Organizational Culture

Primary Embedding Mechanisms

1. What leaders pay attention to, measure, and control
2. Leader reactions to critical incidents and organizational crises
3. Deliberate role modeling, teaching, and coaching
4. Criteria for allocation of rewards and status
5. Criteria for recruitment, selection, promotion, retirement, and excommunication

Secondary Articulation and Reinforcement Mechanisms

1. Organization design and structure
2. Organizational systems and procedures
3. Design of physical space, facades, buildings
4. Stories about important events and people
5. Formal statements of organizational philosophy, creeds, charters

Source: Reprinted with permission from E. H. Schein, *Organizational Culture and Leadership.* Copyright © 1985 Jossey-Bass, Inc. A subsidiary of John Wiley & Sons, Inc. All rights reserved.

5. *Make your HR procedures and criteria consistent with the values you espouse.* When he became chairperson and CEO of IBM, Gerstner brought in a new top management team whose values were consistent with shaking up IBM's traditionally bureaucratic and politicized culture.

Schein suggests not stopping there. As you can see in Table 4-1, he also recommends using secondary mechanisms—such as redesigning the organizational structure, using new organizational systems, and redesigning physical space—to further reinforce the desired cultural changes. However, Schein believes that these secondary mechanisms are just that—secondary—because they work only if they are consistent with the five primary mechanisms.

S U M M A R Y   ■

1. Managers in their leadership roles can focus on various change targets. They can change the strategy, culture, structure, tasks, technologies, or attitudes and skills of the people in the organization.

2. The hardest part of leading a change is overcoming resistance. Resistance stems from several sources: habit, resource limitations, threats to power and influence, fear of the unknown, and altering employees' personal compacts.

3. Methods of dealing with resistance include education and communication, facilitation and support, participation and involvement, negotiation and agreement, manipulation and co-optation, and coercion. Psychologist Kurt Lewin suggests unfreezing the situation, perhaps by using a dramatic event to get people to recognize the need for change.

4. Implementing a change is basically like solving any problem: The manager must recognize that there's a problem, diagnose the problem, and then formulate and implement a solution.

5. Conflict can have dysfunctional effects on an organization and its people, although it can be a positive force as well. At least three types of conflict can be identified in organizations: individual, interpersonal, and intergroup. Intergroup conflicts often stem from interdependencies and shared resources; intergroup differences in goals, values, or perceptions; authority imbalances; or ambiguity. Problems like these can be solved by establishing superordinate goals, eliminating interdependencies, using one or more conflict-resolution modes, or through OD conflict-resolution techniques like confrontation meetings.

TYING IT ALL TOGETHER ■

Managers plan, organize, lead, and control. Planning involves making decisions, laying plans and setting goals, and developing a strategy and mission for the firm. Organizing means putting an organization in place to implement those plans by creating reporting relationships, delegating authority, writing job descriptions, and hiring and training the employees who will staff those positions and implement the plans. With the employees in place, the manager's leadership role becomes more important. Organizations are not just organization charts and machines, but people, and the manager in his or her leadership role is responsible for influencing and motivating the company's employees to achieve their goals.

Leadership therefore involves the distinctly interpersonal aspects of what managers do. We will therefore focus on the people side of the manager's job, including leadership style, motivation, communication, groups and teams, and now, in the current section, on leading organizational and cultural change.

In the next section we'll turn to the fourth, and last, of a manager's main functions. But in fact controlling is, in most respects, inseparable from and largely an extension of the other three functions. Controlling, for instance, traditionally means setting standards, measuring performance, and then taking corrective action as required. Thinking of controlling separately from planning (and setting standards) is therefore somewhat meaningless. Similarly, "controlling someone" is, to a large extent, an extension of the manager's leadership or people-oriented duties.

You know from your own experience that the best way to control someone is to get that person to control himself or herself so that they do the job right because they want to. To that extent controlling, as we'll see, really calls on all the leadership skills you can muster. Indeed, particularly in today's fast-changing, empowered companies, it's best not to think of control as a mechanical process imposed on employees. Keeping track of what's happening in the organization will always be important, of course, but now, more often than not, the key to control is getting employees to want to excel.

EXPERIENTIAL EXERCISES ■

1. You are now a citizen of the 21st century. The rules of the job and career game appear to be changing rapidly as machines such as ATMs replace bank tellers, you can bank and pay bills with your computer, and you can even order products, including groceries, over the Internet. In groups of 5 students, preferably from different majors, explore how you think the profession you are now preparing for will look like in the future, 10 years from now and then 30 years from now. Be prepared to share your discussion with other groups.

2. In *Owning the Future* (Houghton-Mifflin, 1999) Seth Shulman warns that freely shared knowledge is fast becoming a valuable asset. We face imminent threats from new monopolies that concentrate vital information in the hands of a few. Shulman writes of today's battles for con-

trol over the intangible new assets—genes, software, databases, and scientific information—that make up the lifeblood of our new economy. What do you think of his

warnings? Interview five people who are involved in one of these subjects (genes, software, databases, or scientific information), and be prepared to discuss what you find.

C A S E 4 - 3
JOB SURFING: CATCHING
THE NEW WAVE

Switching jobs is no longer viewed as irresponsible behavior. In fact, it makes sense to stay mobile and increase your skills whenever you can.

David Friedensohn is a case in point. Over the last decade he has worked for four different employers, including Citicorp and Viacom. In addition, he has been a self-employed consultant. David has continually learned new skills, increased his responsibilities, and bumped up his income. Currently, he is vice president for new business at Prodigy, running a couple of the online service's startup ventures in New York City and earning a steady six-figure income. His advice: "You have to be disciplined to get the skills to stay in the race. You can't force the ocean to throw a

good wave at you either. You have to seize opportunities when they come."

Questions

1. What are the implications of David's philosophy for leading organizational change today?

2. Why do you think David does not resist change but rather embraces it?

3. Could you manage your career as does David?

4. Do you think constant change is the wave of the future for most job seekers? Why or why not?

Source: Justin Martin, "Job Surfing: Move On to Move Up." *Fortune*, 13 January 1997, 50–4.

SECTION FIVE

MANAGING ORGANIZATIONAL AND CULTURAL CHANGE

Recall the Kodak example from the previous section. Why did Kodak have to change? Because companies that don't adapt to their environments don't survive.[1] For years prior to Fisher's arrival, Kodak was run almost like it had no competition, and it grew slow and unresponsive in the process. For many of these years Kodak in fact had little or no competition, and indeed (particularly in the United States) "Kodak" and "film" were almost synonymous. What the pre-Fisher management didn't recognize, however, was that global competition from firms like Fuji was a growing threat. Unless Kodak changed—unless it began cutting costs and introducing new and innovative products—it could find itself a distant second in the worldwide picture-taking market.

THIS SECTION FOCUSES ON THE FOLLOWING:

- The things managers can change in organizations

- Why employees resist change

- The eight steps for leading organizational change

- How to use five organizational development techniques to change organizations

▶ THE CHALLENGE OF ORGANIZATIONAL CHANGE

Technological change and intense global competition (as embodied by firms like Fuji film) have made managing organizational change an absolute requirement for millions of companies. We've seen in this text that from small companies like Rosenbluth International to giants like IBM and GE, company after company is downsizing and networking their organizations. And, they are creating self-managing teams, opening up communications (by using techniques like upward appraisals and workout forums), and installing Internet-based decision support systems.

Competition, in a nutshell, means companies have to be leaner and faster. Rapid technological change and intense competition means you either change and adapt, or you die. Here's how the *Harvard Business Review* recently put it, "Companies achieve real agility only when every function, office, strategy, goal, and process—when every person—is able and eager to rise to every challenge. This type and degree of fundamental change, commonly called *revitalization* or *transformation*, is what more and more companies seek but all too rarely achieve."[2]

We've seen how leaders motivate and influence individuals and teams. Now we'll turn to an explanation of how managers lead and influence organizational and cultural change.

What to Change?

When we say "organizational change," what is it exactly that a manager can change? The answer is the company's strategy, culture, structure, tasks, technologies, and the attitudes and skills of the company's people.

Strategic Change   **Strategic change** refers to a shift in the firm's strategy, mission, and vision. A strategic change may then lead to other organizational changes—for instance, in the firm's technology, structure, or culture.

We've already touched on strategic change examples elsewhere in this text. On becoming Kodak's CEO, for instance, one of Fisher's first strategic changes was to refocus the firm more fully on digital cameras and photography. When Steve Jobs assumed the interim CEO title at Apple Computer several years ago, one of his first strategic moves was to refocus Apple on a much narrower set of products and to emphasize the reemergence of the Macintosh (iMac) computer. Previously focused on PCs, Microsoft's new strategy is to provide the software people need to run their computers "anytime, anywhere"—including, for instance, cell-phone–based Web browsers—to do Internet-based computing. Entrepreneurs must change strategies too, as the *Entrepreneurs in Action* box illustrates.

Entrepreneurs in Action

Netiva's New Web Portal Strategy

▶ As you can imagine, fast-changing Internet companies also make strategic changes, but at breakneck speed. The experience of Gary Steele, the new CEO of the Internet firm Netiva, is a good example. When he joined Netiva in June 1997, the company seemed a sure bet. It produced and sold an Internet application system that let large companies use the Java programming language to build Web databases.[3]

But after a few months, it became obvious to Steele that something was very wrong. For one thing, technical support was gobbling up Netiva's profits. Netiva had designed its applications for the customer to run and maintain, but Netiva's technical people had to spend days with each customer to get the application up to speed. To make matters worse, the original strategy assumed that customers would

Entrepreneurs in Action

Netiva's New Web Portal Strategy (continued)

develop multiple applications using Netiva's software, and would therefore have to pay multiple license fees. But that wasn't happening: "They were just buying one [license]," said Steele, "so we were doing a lot of work for just $25,000."

By April 1998 Steele knew he was going to have to take drastic measures. Within one week, 40% of the company's employees—including most of the sales and marketing staff—were gone. The next day he met with his executive team to tell them Netiva would no longer be selling Java-based database tools. He spent the rest of the meeting outlining an eight-step plan of action for reformulating the company's strategy over the next six weeks.

Steel and his four executives held 75 fact-finding meetings with executives at-large and midsize companies and swapped notes about what they'd found. One thing they found was that their customers wanted technology, but they wanted that technology without the hassle of installing and endlessly maintaining software. What they wanted, in other words, were "hosted services," where the software vendor runs and maintains complicated applications on its own servers, and the customer's employees access them via the Internet.

Netiva has now changed its name to Portera, and its new product is called ServicePort. Using a Web browser, a customer's employees can use ServicePort to do things like share client reports, schedule group meetings, and get press releases and news. The company has jumped to 70 employees, and a venture capitalist just invested $14 million to help Portera reach the next level.

Strategic changes like those at Apple, Kodak, and Netiva redefine a company's basic direction and are thus among the riskiest (but most important) changes managers can make. What triggers such changes, and why are they so risky? We can summarize some recent research findings as follows:

1. *Strategic changes are usually triggered by factors outside the company*. External threats or challenges, such as deregulation, intensified global competition, and dramatic technological innovations like the Internet are usually the ones that prompt organizations to embark on companywide, strategic changes.[4]

2. *Strategic changes are often required for survival*. Researchers found that making a strategic change did not guarantee success, but that firms which failed to change generally failed to survive. This was especially true when what they called "discontinuous" environmental change—change of an unexpected nature, such as happened when the Internet made bookselling more competitive—required quick and effective strategic change for the firms to survive.

3. *Strategic changes implemented under crisis conditions are highly risky*. Of all organizational changes, strategic, organizationwide ones initiated under crisis conditions and with short time constraints (like those of Kodak and Apple) were the riskiest. They eventually require changing more aspects of the organization, including its core values.[5] Core values tend to be hard to change, so changing them tends to trigger the most resistance from employees.

Other organizational changes may be required as well, either as a result of the strategic change or for some other reason. For example, it may be impossible to fully implement the strategic change without changing the *culture*—the shared values—of the firm's employees. When Louis Gerstner took over as CEO of IBM, one of his first tasks was refocusing employees' attention on core values like competitiveness, open communications, and moving fast. Similarly, the new strategy may precipitate a new *structure*: For instance, given Fisher's strategy of emphasizing digital photography, one of his first organizational moves was to group together in one new division all Kodak's digital product teams. Reorganizing is, as we've seen, an increasingly popular approach to change, with companies around the world generally moving to more responsive, team-based, boundaryless type organizations.

In turn, a new organization structure may require a change in tasks, or what experts call *task redesign*. The day-to-day tasks of team members in newly organized teams are generally different than they were when the firm was organized around traditional functions. Many of the preceding changes result from *technological change*, in other words from modifications to the work methods the organization uses to accomplish its tasks, as when a computerized payroll system is installed to replace an antiquated manual system.

Finally, it may be the *employees* themselves who have to change. Perhaps they haven't the skills to do their new jobs, for instance, or morale is so low that steps must be taken to improve attitudes. This is where managers call on training and development techniques like lectures, conferences, and computer-based training to improve employees skills. At other times, the "people" problems stem from misunderstandings or conflicts; in this case organizational development interventions like those discussed below may be used to try to change attitudes and thereby behavior.

Organizational changes differ in their breadth and urgency—changes can range from big to little, in other words. Some changes are *incremental*: They may require reorganizing just one department or establishing work teams in a single plant. At the other extreme, *strategic organizational changes* affect the entire company and usually change not just the company's strategy, but also its structure, culture, people, and processes.[9]

Managing @ the Speed of Thought
■ Business Process Reengineering

Today, "reorganizing" and task redesign usually doesn't just mean pushing boxes around on an organization chart. Instead, it means reorganizing the company in order to take advantage of some new technology. Business reengineering is one example.

Business reengineering has been defined as "the radical redesign of business processes, combining steps to cut waste and eliminate repetitive, paper-intensive tasks in order to improve cost, quality, and service, and to maximize the benefits of information technology."[6] The approach is to (1) identify a business process to be redesigned (such as approving a mortgage application), (2) measure the performance of the existing processes, (3) identify opportunities to improve these processes, and (4) redesign and implement a new way of doing the work.

Companies' experience with reengineering underscores the importance of the organizational change process. While reengineering with the aid of information technology has had its share of successes, some estimate failure rates to be as high as 70%.[7] When a reengineering effort does fail, it is often due to behavioral factors. Sometimes (as in other change efforts) employees resist the change and deliberately undermine the revised procedures. If business processes are reengineered without considering the new skill requirements, training, and reporting relationships involved, the usual employee resistance problems can be exacerbated. As John Champy, a long-time reengineering proponent, has said, "In short, reducing hierarchy, bureaucracy, and the rest of it is not just a matter of rearranging the furniture to face our customers and markets. It is a matter of rearranging the quality of people's attachments—to their work and to each other. These are *cultural* matters."[8]

Why Do People Resist Change?

Overcoming resistance is often the hardest part of leading a change. As Niccolò Machiavelli, a shrewd observer of 16th-century Italian politics, once said: "There is nothing so difficult to implement as change, since those in favor of the change will often be small in number while those opposing the change will be numerous and enthusiastic in their resistance to change."[10] Indeed, even the best leaders would agree that implementing large-scale change is enormously challenging. GE's Jack Welch once said that even after 10 years of continual change, he expected that it would take at least 10 more years to rejuvenate GE's culture.[11]

The fact that a change is advisable or even mandatory doesn't mean employees will accept it. In fact, it's often the company's key people—perhaps even some top and middle managers—who are the most resistant; they may just prefer the status quo.

It's easy to see how such resistance might arise. Take a personal example: Suppose you've been attending a college class in management, with the college's best professor, and several weeks into the semester the dean comes in and announces that some students will have to be moved to another professor and class because the fire marshal says the lecture hall is overcrowded. You've been asked to move. How would you react? What would go through your mind? Probably several things: that your grade might be adversely affected; that you don't want to leave the·friends you've made in this class and start all over again; that it might be just a tad embarrassing to have to get up and leave (although obviously it's not your fault); and that it's not fair that you should be one of those singled out to leave. You don't want to go!

In his book *Beyond the Wall of Resistance*, author-consultant Rick Maurer says resistance can stem from two sets of things. What he calls Level 1 resistance is based on lack of information or on honest disagreement over the facts. In this case, everything is on the table, and there are no hidden agendas. Level 2 resistance is more personal and emotional. Here, people are afraid—that the change may cost them their jobs, or to lose face, or reduce their control (or in our case, lower their grades). Maurer points out that treating all resistance as if it were Level 1 (and simply caused by an honest disagreement and lack of information) can make a company miss the mark in its change efforts. For example, using "slick visual presentations to explain change with nice neat facts, charts, and time lines, when what people really want to hear is: 'what does this mean to them?'" can be a recipe for disaster.[12]

Years ago, Professor Paul Lawrence said it's usually not the technical aspects of a change that employees resist, but its social consequences, "the changes in their human relationships that generally accompany the technical change."[13] Thus, they may see in the change diminished responsibilities for themselves and therefore lower status in the organization and less job security. Sometimes it's not fear of the obvious consequence, but rather apprehension about the unknown consequences that produces resistance. For example, how much do you know about the professor who'll be teaching that new class you're being moved to, and about the new classmates you'll be joining? Not much, unfortunately.

You've also probably noticed that some people are inherently more resistant to change than others. At the extreme, in fact, some people are simply recalcitrant, which basically means they'll almost always resist change as a knee-jerk reaction. People like these are continually "fighting the system." As you might imagine, they are usually not the sorts of employees who contribute in a positive way to organizational change.

One recent study took place in six organizations—two large European companies, two Australian banks, a large U.S. university, and a Korean manufacturing firm. Its aim was to determine the extent to which managers' responses to organizational change were influenced by various personality traits. Three personality traits—tolerance for ambiguity, having a positive self-concept, and being more tolerant of risk—significantly predicted effectiveness in coping with change.[14] Those with the lowest self-image, least tolerance for ambiguity, and least tolerance for risk appeared, as expected, to be the most resistant.

Overcoming Resistance to Change

What tools are available to overcome resistance? In Table 5-1, John Kotter and Leonard Schlesinger summarize the pros and cons of some methods leaders use to deal with resistance to change. For example, education and communication are appropriate where inaccurate or missing information is contributing to employee resistance. Negotiation and agreement may be appropriate if one group will clearly lose by the change and that group has considerable power to resist. Coercion—forcing the change—can be a fast way of pushing through a change and is widely used, particularly when speed is essential. It can be effective when the manager has the power to force the change, but risky if it leaves influential employees with a residue of ill will.

Psychologist Kurt Lewin proposed a famous model to summarize the basic process for implementing a change with minimal resistance. To Lewin, all behavior in organizations was a product of two kinds of forces: those striving to maintain the status quo, and those pushing for change. Implementing change thus meant either reducing the forces for the status quo or building up the forces for change. Lewin's process consists of three steps: unfreezing, moving, and refreezing.

Unfreezing means reducing the forces that are striving to maintain the status quo, usually by presenting a provocative problem or event to get people to recognize the need for change and to search for new solutions. Without unfreezing, said Lewin, change will not occur. Attitude surveys, interview results, or participatory informational meetings are often used to provide such provocative events. For example, when he took over as CEO of the Dutch electronics firm Philips, Jan Timmer invited the company's top 100 managers to an off-site retreat. Here he gave them a shock: a hypothetical press release that said Philips was bankrupt and that it was up to the 100 managers to bring the company back from the brink.[15] In the fast-changing electronics industry, Timmer then got a shock of his own: Within three years he was replaced by Cor Boostra, who pledged to make the ruthless cost-cutting changes that Timmer—despite his start—failed to implement.[16]

Lewin's second step aims to shift or alter the behavior of the people in the department or organization in which the changes are to take place. **Moving** means developing new behaviors, values, and attitudes, sometimes through structure changes, and sometimes through the sorts of change and development techniques in Table 5-1, and which we'll discuss later in this section.

Lewin assumed that organizations tended to revert to their old ways of doing things unless the new ways were continually reinforced. This reinforcement is accomplished by **refreezing** the organization into its new state of equilibrium. Lewin advocated instituting new systems and procedures that would support and maintain the changes that were made. For example, Gerstner installed new pay and incentive plans at IBM to emphasize the superiority of performance over seniority.

T A B L E   5 - 1   Six Methods for Dealing with Resistance to Change

Method	Commonly Used in Situations	Advantages	Drawbacks
Education + communication	Where there is a lack of information or inaccurate information and analysis.	Once persuaded, people will often help with the implementation of the change.	Can be very time-consuming if lots of people are involved.
Participation + involvement	Where the initiators do not have all the information they need to design the change, and where others have considerable power to resist.	People who participate will be committed to implementing change, and any relevant information they have will be integrated into the change plan.	Can be very time-consuming if participators design an inappropriate change.
Facilitation + support	Where people are resisting because of fear and anxiety.	No other approach works as well with employee adjustment problems.	Can be time-consuming and expensive, yet still fail.
Negotiation + agreement	Where someone or some group will clearly lose out in a change, and where that group has considerable power to resist.	Sometimes it is a relatively easy way to avoid major resistance.	Can be too expensive in many cases if it prompts others to negotiate.
Manipulation + co-optation	Where other tactics will not work or are too expensive.	It can be a relatively quick and inexpensive solution to resistance problems.	Can lead to future problems if people feel manipulated.
Coercion	Where speed is essential, and the change initiators possess considerable power.	It is speedy and can overcome any kind of resistance.	Can be risky if it leaves people angry at the initiators.

Source: Adapted and reprinted by permission of *Harvard Business Review.* "Six Methods for Dealing with Change," from "Choosing Strategies for Change," by John P. Kotter and Leonard A. Schlesinger, March–April 1979. Copyright © 1979 by the President and Fellows of Harvard College; all rights reserved.

▶ AN EIGHT-STEP PROCESS FOR LEADING ORGANIZATIONAL CHANGE

Changes may involve the firm's strategy, culture, structure, tasks, or technologies, or the attitudes and skills of its people. The changes may have to be incremental or strategic. And they may trigger various levels of resistance. In any case, the manager needs a basic process for leading and implementing the organizational change. In this section we focus on an eight-step process: creating a sense of urgency; creating a guiding coalition and mobilizing commitment; developing and then communicating a shared vision; empowering employees; generating short-term wins; consolidating gain; anchoring the new ways of doing things; and monitoring progress and adjusting the vision. In applying this 8-step process, keep in mind that implementing a change is like solving any problem: You have to recognize the problem, diagnose it, and then formulate and implement a solution.

Create a Sense of Urgency

You've become aware of the need for change, what do you do now? Do you simply paper over the problems, or do you take more positive steps? Most experienced leaders instinctively know they've got to unfreeze the old habits, often by creating a sense of urgency. Timmer knew he had to rouse his top managers out of their status-quo thinking. He did this with his hypothetical bankruptcy press release.

Urgency does more than overcome employees' traditional reasons for resisting change: It can also jar them out of their complacency. In organizations, several things can leave employees feeling complacent.[17] These include the absence of a major and visible crisis, too many visible resources, low overall performance standards, and a lack of sufficient performance feedback from external sources. When complacency sets in (as it did in many companies, including IBM and Kodak in the 1980s), something must be done to create a sense of urgency so that employees will be more open to change. How do you create such a sense of urgency?[18] A partial list includes the following:

- Create a crisis by allowing a financial loss or exposing managers to major weaknesses relative to competitors.
- Eliminate obvious examples of excess such as company-owned country club facilities, numerous aircraft, or gourmet executive dining rooms.
- Set targets for revenue, income, productivity, customer satisfaction, and product development cycle time so high that they can't be reached by conducting business as usual.
- Send more data about customer satisfaction and financial performance to more employees, especially information that demonstrates weaknesses relative to competitors.

Create a Guiding Coalition and Mobilize Commitment

Major transformations—such as Fisher accomplished in 1998 by transforming Kodak into an Internet- and digital-oriented company—are often associated with one highly visible leader. But no leader can accomplish any major change alone. That's why most leaders create a guiding coalition of influential people who can be missionaries and implementers of change. The coalition should include people with enough power to lead the change effort, and it's essential to encourage the group to work together as a team.

In this process, the managers have to choose the right lieutenants. One reason to create the coalition is to gather political support; the leader therefore has to ensure that there are enough key players on board so that those left out can't easily block progress.[19] The coalition's members should also have the expertise, credibility, and leadership skills to explain and implement the change.

Many leaders then create one or more broad, employee-based task forces to diagnose the company's problems. This can produce a shared understanding of what can and must be improved, and thus mobilize the commitment of those who must actually implement the change.

Develop and Communicate a Shared Vision

We saw that it's the leader's job to provide direction. Whether that "direction" is a statement of vision, mission, or objectives depends on what the leader wants to achieve and the level at which he or she is acting.

To transform an organization, a new vision is usually required, "a general statement of the organization's intended direction that evokes emotional feelings in organization members." For example, when Barry Gibbons became CEO of a drifting Spec's Music retail chain, its employees, owners, and bankers—all its stakeholders—required a vision of a renewed Spec's around which they could rally. Gibbons's vision of a leaner Spec's offering a diversified blend of concerts and retail music helped to provide the sense of direction they all required.

Change expert Kotter says that "the real power of a vision is unleashed only when most of those involved in an enterprise or activity have a common understanding of its goals and direction."[20] In other words, fostering support for the new vision is impossible unless the vision has been effectively communicated. What are the key steps in effectively communicating a vision? They include the following:

- *Keep it simple.* Here is an example of a good statement of vision: "We are going to become faster than anyone else in our industry at satisfying customer needs."

- *Use multiple forums.* Try to use every channel possible—big meetings and small, memos and newspapers, formal and informal interaction—to spread the word.

- *Use repetition.* Ideas sink in deeply only after they have been heard many times.

- *Lead by example.* "Walk the talk" so that your behaviors and decisions are consistent with the vision you espouse.

Empower Employees to Make the Change

Accomplishing a change that transforms an organization usually requires the assistance of the employees themselves. To get that assistance, change experts advise empowering the employees. As one expert explains:

> Major internal transformation rarely happens unless many people assist. Yet employees generally won't help, or can't help, if they feel relatively powerless. Hence the relevance of empowerment.[21]

The next step, therefore, is to empower employees, to give them the wherewithal to help make the change. This starts with removing the barriers to empowerment. This idea is summarized in Figure 5-1. By now employees understand the vision and want to make it a reality, but they're boxed in: lack of skills means they can't act; formal structures and systems make it difficult to act; or bosses may discourage implementing the new vision. The leader's job is to see that such barriers are removed.

There are many potential barriers, and therefore many ways to remove them. When he took over as CEO of Sony and its loss-making movie studios, Nobuyuki Idei proceeded, in a most un-Japanese way, to fire all the studio executives and install a new team of industry veterans, with a mandate to fix Sony's movie business.[22] At Allied Signal, CEO Lawrence Bossidy put all of his 80,000 people through quality training within two years. He also created area "councils" (for instance, for Asia), so that employees who were undertaking initiatives in those areas could get together, share market intelligence, and compare notes.[23]

Jacques Nasser, Ford Motor Company's newly appointed CEO, took a similar approach. His vision at Ford was aimed at getting employees to think like shareholders and at having the company as a whole respond swiftly to and anticipate customers' needs. Ensuring that Ford's employees had the knowledge and skills they needed to operate at this level was central to Nassers transformation; he therefore implemented an extensive program of what he called "teaching" throughout the giant corporation. As he put it, "the programs we use are many and varied—Capstone, the Business Leadership Initiative, and Executive Partnering, to name just three."[24]

► FIGURE 5-1

Barriers to Empowerment

Source: Reprinted by permission of Harvard Business School Press. From *Leading Change* by John P. Kotter. Boston, MA, 1996, p. 102. Copyright © 1996 by the President and Fellows of Harvard College; all rights reserved.

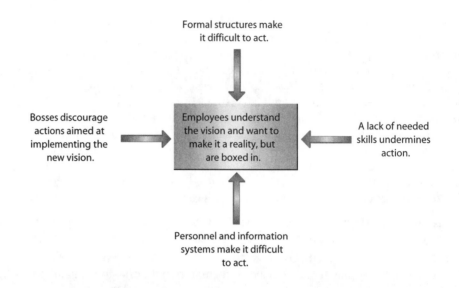

Table 5-2 summarizes four of the most widely used programs in the new curriculum at Ford. The Business Leadership Initiative, for example, is open to all salaried employees. In this program, the employees' managers provide three days of teaching and discussion on such matters as the contrast between the old and new Ford Motor Company.

Chevron uses a change process it calls "direct participation" to help strip away the barriers and give its employees what they need to help with the change. Large-scale conferences—basically two- to three-day events—are at the heart of the direct participation process. During these conferences, large numbers of employees and other participants meet to address a problem or an issue that calls for change, and to produce detailed recommendations that can be implemented fast. In addition to the exhilaration that can result from participating in such an exercise, direct participation conferences like these "bring multiple perspectives to bear on the problem and identify the changes needed to resolve it."[25]

Sometimes empowerment just means letting the employees find their own way, rather than forcing the changes on them. In one successful change, an engineering department spent nearly a year analyzing how to implement the team concept: The engineers conducted surveys, held off-site meetings, and analyzed various alternatives before deciding on a matrix management approach that the department members felt would work for them.[26]

Generate Short-Term Wins

Transforming a company can take time, but most people need reinforcement periodically to see that their efforts are working. Maintaining employees' motivation to stay involved in the change therefore requires planning for and creating short-term wins.

The leader can't just hope that short-term wins will materialize.[27] For example, the guiding coalition in one manufacturing company intentionally set its sights on producing one highly visible and successful new product about 20 months after the start of an organizational renewal effort.[28] The new product was selected in part because the coalition knew that its introduction was doable. And they knew that the introduction would provide the positive feedback required to renew the sense of urgency and motivation.

T A B L E   5 - 2   **The New Curriculum at Ford**

Program	Participants	Teachers	Components
Capstone	24 senior executives at a time	Jacques Nasser and his leadership team	■ Conducted once a year ■ About 20 days of teaching and discussion ■ Teams given six months to solve major strategic challenges ■ 360-degree feedback ■ Community service
Business Leadership Initiative	All Ford salaried employees—55,000 to date	The participants' managers	■ Three days of teaching and discussion ■ Teams assigned to 100-day projects ■ Community service ■ 360-degree feedback ■ Participants make videos that contrast the old with the new Ford
Executive Partnering	Promising young managers—12 so far	Nasser and his leadership team	■ Participants spend eight weeks shadowing seven senior executives
Let's Chat About the Business	Everyone who receives e-mail at Ford—about 100,000 employees	Nasser	■ Weekly e-mails describing Ford's new approach to business

Source: Reprinted by permission of the Harvard Business Review, An exhibit from "Driving Change: An Interview with Ford Motor Company's Jacques Nasser" by Jacques Nasser and Suzy Wetlaufer, March–April 1999 Copyright © 1999 by the President and Fellows of Harvard College; all rights reserved.

Consolidate Gains and Produce More Change

As momentum builds and changes are made, the leader has to guard against renewed complacency. That's why it's crucial, while employees are generating short-term wins, to consolidate the gains that have been made and produce even more change. How?

One approach is to use the increased credibility that comes from short-term wins to change all the systems, structures, and policies that don't fit well with the company's new vision. In one company, for example, when a vice president for operations saw the writing on the wall and left the firm, the position was left vacant; the two departments that had reported to him—engineering and manufacturing—now reported to the general manager. This helped to formalize the cross-functional nature of the new team approach at this firm.[29]

Anchor the New Ways of Doing Things in the Company Culture

The organizational change won't survive without a corresponding change in employees' shared values. A "team-based, quality-oriented, adaptable organization" is not going to happen if the company's shared values still emphasize selfishness, mediocrity, and bureaucratic behavior. We'll look more closely at how to mold culture in the following pages.

Monitor Progress and Adjust the Vision as Required

Finally, it's essential that the company have a mechanism for monitoring the effectiveness of the change and for recommending remedial actions. One firm appointed an oversight team composed of managers, a union representative, an engineer, and several others to monitor the functioning of its new self-managing teams. In another firm, regular morale surveys were used to monitor employee attitudes.

Change in Action: Becoming an E-Business

Every business is becoming an e-business today. As *Fortune* recently put it, "e or be eaten": Either link your business to the Web, or say goodbye to your business.

As a result, just about every business today—not just familiar e-businesses like Amazon.com—is getting on the Web. GM, Ford, and the other automakers are marketing cars over the Web, and will soon purchase all or most of their billions of dollars of supplies via Internet links with suppliers. Banc One recently sponsored an "immersion day" in New York City to introduce the press to its new online spin-off—an Internet bank called wingspanbank.com.[30] At Sears, CEO Arthur C. Martinez said he was "a serious skeptic for a long time," but Sears too has jumped on the e-business bandwagon, as have Procter & Gamble, Toys "Я" Us, Southwest Airlines, Lands' End, and even the U.S. Postal Service.

The problem, as one observer put it, is that "blending old business and e-business—'clicks and mortar' as some call it—is for the most part a difficult, awkward process."[31] For one thing, the cultures are often widely different. Most Sears headquarters employees are housed in comfortable offices in company headquarters. In their Internet division at Hoffman Estates, Illinois, Sears's e-employees, including its former treasurer, have small cubicles and "boxes lie everywhere."[32]

Major strategic and structural changes may be required when moving into e-business as well. For example, when Charles Schwab first established its Internet-based trading system, the strategy was to run it as a separate business from its conventional office-based trading network. Within two years, however, it became apparent that the two were competing, so Schwab had to take the painful steps required to actually merge two different businesses.

What sorts of organizational changes can you expect when moving from a conventional to an Internet-based business? "Entering the e-commerce realm is like managing at 90 mph. E-business affects finance, human resources, training, supply-chain management, customer-resource management, and just about every other corporate function. This puts the managers of these departments in a new light," says the chief strategist for one e-business.[33]

For example, you have to decide whether to blend the new e-business into the company's existing structure or organize the e-commerce operation as a completely separate entity. If the decision is made to blend the two entities, some argue that rather than assigning one manager the job of coming up with an e-strategy, "it's far better to develop an organizational structure that puts the Web and e business at the central focus of a cross-departmental business group, rather than merely adding Web responsibilities to a preexisting task list."[34] Greg Rogers, who heads up Whirlpool Corporation's e-commerce operation, points out that the company's strategy will have to change, too: "Internet strategy is really business strategy."[35] The company's new business strategy will have to reflect the fact that the company now embraces e-commerce as part of its competitive advantage.

As with any major change, there is resistance.[36] For example, "one of the early organizational barriers (Michael) Dell had to overcome was convincing everybody that the Web wasn't just a science project—that the Web could be used to conduct a real business," says the director of Dell Online. That means, of course, that top executives need to understand and be committed to the Web and then take a leadership role in overcoming resistance.

SUMMARY ■

1. Thinking like a leader involves reviewing a leadership situation and identifying what is happening, accounting for what is happening (in terms of leadership and other behavioral science theories and concepts), and formulating leader actions. Knowledge of organizational change and development can be useful tools.

2. An eight-step process for actually leading organizational change includes creating a sense of urgency; creating a guiding coalition and mobilizing commitment to change through joint diagnosis of business problems; developing and then communicating a shared vision; removing barriers to the change and empowering employees; generating short-term wins; consolidating gains and producing more change; anchoring the new ways of doing things in the company's culture; and monitoring progress and adjusting the vision as required.

3. Organizational changes almost never take place spontaneously; instead, they are pushed or driven by leaders. If you are a change leader, important functions to keep in mind include the need for charismatic leadership, instrumental leadership, missionary leadership, and transformational leadership.

4. Organizational development is a special approach to organizational change that basically involves letting the employees themselves formulate and implement the change that's required, often with the assistance of a trained consultant. Types of OD applications include human process applications, technostructural interventions, HR management applications, and strategic applications.

CONTROLLING AND BUILDING COMMITMENT

WHAT'S AHEAD?

Craig Miller, CEO of MM & A Group, was getting a sinking feeling. Not long ago, the fast-growing software consulting and personnel placement firm in Atlanta was overwhelmed with information—by phone, mail, fax, and e-mail—flooding in from customer orders and invoices, and from financial and legal documents. He knew his firm wouldn't be able to fill software engineering positions for its corporate clients or complete its own consulting projects if he didn't get control of all that data.[1] Craig knew he had to keep track of what was happening in his company, and knew he needed the information in a form that would enable him to take fast corrective action if corrective action was required. He also knew that installing a system to control what was happening at his firm was therefore one of the most important things he could do as a manager.

THIS SECTION FOCUSES ON THE FOLLOWING:

- The three steps in the traditional control process

- Traditional control methods and commitment-based control methods

- Traditional diagnostic, boundary, and interactive control methods

- The unintended behavioral consequences of control

- How managers can use belief systems and employee commitment to maintain better control

► THE ROLE OF CONTROL IN THE MANAGEMENT PROCESS

Craig Miller is only one of millions of managers trying to deal with the question of how to keep his or her business under control. Sometimes being out of control doesn't have especially serious consequences, as when your dry cleaner is "only" an hour late in finding your freshly cleaned blouse. Often, though, the consequences are more severe, as when Barings, the British banking firm, saw its business ruined by multimillion-dollar losses run up unnoticed by one of its traders in Asia. Upon assuming responsibility for a unit, managers decide "where we're going" (Planning), who will do what (Organizing), and how to motivate their troops (Leading). Now we'll see how to keep things under control.

Control is the task of ensuring that activities are providing the desired results. In its most general sense, *controlling* means setting a target, measuring performance, and taking corrective action as required. As control expert Kenneth Merchant says, "The goal [of the control system] is to have no unpleasant surprises in the future."[2]

Why Control Is Required

If managers could be sure that every plan they made and every task they assigned would be perfectly executed, they really wouldn't need to "control." All the results could be expected to be as planned, with no unpleasant surprises. But things rarely go this smoothly. Most plans are executed by people, and people vary widely in abilities, motivation, and even honesty. Furthermore, particularly in today's fast-changing business environment, who can assume that the plans themselves might not suddenly become outdated? (One can only imagine the kind of scrambling booksellers like Barnes & Noble had to do to change their five-year plans when Amazon.com was first introduced, for instance). So even the validity of the plans themselves and the results originally desired must be monitored and controlled.

Making Sure There's a Timely Response

As Kenneth Merchant said, the manager's aim is to have no unpleasant surprises, and so the manager has to be sure he or she can make a timely response. It would surely do Craig Miller no good, for instance, to find out in June that in March a large client had called to ask Craig to fill a position.

When it comes to being able to take timely action, some controls are more timely than others. For example, experts distinguish between steering controls, yes/no controls, and post-action controls. With **steering controls**, corrective action is taken before the operation or project has been completed.[3] For example, the flight path of a spacecraft aimed at Mars is tracked continuously, since you would not want to find out after the fact that you missed your mark. Its trajectory is modified so that flight path corrections can be made days before the spacecraft is due to reach a target. In the same way, most managers set intermediate milestones so they can check progress long before a project is to be completed. If a problem is found, it can be corrected in time to save the project.

A **yes/no control** means work may not proceed until it passes an intermediate control step. For example, most companies have a rule forbidding employees from entering into contracts with suppliers or customers unless the agreements have been approved ahead of time by the firm's legal staff. Yes/no controls help to head off problems before they occur.

Post-action controls are ones in which results are compared to the standard after the project has been finished. Budgets are examples of post-action controls, as are the end of term grades students receive. The problem with post-action controls, as with grades, is that you usually can't do much to remedy the situation once the time period is over and the results are in. Most students therefore prefer finding out how they're doing during the semester. Similarly, with things changing so fast, Craig Miller doesn't want to find out after the fact that his plans were ill-conceived or his employees didn't follow through. Most managers try to build in the timeliness provided by steering controls, such as by monitoring weekly or monthly performance reports. This can help identify problems before they get out of hand.

Everything Managers Do Relates to Control

Since managing involves planning, organizing, leading, and controlling, one might easily get the impression that maintaining control is just something managers do after they're finished planning, organizing, and leading, but in fact nothing could be further from the truth. In fact, just about everything managers do that we've touched on relates to control. For example, controlling always requires that some desirable outcomes like targets, standards, or goals be set, so that the word *planning* is almost always used along with the word *control*. Similarly, "how to control" is often an underlying concern when decisions are made regarding how to *organize*. For example, self-contained autonomous divisions (like GM's Saturn division) can, due to their relative freedom, easily overspend and spin out of control unless their profits and other results are carefully monitored. And even the most sophisticated, computerized control system won't prevent unpleasant surprises if the company's

Managing @ the Speed of Thought
■ Controlling on Internet Time

As you can imagine, the Internet has improved managers' abilities to make timely mid-course corrections if they see activities trending out of control. Boeing's use of the Web is a good example. Boeing has an Internet-based network used by 1,000 other companies, including aluminum supplier Alcoa, Inc.[4] To gain access to this network, external users (including most of Boeing's suppliers and customers) receive "digital certificates" from Boeing, with passwords authorizing them to access the network.

The network allows both Boeing and its suppliers to maintain better, more timely control, "by reducing the number of misunderstandings with business partners and customers," according to Boeing's Web program manager. Access to the e-network means suppliers can continually get real-time updates regarding required delivery dates and schedule changes, and can make course corrections if these are required. And, since Boeing's e-commerce system is linked to tracking tools supplied by delivery services such as FedEx, customers can view the status of their orders at anytime over the Web. Delivery surprises are thus kept to a minimum.

Boeing's Internet-based system has improved the timeliness of the company's control system in many other ways. For example, employees can use the system to monitor production lines:"We use the Web to keep track of shortages on airplane production lines so that everyone in the whole organization can know where the hot spots are, not just management."[5]

The system even made it easier to control activities in more specific areas, such as training. For example, as soon as each instructor was required to publish his or her course lists on the Internet-based system, the training department realized different instructors were sometimes teaching the same thing. This allowed the training department to eliminate redundant courses and better control the costs of the courses the company makes available to its employees.

staffing—hiring people with the right skills and then giving them the training and orientation that they need—is not up to par.

Similarly, much of what managers do when they have their *leadership* hats on involves making sure that employees are doing and will do the things they're supposed to do. For instance, close supervision—literally monitoring each and every thing employees do—is certainly one way to accomplish that. However, today the sort of self-motivation that derives from empowering teams and putting them in charge is often the better alternative. Let's look more closely at how managers maintain control.

▶ TWO APPROACHES TO MAINTAINING CONTROL

What is the best way to stay in control? We'll see in this section that there are two basic options: **traditional** and **commitment-based control methods**. Let's look at each.

The Traditional Control Process

What's the first thing you think of when someone mentions the word *control*? Chances are, you think of somehow exerting influence to ensure that some person or group is doing what he or she is supposed to do. When most people think of control, in other words, they generally think of some kind of external process that's somehow used to keep a person's behavior in line. Whether you're controlling your neighbor down the block, or the sales team at your company, or the City of New York, control traditionally includes three steps:

1. Establishing a standard, goal, or target so that you know in advance what the results ought to be.

2. Using some type of external monitoring system (such as personal observation or a budget) to compare actual performance to that standard.

3. Taking corrective action, if necessary, to get the actual performance in line with what you planned.[6] Let's look at the three traditional steps in control in more detail.

Step 1: Establish a Standard   Standards can be expressed in terms of money, time, quantity, or quality (or a combination of these). Thus, a salesperson might get a dollar-based quota of $8,000 worth of products per month, or a production supervisor might be told to cut costs by $2,000 per week. Performance standards are also expressed in terms of time—a person might have to meet a certain sales quota in a week or complete a report by May 1.

Some standards are quantity based. For example, production supervisors are usually responsible for producing a specified number of units of product per week. Sometimes standards are qualitative, such as the reject rates in quality control, the grades of products sold (such as "grade A"), or the quality of a student's report.

Whatever the category—quantity, quality, timeliness, dollars—the usual procedure is to choose a specific yardstick and then set a standard, as shown in Figure 5-2. For quantity, yardsticks include units produced per shift and grievances filed per month.[7] Specific quantitative goals then might be set for each.

Step 2: Measure Actual Performance and Compare It to the Standard   The next step is to install a "control system" and then use it to measure actual performance or results.[8] Personal observation is the simplest and most common way of comparing

▶ F I G U R E   5 - 2

Examples of Control Standards

AREA TO CONTROL	POSSIBLE YARDSTICK	STANDARD/GOAL TO ACHIEVE
Quantity	Number of products produced	Produce 14 units per month
Quality	Number of rejects	No more than 10 rejects per day
Timeliness	Percentage of sales reports in on time	Return 90% of sales reports on time
Dollars	Percentage of deviation from budget	Do not exceed budgeted expenses by more than 5% during year

actual performance to standards: You keep monitoring subordinates to make sure things are being done right.

While nothing substitutes for the interactive give-and-take of this sort of personal supervision, it becomes increasingly difficult to monitor everyone personally as the manager assumes more responsibilities. One way to handle this is to add supervisors; for example, a hospital director might hire two assistant directors to observe employees on different floors. But in practice, personal control must at some point be supplemented by formal, more impersonal control systems. Budgetary and financial reports, quality control reports, and inventory control reports are three examples of traditional control systems used to measure and compare actual performance to standards.

Step 3: Take Corrective Action   Taking corrective action is essentially a problem-solving activity. In some instances the deviation—such as sales that are too low—can be easily explained. However, things are often not what they seem. Perhaps the sales target was too high, or your firm could not supply the products or couldn't supply them on time. The point is that a deviation from the standard merely flags a problem that may or may not require further analysis. You may then have to diagnose and solve the problem.

Commitment-Based Control

As companies expand worldwide and compete in fast-changing markets, the problems of relying on traditional controls like budgets have become increasingly apparent. Sears, Roebuck, and Company took a $60 million charge against earnings after it admitted that some of its service writers and mechanics recommended unnecessary automobile repairs to customers. Kidder, Peabody & Company lost $350 million when a trader allegedly reported fictitious profits.

Problems like these were not—and probably could not have been—anticipated with traditional controls. Particularly today, when markets change quickly and more employees are empowered, managers need a way to ensure that their employees won't let activities slip out of control, or that, if they do, the managers will discover it before catastrophe strikes. Harvard professor and control expert Robert Simons puts it this way:

A fundamental problem facing managers [today] is how to exercise adequate control in organizations that demand flexibility, innovation, and creativity. . . . In most organizations operating in dynamic and highly competitive markets, managers cannot spend all their time and effort making sure that everyone is doing what is expected. Nor is it realistic to think that managers can achieve control by simply hiring good people, aligning incentives, and hoping for the best. Instead, today's managers must encourage employees to initiate process improvements and new ways of responding to customers' needs—but in a controlled way.[9]

Companies are therefore increasingly relying on employees' commitment and self-control to keep things under control. One sign of this is the widespread use of self-managing teams, wherein employees are given the self-confidence, tools, training, and information they need to do their jobs as if they owned the firm. The idea here is that the best way to keep things on track is to get the employee to want to do so.

This leaves us with two basic ways to maintain control. While any classification scheme is bound to be somewhat arbitrary, we can conveniently distinguish (see Figure 5-3) between traditional control systems and commitment-based control systems:

■ Traditional control systems, as we've seen, are based on setting standards and then monitoring performance. These systems include three categories of controls: diagnostic controls, boundary systems and interactive controls.[10] **Diagnostic control systems** (such as budgets) allow managers to determine whether important targets have been met and, if necessary, to figure out why they haven't been. **Boundary control systems** are policies that identify the boundaries within which employees are to operate. Ethical rules against accepting gifts from suppliers are an example. **Interactive control systems** involve controlling employees interactively, by questioning them face to face.

■ Commitment-based control systems rely on getting the employees themselves to want to do things right—they emphasize self-control, in other words. For example, companies like Toyota and Saturn work hard to socialize all employees in the companies' belief systems and values, such as the importance of teamwork, quality, and respect for people, to foster self-control. The employees then, they hope, are more inclined to control their own actions. Other companies

▼ **FIGURE 5-3**   **Two Basic Categories of Control Systems**

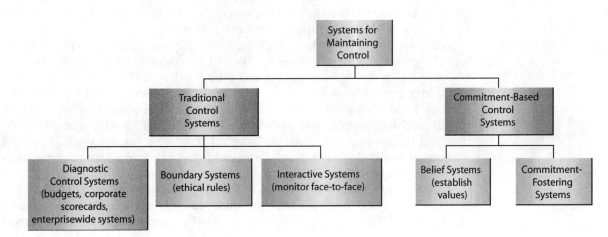

emphasize systems for building commitment to doing what is best for the company, and doing it right.

Let's look at these two types of systems in more detail.

►TRADITIONAL CONTROL SYSTEMS

We can start by exploring the three main types of traditional control systems: diagnostic control systems, boundary control systems, and interactive control systems.

Diagnostic-Control Systems

When most people think of controls, they think of *diagnostic control systems*. These aim to ensure that the firm's targets and goals are being met and that any discrepancies can be diagnosed and explained. Budgets and performance reports are examples. Semi-annual performance reviews are another.

Diagnostic controls reduce the need for managers to constantly monitor everything.[11] Once targets have been set, managers can (at least in theory) leave the employees to pursue the goals, supposedly secure in the knowledge that if the goals aren't met, the deviations will show up as variances that must be explained. This idea is at the heart of what managers call the principle of exception. The **principle of exception** (or management by exception) holds that to conserve managers' time, only significant deviations or exceptions from the standard, "both the especially good and bad exceptions," should be brought to the manager's attention.[12]

The Basic Management Control System   There are any number of things that a manager might want to control, ranging from employees' performance to the progress of a report. However, there's no doubt that in virtually every organization it's the financial aspects of how the company is doing that's the bottom line of what needs to be controlled. At the end of the day, it's usually whether the manager achieved his or her sales, expense, and profit targets that largely determines whether or not that person succeeded in the past year or not. The basic management control system is therefore usually financially based.

As a result, the management functions of planning and controlling are inseparable. Planning generally begins with formulating a strategic plan for the enterprise, including a strategy or course of action that explains how the enterprise will move from the business it's in now to the business it wants to be in. This provides an overall direction for the enterprise and creates a framework within which the rest of the planning process can take place.

Subsidiary, lower-level plans and a hierarchy of goals are then produced. At the top, the president and his or her staff might set strategic goals (such as to have 50% of sales revenue from customized products by 2001), to which each vice president's goal is then tied. A chain or hierarchy of supporting departmental goals and short-term operational goals can then be formulated. At each step in this hierarchical process, the goals and plans are almost always translated into financial targets and embodied in financial reports of various kinds. Financial statements and budgets comprise the heart of the basic management control system. Let's look more closely at these statements and budgets.

Budgets are formal financial expressions of a manager's plans. They show targets for things such as sales, cost of materials, production levels, and profit, usually expressed in dollars. These planned targets are the standards against which actual performance is compared and controlled. The first step in budgeting is generally to develop a sales forecast and sales budget. The **sales budget** shows the number of units to be shipped in each period (usually per month) or in general the sales activity to be achieved, and the revenue expected from the sales.

Various operating budgets can then be produced. **Operating budgets** show the expected sales and/or expenses for each of the company's departments for the planning period in question. For example, a **production and materials budget** or plan might show what the company plans to spend for materials, labor, administration, and so forth in order to fulfill the requirements of the sales budget.

For the organization as a whole, the data from all of these budgets or plans are generally compiled into a tentative profit plan for the coming year. This tentative profit plan is usually called the budgeted **income statement** or pro forma income statement. It shows expected sales, expected expenses, and expected income or profit for the year. In practice, cash from sales usually doesn't flow into the firm in such a way as to coincide precisely with cash disbursements. (Some customers may take 35 days to pay their bills, for instance, but employees expect to be paid every week). The **cash budget** or plan shows, for each month, the amount of cash the company can expect to receive and the amount it can expect to disperse. Any expected cash shortage can then be planned for, perhaps with a short-term loan.

There will also probably be a budgeted **balance sheet** for the company. This is a projected statement of the financial position of the firm; it shows assets (such as cash and equipment), liabilities (such as long-term debt), and net worth, (the excess of assets over other liabilities). The budgeted balance sheet shows managers, owners, and creditors what the company's projected financial picture should be at the end of the year.

Budgets are probably the most widely used control device. Each manager, from first-line supervisor to company president, usually has an operating budget to use as a standard of comparison. Remember, however, that creating the budget (as shown in Figure 5-4) is just the standard-setting step in the three-step control process. Actual performance still must be measured and compared to the budgeted standards and, if necessary, the problem diagnosed and corrective action taken.

The organization's accountants are responsible for collecting data on actual performance. They compile the financial information and feed it back to the appropriate managers. The most common form of feedback is a performance report, such as the one in Figure 5-5. The manager typically receives a report like this for his or her unit at the end of some time period (say, each month).

BUDGET FOR MACHINERY DEPARTMENT, JUNE 2000	
Budgeted Expenses	**Budget**
Direct Labor	$2,107
Supplies	$3,826
Repairs	$ 402
Overhead (electricity, etc.)	$ 500
TOTAL EXPENSES	$6,835

◀ **FIGURE 5-4**
Example of a Budget

► **FIGURE 5 - 5**

Example of a Performance Report

PERFORMANCE REPORT FOR MACHINERY DEPARTMENT, JUNE 2000

	Budget	Actual	Variance	Explanation
Direct Labor	$2,107	$2,480	$373 over	Had to put workers on overtime.
Supplies	$3,826	$4,200	$374 over	Wasted two crates of material.
Repairs	$ 402	$ 150	$252 under	
Overhead (electricity, etc.)	$ 500	$ 500	0	
TOTAL	$6,835	$7,330	$495 over	

As in Figure 5-5, the performance report shows budgeted or planned targets. Next to these numbers, it shows the department's actual performance. The report also lists the differences between budgeted and actual amounts; these are usually called **variances**. A space is sometimes provided for the manager to explain any variances. After reviewing the performance report, the manager can take corrective action. The firm's accountants will also conduct an audit of the firm's financial statements and financial results. An **audit** is a systematic process of objectively obtaining and evaluating evidence regarding important aspects of the firm's performance, judging the accuracy and validity of the data, and communicating the results to interested users such as the board of directors and the company's banks.[13] The purpose of the audit is to make sure the firm's financial statements accurately reflect its performance.

Ratio Analysis and Return on Investment   Most managers and accountants maintain control in part by monitoring various **financial ratios**, which compare one financial indicator on a financial statement to another. The rate of return on investment (ROI) is one such ratio: It is a measure of overall company performance and equals net profit divided by total investment. Return on investment measures net profit not as an absolute figure, but rather in relation to the total investment in the business. A $1 million profit, for example, would be more impressive in a business with a $10 million investment than in one with a $100 million investment. Figure 5-6 presents some commonly used financial ratios.

Figure 5-7 shows how financial ratios can be used to analyze a firm's performance. For example, a missed net income target may be due to low sales or high sales costs. Similarly, earnings divided by sales (the profit margin) reflects management's success or failure in maintaining satisfactory cost controls. As another example, a low ROI can be influenced by factors like excessive investment. In turn, excessive investment might reflect inadequate inventory control, accounts receivable, or cash.[14]

Financial Responsibility Centers   Particularly in larger departments, the managers' operating budgets usually reflect the fact that the managers are in charge of financial responsibility centers. **Financial responsibility centers** are individuals or units who are responsible for and measured based on a specific set of financial activities. For example, **profit centers** are responsibility centers whose managers are held accountable for profit, which is a measure of the difference between the revenues generated and the cost of generating those revenues.[15] The Saturn division of General Motors is a profit center and the performance of the person managing that division is controlled in large part in terms of whether or not he or she meets the division's profit goals. **Revenue**

NAME OF RATIO	FORMULA	INDUSTRY NORM (AS ILLUSTRATION)
1. Liquidity Ratios (measuring the ability of the firm to meet its short-term obligations)		
Current ratio	$\dfrac{\text{Current assets}}{\text{Current liabilities}}$	2.6
Acid-test ratio	$\dfrac{\text{Cash and equivalent}}{\text{Current liability}}$	1.0
Cash velocity	$\dfrac{\text{Sales}}{\text{Cash and equivalent}}$	12 times
Inventory to net working capital	$\dfrac{\text{Inventory}}{\text{Current assets} - \text{Current liabilities}}$	85%
2. Leverage Ratios (measures the contributions of financing by owners compared with financing provided by creditors)		
Debt to equity	$\dfrac{\text{Total debt}}{\text{Net worth}}$	56%
Coverage of fixed charges	$\dfrac{\text{Net profit before fixed charges}}{\text{Fixed charges}}$	6 times
Current liability to net worth	$\dfrac{\text{Current liability}}{\text{Net worth}}$	32%
Fixed assets to net worth	$\dfrac{\text{Fixed assets}}{\text{Net worth}}$	60%
3. Activities Ratios (measures the effectiveness of the employment of resources)		
Inventory turnover	$\dfrac{\text{Sales}}{\text{Inventory}}$	7 times
Net working capital turnover	$\dfrac{\text{Sales}}{\text{Net working capital}}$	5 times
Fixed-assets turnover	$\dfrac{\text{Sales}}{\text{Fixed assets}}$	6 times
Average collection period	$\dfrac{\text{Receivables}}{\text{Average sales per day}}$	20 days
Equity capital turnover	$\dfrac{\text{Sales}}{\text{Net worth}}$	3 times
Total capital turnover	$\dfrac{\text{Sales}}{\text{Total assets}}$	2 times
4. Profitability Ratios (indicates degree of success in achieving desired profit levels)		
Gross operating margin	$\dfrac{\text{Gross operating profit}}{\text{Sales}}$	30%
Net operating margin	$\dfrac{\text{Net operating profit}}{\text{Sales}}$	6.5%
Sales (profit) margin	$\dfrac{\text{Net profit after taxes}}{\text{Sales}}$	3.2%
Productivity of assets	$\dfrac{\text{Gross income less taxes}}{\text{Total assets}}$	10%
Return on investment	$\dfrac{\text{Net profit after taxes}}{\text{Total investment}}$	7.5%
Net profit on working capital	$\dfrac{\text{Net operating profit}}{\text{Net working capital}}$	14.5%

▶ **FIGURE 5-7**

Relationship of Factors Affecting Return on Investment

The firm's overall profitability—its return on total investments—can be better understood by analyzing its components, including earnings as a percentage of sales and turnover.

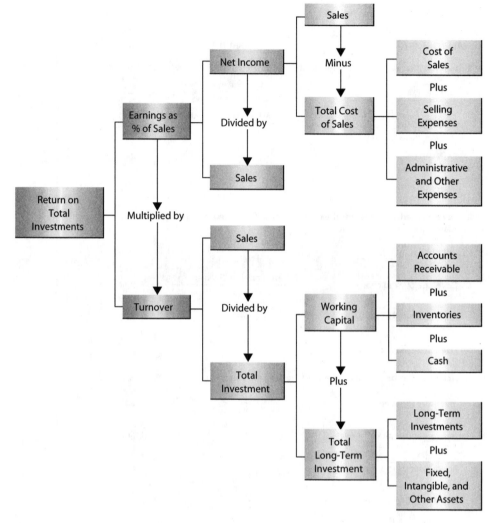

centers are responsibility centers whose managers are held accountable for generating revenues, which is a financial measure of output. Sales managers are generally measured in terms of the sales produced by their revenue center/ departments.

The Corporate Scorecard   Today, more and more companies are experimenting with a diagnostic control tool called a **corporate scorecard**. Its basic purpose is to provide managers with an overall impression of how their companies are doing.[16]

Corporate scorecards are basically computerized models. Like other traditional diagnostic control tools, they measure how the company has been doing and help managers diagnose exactly what (if anything) has gone wrong. However, they differ from their simpler control cousins, such as budgets, in several ways. First, they mathematically trace a multitude of performance measures simultaneously, and show the relationships between these various measures.

Managing @ the Speed of Thought
■ Using Technology to Stay in Control at UPS

UPS is the world's largest air and ground package distribution company, delivering close to three billion parcels and documents each year in the United States and more than 185 other countries. Critical to its success has been the $1.8 billion UPS invested in the mid 1990s in information technology. Each UPS driver uses a hand-held computer called a Delivery Information Acquisition Device (pictured below) to capture customers' signatures along with pick-up, delivery, and time card information and automatically transmit this information to headquarters via a cellular telephone network.

Through TotalTrack, its automated package-tracking system, UPS can control packages throughout the delivery process. And with its own global communication network called UPSnet, UPS not only tracks its packages, but electronically transmits documentation on each shipment directly to customs officials prior to arrival. Shipments are therefore either cleared for shipment or flagged for inspection when they arrive.

Today, UPS uses the Internet to help it and its customers monitor and control the progress of all those millions and millions of packages. For example, the UPS Internet-based tracking system lets a customer store up to 25 tracking numbers and then monitor the progress of each package. That not only lets the customer (and UPS) keep on top of each package's progress, but it is also a "value added" feature for the customer, which can easily keep its customers informed about the progress of the ultimate customer's package.

The manager therefore generally gets several measures of overall performance, rather than just one or two. At Shell Oil, for instance, the Shell Business Model (as Shell's scorecard is called) shows revenue growth, overall company market value, rate of return compared to the cost of borrowing money, and rate of return of the firm as a whole.

Like the dials on your car's dashboard, corporate scorecards help managers better analyze and control what's happening in their companies. For example, before using the Shell Business Model, Shell's managers didn't understand the mathematical link between revenue growth and shareholder value (especially stock price). As a result, they wouldn't try to rush a new oil rig into operation, since fast growth was not so important to them. With the new scorecard model, they could see that faster growth translates into higher shareholder value, so they're more anxious to get those oil rigs on-line fast.

Enterprise Resource Planning Systems Corporate scorecards are actually components of larger control systems known as **enterprise resource planning systems**. Systems like these are produced by companies like SAP of Germany, Oracle, and PeopleSoft. They are basically companywide integrated computer systems that integrate a firm's individual control systems (such as order processing, production control, and accounting) in order to give managers real-time, instantaneous information regarding the costs and status of every activity and project in the business.[17]

Using one of these products, for example, the check-printing company Deluxe Paper Payment Systems was able to "get a clearer picture of which of its customers were profitable and which were not."[18] When it discovered how much more profitable an order from a bank for checks could be when it came via electronic ordering, the company launched a campaign to increase electronic ordering—particularly by its 18,000 bank and small-business customers.

As a result, the number of checks ordered electronically jumped from 48% to 62% in just a few months, dramatically improving profits at Deluxe. The box below shows another example.

With results like that, some glowingly refer to enterprise software as "the stuff that puts the information age to work for corporations.[19] By integrating all the company's various control systems, "managers will now be able to receive daily online reports about the costs of specific business processes, for example, and on the real-time profitability of individual products and customers."[20]

Entrepreneurs in Action

Using Enterprise Software to Get in Control

■ While enterprise software systems can be very expensive—one Fortune 500 company reportedly spent $30 million in license fees and $200 million in consulting fees to install one—smaller firms are increasingly using them, too.[21] For example, thanks to its new enterprise software system, "three people at Harman Music Group that once worked nearly full-time planning what products to make at its factory [have been replaced by] two people who do that work part time each week."[22]

According to Harman's director of operations, Matthew Bush, the stacks of reports (including production schedules, orders, and inventory reports) that he used to analyze each day to begin developing his production plans now come right off his personal computer:"I just call it up and, in a matter of seconds, there it is."

Harman hired Hewlett-Packard to install its new software, and Hewlett-Packard assigned a five-person full-time team to the project. The team began by developing a blueprint of how Harman music operates by interviewing employees

and by mapping out exactly how information (such as a new order) went from one activity to another, and analyzing which managers needed what kind of information.

The team made some interesting discoveries along the way. For example, they discovered that three people at Harman spent part of their workday literally "taking out the trash," getting rid of scrap and obsolete inventory. When it became obvious how expensive that basically unproductive activity was, the process was streamlined.

There were other discoveries, and many other benefits. For example, while the company reportedly always knew how many units of a model it planned to build in any given week, and how many were in stock and how many were ordered, "there was a lot of guesswork" in matching all that information. The new enterprise system updates the forecast whenever the company gets an order. It also automatically updates production plans, while providing Harman's managers with a real-time estimate of the profitability of each of its products. Now that's control!

On September 30, 1999, SAP launched a new Web site called mysap.com. Companies can use the site to download SAP software components, as well as to link with other companies using SAP—for instance, to link their sales and inventory systems—and interact more seamlessly with them.[23]

Boundary Control Systems

Boundary control systems are a second traditional category of ways to maintain control. They "establish the rules of the game and identify actions and pitfalls that employees must avoid."[24] In other words, they set the boundaries within which employees should operate. Examples include standards of ethical behavior and the codes of conduct to which employees are told to adhere.

Johnson & Johnson's credo illustrates the heart of a boundary control system. It contains fundamental ethical guidelines (such as, "We believe our first responsibility is to the doctors, nurses, and patients . . . who use our products" and "Our suppliers and distributors must have an opportunity to make a fair profit"). These are supposed to provide the boundaries within which Johnson & Johnson employees are to keep. Selling a product that might be harmful, for example, would obviously be out of bounds. This helps explain why when several bottles of poisoned Tylenol were found some years back, Johnson & Johnson decided to recall the entire stock of the product.

Ethical or boundary control systems require more than just drawing up a list of guidelines. For instance, we emphasized that fostering ethics at work involves at least five steps.

1. Emphasize top management's commitment.

2. Publish a code.

3. Establish compliance mechanisms.

4. Involve personnel at all levels.

5. Measure results.

Boundary control systems are important for any company, but they're especially important for firms that depend on trust.[25] Large consulting firms like McKinsey & Company and the Boston Consulting Group must be able to assure clients that the highly proprietary strategic data they'll see will never be compromised. They must therefore enforce strict rules "that forbid consultants to reveal information—even the names of clients—to anyone not employed by the firm, including spouses."[26]

The boundaries a firm lays down are not limited to ethical guidelines: "Strategic boundaries focus on ensuring that people steer clear of opportunities that could diminish the business's competitive position."[27] Thus managers at Automatic Data Processing (ADP) use a strategic boundary list that lays out the types of business opportunities ADP managers should avoid. Another company, a large Netherlands-based multinational, has a strategic policy of discouraging its executives from forming joint ventures with firms in the United States because of the greater possibility of litigation in U.S. courts. The basic idea of such rules and policies is to delineate and control the boundaries within which employees should stay.

Interactive Control Systems

The typical small, entrepreneurial company has at least one big control advantage over its huge multinational competitors: Mom and Pop can talk face to face with almost everyone in the firm to find out immediately how everything is going. Indeed, such face-to-face interaction is at the heart of how most smaller companies traditionally maintain control. It is perhaps the most basic traditional way to stay in control.

Of course, as companies grow, this kind of direct interaction becomes more difficult. However, most firms still use these controls. Interactive strategic control is one example. It is a real-time, usually face-to-face method of monitoring both a strategy's effectiveness and the underlying assumptions on which the strategy is built.[28]

Senior managers at *USA Today* use interactive control.[29] Three weekly reports delivered each Friday give senior managers an overview of how they have done in the previous week and what they may expect in the next few weeks. This "Friday packet" includes information ranging from year-to-date advertising and sales figures to specific information regarding particular advertisers.

Weekly face-to-face meetings among senior managers and key subordinates are part of interactive control at *USA Today*. Regular meeting topics include advertising volume compared to plan, and new business by type of client. Senior managers don't just look for unexpected shortfalls; they also look for unexpected successes that might suggest putting more emphasis on particular areas, such as approaching more software suppliers to advertise. Several strategic innovations have emerged from these meetings. Among them are exclusive advertising inserts dedicated to specific customers and products, and a new market-survey service for automotive clients.

How does information like this help *USA Today*'s senior managers? It helps them to look at the big picture regarding how the paper is doing versus its competitors. And it helps them identify trends, such as decreasing or increasing advertising expenditures by specific advertisers, or changing sales patterns in various states. At *USA Today*, interactive controls give senior managers a formal procedure through which they can monitor strategic information and get a feel for the importance of that information by interacting face to face with key subordinates.

▶ HOW DO PEOPLE REACT TO CONTROL?

Every organization has to ensure that its employees are performing as planned. Every day managers face questions like "How can I make sure that Marie files her sales reports on time?" and "How can I make sure John doesn't close the store before 10:00 P.M.?" To a large extent, the answer to both questions is to impose controls. Unfortunately, relying on controls is not as easy as it may seem.

The Negative Side of Control

If controlling employees' behavior were the only (or the best) way to ensure effective performance, we could disregard much of this text. For example, we wouldn't need to know much about what motivates people, what leadership style is best, or how to win employee commitment. We could just "control" employees' work.

But the fact is that managers can't just rely on controls for keeping employees in line. For one thing, from a practical point of view, it's impossible to have a system of rules and controls so complete that you can track everything employees say or do, even with enterprise software. For another, employees often short-circuit the controls, sometimes with ingenious techniques. Let's look more closely at this second problem.

Some Unintended Behavioral Consequences of Controls

How can employees evade controls? One expert classifies these employee tactics as behavioral displacement, gamesmanship, operating delays, and negative attitudes.[30]

Behavioral Displacement   **Behavioral displacement** occurs when the behaviors encouraged by the controls are inconsistent with what the company actually wants to accomplish. "You get what you measure," in other words. Employees focus their efforts where results are measured and disregard the company's more important goals.

The problem stems mostly from limiting the measures to just one or two control standards. For example, Nordstrom, a retailer famed for its extraordinary customer service, found itself involved in a lawsuit related to its policy of measuring employees in terms of sales per hour of performance.[31] Unfortunately, tracking its salespeople's performance by simply monitoring sales per hour backfired. Without other measures, the sales-per-hour system didn't work. Some employees claimed their supervisors were pressuring them to underreport hours on the job to boost reported sales per hour. Nordstrom ended up settling the claims for over $15 million.

Gamesmanship **Gamesmanship** refers to management actions aimed at improving the manager's performance in terms of the control system, without producing any economic benefits for the firm. For example, one manager depleted his stocks of spare parts and heating oil at year's end, although he knew these stocks would have to be replenished shortly thereafter at higher prices. By reducing his stocks, the manager reduced his expenses for the year and made his end-of-year results look better, although in the long run the company spent more than it had to.[32] In another example, a division overshipped products to distributors at year-end. The aim was to ensure that management could meet its budgeted sales targets, even though the managers knew the products would be returned.[33]

Operating Delays Operating delays are another unintended consequence of control, and they are especially dangerous when quick, responsive decisions are required. When he became CEO of GE, for instance, Jack Welch knew that it sometimes took a year or more for division managers to get approval to introduce new products; the problem was the long list of approvals required by GE's control system. Flattening the organization and streamlining the approval process are two ways to solve this problem.

Negative Attitudes In addition to displacement, gamesmanship, and operating delays, controls can have more insidious effects by undermining employee attitudes. One study that focused on first-line supervisors' reactions to budgets found that the budgets were viewed as pressure devices. Supervisors came to see them as prods by top management and in turn used them to prod their own subordinates. As a result of this pressure, employees formed antimanagement work groups, and the supervisors reacted by increasing their compliance efforts.[34]

"Intelligent" employee ID badges provide a more high-tech example. Italy's Olivetti holds the basic patent on the Active-Badge System and began marketing it commercially in the early 1990s. The Active Badge looks like a clip-on ID card. It's actually a small computer that emits infrared signals to strategically located sensors, which can then track the wearer anywhere within an equipped facility. The system can also keep tabs on visitors. Knowing where people are avoids interruptions, wasted phone calls, and useless trips to empty offices. But questions arise: How much privacy can managers expect employees to surrender in the name of control? How much control is too much? And what effect will these badges have on morale? Proponents say effective safeguards can be implemented. Critics fear that once such a system is in place, there will be no defense against abuse.[35] Let's look more closely at this.

► USING COMMITMENT-BASED CONTROL SYSTEMS

This all presents an interesting dilemma for those managing today's organizations. For one thing, globalized and team-based organizations complicate the task of keeping everything under control: Distance makes monitoring what your employees are doing day-to-day much more difficult, especially since there's a tendency to try to evade the control system. A second problem is that imposing too much control on self-managing teams may well backfire: How can you feel empowered if someone else is controlling everything you do?

How then do today's managers ensure that everyone does what they're supposed to do and that things stay under control? Increasingly, the answer is by supplementing traditional controls with systems that encourage employees to exercise self-control. The idea here is that employees are then driven to do what they're supposed to do not because they have to, but because they want to. As management guru Tom Peters once put it:

> You are out of control when you are "in control." You are in control when you are "out of control." [The executive] who knows everything and who is surrounded by layers of staffers and inundated with thousands of pages of analyses from below may be "in control" in the classic sense but in fact really only has the illusion of control. The manager has tons of after-the-fact reports on everything, but (almost) invariably a control system and organization that's

The People Side of Managing

■ Electronic Performance Monitoring and Control

When it comes to monitoring employees electronically, computerized badges are the tip of the iceberg. As two researchers recently put it: "As many as 26 million workers in the United States are subject to electronic performance monitoring (EPM)—such as having supervisors monitor through electronic means the amount of computerized data an employee is processing per day—on the job."[36]

Jeffrey Stanton and Janet Barnes-Farrell studied the effects of such monitoring on individuals working on computers in an officelike environment.[37] The 108 participants were recruited from introductory psychology classes. The researchers wanted to study several things: one was whether a worker's feelings of personal control were affected by having the ability to lock out the performance monitoring; another was whether informing the person he or she was being monitored affected performance.

The results show why it's important for employees to believe they have some personal control over their environments. "Participants with the ability to delay or prevent electronic performance monitoring indicated higher feelings of personal control and demonstrated superior task performance."[38] The findings also suggest that if you *are* going to monitor employees' performance electronically, it's probably best not to let them know when they're actually being monitored. Participants who knew exactly when they were being monitored expressed lower feelings of personal control than did those who were not told when they were being monitored.

By the way, don't assume that electronic performance monitoring will apply only to subordinates and not to bosses. For example, the Japanese company that controls 7-Eleven is gradually trying to impose an EPM system on its store managers in Japan and in the United States. Like all 7-Eleven stores, the ones belonging to Michiharu Endo use a point-of-sale computer to let headquarters know each time he makes a sale. In the case of 7-Eleven's new system, headquarters monitors how much time Endo spends using the analytical tools built into the computerized cash register to track product sales, and how effective he is at weaning out poor sellers. Headquarters then ranks stores by how often their operators use the computer as a measure of how efficient they are.

The system has run into particular resistance in the United States. Many 7-Eleven managers, thinking they escaped the bureaucratic ratrace by taking over their own stores, have been surprised at the degree of control this new EPM system has exposed them to.[39]

so ponderous that it's virtually impossible to respond fast enough even if a deviation is finally detected. . . .

In fact, you really are in control when thousands upon thousands of people, unbeknownst to you, are taking initiatives, going beyond job descriptions and the constraints of their box on the organization chart, to serve the customer better, improve the process, [or] work quickly with a supplier to nullify a defect.[40]

There are at least three approaches managers can use to encourage self-control and employee commitment: motivation techniques, belief systems, and commitment-building systems. Obviously, highly motivated employees are generally more likely to do their jobs right. In the remainder of this section, we'll look at how managers use *belief systems* and *commitment-building systems* to encourage and foster employee self-control.

Using Belief Systems and Values to Foster Self-Control

We've seen at several points in this text that a person's behavior tends to be a function of his or her values and beliefs. For example, if one of your values is "always do your best at everything you do, and never do more than you can do well," you'll probably do a better job than someone who takes a more flippant approach to the quality of his or her work. Since values can have a powerful influence on controlling one's behavior, managers often try to instill the right values in their employees.

This helps to explain why companies work hard to create a belief system—a culture—that is consistent with what the company wants to achieve. At the Toyota Manufacturing plant in Lexington, Kentucky, for instance, quality and teamwork are crucial to everything the facility wants to do. Its managers therefore steep their employees in the culture and values of quality and teamwork. They do this by selecting new employees based on the extent to which they evidence such traits, and then by emphasizing quality and teamwork in orientation, training, and appraisal and incentive systems. To a large extent, in other words, the superior quality and high productivity that characterizes Toyota's Lexington facility is a result not of technology (since all auto plants have similar machines), but of the employees' dedication to a handful of core values that drive their behavior.

It's hard to overestimate how important shared values like these can be in managing far-flung global operations. Shared values like Wal-Mart's "hard work, honesty, neighborliness, and thrift" provide it's employees with a common ideology or way of looking at the world. They give Wal-Mart's employees a sort of built-in compass, one that gives them the direction and sense of purpose that's required to do the job right, no matter how far from headquarters they are, and without a rulebook or supervisor to watch their every move.

In a study of successful and long-lived companies, James Collins and Jerry Porras made similar observations. In their book *Built to Last*, they describe how firms like Boeing, Disney, GE, Merck, and Motorola put enormous effort into creating shared values, values that answer questions such as "What are we trying to achieve together?" and "What does this organization stand for?"[41] As they say,

More than at any time in the past companies will not be able to hold themselves together with the traditional methods of control: hierarchy, systems, budgets, and the like. Even "going into the office" will become less relevant as technology enables people to work from remote sites. The bonding glue will increasingly become *ideological*.[42]

In explaining why shared values are so important for managing today, Collins and Porras emphasize that a strong set of shared values "allows for coordination without control, adaptation without chaos."[43] In other words, employees who buy into the company's values don't need to be coaxed, prodded, or controlled into doing the right thing: They'll do the right thing because they believe it's the right thing to do. They'll control themselves.

This helps to explain why organizational change efforts often put a premium on achieving cultural change. When Louis Gerstner took over as IBM's CEO, he knew that reorganizing and instituting a new strategy wouldn't be enough to transform his giant company into a highly responsive and efficient competitor. In many parts of the company, more lethargic values had taken root: these emphasized, for instance, seniority rather than performance; waiting for approvals rather than acting; and sticking to the chain of command. It took several years of Gerstner leading by example, instituting new systems (such as performance-based pay), and evangalizing about the firm's new values before IBM's new culture could emerge.

Today, at IBM as at many other change-oriented companies, the values that tend to be cherished include beliefs in teamwork, openness, candor, trust, and being number one. To the extent that employees share these values, the task of controlling what employees do becomes easier: Again, for example, assemblers at Toyota's Camry plant in Lexington, Kentucky, build quality into their cars not because they're being supervised or told to do so, but because they're driven to do so by their own deep-seated beliefs.

Using Commitment-Building Systems to Foster Self-Control

Fostering the right values is one way to encourage self-control; building employees' commitment is another.

Viacom several years ago reached agreement to sell its Prentice Hall publishing operations to Pearson PLC, for $4.6 billion. In announcing the sale, Prentice Hall's president thanked its employees for their past hard work and dedication, and reminded them that during the transition, "It's more important than ever to focus on our individual responsibilities to ensure that our company performs at the highest levels."[44] His message spotlights a dilemma all managers have today: maintaining employee **commitment**—an employee's identification with and agreement to pursue the company's or the unit's mission—in the face of downsizings, mergers, and turbulent change.[45] In other words, how do you get your employees to exercise self-control and do their jobs as if they own the company at a time when loyalty seems to be going out of style?

Over the past 30 years or so, we've learned quite a bit about how to earn employee commitment. The evidence suggests that doing so requires a comprehensive, multifaceted management system, one that draws on all the managers' planning, organizing, leading, and controlling skills, and one consisting of an integrated package of concrete managerial actions. These actions would include the following: foster people-first values, guarantee organizational justice, build a sense of community, communicate your vision, use value-based hiring, plus financial rewards, and encourage personal development and self-actualization.

Foster People-First Values Building employee commitment usually starts by establishing a strong foundation of "people-first values." Firms that hold to these values literally put their people first: They trust their employees, assume their employees are their most important assets, believe strongly in respecting their employees as individuals and treating them fairly, and maintain a relentless commitment to each employee's welfare. As one United Auto Workers (UAW) officer at Saturn Corporation's Spring Hill, Tennessee, plant put it:

> Our philosophy is, we care about people—and it shows. We involve people in decisions that affect them. I came from the Messina, New York, GM foundry, and managers there, like a lot of the other managers you'll come across, take the position that "I'll tell you what to do, and that's what you'll do." In fact, some of those managers from the foundry are here now. But on the whole those who are here now are different, and the basic difference is wrapped up in the question "Do you really believe in people?" Saturn's commitment really comes down to how you feel about people—your attitudes—more than anything, because all the other Saturn programs—the work teams, the extensive training, the way people are paid—all stem from these people attitudes.[46]

One way firms like Saturn foster such people-first values is by emphasizing them in all their communications to employees. For example, all Saturn employees carry a card that lists the firm's values, one of which is:

> Trust and respect for the individual: We have nothing of greater value than our people. We believe that demonstrating respect for the uniqueness of every individual builds a team of confident, creative members possessing a high degree of initiative, self-respect, and self-discipline.[47]

The UAW officer's comment that "commitment really comes down to how you feel about people" underscores another way in which people-first values are institutionalized throughout these firms: They hire managers who already have people-first values, and then promote them in part based on their people skills. In fact, it's almost impossible for antisocial people to move into management at such firms—or to stay. People-first values permeate everything these managers say and do. The idea that these values should be applied to every one of its decisions was summed up by one officer at JC Penney this way:

> Our people's high commitment stems from our commitment to them, and that commitment boils down to the fundamental respect for the individual that we all share. That respect goes back to the Penney idea—"To test every act in this wise: Does it square with what is right and just?" As a result, the value of respect for the individual is brought into our management process on a regular basis and is a standard against which we measure each and every decision that we make.[48]

Guarantee Organizational Justice   Commitment is built on trust, and trust requires being treated fairly. Managers in firms like Saturn, FedEx, and GE do more than express a willingness to hear and be heard. They also establish programs that guarantee employees will be treated fairly. These programs include: guaranteed fair treatment programs for filing grievances and complaints; "speak up" programs for voicing concerns and making inquiries; periodic survey programs for expressing opinions; and various top-down programs for keeping employees informed.

Build a Sense of Shared Fate and Community   High-commitment firms also work hard to encourage a sense of community and shared fate, a sense that "we're all in this together." They do so by pursuing what Rosabeth Moss Kanter calls commonality, communal work, and regular work contact and ritual.[49]

For one thing, they try to minimize status differences. In many new Internet firms, for instance, all managers and employees share one large space, perhaps (as at Sears) with some movable cubicles. Other employers have eliminated status differences like executive washrooms and executive parking spaces; these too are usually efforts at building a sense of community.

Managers further emphasize this sense of community by encouraging joint effort and communal work. At Saturn new employees are quickly steeped in the terminology and techniques of teamwork: There are no employees in the plant, only team members working together on their communal tasks (like installing all dashboard components). Team training starts with the employee's initial orientation, as new members meet their teams and are trained in the interpersonal techniques that make for good teamwork. The resulting closeness is then enhanced by empowering work teams to recruit and select their own new members. Periodic job rotation reinforces the sense that everyone is sharing all the work.

Kanter found that the feeling of "we're all in this together" is further enhanced by bringing individual employees into regular contact with the group as a whole.[50] Ben & Jerry's hosts monthly staff meetings in the receiving bay of its Waterbury, Vermont, plant. It also has a "joy gang," whose function is to organize regular "joy events," including Cajun parties, ping-pong contests, and manufacturing appreciation day.

Thanks to the Internet, employees don't necessarily have to be at the same location to cultivate the feeling that they're part of a close-knit community. Using Internet-based group communication systems such as Tribal Voice, companies can build virtual communities by letting teams of employees communicate easily and in real-time, even if they are dispersed around the globe.[51] As one expert puts it, "The sales department could hold forums and share information in an interactive community." Said another, "When people interact in a virtual community, there is an exchange of ideas and information, which becomes powerful and generates excitement."[52]

Communicate Your Vision Committed employees need missions and visions to which to be committed, preferably missions and visions that they can say "are bigger than we are." With such missions to commit to, workers at firms like Saturn and Ben & Jerry's become almost soldiers in a crusade, one that allows them to redefine themselves in terms of the mission. In that way, says Kanter, the employee can "find himself anew in something larger and greater."[53] Employee commitment in high-commitment firms thus derives in part from the power of the firm's mission and from the willingness of the employees to acquiesce, if need be, to the needs of the firm for the good of achieving its mission.

Ben & Jerry's is an example. The company's mission still symbolizes its founders' idea of what a business should be and provides the firm and its employees with an ideology that represents a higher calling to which they can commit themselves. The mission is presented in Figure 5-8. Ben & Jerry's employees don't just make ice cream, in other words: They are out to change the world.

Use Value-Based Hiring Many firms today also practice **value-based hiring**. Instead of just looking for job-related skills, they try to get a sense of the applicant's personal values. To do this, they look for common experiences and values that may signal the applicant's fit with the firm and give applicants realistic previews of what to expect when they come to work there. At UPS and Delta Airlines, for instance, you must be ready to start at the bottom. At UPS, you may have a new college degree, but chances are you'll start working on a delivery truck. At Delta you may

Ben & Jerry's mission consists of three interrelated parts:
Product Mission: Making, selling, and distributing the best all-natural ice cream and related products in a wide variety of innovative flavors made from Vermont dairy products.
Social Mission: Operating the company in a way that actively recognizes the central role that business plays in the structure of a society by initiating new ways to improve the quality of life of the broad community, including local, national, and international.
Economic Mission: Operating the company on a sound financial basis of profitable growth, increasing value for our shareholders and creating career opportunities and financial rewards for our employees.

◀ **FIGURE 5-8**

Some Elements of Ben & Jerry's Mission

Ben & Jerry's mission is "charismatic" in that it links employees' actions with the transcendent goal of helping humankind.
Source: Adapted from Ben & Jerry's Homemade, Inc., *Employee Handbook.*

well start cleaning planes. That may seem onerous to some, but it does help sift out people who may not fit with those firms' ways of doing things. The idea is that if you don't fit in, you probably won't become committed to the company.

Use Financial Rewards and Profit Sharing   You may not be able to buy commitment, but most firms don't try to build commitment without good financial rewards. Intrinsic motivators like work involvement, a sense of achievement, and the feeling of oneness are usually not enough. To paraphrase psychologist Abraham Maslow, you can't appeal to someone's need to achieve until you've filled his or her belly and made the person secure. That is why Kanter says "Entrepreneurial incentives that give teams a piece of the action are highly appropriate in collaborative companies."[54] Firms like these generally provide above-average pay and incentives. FedEx, for instance, provides a half-dozen types of incentive awards, including "Bravo-Zulu," that a manager can award on the spot.

Encourage Employee Development and Self-Actualization   Few needs are as strong as the need to fulfill our dreams, to become all we are capable of being. We discussed Maslow's theory that "the desire to become more and more what one is, to become everything that one is capable of becoming" is the ultimate need. Self-actualization, to Maslow, means that "what man can be, he *must* be . . . it refers to the desire for self-fulfillment, namely, to this tendency for him to become actualized in what he is potentially.[55]

At work, promotions are important. But the real question is whether employees get the opportunity to develop and use all their skills and become, as Maslow would say, all they can be. Training employees to expand their skills and to solve problems, enriching their jobs, empowering employees to plan and inspect their own work, and helping them to continue their education and to grow are some other ways to accomplish employee self-actualization, as we've seen in earlier sections.

Having the company explicitly commit to the goal of helping workers to self-actualize is an important part of the process. Here's what one Saturn assembler said:

I'm committed to Saturn in part for what they did for me; for the 300 hours of training in problem solving and leadership that help me expand my personal horizons; for the firm's Excel program that helps me push myself to the limit; and because I know that at Saturn I can go as far as I can go—this company wants its people to be all that they can be. But I'm also committed to Saturn for what I saw where I came from: the burned out workers, the people who were so pressed down by the system that even if they saw their machines were about to break from poor maintenance, they'd say, "Leave it alone. Let management handle it." This is like a different world.[56]

Similarly, one FedEx manager described his firm's commitment to actualizing employees as follows:

At Federal Express, the best I can be is what I can be here. I have been allowed to grow with Federal Express. For the people at Federal Express, it's not the money that draws us to the firm. The biggest benefit is that Federal Express made me a man. It gave me the confidence and self-esteem to become the person I had the potential to become.[57]

Summary: How Do You Foster Employees' Self-Control?

In today's globalized, quality-conscious, and teamwork-based world, managers can't rely on traditional control systems to ensure that results are up to par. Financial statements, budgets, and profit centers—all those elements of traditional control systems—only go so far. They can't easily monitor what a young trader is buying and selling in Asia (as Barings discovered to its chagrin). And they can't ensure the kind of continuous attention to detail and initiative that producing high-quality Camry cars or a new Windows application requires of the teams that are working on these projects. Today, you have to supplement traditional control systems with employee self-control. You have to make the workers want to do their jobs as if they own the company.

We've looked at several ways to do this. Motivation techniques can certainly help, since motivated employees can usually be expected to perform better. Fostering the right culture of shared values can be useful too. What people do tends to reflect what they believe, and if employees believe, for instance, in doing high-quality work, then their performance will more likely reflect such values.

Finally, we've seen on the last few pages that fostering commitment is another powerful way to encourage employee self-control. Committed employees, by definition, identify with and agree to pursue the company's or the unit's mission. They exercise self-control because, in a very real sense, their companies' missions are their own, and because they do their jobs as if they own the company. Getting employees to actually think of the company's goals as their own isn't easy. It requires most of your management skills, and the creation of an integrated, commitment-oriented management system. You must:

Foster people-first values

Encourage extensive two-way communications

Build a sense of shared fate and community

Provide a vision

Use value-based hiring

Use financial rewards and profit sharing

Encourage self-actualizing

SUMMARY ■

1. Control is the task of ensuring that activities are providing the desired results. In its most general sense, controlling therefore means setting a target, measuring performance, and taking corrective action. Experts distinguish between steering controls, yes/no controls, and post-action controls.

2. As companies expand worldwide and compete in fast-changing markets, the problems of relying on a traditional control system (set standards, compare actual to standard, and take corrective action) have become increasingly apparent. Employees have had to become more empowered to be more responsive, and "controlling" can detract from that.

3. While the classification is somewhat arbitrary, there are three types of traditional control methods. Diagnostic control systems like budgets and performance reports are intended to ensure that goals are being achieved and that variances, if any, are explained. Boundary control systems establish the rules of the game and identify actions and pitfalls employees must avoid. Interactive control systems are real-time, usually face-to-face methods of monitoring both a plan's effectiveness and the underlying assumptions on which the plan was built.

4. Budgets and ratio analysis are among the most widely used diagnostic control tools. Budgets are formal financial expressions of a manager's plan and show targets for yardsticks such as revenues, cost of materials, and profits, usually expressed in dollars. Most managers also achieve control by monitoring various financial ratios.

5. A big problem with relying on traditional controls is that they can lead to unintended, undesirable, and often harmful employee reactions, such as behavioral displacement, gamesmanship, operating delays, negative attitudes, and reduced empowerment.

6. Achieving control in an age of empowerment relies on employees' self-control. Motivation techniques and building value systems are two important ways to tap such self-control. Another powerful way is to get employees to think of the company's goals as their own—to earn their commitment.

TYING IT ALL TOGETHER ■

In this text we have talked about the management process—namely, planning, organizing, leading, and controlling. Since this is a textbook, we necessarily covered the topics sequentially, one topic at a time. But as you can probably imagine, that's not the way managers really manage day to day. In other words, you generally won't have the luxury to spend Monday planning, Tuesday organizing, Wednesday and Thursday leading, and Friday controlling. Instead, you'll be doing all these tasks simultaneously. For example, as part of your planning function you'll be sitting with your subordinates trying to formulate goals and to motivate them to accept them. You may be monitoring and controlling the progress of a project, only to discover that the people staffing the project are not up to the job, or that the milestones you set when the project was planned are no longer valid. Management is really an integrated, "tying it altogether" process, in other words.

That fact is particularly evident when it comes to controlling and building commitment. For one thing, planning and controlling are merely two sides of the same coin: what you control and how you're doing depends entirely on where you want to go, so that deciding where planning leaves off and controlling begins is bound to be somewhat arbitrary.

Similarly, effectively controlling your organization will demand all the people skills you can muster. Employees can be enormously creative when it comes to getting around control systems, and getting them to *not* want to get around those systems is therefore a very demanding task.

Also, and perhaps more important, controlling someone is usually not the best way to stay in control. You can lower your "control costs"—not to mention your aggravation level—enormously by getting your employees to want to do a great job. Doing this of course is essentially a behavioral, not a technical, process.

When you ask most people how they maintain control, their first reaction might be "we use budgets," "we use timeclocks," or "we watch what our people are doing." But getting employees to want to do a great job is in many respects the best way to keep your firm under control, and doing so, as we have seen, relies on behavioral activities like fostering people-first values and building a sense of shared fate and community. And it's just such an "integrating the people side of managing into all that they do" that top managers do best.

Skills and Study Materials

CRITICAL THINKING EXERCISES   ■

1. The budget is a traditional means of control, usually established by the top management. Now think about establishing a budget for a company by using committed and empowered employees to develop it. Who would be involved and why? How would your approach differ from traditional budgeting?

2. We are increasingly dependent on technology and the flow of information provided by means such as the Internet. Yet there is ongoing debate about the control and privacy aspects of both the Internet and intranets. What do you think about using electronic monitoring technology as a control device? What about the privacy issues? Should our boss be able to monitor us and our use of computers?

EXPERIENTIAL EXERCISES   ■

1. You are one of the founding engineers in your 6-month-old firm, and you brought to the firm values of environmental awareness, quality, and excellence. These values have united the original members, but you are concerned that they might change with the addition of 50 new people needed by your fast-growing company to meet demand. What type of control system would you develop to ensure your values are adhered to, based on the concepts in this section?

2. When you next eat at a fast food restaurant, or go to the gas station to fill up your tank or get service, or go shopping at the grocery store, note the control systems in place. Then be prepared to discuss them in terms of what you have read in this section.

CASE 5-1
CONTROLLING QUALITY
WITH COMMITTED EMPLOYEES
AT RITZ-CARLTON

Many consider business hotels as offering a generic service—a safe, clean, comfortable room in a city away from home. Ritz-Carlton Hotel Company viewed its business differently. Targeting industry executives, meeting and corporate travel planners, and affluent travelers, the Atlanta-based company manages 25 luxury hotels that pursue the goal of being the very best in each market. Ritz-Carlton succeeded with more than just travelers; it was awarded the U.S. government's Malcom Baldrige National Quality Award. Given a mission of true excellence in service, what types of control systems did Ritz-Carlton need to achieve its goals?

In the presentation of the Baldrige award, the committee commended Ritz-Carlton for a management program that included participatory leadership, thorough information gathering, coordinated planning and execution, and a trained workforce empowered "to move heaven and earth" to satisfy customers. Of all the elements in the system, Ritz-Carlton felt the most important control mechanism was committed employees.

All employees are trained in the company's "Gold Standards," which set out Ritz-Carlton's service credo and the basics of premium service. The company has translated key product and service requirements into a credo, and 20 "Ritz-Carlton Basics." Each employee is expected to understand and adhere to these standards, which describe processes for solving any problem guests may have.

The corporate motto is "ladies and gentlemen serving ladies and gentlemen." Like many companies, Ritz-Carlton gives new employees an orientation followed by on-the-job training. Unlike other hotel firms, Ritz-Carlton then "certifies" employees. Corporate values are reinforced continuously by daily "line ups," frequent recognition for extraordinary achievement, and a performance appraisal based on expectations explained during the orientation, training, and certification processes.

All workers are required to act at the first sign of a problem, regardless of the type of problem or customer complaint. Employees are empowered to do whatever it takes to provide "instant pacification." Other employees must assist if a coworker requests aid in responding to a guest's complaint or wish. There is never an excuse for not solving a customer problem.

Responsibility for ensuring high-quality guest services and accommodations rests largely with employees. All employees are surveyed annually to determine their understanding of quality standards and their personal satisfaction as a Ritz-Carlton employee. In one case, 96% of all employees surveyed singled out excellence in guest services as the key priority.

Discussion Questions

1. What steps does Ritz-Carlton take to control the quality of its service?

2. What does Ritz-Carlton do to foster its employees' high level of commitment?

3. How does the company's value system foster employee self-control?

MANAGING WITH INFORMATION TECHNOLOGY

WHAT'S AHEAD?

While most people don't know it, buying a pair of Levi's jeans at a big chain like Macy's makes the consumer a part of the Levi's information system—at least for a moment. As we'll see in this module, Levi's has installed a vast information network to help it manage and control its sales, and that network begins, in a sense, with the point of sale cash register where you pay for those jeans. That sale automatically triggers a series of automated decisions—for instance, telling Levi's computer systems to produce another pair of jeans in that size and model, and to ship them to that store to replace its inventory. We'll see in this module that, as at Levi's, information technology—combining telecommunications systems and computers—is today an integral part of the way that firms do business, and an essential ingredient in managing change.

THIS SECTION FOCUSES ON THE FOLLOWING:

- Why managers at different organizational levels require different types of information

- Information systems used by managers

- Telecommunication's role in managing organizations

- How information technology and the Internet can help managers plan, organize, lead, and control more effectively

Throughout this text (and particularly in the "Managing @ the Speed of Thought" sections), we've seen how managers are using information technology like computers and the Internet today. In this module we'll take a more comprehensive look at information technology and management, and particularly at what information technology is and how it's used to manage organizations.

▶ MANAGEMENT IN THE INFORMATION AGE

Information technology refers to any processes, practices, or systems that facilitate processing and transporting information. You are no doubt already very familiar with information technology's modern components. For example, you probably use a personal computer and are familiar with management information systems from the work you do. You probably use cellular phones, facsimile machines, and e-mail and voice-mail systems. Information technologies like these have dramatically altered the way people do their jobs and the way companies are managed.

The Nature of Information

Information is data presented in a form that is meaningful to the recipient.[1] "Information," as Peter Drucker said, "is data endowed with relevance and purpose."[2] Knowledge, on the other hand, has been defined as "information . . . distilled via study or research and augmented by judgment and experience."[3]

To put these definitions into managerial terms, consider this example. PepsiCo Inc., wants to determine why consumers are not buying its new Pepsi Light drink. To search for an answer, the company's market researchers conduct a survey containing 25 multiple-choice questions. The answers to the questions are put on computer disks, where by themselves they would appear to the untrained eye as nothing but long streams of unrelated numbers.

When market researchers summarize these *data* for presentation to management, the result is *information*, such as graphs showing average responses by age level and other demographic traits for each question. The marketing department can then apply its *knowledge* to draw meaningful conclusions, such as (in PepsiCo's case), a hypothesis about why older consumers seem less inclined to purchase Pepsi Light than younger ones.

What Is "Information Quality"

Managers are, of course, inundated with information all the time. What they need is high-quality information. High-quality information has several characteristics.[4] As in the PepsiCo example, good information must be *pertinent* and related to the problem at hand. It must also be *timely*. For example, the Pepsi Light survey information would be useless if it came rolling in two years after the product was pulled off the shelf. Good information must also be *accurate*. Finally, good information reduces *uncertainty*, which we can define as the absence of information about a particular area of concern.[5]

In the PepsiCo example, to meet these last criteria, the survey information should help the marketing manager answer the question "Why aren't people buying Pepsi Light the way we thought they would?"

Yet, even good information is relatively useless without the knowledge that comes from analysis, interpretation, and explanation.[6] Managers are, as we said, deluged by information—on competitors' practices, consumers' buying habits, machinery breakdowns, and many other relevant issues. The role of information technology today is thus not just to generate and transfer more (or even better-quality) information. It is to contribute to the manager's knowledge of what is happening, through analysis, interpretation, and explanation. Its ultimate aim is to make the manager's company more competitive.

Data mining is one example.[7] This means using special computer software to analyze vast amounts of customer data stored in a company's data banks to obtain information the firm can use to be more competitive. When it comes to making decisions, managers don't want to be deluged by truckloads of numbers; they want to receive reports that let them see meaningful patterns and relationships. New data-mining software products like Intelligent Miner from IBM let them do just that.

For example, like most phone companies, MCI Worldcom Communications Corp. wants to keep its best customers. To do this, it's helpful to identify early those customers who might be thinking of jumping to another long-distance carrier. But how do you screen telephone data on more than 100 million households to try to find patterns in characteristics like lifestyle and past calling habits that may suggest the customer is a likely candidate for switching phone companies? In this case, MCI Worldcom uses its IBM supercomputer and special data-mining software to analyze a set of 22 detailed and highly secret statistical profiles of customers to monitor the patterns that it believes can help identify customers' intentions.

Knowledge Management

Knowledge—no matter how high-quality it is—is totally useless if the people who need that knowledge don't know it exists or can't get to it. This fact has given rise to a new area called knowledge management, which one expert refers to as "the task of developing and exploiting an organization's tangible and intangible knowledge resources".[8] The company's tangible knowledge assets include things like patents, licenses, and information on customers and competitors. Intangible knowledge assets are the knowledge employees possess, including their experiences and the methods they've discovered for solving problems. The basic purpose of knowledge management "is to leverage and reuse resources that already exist in the organization so that people will seek out best practices rather than reinvent the wheel."[9]

As we noted in earlier sections, using computerized systems to enable employees to easily access their companies' knowledge bases has proved to be a boon to companies. For example, IBM consultants reportedly cut their proposal-writing time from an average of 200 hours to 30 because they can now share information.[10] Sales and technical support reps at Dell Computer's call centers solve more problems more easily thanks to a central knowledge base that advises them on what questions to ask and what solutions to suggest. As we saw earlier, Xerox Corp.'s copier repairers have reduced average repair time by 50% thanks to a knowledge base comprised of suggestions and solutions from the company's repair staff.

Managers' Requirements for Information

Managers at different levels in the organization require different types of information.[11] First-line managers (like the front-desk manager at a Hilton Hotel) tend to focus on short-term, operational decisions. At this level, information should emphasize activities such as accounts receivables, order entry, inventory control, and cash management.

Middle managers tend to focus more on intermediate-range decisions, like events that might affect the company in the coming year or so. They therefore require information for use in budget analysis, short-term forecasting, and variance analysis. A marketing manager needs consumer data to plan her next ad campaign, for instance.

Top managers (including the firm's CEO and vice presidents) focus more on long-range strategic decisions. They therefore need information that enables them to make, for example, factory location decisions, merger and acquisition decisions, and new-product planning decisions.

Because of these different information requirements, different types of information systems are needed at each level of the organization, as we'll see next.

▶ INFORMATION SYSTEMS FOR MANAGING ORGANIZATIONS

What Is an Information System?

An **information system** is a set of people, data, technology, and organizational procedures that work together to retrieve, process, store, and disseminate information to support decision making and control.[12] We'll focus here on *managerial* information systems, which are systems that support managerial decision making and control.

Information systems are more than computers. The information system also usually includes major parts of the organization, such as the employees who input data into the system and retrieve its output. Managers are (or should be) part of the information system too, since it's their specific needs for information (like an MCI Worldcom managers' need for information about customers' calling patterns) that the information system is designed to serve.

Information Systems = Technology + People Recent changes at Schneider National, North America's biggest carrier of full truckload cargoes, help show why information systems include technology, people, and organizations.

After deregulation revolutionized the trucking industry, Schneider National knew it had to do something quickly to get itself into more competitive shape.[13] The regulations that had made it difficult for customers to change carriers were gone, so the firm suddenly faced more competition than ever before.

Schneider National managers decided on a two-pronged strategy. First, to prepare the organization for other changes to come, management focused on making sweeping changes in its corporate culture. The main aim was to replace its "regulated-utility" mentality with a sense of urgency to get things done fast.

The company's CEO took several steps to change the culture and values of the company: He encouraged everyone from drivers on up to suggest ways to improve operations, eliminated status symbols like reserved parking spaces, began calling all employees *associates*, and drew attention to the new emphasis on performance by awarding bonus paychecks based solely on performance.

Information technology changes were then built on this new cultural foundation. All trucks were equipped with computers and rotating antennas, so that a satellite could track every rig and make sure it stuck to its schedule. When a customer called to request a pick-up, dispatchers knew exactly which truck to assign to the job. The order was sent directly to that driver's on-board terminal, complete with directions to the destination and instructions about what gate to use.

The new information system has been very successful. However, it's doubtful that it would have been if management hadn't had the wisdom to design the system around the people—by changing the culture, by making sure the drivers who had to use the system were made to feel like involved participants in the process, and by designing a system the drivers wanted to use.

Levels of Information Systems Because information requirements at each organizational level tend to be unique to that level, there is a corresponding hierarchy of information systems, from strategic-level systems at the top, to operational systems at the bottom.[14]

As in Figure 5-9, **executive support systems** provide information for strategic-level decisions on matters such as five-year operating plans. **Management information systems** and *decision support systems* provide middle managers with reports regarding matters such as current versus historical sales levels. **Transaction processing systems** provide detailed information about the most short-term, daily activities, such as accounts payables and order status. We'll look more closely at each type of system.

▼ **FIGURE 5-9** Applications of Information Systems for Each Organizational Level

Managers at each level of the organization have unique information requirements. Various types of information systems have thus been developed to serve the needs at each management level.

TYPES OF SYSTEMS

Executive Support Systems (ESS)

STRATEGIC-LEVEL SYSTEMS				
Sales and Marketing	Manufacturing	Finance	Accounting	Human Resources
5-year sales trend forecasting	5-year operating plan	5-year budget forecasting	Profit planning	Manpower planning

Management Information Systems (MIS)

Decision-Support Systems (DSS)

MANAGEMENT-LEVEL SYSTEMS				
Sales and Marketing	Manufacturing	Finance	Accounting	Human Resources
Sales management	Inventory control	Annual budgeting	Capital investment analysis	Relocation analysis
Sales region analysis	Production scheduling	Cost analysis	Pricing/ profitability analysis	Contract cost analysis

Knowledge-Level Work Systems (KWS)

Office Automation Systems (OAS)

KNOWLEDGE-LEVEL SYSTEMS		
Sales and Marketing	Finance	Human Resources
Engineering workstations	Graphics workstations	Managerial workstations
Word processing	Document imaging	Electronic calendars

Transaction Processing Systems (TPS)

OPERATIONAL-LEVEL SYSTEMS				
Sales and Marketing	Manufacturing	Finance	Accounting	Human Resources
	Machine control	Securities trading	Payroll	Compensation
Order tracking	Plant scheduling		Accounts payable	Training & development
Order processing	Material movement control	Cash management	Accounts receivable	Employee record keeping

Source: Adapted from Laudon and Laudon, *Management Information Systems* 6th ed. (Upper Saddle River, NJ; Prentice Hall, 1998), p 39.

Transaction Processing Systems

A *transaction* is an event that affects the business. Hiring an employee, selling merchandise, paying an employee, and ordering supplies are transactions. In essence, transaction processing systems collect and maintain detailed records regarding the organization's transactions. These records are generally used for making operational-level decisions. For example, a university must know which students have registered, which have paid fees, which members of the faculty are teaching, and what secretaries are employed in order to conduct its business.

The collection and maintenance of such day-to-day transactions were two of the first procedures to be computerized in organizations. As is still the case today, early transaction processing systems automated the collection, maintenance, and processing of mostly repetitive transactions. Examples include computing withholding taxes and net pay, and processing accounts payable checks.

Transaction processing systems (TPSs) can be put to five uses.[15] They may have to classify data based on common characteristics of a group (such as finding all sales employees with five years' service, for instance). They are used to do routine calculations (such as computing net pay after taxes and deductions for each employee) and can be used for sorting (for instance, grouping invoices by zip code). The TPS can also be used for summarization (such as summarizing for each department's manager what his or her average payroll is compared to the other departments). Finally, the TPS can be used for storage (for example, storing payroll information for, say, the past five years).

Management Information Systems

A management information system (MIS) provides decision support for managers by producing standardized, summarized reports on a regular basis.[16] It generally produces management level reports, reports for longer-term purposes than typical transaction processing systems.

In a university, for instance, a TPS is used to print class rolls and grade rolls. An MIS, in contrast, can measure and report class size and enrollment trends by department and by college. The deans (who are midway between the president and other executives, and operating managers such as department heads) can then use the MIS reports to increase or decrease class sizes or to drop some courses from next semester's schedule while adding others. MISs condense, summarize, and manipulate information derived from the organization's TPS. They then present the results in the form of routine summary reports to management, often with exceptions flagged for control purposes.[17]

Decision Support Systems

Decision support systems (DSSs) "assist management decision making by combining data, sophisticated analytical models, and user-friendly software into a single powerful system that can support semi-structured or unstructured decision making."[18] In other words, systems like these can help managers (again, usually midlevel managers but occasionally executives) make decisions that are relatively unstructured when compared to those addressed by the typical MIS.

At the university, for instance, an MIS is used to make course addition and deletion decisions, decisions that are fairly routine. However, suppose the university's faculty

T A B L E   5 - 3   **How Firms Use Their DSS**

American Airlines	Price and route selection
Champlin Petroleum	Corporate planning and forecasting
Equico Capital Corporation	Investment evaluation
Frito-Lay, Inc.	Price, advertising, and promotion selection
General Dynamics	Price evaluation
Juniper Lumber	Production optimization
Kmart	Price evaluation
National Gypsum	Corporate planning and forecasting
Southern Railway	Train dispatching and routing
Texas Oil and Gas Corporation	Evaluation of potential drilling sites
United Airlines	Flight scheduling
U.S. Department of Defense	Defense contract analysis

threatens to strike. The university could use a decision support system to estimate the impact on university revenues of having to drop various combinations of classes.

An MIS differs from a DSS in several ways.[19] A DSS is more capable of analyzing alternatives. This is because decision support systems let the user (in this case, the vice president for academic affairs) include subprograms showing how various components of the university (such as revenues and enrollments in various courses) are related. Furthermore, a DSS does not rely just on internal information from the TPS the way the MIS typically does. Instead, a DSS is built to absorb new external information into the analysis.

Thus, the university's academic vice president, faced with a strike, may want to include in her or his analysis an estimate of the likelihood that a number of the university's students will move across town to a competing school, given the competing school's ability (or inability) to expand its class offerings.

Table 5-3 gives some examples of how companies use DSS systems. For example, American Airlines uses its system for price and route selection, General Dynamics for price evaluation, and Southern Railway for train dispatching and routing.

Executive Support Systems

Executive support systems (ESS) are information systems designed to help top-level executives acquire, manipulate, and use the information they need to maintain the overall strategic effectiveness of the company. Such systems often focus on providing top management with information for making strategic decisions. They help top management match changes in the firm's environment with the firm's existing and potential strengths and weaknesses.[20]

Executive support systems perform several specific tasks. Executives such as Cypress Semiconductor's president use their ESS for keeping informed about and monitoring the pulse of their organizations. For example Cypress monitors the weekly compliance of all its 4,000 employees (for instance, how each worker stands in terms of project progress or sales productivity). Second, executives use ESS to quickly identify and understand evolving competitive situations.

A university president could thus use an ESS to keep tabs on and analyze the following questions:

- Is the average student taking fewer courses?
- Are costs for maintenance labor substantially higher than they have been in the past?
- Is there a significant shift in the zip codes from which most of our students come?

An ESS also makes it easy for executives to browse through the data. One executive describes the capability this way:

> I like to take a few minutes to review details about our customers, our manufacturers or our financial activities first hand. Having the details flow across the screen gives me a feel for how things are going. I don't look at each record, but glance at certain elements as they scroll by. If something looks unusual, it will almost jump out at me and I can find out more about it. But if nothing is unusual, I will know that, too.[21]

A top executive can also use an ESS to monitor a situation. Thus, a university president could use an ESS to monitor the new dining facilities management firm running the student cafeteria by reviewing information such as student usage, student complaints, and revenues. Executives also use ESSs to facilitate environmental scanning. For example, a wealth of information is available in commercial computerized data banks, including financial information on tens of thousands of U.S. companies. Executives can use an ESS to tap into such data banks in order to glean competitive data regarding other firms in their industry.

An ESS can also support analytical needs. For example, it may allow the university president to create what-if scenarios that show the probable effects on revenues of increasing faculty salaries or adding new programs. Finally, an ESS may enable the executive to get at data directly. Using terminals and telephone lines, executives can use an executive support system to tap directly into the company's data files in order to get specific information that may be of interest, without waiting for others to assemble it.[22]

Enterprisewide Information Systems and the Company's "Digital Nervous System"

Companies today are increasingly implementing enterprisewide information systems. Basically, systems like these—produced by companies like SAP of Germany—are companywide integrated computer systems that integrate a firm's individual systems (such as order processing, production control, and accounting) in order to give managers real-time, instantaneous information regarding the costs and status of every activity and project in the business.

Today, in other words, more and more managers don't rely just on the sorts of executive, management, and transaction information systems that parallel the company's executive, managerial, and operational levels. Instead, enterprisewide systems are being used to integrate these various systems. For example, a point-of-sale device at a Wal-Mart store might signal Levi Strauss to produce 50 more size 34 501 jeans. Levi's enterprisewide system than automatically acknowledges the order, produces a production schedule, monitors the order's progress, and provides top managers with real-time information regarding the profitability of that order as well as total Wal-Mart orders by geographic region for that day.

Microsoft chairman Bill Gates, says that "like a human being, the company has to have an internal communication mechanism, a 'nervous system,' to coordinate its actions."[23] Like world-class athletes, world-class companies need superfast reflexes. And just as it's hard for someone to have great reflexes with a malfunctioning nervous system, companies with inadequate "digital nervous systems" can't respond fast enough to customers' requests or competitors' moves. Enterprisewide information systems like the one at Levi can form the backbone of the company's digital nervous system. It's easier for companies with systems like these to literally "do business at the speed of thought."

Systems like these are already in place and working effectively at many firms. For example, you'll recall that Harmon Music Group uses a type of enterprisewide system to integrate its order processing, production scheduling, and accounting systems and to thereby run its business very efficiently. Similarly, Deluxe Paper Payment systems was able to dramatically improve its profitability by using information from its enterprisewide information systems to get many of its smaller customers to switch to electronic check ordering.

Yet installing one of these highly integrated systems can also be fraught with peril. For example, October 31, 1999 turned out to be a scary Halloween for Hershey Foods, the largest U.S. candymaker. During the summer, "Hershey flipped the switch on a $112 million computer system that was supposed to automate and modernize everything from taking candy orders to putting palettes on trucks."[24] But instead of speeding the flow of orders and information, the system has apparently gummed up the works. Orders, even from huge customers like Wal-Mart, were being delayed, and Hershey sales reps actually had to call customers to find out what products they'd received, because the new information system couldn't tell which orders Hershey had delivered and which it had not. The mix up was a boon to competitors like Mars Inc. and Nestle USA, both of which saw their Halloween chocolate orders jump as customers scrambled to keep their shelves stocked with candies.

Part of the problem, experts now say, may be that Hershey tried to implement its system all at once, putting it online in what computer people call a "big bang" approach. Whatever the cause, it's apparent that while enterprisewide information systems can certainly help managers manage, implementing a project of that magnitude requires the most effective planning, organizing, leading, and controlling (in other words, management) skills the company can muster.

▶ NETWORKS FOR MANAGING ORGANIZATIONS

Organizations make extensive use of networks to better manage their operations. A **network** "is a group of interconnected computers, work stations or computer devices (such as printers and data storage systems)."[25] Local area networks, wide area networks, and distributed networks are three examples of managerial networks.

Local Area Networks

A **local area network (LAN)** spans a limited distance, such as a building or several adjacent buildings, using the company's own telecommunications links (rather than common-carrier links such as those provided by AT&T's phone lines). In an office, a LAN may be used to support a workgroup information system such as e-mail, and a factory may use a LAN to link computers with computer-controlled production equipment.

More generally, LANs are used for one or more of the following reasons: to distribute information and messages (including e-mail); to drive computer-controlled manufacturing equipment; to distribute documents (such as engineering drawings from one department to another); to interconnect the LAN's computers with those of a public network such as Prodigy or the Internet; and, given the high cost of certain equipment such as laser printers, to make equipment sharing possible (including not just printers but disk storage file servers, for instance).

Wide Area Networks

Wide area networks (WANs) are networks that serve microcomputers over larger geographic areas, spanning distances that can cover a few miles or circle the globe. Early WANs utilized common carrier networks, such as the telephone links provided by AT&T. However, many firms today operate their own WANs, which are essentially private, computerized telecommunications systems.

The Benetton retail store chain uses its WAN to enable both store managers and headquarters staff to identify local trends and improve inventory and production management. The stores accumulate sales data during the day and keep them on computer disks. At night, another, larger computer at corporate headquarters polls the individual retail stores' computers, accessing data that are then transmitted over telephone lines back to headquarters. Here, the information is processed and a summary of sales trends is forwarded to headquarters and individual store managers.[26]

As at Benetton, WANs are often used to achieve distributed processing. **Distributed processing** generally uses small local computers (such as point-of-sale systems) to collect, store, and process information, with summary reports and information sent to headquarters as needed.[27]

Managing and The Internet

While you're reading this page, millions of people around the world are "on the Internet," searching through libraries, talking to friends, and buying and selling products and services, from firms ranging from Amazon.com to Sony to Deutsche Telecom. The value of the Internet lies in its ability to easily and inexpensively connect so many people from so many places; the miracle of the Internet is that no one owns it and it has no formal management organization. Instead, to become part of the Internet, an existing network simply pays a small registration fee and agrees to comply with certain electronic standards, such as Transmission Control Protocol/Internet Protocol (TCP/IP), originally developed by the U.S. Department of Defense.

As most of us are aware, the boom in e-commerce has turned most business people into Web believers. It's probably harder to find companies that don't use the Web today than those that do. Hundreds of thousands of merchants around the world now sell products or services via the Web. Hershey Foods, for instance, offers a personal address book and a service that reminds users of special dates and anniversaries, thus allowing them to conveniently send Herhsey products to mark special occasions. In July 1999, BarnesandNoble.com launched its music site. Another site, onlineofficesupplies.com, is open 24 hours a day, seven days a week, offering more than 30,000 products at reduced prices.[28] Business sales (if not profits) are thus booming on the Internet.

But all those Internet-based sales sites are only the tip of the iceberg when it comes to managerial uses of the Internet. For one thing, since companies can, in a sense, get a "free ride" on the Internet, they can substantially reduce their communications costs by building their management systems around the Internet.

This text's "Managing @ the Speed of Thought" features and Webnotes present many examples of how managers use the Internet. Remember, for instance, how the New York real estate firm Cushman & Wakefield uses the Internet to let its 2,000 employees around the world communicate with each other and with the headquarters staff. Similarly, Schlumberger Ltd., the New York and Paris oil drilling equipment company, relies on the Internet to communicate with and stay in control of vast projects in 85 countries.

Other companies use the Internet for strategic planning. With so many firms having Web sites today, the Internet has become a useful device for collecting information on competitors, for example. (One company, visiting a competitor's site, reportedly found a preview of an upcoming promotional campaign, and was able to quickly revise its own plans and get the jump on its competitor).[29] Other companies actually build Web pages to help employees gather information about competitors or customers; the Web pages contain, for instance, links to published news accounts, press releases, and government statistics.[30]

The bottom line is that information technology and the Internet are literally helping managers to "manage @ the speed of thought." Many or most of today's virtual corporations and strategic alliances—all of which depend for their existence on rapid, relatively inexpensive multimedia communications—would be impossible without such tools. Similarly, many team-based organizations would be unmanageable without systems such as Lotus Notes groupware, through which geographically dispersed team members can communicate virtually "face-to-face." Indeed, when it comes to leading and influencing employees, information technology and the Internet now almost always play a major role.

When the president of Xerox recently wanted to motivate his troops, he sent them all what Xerox calls a "vmail," a voicemail note that goes automatically to each employee's voicemail box. Dell Computer, the direct sales computer firm, relies heavily on information technology to stay close to its customers and to control the progress of its orders. For example, employees who take customers' calls work on PCs linked by a network to a large central computer that contains the company's customer database. As the calls come in, the telephone representatives input the information to the database, and follow up inquiries by triggering the mailing of customized sales letters to inquiry customers. Customers can then easily track the progress of their orders on Dell's Web site and can do this without tying up a Dell telephone representative's time. Thus, whether it's planning, organizing, leading, or controlling, information technology and the Internet are vital management tools today.

SUMMARY ∎

1. Information technology refers to any processes, practices, or systems that facilitate the processing and transportation of data and information. The increasingly rapid deployment of information technology in organizations has sped the transformation of many businesses today into information-based organizations.

2. Information is data presented in a form that is meaningful to the recipient. Knowledge, on the other hand, has been defined as information distilled via study or research and augmented by judgment and experience. Good-quality information must be pertinent, timely, and accurate and reduce uncertainty. But even good information is relatively useless without knowledge. The role of information technology at work is to contribute to the manager's knowledge of what is happening through analysis, interpretation, and explanation.

3. Managers at different levels in the organization require different types of information. First-line managers tend to focus on short-term, operational decisions and therefore need information that focuses on operational activities. Middle managers tend to concentrate on the intermediate range and so require information for use in such tasks as budget analysis, short-term forecasting, and variance analysis. Top managers make long-range plans and, therefore, require information that will enable them to make better strategic decisions.

4. Information systems are people, data, hardware, and procedures that work together to retrieve, process, store, and disseminate information to support decision making and control. The hierarchy of information systems used in management includes executive support systems, management information and decision support systems, and transaction processing systems.

5. Managers today rely heavily on telecommunication-based networks such as LANs, WANs and the Internet. We've seen in this text's *Managing @ the Speed of Thought* features that all management functions—from planning to organizing to leading to control—are often Internet-assisted today.

ENDNOTES

SECTION ONE
MANAGING IN THE 21ST CENTURY

1   David Kirkpatrick, "The Second Coming of Apple," *Fortune*, 9 November 1998, pp. 87–104.

2   David Kirkpatrick, "IBM: From Blue Dinosaur to E-Business Animal," *Fortune*, 26 April 1999, pp. 119–125.

3   Joan Magretta, "The Power of Virtual Integration: An Interview with Dell Computer's Michael Dell," *Harvard Business Review*, March–April 1998, pp. 73–84.

4   Henry Mintzberg, "The Manager's Job: Folklore and Fact," *Harvard Business Review*, July–August 1975, pp. 489–561.

5   See, for example, ibid.; and George Copeman, *The Chief Executive* (London: Leviathan House, 1971), p. 271. See also George Weathersby, "Facing Today's Sea Changes," *Management Review*, June 1999, p. 5; and David Kirkpatrick, "The Second Coming of Apple," *Fortune*, 9 November 1998, pp. 86–104; and Jenny McCune, "The Changemakers," Management Review, May 1999, pp. 16–22.

6   Peter Drucker, "The Coming of the New Organization," *Harvard Business Review*, January–February 1988, p. 45. See also Fred Andrews, "The Sage of Value and Service," *New York Times*, 17 November 1999, pp. C-1, C14.

7   Geoffrey Colvin, "How to be a great ECEO," *Fortune*, 24 May 1999, pp. 104–110.

8   G. William Dauphinais and Colin Price, "The CEO as a Psychologist," Management Review, September 1998, pp. 1–15.

9   Claudia H. Deutsch, "A Hands-on-the-Helm Leader," *New York Times*, 13 June 1999, Money and Business Section, p. 2.

10 Noel Tichy and Ram Charan, "The CEO as Coach: An Interview with Allied-Signal's Lawrence A. Bossidy," *Harvard Business Review*, March–April 1995, pp. 69–78.

11 Ibid., p. 70.

12 Ibid., p. 73.

13 Ibid., p. 70.

14 Ibid.

15 Ibid., p. 76.

16 These are based on Henry Mintzberg, "The Manager's Job: Folklore and Fact."

17 Sumatra Ghoshal and Christopher Bartlett, "Changing the Role of Top Management: Beyond Structure to Processes," *Harvard Business Review*, January–February 1995, pp. 86–96.

18 Ibid., p. 89.

19 Ibid., p. 91.

20 Ibid., p. 96.

21 Ibid., p. 94.

22 John Holland, *Making Vocational Choices: A Theory of Careers* (Upper Saddle River, NJ: Prentice-Hall, 1973); see also John Holland, *Assessment Booklet: A Guide to Educational and Career Planning* (Odessa, FL: Psychological Assessment Resources, Inc., 1990).

23 Edgar Schein, *Career Dynamics: Matching Individual and Organizational Needs* (Reading, MA: Addison-Wesley, 1978), pp. 128–129.

24 A. Howard and D. W. Bray, *Managerial Lives in Transition: Advancing Age and Changing Times* (New York: Guilford, 1988); discussed in Dwayne Schultz and Sydney Ellen Schultz, *Psychology and Work Today* (New York: Macmillan Publishing Co., 1994), pp. 103–104.

25 Ibid., Schultz and Schultz, p. 104.

26 Ibid.

27 "Riding the Storm," *Economist*, 6 November 1999.

28 Rebecca Buckman, "Wall Street Is Rocked by Merrill's On-Line Moves," *Wall Street Journal*, 2 June 1999, p. C1.

29 Nina Munk, "How Levi's Trashed a Great American Brand," *Fortune*, 12 April 1999, pp. 83–90.

30 Henry Mintzberg, "The Manager's Job: Folklore and Fact," *Harvard Business Review*, July–August 1975, 489–561. For a discussion of critical management trends, see Sharon Lobel, et al, "The Future of Work and Family: Critical Trends for Policy, Practice, and Research," *Human Resource Management*, Fall 1999, pp. 243–254.

31 See, for example, ibid.; and Copeman, p. 271. See also Weathersby, p. 5.

32 Thomas Stewart, "Welcome to the Revolution," *Fortune*, 13 December 1993, p. 66.

33 Charles W. Hill, *International Business* (Burr Ridge, IL: Irwin, 1994), p. 6.

34 Ibid., p. 9.

35 Amy Barrett, Peter Elstrom, and Catherine Arnst, "Vaulting the Walls with Wireless," *Business Week*, 20 January 1997, pp. 85, 88.

36 Bryan O'Reilly, "Your New Global Workforce," *Fortune*, 14 December 1992, pp. 52–66. See also "Charting the Projections: 1996–2006," *Occupational Outook Quarterly*, Winter 1997–1998, pp. 2–5. See also Floyd Kemske, "HR 2008: A Forecast Based on our Exclusive Study," *Workforce*, January 1998, pp. 46–58.

37 Richard Crawford, *In the Era of Human Capital* (New York: Harper, 1991), p. 10. See also Kemske, pp. 46–58. See also Sharon Lobel, Bradley Googins, and Ellen Bankert, "The Future of Work and Family: Critical Trends for Policy, Practice, and Research," *Human Resource Management*, Fall 1999, pp. 243–254.

38 Ibid.

39 "Charting the Projections: 1996–2006," *Occupational Outlook Quarterly*, Winter 1997–1998, pp. 2–24.

40 Ibid., p. 26.

41 Thomas Stewart, "Brain Power," *Fortune*, June 3, 1991, p. 44; See also Thomas Stewart, "Brain Power," *Fortune*, 17 March 1997, pp. 105–10.

42 James Brian Quinn, *Intelligent Enterprise* (New York: The Free Press, 1992), p. 3.

43 Bill Gates, *Business @ the Speed of Thought* (New York: Warner Books, 1999), p. 289.

44 Francis Fukuyama, "Are We at the End of History?" *Fortune*, 15 January 1990, p. 68.

45 Peter Drucker, "The Coming of the New Organization," *Harvard Business Review*, January–February 1988, p. 45.

46 Joan Magretta, "The Power of a Virtual Integration: An Interview with Dell Computers Michael Dell," *Harvard Business Review*, March–April 1998, pp. 73–84.

47 Ibid., p. 74.

48 Ibid., p. 82.

49 Ibid.

50 Ibid., p. 76.

51 Ibid., p. 75.

52 Bryan Dumaine, "What the Leaders of Tomorrow See," *Fortune*, 3 July 1989, p. 58. See also Weathersby, p. 5. See also, Gary Hamel and Jeff Sampler, "The eCorp.: Building a New Industrial" *Fortune*, 7 December 1998, pp. 80–112.

53 These are based on Walter Kiechel III, "How We Will Work in the Year 2000," *Fortune*, 17 May 1993, p. 79.

54 Karl Albrecht, *At America's Service: How Corporations Can Revolutionize the Way They Treat Their Customers* (Homewood, IL: Dow-Jones Irwin, 1998).

55 Bryan Dumaine, "What the Leaders of Tomorrow See," *Fortune*, 3 July 1989, p. 51.

56 Rosabeth Moss Kanter, "The New Managerial Work," *Harvard Business Review*, November–December 1989, p. 88.

57 Ibid.

58 Drucker, "The Coming of the New Organization," p. 45.

59 Peters, *Liberation Management*.

60 Bryan Dumaine, "The New Non-Managers," Fortune, 22 February 1993, p. 81. See also David Kirkpatrick, "IBM: from Big Blue Dinosaur to e-Business Animal," Fortune, 26 April 1999, pp. 116–127. See also McCune, pp. 16–22. See also Brent Schlender, "Larry Ellison: Oracle at Web Speed," Fortune, 24 May 1999, pp. 128–137.

61 Thomas Stewart, "How GE Keeps Those Ideas Coming," Fortune, 12 August 1991, p. 42. See also Kirkpatrick, "IBM: from Big Blue Dinosaur to e-Business Animal," pp. 116–127; and Kirkpatrick, "The Second Coming of Apple," Fortune, pp. 86–104.

62 Peter Drucker, "The Coming of the New Organization," p. 43.

63 Stratford Sherman, "A Master Class in Radical Change," Fortune, 13 December 1993, p. 82. See also McCune, pp. 16–22.

64 Michael Dorf, Knitting Music (New York: Knitting Factory Works, 1992) p. 4.

FOUNDATIONS OF MODERN MANAGEMENT

1 Alvin Toffler, Future Shock (New York: Bantam Books, 1971), p. 43.

2 Adam Smith, An Inquiry into the Nature and Causes of Wealth of Nations, ed., Edward Cannan, 4th ed. (London: Methuen, 1925). Published originally in 1776.

3 Alfred Chandler, Strategy and Structure (Cambridge, MA: MIT Press); see also Daniel Wren, The Evolution of Management Thought (New York: John Wiley, 1979).

4 D. S. Pugh, Organization Theory (Baltimore: Penguin, 1971), pp. 126–127.

5 Claude George, Jr., The History of Management Thought (Upper Saddle River, NJ: Prentice-Hall, 1972), pp. 99–101.

6 Richard Hopeman, Production (Columbus, OH: Charles Merrill, 1965), pp. 478–485.

7 Henri Fayol, General and Industrial Management, translated by Constance Storrs (London: Sir Isaac Pitman, 1949), pp. 42–43.

8 Based on Richard Hall, "Intra-Organizational Structural Variation: Application of the Bureaucratic Model," Administrative Science Quarterly, December 1962, pp. 295–308.

9 William Scott, Organization Theory (Homewood, IL: Richard D. Irwin, 1967).

10 F. L. Roethlisberger and William Dickson, Management and Worker (Boston: Harvard University Graduate School of Business, 1947), p. 21.

11 Chandler, Strategy and Structure, pp. 19–51.

12 Warren G. Bennis, "Organizational Development and the Fate of Bureaucracy." Address at the Division of Industrial and Business Psychology, American Psychological Association, 5 September 1964. Reprinted in L. L. Cummings and W. E. Scott, Jr., Organizational Behavior and Human Performance (Homewood, IL: Richard D. Irwin and Dorsey, 1969), p. 436.

13 Douglas McGregor, "The Human Side of Enterprise," Edward Deci, B. Von Haller Gilmer, and Harry Kairn, Readings in Industrial and Organizational Psychology (New York: McGraw-Hill, 1972), p. 123.

14 R. Likert, New Patterns of Management (New York: McGraw-Hill, 1961), p. 6.

15 Ibid., p. 103.

16 Chris Argyris, Integrating the Individual and the Organization (New York: John Wiley, 1964).

17 Likert, New Patterns of Management, p. 91.

18 Ibid., p. 100.

19 Ibid.

20 Ibid.

21 Chester Barnard, The Functions of the Executive (Cambridge: Harvard University Press, 1968), p. 84.

22 Ibid., p. 167.

23 Ibid., p. 143.

24 Herbert A. Simon, Administrative Behavior (New York: Free Press, 1976), p. 11.

25 C. West Churchman, Russell Ackoff, and E. Leonard Arnoff, Introduction to Operations Research (New York: John Wiley, 1957), p. 18.

26 Daniel Wren, The Evolution of Management Thought (New York: John Wiley, 1979), p. 512.

27 C. West Churchman, The Systems Approach (New York: Delta, 1968).

28 Joan Woodward, Industrial Organizations: Theory and Practice (London: Oxford University Press, 1965), pp. 64–65.

MANAGING IN A GLOBAL ENVIRONMENT

1 Jeremy Kahn, "Wal-Mart Goes Shopping in Europe," Fortune, 7 June 1999, pp. 105–12.

2 Hill, p. 4; Dawn Anfuso, "Colgate's Global HR United Under One Strategy," Personnel Journal, October 1995, p. 44ff; See also Marlene Piturro, "What Are You Doing About the New Global Realities?" Management Review, March 1999, pp. 16–22; and Maureen Minehan, "Changing Conditions in Emerging Markets," HR Magazine, January 1998, p. 160.

3 For a discussion see, for example, Arvind Phatak, International Dimensions of Management (Boston: PWS-Kent, 1989), p. 2.

4 Paul Doremus, William Keller, Louis Pauly, and Simon Reich, The Myth of the Global Corporation (Princeton: Princeton University Press, 1998).

5 Theodore Levitt, "The Globalization of Markets," Harvard Business Review, May–June 1983, pp. 92–102; For an example see Thomas Stewart, "See Jack. See Jack Run Europe," Fortune, 27 September 1999, pp. 124–127.

6 Note that there are few, if any, "pure" market economies or command economies anymore. For example, much of the French banking system is still under government control. And it was only several years ago that the government of England privatized (sold to private investors) British Airways.

7 Jeffrey Garten, "Troubles Ahead in Emerging Markets," Harvard Business Review, May–June 1997, pp. 38–48.

8 "Countries with Highest Gross Domestic Product and Per-Capita GDP," The World Almanac and Book of Facts, 1998 (Mahwah, NJ: K-III Reference Corporation, 1997), p. 112.

9 David Kemme, "The World Economic Outlook for 1999," Business Perspectives, January 1999, pp. 6–9.

10 For a discussion see, for example, Czinkota et al., Chapter 2, James Flanigan, "Asian Crisis Could Bring New Threat: Protectionism," Los Angeles Times, 3 February 1999, p. N1.

11 Ibid., p. 116.

12 Daniels and Radebaugh, p. 409.

13 Molly O'Meara, "Riding the Dragon," World Watch, March/April 1997, pp. 8–18.

14 See, for example, Susan Lee, "Are We Building New Berlin Walls?" Forbes, January 1991, pp. 86–89; Tom Reilly, "The Harmonization of Standards in the European Union and the Impact on U.S. Business," Business Horizons, March–April 1995.

15 Bryan Moskal, "The World Trade Topography: How Level Is It?" Industry Week, 18, May 1992, pp. 24–36.

16 Daniels and Radebaugh, p. 138.

17 Czinkota et al., p. 640.

18 Benjamin Weiner, "What Executives Should Know About Political Risk," Management Review, January 1992, pp. 19–22; see also Maria Kielnas, "Political Risks Emerged as Global Landscape Changes: Managing Risks of Doing Business Internationally Requires Knowledge of Culture and Infrastructure," Business Insurance, 14 June 1999, p. G2.

19 Laura Pincus and James Belohlav, "Legal Issues in Multinational Business Strategy: To Play the Game, You Have to

Know the Rules," *Academy of Management Executive*, (November 1996), pp. 52–61.

20 Ibid., pp. 53–54.

21 Ibid., p. 53.

22 Philip Harris and Robert Moran, *Managing Cultural Differences*, pp. 227–228. See also Jack N. Behrman, "Cross-Cultural Impacts on International Competitiveness," *Business and the Contemporary World*, 1995, pp. 93–113 and Lorna Wrighte, "Building Cultural Competence," *Canadian Business Review*, Spring 1996, p. 29ff.

23 Catherine Tinsley, "Models of Conflict Resolution in Japanese, German, and American Cultures," *Journal of Applied Psychology*, Month 1998, pp. 316–322.

24 Ibid., p. 321.

25 Geert Hofstede, "Cultural Dimensions in People Management," in Vladimir Pucik, Noel Tichy, and Carole Barnett, eds., *Globalizing Management*, (New York: John Wiley & Sons, Inc., 1992), 139–158.

26 Ibid., p. 143.

27 Ibid.

28 Ibid., p. 147.

29 "Hard Labor," *Economist*, 27 February 1999, p. 62.

30 "Sweatshop Wars," *Economist*, 27 February 1999, p. 62.

31 Czinkota et al., 205.

32 United Nations, Draft International Code of Conduct on the Transfer of Technology (New York: United Nations, 1981), p. 3; quoted in Michael Czinkota et al., *International Business*, p. 313.

33 Czinkota et al., p. 314.

34 Jeremy Main, "How to Go Global—and Why," *Fortune*, 28 August 1989, p. 70, See also Kasra Ferdows, "Making the Most of Foreign Markets," *Harvard Business Review*, March–April 1997, pp. 73–88 and Liane Ladarba, "A.M. Report: Olivetti Reshapes Global Landscape," *Telephony*, 31 May 1999.

35 www.wal-mart.com/newsroom/firstquarter99.html.

36 Hill, pp. 5–6.

37 Ibid., p. 6; and Michael McGrath and Richard Hoole, "Manufacturing's New Economies of Scale," *Harvard Business Review*, May–June 1992, p. 94; See also Thomas Kochan and Russell Lansbury, "Lean Production and Changing Employment Relations in the International Auto Industry," *Economic and Industrial Democracy*, November 1997, pp. 597–620 and John Sheridan, "Bridging the Enterprise," *Industry Week*, 5 April 1999, p. 17.

38 Based on McGrath and Hoole, pp. 94–102.

39 Kasra Ferdows, "Making the Most of Foreign Factories," *Harvard Business Review*, March–April 1997, pp. 80–81.

40 Kenneth Laudon and Jane Laudon, *Management Information Systems* (Upper Saddle River, NJ: Prentice Hall 1998), p. 348.

41 Ibid., p. 348.

42 Based on Brian O'Reilly, "Your New Global Workforce," *Fortune*, December 1992, pp. 52–66, See also Charlene Solomon, "Don't Get Burned by Hot New Markets," *Global Workforce*, a supplement to *Workforce*, January 1998, p. 12.

43 Ibid., p. 64. See also Shirley R. Fishman, "Developing a Global Workforce," *Canadian Business Review*, Spring 1996, pp. 18–21.

44 See Mariah E. DeForest, "Thinking of a Plant in Mexico?" *Academy of Management Executive*, February 1994, pp. 33–40.

45 Ibid., p. 34.

46 Ibid., p. 37.

47 Ibid., p. 38. See also Randall S. Schuler, Susan E. Jackson, Ellen Jackofsky, and John W. Slocum, "Managing Human Resources in Mexico: A Cultural Understanding," *Business Horizons*, May 1996, pp. 55–61.

48 Robert Reich, "Who Is Them?" *Harvard Business Review*, March–April 1991, pp. 77–88.

49 Philip Harris and Robert Moran, *Managing Cultural Differences* (Houston: Gulf Publishing Company, 1979), p. 1.

50 "On a Wing and a Hotel Room," *Economist*, 9 January 1999, p. 64.

51 Ibid., p. 64.

52 Gail Dutton, "Building a Global Brain," *Management Review*, May 1999, pp. 34–38.

53 Ibid., p. 35.

54 Ibid., p. 36.

55 Ibid., p. 37.

56 Ibid., p. 35.

57 Ibid., p. 35.

58 Ibid., p. 35.

59 Gretchen Spreitzer, Morgan McCall, Jr., and Joan Mahoney, "Early Identification of International Executive Potential," *Journal of Applied Psychology*, February 1997, pp. 6–29.

60 Phatak, pp. 46–49.

61 John Rossant, "After the Scandals," *Business Week*, 22 November 1993, pp. 56–57; William Duggan, "Global Dangers: Political Risks," *Risk Management*, September 1999, p. 13.

62 Anant Negandhi, *International Management* (Newton, MA: Allyn & Bacon, Inc., 1987), 61. See also Keith W. Glaister and Peter J. Buckley, "Strategic Motives for International Alliance Formation," *Journal of Management Studies*, May 1996, pp. 301–322.

63 Richard D. Robinson, *Internationalization of Business: An Introduction* (Hillsdale, IL: The Dryden Press, 1984), pp. 227–28; See also "Organizing for Europe," *International Journal of Retail and Distribution Management*, Winter 1993, pp. 15–16.

64 PR Newswire, 27 March 1997, "Reynolds Metal Announces Organizational and Management Changes."

65 See, for example, S. M. Davis, "Managing and Organizing Multinational Corporations," in C. A. Bartlett and S. Ghoshal, eds. *Transnational Management* (Homewood, IL: Richard D. Irwin, 1992). See also Oliver Gassnann and Maximilian von Zedtwitz, "New Concepts and Trends in International are & the Organization," *Research Policy*, March 1999, pp. 231–232.

66 Paul Blocklyn, "Developing the International Executive," *Personnel*, March 1989, p. 44. Overseas assignments can also be risky for the managers who are sent abroad, with one recent study concluding that these managers' employers don't reward their international experience. See Linda Grant, "That Overseas Job Could Derail Your Career," *Fortune*, 14 April 1997, p. 167; see also Martha I. Finney, "Global Success Rides on Keeping Top Talent," *HRMagazine*, April 1996, pp. 69–72; and Reyer A. Swaak, "Expatriate Failures: Too Many, Too Much Cost, Too Little Planning," *Compensation and Benefits Review*, November 1995, pp. 47–55.

67 Jackqueline Heidelberg, "When Sexual Harassment Is a Foreign Affair," *Personnel Journal*, April 1996.

68 Madelyn Callahan, "Preparing the New Global Manager," *Training and Development Journal*, March 1989, p. 30. See also Charlene Marmer Solomon, "Big Mac's McGlobal HR Secrets," *Personnel Journal*, April 1996, p. 46ff; and Lorna Wrighte, "Building Cultural Competence," *Canadian Business Review*, Spring 1996, p. 29ff.

69 Joseph Fucini and Suzy Fucini, *Working for the Japanese* (New York: The Free Press, 1990), pp. 122–123. See also Richard Kustin and Robert Jones, "The Influence of Corporate Headquarters on Leadership Styles in Japanese and US Subsidiary Companies," *Leadership Organizational Development Journal*, 1995, pp. 11–15.

70 Ken Siegmann, "Workforce," *Profit*, November 1999, p. 47.

MANAGING IN A CULTURAL AND ETHICAL ENVIRONMENT

1 "A Global War Against Bribery," *Economist*, 16 January 1999, pp. 22–24.

2 Manuel Velasquez, *Business Ethics: Concepts and Cases* (Upper Saddle River, NJ: Prentice-Hall, 1992), p. 9; Kate Walter, "Ethics Hot Lines Tap into More Than Wrongdoing," *HRMagazine*, September 1995, pp. 79–85. See also Skip Kaltenheuser, "Bribery Is Being Outlawed Virtually Worldwide," *Business Ethics*, May 1998, p. 11.

3 The following, except as noted, is based on Manuel Velasquez, *Business Ethics*, pp. 9–12.

4 Ibid., p. 9.

5 This is based on ibid., pp. 12–14.

6 Ibid., p. 12. For further discussion see Kurt Baier, *Moral Points of View*, abbr. ed. (New York: Random House, 1965), p. 88. See also Milton Bordwin, "The 3 R's of Ethics," *Management Review*, June 1998, pp. 59–61.

7 For further discussion of ethics and morality see Tom Beauchamp and Norman Bowie, *Ethical Theory and Business* (Upper Saddle River, NJ: Prentice Hall, 1993), pp. 1–19.

8 See Michael McCarthy, "James Bond Hits the Supermarket: Stores Snoop on Shoppers' Habits to Boost Sales," *Wall Street Journal*, 25 August 1993, p. B12. See also Rene Bos, "Business Ethics and Human Ethics," *Organization Studies*, vol. 18, no. 6, 1997, pp. 997–1014.

9 Sara Morris et al., "A Test of Environmental, Situational, and Personal Influences on the Ethical Intentions of CEOs," *Business and Society*, August 1995, pp. 119–147.

10 Justin Longnecker, Joseph McKinney, and Carlos Moore, "The Generation Gap in Business Ethics," *Business Horizons*, September–October 1989, pp. 9–14.

11 Ibid., 10. For a discussion of the development of a scale for measuring individual beliefs about organizational ethics, see Kristina Froelich and Janet Kottke, "Measuring Individual Beliefs About Organizational Ethics," *Educational and Psychological Measurement*, vol. 51, 1991, pp. 377–383.

12 Thomas Tyson, "Does Believing that Everyone Else is Less Ethical Have an Impact on Work Behavior?" *Journal of Business Ethics*, vol. 11, 1992, pp. 707–717. See also Basil Orsini and Diane McDougall, "Fraud Busting Ethics," *CMA 1973*, June 1999, pp. 18–21.

13 For a discussion see, for example, Alan Rowe et al., *Strategic Management: A Methodological Approach* (Reading, MA: Addison-Wesley Publishing Co., 1994), p. 101.

14 Ibid., 6.

15 Kate Walter, "Ethics Hot Lines Tap into More Than Wrongdoing," *HRMagazine*, September 1995, pp. 79–85.

16 Rowe et al., *Strategic Management*, p. 7; see also John J. Quinn, "The Role of 'Good Conversation' in Strategic Control," *Journal of Management Studies*, May 1996, pp. 381–395.

17 Ibid., p. 9.

18 Sandra Gray, "Audit Your Ethics," *Association Management*, September 1996, p. 188.

19 James G. Hunt, *Leadership* (Newbury Park, CA: Sage Publications, 1991), pp. 220–224. One somewhat tongue-in-cheek writer describes culture as a sort of "organizational DNA," since "it's the stuff, mostly intangible, that determines the basic character of a business." See James Moore, "How Companies Have Sex," *Fast Company*, October–November 1997, pp. 66–68.

20 Hunt, p. 221. For a recent discussion of types of cultures see, for example, "A Quadrant of Corporate Cultures," *Management Decision*, September 1996, pp. 37–40.

21 *Blueprints for Service Quality: The Federal Express Approach* (New York: AMA Membership Publications, 1991), p. 13.

22 Richard Osborne, "Core Value Statements: The Corporate Compass," *Business Horizons*, September–October 1991, p. 29.

23 Ibid., p. 29.

24 Gary Dessler, *Winning Commitment: How to Build and Keep a Competitive Work Force* (New York: McGraw-Hill, 1993), p. 85.

25 Ibid., p. 85.

26 Daniel Denison, *Corporate Culture and Organizational Effectiveness* (New York: John Wiley and Sons, 1990), p. 12. For a recent discussion see also Daniel Denison, "What Is the Difference between Organizational Culture and Organizational Climate? A Native's Point of View on a Decade of Paradigm Wars," *Academy of Management Review*, July 1996, pp. 619–654.

27 Example is based on Daniel Denison, *Corporate Culture and Organizational Effectiveness*, pp. 147–174.

28 Ibid., p. 148.

29 Ibid.

30 Ibid., p. 151.

31 Ibid.

32 Ibid.

33 Ibid., p. 154.

34 Ibid., p. 155.

35 "Sweatshop Wars," *Economist*, 27 February 1999, pp. 62–63.

36 Ben & Jerry's Homemade, Inc., *Employee Handbook*.

37 Ben & Jerry's *Public Relations Release*, 5 October 1990.

38 Milton Friedman, *Capitalism and Freedom* (Chicago: University of Chicago Press, 1962), p. 133. See also Charles Handy, "A Better Capitalism," *Across the Board*, April 1998, pp. 16–22. See also Robert Reich, "The New Meaning of Corporate Social Responsibility," *California Management Review*, Winter 1998, pp. 8–17. Reich also believes that because of pressure from investors, nonowner stakeholders are being neglected, and that the government should step in to protect them.

39 Tom Beauchamp and Norman Bowie, *Ethical Theory and Business*, pp. 49–52. See also Marjorie Kelly, "Do Stockholders "Own" Corporations?" *Business Ethics*, June 1999, pp. 4–5.

40 Ibid., p. 79.

41 Ibid., p. 60.

42 Ibid., p. 54.

43 William Evan and R. Edward Freeman, "A Stakeholder Theory of the Modern Corporation: Kantian Capitalism," *Ethical Theory of Business*, p. 82. See also Kenneth Goodpaster, "Business Ethics and Stakeholder Analysis," *Business Ethics Quarterly*, January 1991, pp. 53–73. See also Courtney Pratt, "Business Accountability: To Whom?" *CMA*, January 1998, p. 8.

44 John Simon, Charles Powers, and John Gunnermann, "The Responsibilities of Corporations and Their Owners," *The Ethical Investor: Universities and Corporate Responsibility* (New Haven, CT: Yale University Press, 1972); reprinted in Beauchamp and Bowie, pp. 60–65. See also Roger Kaufman et al., "The Changing Corporate Mind: Organizations, Vision, Missions, Purposes, and Indicators on the Move Toward Societal Payoffs," *Performance Improvement Quarterly*, vol. 11, no. 3, 1998, pp. 32–44.

45 Jo-Ann Johnston, "Social Auditors: The New Breed of Expert," *Business Ethics*, March 1996, p. 27.

46 Karen Paul and Steven Ludenberg, "Applications of Corporate Social Monitoring Systems: Types, Dimensions and Goals," *Journal of Business Ethics*, vol. 11, 1992, pp. 1–10.

47 Karen Paul, "Corporate Social Monitoring in South Africa: A Decade of Achievement, An Uncertain Future," *Journal of Business Ethics*, vol. 8, 1989, p. 464. See also Bernadette Ruf et al. "The Development of a Systematic, Aggregate Measure of Corporate Social Performance," *Journal of Management*, vol. 24, no. 1, 1998, pp. 119–133.

48 Ibid. See also John S. North, "Living Under a Social Code of Ethics: Eli Lilly in South Africa Operating Under the Sullivan Principles," *Business and the Contemporary World*, vol. 8, no. 1, 1996, pp. 168–80; and S. Prakash Sethi, "Working With International Codes of Conduct: Experience of U.S. Companies Operating in South Africa Under the Sullivan Principles," *Business and the Contemporary World*, vol. 8, no. 1, 1996, pp. 129–50. Standards similar to the international quality standards that have been used for some time have been put in place for social accountability areas such as child labor and health and safety. See Ruth Thaler-Carter, "Social Accountability 8000: A Social Guide for Companies or Another Layer of Bureaucracy?" *HRMagazine*, June 1999, pp. 106–108.

49 Janet Near, "Whistle-Blowing: Encourage It!" *Business Horizons*, January-February, 1989, p. 5. See also Robert J. Paul and James B. Townsend, "Don't Kill the Messenger! Whistle-Blowing in America: A Review with Recommendations," *Employee Responsibilities and Rights*, June 1996, pp. 149–61. Nick Perry, "Indecent Exposures: Theorizing Whistle Blowing," *Organization Studies*, vol. 19, no. 2, 1998, pp. 235–257.

50 Near, p. 5. See also Fraser Younson, "Spilling the Beans," *People Management*, 11 June 1998, pp. 25–26.

51 Ibid., p. 6. See also David Lewis, "Whistle Blowing at Work: Ingredients for an Effective Procedure," *Human Resource Management Journal*, vol. 7, no. 4, 1997, pp. 5–11.

52 Patricia Digh, "Coming to Terms with Diversity," *HRMagazine*, November 1998, p. 119.

53 Cox, p. 236.

54 Digh, p. 119.

55 K. Kram, *Mentoring at Work* (Glenview, IL: Scott Foresman, 1985); Cox, p. 198. See also Ian Cunningham and Linda Honold, "Everyone Can Be a Coach," *HRMagazine*, June 1998, pp. 63–66.

56 See, for example, G. F. Dreher and R. A. Ash, "A Comparative Study of Mentoring among Men and Women in Managerial, Professional, and Technical Positions," *Journal of Applied Psychology*, vol. 75, no. 5, 1990, pp. 1–8.

57 "A Report Card on Diversity," *Harvard Business Review*, January–February 1999, p. 43.

58 "The Impact of Diversity on Education," *Harvard Business Review*, January–February 1999, p. 143.

59 Benjamin Hoff, *The Tao of Pooh* (New York: Dutton, 1992), pp. 109–110.

60 Ibid.

SECTION TWO
PLANNING AND SETTING OBJECTIVES

1 Kenneth Laudon and Jane Laudon, *Management Information Systems* (Upper Saddle River, NJ: Prentice Hall), p. 598; "Wal-Mart to Triple the Size of Data Warehouse," TechWeb <*http://192.21.17.45/newsflash/nf617/0210—st6.htm*> 10 February 1999.

2 George L. Morrisey, *A Guide to Tactical Planning* (San Francisco: Jossey-Bass, 1996), p. 61.

3 Leonard Goodstein, Timothy Nolan, and Jay William Pfeiffer, *Applied Strategic Planning* (New York: McGraw-Hill, Inc., 1993), p. 3.

4 R. R. Donnelley and Sons Company Web site, 10 November 1999. <*wwwrrdonnelley.com*>

5 Ronald Henkoff, "How to Plan for 1995," *Fortune*, 31 December 1990, p. 74.

6 Peter Drucker, "Long Range Planning," *Management Science 5*, (1959), pp. 238–49. See also in Bristol Voss, "Cover to Cover Drucker," *Journal of Business Strategy*, May–June 1999, fall 1991, pp. 1–9.

7 Harvey Kahalas, "A Look at Planning and Its Components," *Managerial Planning*, January-February 1982, pp. 13–16; reprinted in Phillip DuBose, *Readings in Management* (Upper Saddle River, NJ: Prentice Hall, Inc., 1988), pp. 49–50. See also Mary M. Crossan, Henry W. Lane, Roderick E. White, and Leo Klus, "The Improvising Organization: Where Planning Meets Opportunity," *Organization Dynamics*, Spring 1996, pp. 20–35.

8 Peter F. Drucker, *The Effective Executive* (New York: Harper & Row, 1966); quoted in Keith Curtis, *From Management Goal Setting to Organizational Results* (Westport, CT: Quorum Books, 1994), p. 101.

9 Peter F. Drucker, *The Practice of Management* (New York: Harper & Row, 1954), pp. 65–83, 100.

10 Morrisey, p. 25.

11 Steven Carroll and Henry Tosi, *Management by Objectives* (New York: Macmillan, 1973).

12 Mark McConkie, "A Clarification of the Goal Setting and Appraisal Processes in MBO," *Academy of Management Review*, December 1991, pp. 29–40. See also Dawn Winters, "The Effects of Learning vs. Outcome Goals on a Simple vs. a Complex Task," *Group and Organization Management*, June 1996, pp. 236–251.

13 *Webster's Collegiate Dictionary of American English* (New York: Simon & Schuster, Inc., 1988).

14 Murray R. Spiegel, *Statistics* (New York: Schaum Publishing, 1961), p. 283.

15 See, for example, Moore, p. 5.

16 George Kress, *Practical Techniques of Business Forecasting* (Westport, CT: Quorum Books, 1985), p. 13. See also Diane Painter, "The Business Economist at Work: Mobil Corp.," *Business Economics*, April 1999, pp. 52–55.

17 Kenneth Laudon and Jane Laudon, *Management Information Systems* (Upper Saddle River, NJ: Prentice Hall), p. 598; and "Wal-Mart to Triple Size of a Warehouse," TechWeb <*http://192.215.17.45/newsflash/nf617/0210—st6.htm.*> 10 February 1999.

18 A. Chairncross, quoted in Thomas Milne, *Business Forecasting*, p. 42.

19 John Chambers, Santinder Mullick, and Donald Smith, "How to Choose the Right Forecasting Technique," *Harvard Business Review*, July–August 1971, pp. 45–74; and Moore, Handbook of Business Forecasting, pp. 265–290. See also John Mentzer, et al. "Benchmarking Sales Forecasting Management," *Business Horizons*, May–June 1999, pp. 48–57. This study of 20 leading U.S. firms found widespread dissatisfaction regarding their current sales forecasting techniques.

20 Philip Kotler, *Marketing Management* (Upper Saddle River, NJ: Prentice Hall, 1997), p. 113.

21 E. Jerome McCarthy and William Perreault, Jr., *Basic Marketing* (Homewood, IL: Irwin, 1990), pp. 131–132.

22 Stan Crock et al., "They Snoop to Conquer," *Business Week*, 28 October 1996, p. 172.

23 Douglas Frantz, "Journalists, or Detectives? Depends on Who Is Asking," *New York Times*, 28 July 1999, p. A1.

24 Melanie Warner, "Nightmare on Net Street," *Fortune*, 6 September 1999, pp. 285–286.

25 Arthur Little, *Global Strategic Planning* (New York: Business International Corporation, 1991), p. 3.

26 Ibid.

27 General Electric Corporation, *Annual Report*, 1998.

28 Andrew Campbell, "Tailored, Not Benchmarked: A Fresh Look at Corporate Planning," *Harvard Business Review*, March–April 1999, pp. 41–50.

29 Ibid., p. 42.

30 Ibid.

31 Ibid., p. 43.

STRATEGIC MANAGEMENT

1   Peter Drucker, *Management: Tasks, Responsibilities, Practices* (New York: Harper & Row, 1974), p. 611. For an interesting point of view on strategic management, see Daniel W. Greening and Richard A. Johnson, "Do Managers and Strategies Matter? A Study in Crisis," *Journal of Management Studies*, January 1996, pp. 25–52.

2   Andrew Campbell and Marcus Alexander, "What's Wrong with Strategy?" *Harvard Business Review*, November–December 1997, p. 42.

3   Ibid., p. 48.

4   See for example, Allan J. Rowe, Richard O. Mason, Carl E. Dickel, Richard B. Mann, and Robert J. Mockler, *Strategic Management* (Reading, MA: Addison-Wesley Publishing Co., 1989), p. 2; James Higgins and Julian Vincze, *Strategic Management* (Fort Worth, TX: The Dryden Press, 1993), p. 5; Peter Wright, Mark Kroll, and John Parnell, *Strategic Management Concepts* (Upper Saddle River, NJ: Prentice Hall, 1996), pp. 1–15.

5   Arthur Thompson and A. J. Strickland, *Strategic Management* (Homewood, IL: Irwin, 1992), 4; Fred R. David, Concepts of Strategic Management (Upper Saddle River, NJ: Prentice Hall, 1997) 1–27. See also Bob Dust, "Making Mission Statements Meaningful," *Training & Development Journal*, June 1996, p. 53.

6   Higgins and Vincze, p. 5.

7   Warren Bennis and Bert Manus, *Leaders: The Strategies for Taking Charge* (New York: Harper & Row, 1985); quoted in Andrew Campbell and Sally Yeung, "Mission, Vision and Strategic Intent," *Long-Range Planning*, vol. 24, no. 4, p. 145. See also James M. Lucas, "Anatomy of a Vision Statement," *Management Review*, February 1998, pp. 22–26.

8   Melanie Warner, "The Young and the Loaded," *Fortune*, 27 September 1999, pp. 78–118.

9   Thompson and Strickland, p. 4. See also George Morrisey, *A Guide to Strategic Planning* (San Francisco: Jossey-Bass, 1996), p. 7.

10 Ibid., p. 8.

11 This is quoted from, and this section is based on, Allan J. Rowe, et al., pp. 114–116; and Stephen George and Arnold Weimerskirch, *Total Quality Management* (New York: Wiley, 1994), pp. 207–221. See also Jeffrey Sampler and James Short, "Strategy in Dynamic Information—Intensive Environments," *Journal of Management Studies*, July 1998, pp. 429–436.

12 This is based on Higgins and Vincze, pp. 200–204.

13 Rowe et al., pp. 246–247.

14 Thompson and Strickland, p. 169. See also Michael Lubatkin and Sayan Chatterjee, "Extending Portfolio Theory into the Domain of Corporate Diversification: Does It Apply?" *Academy of Management Journal*, February 1994, pp. 109–36.

15 Higgins and Vincze, p. 304.

16 John Byrne, Richard Brandt, and Otis Port, "The Virtual Corporation," *Business Week*, 8 February 1993, p. 99. See also Keith Hammonds, "This Virtual Agency Has Big Ideas," *Fast Company*, November 1999, pp. 70–74.

17 See also J. Carlos Jarillo, "On Strategic Networks," *Strategic Management Journal*," vol. 9, 1988, pp. 31–41; and William Davidow and Michael Malone, "The Virtual Corporation," California Business Review, 12 November 1992, 34–42. See also Hammonds, ibid.

18 Byrne et al., p. 99.

19 Ibid., p. 100.

20 Virtual corporations should not be confused with the Japanese Keiretsus strategy. Keiretsus are tightly knit groups of firms governed by a supra-board of directors concerned with establishing the long-term survivability of the Keiretsus organization. Interlocking boards of directors and shared ownership help distinguish Keiretsus from other forms of strategic alliances, including virtual corporations. See, for example, Byrne et al., p. 101; Thompson and Strickland, p. 216; and Kenichi Ohmae, "The Global Logic of Strategic Alliances," *Harvard Business Review*, March–April 1989, pp. 143–154. See also Richard Oliver, "Killer Keiretsu," *Management Review*, September 1999, pp. 10–11.

21 Katherine Mieszkowski, "The E.-Lance Economy," November 1999, *Fast Company*, pp. 66–68.

22 Ibid., p. 68.

23 Unless otherwise noted, the following is based on Michael E. Porter, *Competitive Strategy: Techniques for Analyzing Industries and Competitions* (New York: The Free Press, 1980); and Michael E. Porter, *Competitive Advantage* (New York: The Free Press, 1985).

24 Porter, *Competitive Advantage*, p. 14.

25 Porter.

26 Porter, *Competitive Strategy*, p. 17.

27 Based on Tomima Edmark, "Power Play," *Entrepreneur*, March 1997, pp. 104–107.

28 Clayton Christensen, Making Strategy: Learning by Doing," *Harvard Business Review*, November–December 1997, pp. 141–156.

29 Gary Hamel, "Killer Strategies That Make Shareholders Rich," *Fortune*, 23 June 1997, p. 83.

30 Ibid., p. 83.

31 Ibid., p. 83.

32 Ibid., p. 69.

33 Ibid., p. 31.

34 Philip Evans and Thomas Wurster, "Strategy and the New Economics of Information," *Harvard Business Review*, September–October 1997, p. 72.

35 This is quoted from, and this section is based on, Rowe et al.

36 This is based on ibid, p. 116; and George and Weimerskirch, pp. 207–221.

37 Watson Wyatt, Work USA 1997, in BNA *Bulletin to Management*, 4 September 1997, p. 281.

38 Amar Bhide, "How Entrepreneurs Craft Strategies That Work," *Harvard Business Review*, March–April 1994, pp. 150–160. One study suggests that about two-thirds of entrepreneurs—at least owners of family businesses—do not have written strategic plans. See "Planning Lessons from Family Business Owners," *Infoseek/Reuters*, 26 March 1997.

SECTION THREE
THE FUNDAMENTALS OF ORGANIZING

1   <www.starbucks.com/company/timeline.asp211hqv=1a>.

2   "How Can Big Companies Keep the Entrepreneurial Spirit Alive?" *Harvard Business Review*, November–December 1995, pp. 188–189. See also Mary Jo Hatch, "Exploring the Empty Spaces of Organizing: How Improvisational Jazz Helps Redescribe Organizational Structure," *Organization Studies*, vol. 20, no. 1, 1999, pp. 75–100.

3   Ernest Dale, *Organization* (New York: AMA, 1967), p. 109. See also Ed Clark, "The Adoption of the Multidivisional Form in Large Czech Enterprises: The Role of Economics, Institutional and Strategic Choice Factors," *Journal of Management Studies*, July 1999, pp. 535–537; and Tom Peters, "Destruction Is Cool . . . ," *Forbes*, 23 February 1998, p. 128.

4   Rekha Bach, "Heinz's Johnson to Divest Operations, Scrap Management of Firm by Region," *Wall Street Journal*, 8 December 1997, pp. B10, B12.

5 Kenneth Laudon and Jane Laudon, *Management Information Systems, 5th edition* (Upper Saddle River, NJ: Prentice Hall, 1998), p. 323.

6 Jana Parker-Pope and Joann Lublin, "P&G Will Make Jager CEO Ahead of Schedule," *Wall Street Journal*, 10 September 1998, pp. B1, B8.

7 See, for example, Lawton Burns and Douglas Wholey, "Adoption and Abandonment of Matrix Management Programs: Effects of Organizational Characteristics and Interorganizational Networks," *Academy of Management Journal*, February 1993, pp. 106–138.

8 *Organizing for International Competitiveness* (New York: Business International Corp., 1985) p. 117.

9 Burns and Wholey, p. 106.

10 For a discussion of this type of organization and its problems, see Stanley Davis and Paul Lawrence, *Matrix* (Reading, MA: Addison-Wesley, 1967); and Davis and Lawrence, "Problems of Matrix Organizations," *Harvard Business Review*, May–June 1978, pp. 131–142. See also Wilma Bernasco, "Balanced Matrix Structure and New Product Development Process at Texas Instruments Materials and Controls Division," *R&D Management*, April 1999, p. 121.

11 John Hunt, "Is Matrix Management a Recipe for Chaos?" *Financial Times*, January 1998, p. 14.

12 Wilma Bernasco, "Balanced Matrix Structure and New Product Development Process at Texas Instruments Materials and Controls Division," *R&D Management*, April 1999, p. 121.

13 Ibid.

14 Ibid.

15 Rob Walker, "Down on the Farm," *Fast Company*, February–March 1997, pp. 112–122.

DESIGNING ORGANIZATIONS TO MANAGE CHANGE

1 Except as noted, the remainder of this section is based on James Shonk, *Team-Based Organizations* (Chicago: Irwin, 1997).

2 Peters, *Thriving on Chaos*, p. 256.

3 Charles Fishman, "Engines of Democracy," *Fast Company*, October 1999, pp. 174–202.

4 Peters, *Liberation Management*, p. 238.

5 William H. Miller, "Chesebrough-Ponds at a Glance," *Industry Week*, 19 October 1992, pp. 14–15.

6 Shonk, pp. 35–38.

7 *Webster's New World Dictionary, 3rd College edition.* (New York: Simon and Schuster, Inc., 1988), p. 911. For a discussion of networked organizations, see James Brian Quinn, Intelligent Enterprise (New York: Free Press, 1992), pp. 213–40.

8 Ram Charan, "How Networks Reshape Organizations—For Results," *Harvard Business Review*, September–October 1991, pp. 104–115.

9 Ibid., pp. 106–107.

10 Ibid., 106; see also Marlene Piturro, "What Are You Doing about the New Global Realities?" *Management Review*, March 1999, p. 16.

11 Ibid., p.108.

12 Christopher Bartlett and Sumantra Ghoshal, "What Is a Global Manager?" *Harvard Business Review*, September–October 1992, pp. 62–74.

13 Cyrus Freidheim, Jr., "The Battle of the Alliances," *Management Review*, September 1999, pp. 46–51.

14 Tom Lester, "The Rise of the Network," *International Management*, June 1992, p. 72.

15 Paul Evans, Yves Doz, and Andre Laurent, *Human Resource Management in International Firms* (London: Macmillan, 1989), p. 123.

16 David Kilpatrick, "Groupware Goes Boom," *Fortune*, 27 December 1993, pp. 99–101.

17 Kenneth Laudon and Jane Laudon, *Essentials of Management Information Systems* (Upper Saddle River, NJ: Prentice Hall, 1997), pp. 413–416.

18 Bob Underwood, "Transforming with Collaborative Computing," *AS/400 Systems Management*, March 1999, p. 59.

19 "Product Development Tool Gets Revamped with Java; Ip Team Integrates Suppliers and Contractors," *Computer World*, 24 May 1999, p. 16.

20 Douglas Johnson, "Discuss Changing Models in Real Time," *Design News*, 3 May 1999, p. 96.

21 Richard Dennis, "Online R&D Management: The Way Forward," *R&D Management*, January 1998, pp. 27–36.

22 Phillip Evans and Thomas Wurster, "Strategy and the New Economics of Information," *Harvard Business Review*, September–October 1997, p. 75.

23 Bill Gates, *Business @ the Speed of Thought* (New York: Warner Books, 1999), pp. 239.

24 Mary Anne Devanna and Noel Tichy, "Creating the Competitive Organization of the 21st Century: The Boundaryless Corporation," *Human Resource Management*, Winter 1990, pp. 455–471.

25 Larry Hirschhorn and Thomas Gilmore, "The New Boundaries of the 'Boundaryless' Company," *Harvard Business Review*, May–June 1992, 104. See also Daniel Denison, Stuart Hart, and Joel Kahn, "From Chimneys to Cross-Functional Teams: Developing and Validating a Diagnostic Model," *Academy of Management Journal*, August 1996, pp. 1005–1023.

26 This is based on Hirschhorn and Gilmore, pp. 104–108.

27 Except as noted, the remainder of this section is based on Hirschhorn and Gilmore, "The New Boundaries," pp. 107–108.

28 Hirschhorn and Gilmore, p. 107.

29 Ibid., p. 108.

30 Ibid., p. 109.

31 Luc Hatlestad, "New Shades of Blue," *Red Herring*, November 1999, p. 126.

STAFFING THE ORGANIZATION

1 Cisco Web site <www.cisco.com.>

2 Catherine Truss and Lynda Gratton, "Strategic Human Resource Management: A Conceptual Approach," *International Journal of Human Resource Management*, September 1994, p. 663.

3 See also James Clifford, "Manage Work Better to Better Manage Human Resources: A Comparative Study of Two Approaches to Job Analysis," *Public Personnel Management*, Spring 1996, pp. 89–103.

4 Donald Harris, "A Matter of Privacy: Managing Personnel Data in Company Computers," *Personnel*, February 1987, p. 37.

5 Shari Caudron, "Low Unemployment Is Causing a Staffing Draught," *Personnel Journal*, November 1996, pp. 59–67.

6 "Tight Labor Markets Bring New Paradigm," *BNA Bulletin to Management*, 23 October 1997, p. 344.

7 "High-Stakes Recruiting in High-Tech," *BNA Bulletin to Management*, 12 February 1998, p. 48.

8 Arthur R. Pell, *Recruiting and Selecting Personnel* (New York: Regents, 1969), pp. 10–12; see also Katherine Tyler, "Employees Can Help Recruiting New Talent," *HRMagazine*, September 1996, pp. 57–61.

9 Ibid., p. 11.

10 Allison Thomson, "The Contingent Work Force," *Occupational Outlook Quarterly*, Spring 1995, p. 45.

11 Amy Kover, "Manufacturing's Hidden Asset: Temp Workers," *Fortune*, 10 November 1997, pp. 28–29.

12 One Bureau of Labor Statistics study suggests that temporary employees produce the equivalent of two or more hours of work per day more than their permanent counterparts. For a discussion, see Shari Caudron, "Contingent Workforce Spurs HR Planning," *Personnel Journal*, July 1994, p. 54; See also Brenda Sunoo, "Temp Firms Turn Up the Heat on Hiring," *Workforce*, April 1999, pp. 50–52.

13 "Search and Destroy," *The Economist*, 27 June 1998, p. 63.

14 Ibid.

15 Ibid.

16 The study on employment referrals was published by Bernard Hodes Advertising, Dept. 100, 555 Madison Avenue, NY, NY 10022. See also Allan Halcrow, "Employees Are Your Best Recruiters," *Personnel Journal*, November 1988, pp. 41–49. See also Andy Hargerstock and Hand Engel, "Six Ways to Boost Employee Referral Programs," *HRMagazine*, December 1994, pp.72ff; See also Katherine Tyler, "Employees Can Help Recruiting New Talent," *HRMagazine*, September 1996, pp. 57–61.

17 "High-Stakes Recruiting in High-Tech," *BNA Bulletin to Management*, 12 February 1998, p. 48.

18 Sara Rynes, Marc Orlitzky, and Robert Bretz, Jr., "Experienced Hiring versus College Recruiting: Practices and Emerging Trends," *Peronnel Psychology*, vol. 50 (1997), pp. 309–339.

19 See, for example, Richard Becker, "Ten Common Mistakes in College Recruiting—or How to Try Without Really Succeeding," *Personnel*, March–April 1975, pp. 19–28. See also Sara Rynes and John Boudreau, "College Recruiting in Large Organizations: Practice, Evaluation, and Research Implications," *Personnel Psychology*, Winter 1986, pp. 729–757.

20 "Internships Provide Workplace Snapshot," *BNA Bulletin to Management*, 22 May 1997, p. 168.

21 Nancy Austin, "First Aide," *Inc.*, September 1999, pp. 68–71.

22 Ibid., p. 78.

23 Ibid., p. 72.

24 "Internet Recruitment Survey," *BNA Bulletin to Management*, 22 May 1997, pp. 164–165.

25 Elaine Appleton, "Recruiting on the Internet," *Datamation*, August 1995, p. 39.

26 Julia King, "Job Networking," *Enterprise Networking*, 26 January 1995; see also David Schulz, "Internet Emerging as a Major Vehicle for Mid-Level Retail Recruiting." *Stores*, June 1999, pp. 70–73.

27 Brenda Paik Sunoo, "Thumbs Up for Staffing Websites," *Workforce*, October 1997, pp. 67–73; See also Katherine Hildebrand, "Recruiting on the Internet," *Colorado Business Magazine*, July 1998, pp. 46–48.

28 Gillian Flynn, "Cisco Turns the Internet Inside (and) Out," *Personnel Journal*, October 1996, pp. 28–34.

29 "Retirees Increasingly Reentering the Workforce," *BNA Bulletin to Management*, 16 January 1997, p. 17.

30 Samuel Greengard, "At Peoplesoft, Client/Server Drives the HR Office of the Future," *Personnel Journal*, May 1996, p. 92; see also Bill Gates, *Business @ the Speed of Thought (New York) Warner Books, 1999), pp. 41–42*.

31 Jennifer Koch, *"Finding Qualified Hispanic Candidates," Recruitment Today*, Spring 1990, p. 35; see also Shelley Coolidge, "Minority Grads Sought for Jobs," *Christian Science Monitor*, 5 December 1997, p. 8.

32 This compares with 21.5% for black job seekers and 23.9% for white job seekers. Michelle Harrison Ports, "Trends in Job Search Methods, 1990–92," *Monthly Labor Review*, October 1993, p. 64.

33 Bill Leonard, "Welfare Reform: A New Deal for HR," *HRMagazine*, March 1997, pp. 78–86; Jennifer Laabs, "Welfare Law: HR's Role in Employment," *Workforce*, January 1998, pp. 30–39.

34 Herbert Greenberg, "A Hidden Source of Talent," *HRMagazine*, March 1997, pp. 88–91.

35 "Welfare-to-Work: No Easy Chore," *BNA Bulletin to Management*, 13 February 1997, p. 56.

36 See for example Ann Fields, "Class Act," *Inc. Technology*, 1997, pp. 55–57.

37 "Industry Report 1999," *Training*, October 1999, pp. 37–60.

38 Jennifer Reese, "Starbuck," *Fortune*, 9 December 1996, 190–200.

39 Kenneth Wexley and Gary Latham, *Developing and Training Human Resources in Organizations* (Glenview, IL: Scott, Foresman, 1981), p. 107.

40 Mary Boone and Susan Schulman, "Teletraining: A High-Tech Alternative," Personnel, May 1985, pp. 4–9. See also Ron Zemke, "The Rediscovery of Video Teleconferencing," *Training*, September 1986, pp. 28–36; and Carol Haig, "Clinics Fill Training Niche," *Personnel Journal*, September 1987, pp. 134–140.

41 Joseph Giusti, David Baker, and Peter Braybash, "Satellites Dish Out Global Training," *Personnel Journal*, June 1991, pp. 80–84.

42 Macy's Goes 'On Air' to Inform Employees," *BNA Bulletin to Management*, May 15, 1997, p. 160.

43 Larry Stevens, "The Internet: Your Newest Training Tool?, *Personnel Journal*, July 1996, pp. 27–31; see also Samuel Greengard, "Web-Based Training Yields Maximum Returns," *Workforce*, February 1999, pp. 95–96.

44 Shari Caudron, "Your Learning Technology Primer," *Personnel Journal*, June 1996, pp. 120–136.

45 Ibid., p. 130.

46 John Aram, *Presumed Superior* (Upper Saddle River, NJ: Prentice Hall).

47 *Sacrmento Bee*, 21 February 1999, Special Report.

48 Gillian Flynn, "It Takes Value to Capitalize on Change," *Workforce*, April 1997, pp. 27–34.

SECTION FOUR
BEING A LEADER

1 Melanie Warner, "Getting up to Internet Speed," *Fortune*, 10 January 2000, pp. 185–186.

2 Ibid., p. 186.

3 Jeffrey McNally, Stephen Gerras, and R. Craig Bullis, "Teaching Leadership at the U.S. Military Academy at West Point," *Journal of Applied Behavioral Science*, June 1996, p. 181.

4 McNally, et al., p. 178.

5 "Steve Job's Apple Gets Way Cooler," *Fortune*, 24 January 2000, pp. 66–76.

6 Ibid., 67.

7 Ibid., 67.

8 M. S. El-Namiki, "Creating a Corporate Vision," *Long-Range Planning*, vol. 25, no. 6, December 1992, p. 25.

9 Ibid.

10 Arthur Thompson and A. J. Strickland, *Strategic Management* (Homewood, IL: Irwin, 1992), p. 7.

11 Shawn Tully, "How Cisco Mastered the Net," *Fortune*, 17 August 1998, pp. 207–210.

12 Tully, p. 210.

13 Shelley Kirkpatrick and Edwin A. Locke, "Leadership: Do Traits Matter?" *Academy of Management Executive*, May 1991, p. 49, and Edwin A. Locke, et al., *The Essence of Leadership: The Four Keys to Leading Successfully* (New York: Lexington/Macmillan, 1991). See also Ruth Tait, "The Attributes of Leadership," *Leadership and Organization Development Journal*, vol. 17, no. 1 (1996), pp. 27–31; David L. Cawthon, "Leadership: The Great Man Theory Revisited," *Business Horizons*, May 1996, pp. 1–4; Robert Baum, "A Longitudinal Study of the Relation of Vision and Vision Communication to Venture Growth in Entrepreneurial Firms," *Journal of Applied Psychology*, February 1998, pp. 43–55.

14 Kirkpatrick and Locke, p. 49.

15 Ibid., p. 50.

16 Except as noted, this section is based on ibid., pp. 48–60; See also Ross Laver, "Building a Better Boss: Studies Show That the Personality of a Chief Executive Can Have a Major Impact on Profits and Productivity," *Maclean's*, 30 September 1996, p. 41.

17 Ibid., p. 53.

18 Ibid., p. 54.

19 Ibid., p. 55.

20 Ibid., pp. 5–6.

21 Daniel Goleman, "What Makes a Leader?" *Harvard Business Review*, November–December 1998, pp. 93–99.

22 Goleman, p. 94.

23 Goleman, p. 99.

24 Chester Barnard, *The Functions of the Executive* (Cambridge, MA: Harvard University Press, 1938). See also Roger Dawson, *Secrets of Power Persuasion* (Upper Saddle River, NJ: Prentice-Hall, 1992); Sydney Finkelstein, "Power in Top Management Teams: Dimensions, Measurement, and Validation," *Academy of Management Journal*, August 1992; and Jeffrey Pfeffer, *Managing with Power: Politics and Influence in Organizations* (Boston: Harvard Business School Press, 1992).

25 Eli Cohen and Noel Tichy, "Operation: Leadership," *Fast Company*, September 1999, p. 280.

26 Cohen and Tichy, p. 280.

27 See, for example, Kirkpatrick and Locke, p. 49.

28 Ibid., p. 56.

29 For a discussion of this issue, see Peter Wissenberg and Michael Kavanagh, "The Independence of Initiating Structure and Consideration: A Review of Evidence," *Personnel Psychology*, vol. 25 (1972) pp. 119–130. See also Gary A. Yukl, *Leadership in Organizations, 3rd ed.* (Upper Saddle River, NJ: Prentice-Hall, 1994). For an interesting example of what can go wrong when the leader uses the wrong leadership style, see Thomas Ricks, "Army at Odds: West Point Posting Becomes a Minefield for 'Warrior' Officer," *Wall Street Journal*, 13 March 1997, pp. A1, A9.

30 Ralph Stogdill and A. E. Koonz, "Leader Behavior: Its Description and Measurement" (Columbus: Bureau of Business Research, Ohio State University, 1957). See also Bernard M. Bass, *Bass & Stogdill's Handbook of Leadership: Theory, Research, & Managerial Applications, 3rd ed.* (New York: The Free Press, 1990).

31 Ralph Stogdill, *Managers, Employees, Organizations* (Columbus: Bureau of Business Research, Ohio State University, 1965).

32 Gary Yukl, "Towards a Behavioral Theory of Leadership," *Organizational Behavior and Human Performance*, July 1971, pp. 414–440. See also Gary A. Yukl, *Leadership in Organizations, 3rd ed.* (Upper Saddle River, NJ: Prentice-Hall, 1994).

33 Hal Lancaster, "Herb Kelleher Has One Main Strategy: Treat Employees Well," *Wall Street Journal*, 31 August 1999, p. B1.

34 Blake and Mouton, *The Managerial Grid*.

35 Chester Schriesheim, Robert J. House, and Steven Kerr, "Leader Initiating Structure: A Reconciliation of Discrepant Research Results and Some Empirical Tests," *Organizational Behavior and Human Performance*, April 1976. See also Bernard M. Bass, *Bass & Stogdill's Handbook of Leadership: Theory, Research, & Managerial Applications, 3rd ed.* (New York: The Free Press, 1990).

36 Victor Vroom and Arthur Jago, "On the Validity of the Vroom-Yetton Model," *Journal of Applied Psychology*, vol. 63, no. 2 (1978), pp. 151–162; Madeleine Heilman et al, "Reactions to Prescribed Leader Behavior as a Function of Role Perspective: The Case of Vroom-Yetton Model," *Journal of Applied*

Psychology, February 1984, pp. 50–60. See also Donna Brown, "Why Participative Management Won't Work Here" *Management Review*, June 1992.

37 Vroom and Jago, pp. 151–162.

38 See, for example, Mark Tubbs and Steven Akeberg, "The Role of Intentions in Work Motivation: Implications for Goal Setting Theory and Research," *Academy of Management Review*, January 1991, pp. 180–199.

39 Rensis Likert, *New Patterns of Management* (New York: McGraw-Hill, 1961).

40 Robert Day and Robert Hamblin, "Some Effects of Close and Punitive Styles of Leadership," *American Journal of Psychology*, vol. 69, (1964), pp. 499–510.

41 See for example, Nancy Morse, *Satisfaction in the White Collar Job* (Ann Arbor, MI: Survey Research Center, University of Michigan, 1953).

42 J. M. Burns, *Leadership* (New York: Harper, 1978).

43 For a discussion, see Ronald Deluga, "Relationship of Transformational and Transactional Leadership with Employee Influencing Strategies," *Group and Organizational Studies*, December 1988, pp. 457–458. See also Philip M. Podsakoff, Scott B. MacKenzie, and William H. Bommer, "Transformational Leader Behaviors as Determinants of Employee Satisfaction, Commitment, Trust, and Organizational Citizenship Behaviors," *Journal of Management*, vol. 22, no. 2 (1996), pp. 259–298.

44 Joseph Seltzer and Bernard Bass, "Transformational Leadership: Beyond Initiation and Consideration," *Journal of Management*, vol. 4, (1990), p. 694. See also Bernard M. Bass, "Theory of Transformational Leadership Redux," *Leadership Quarterly*, Winter 1995, pp. 463–478.

45 Gary Yukl, "Managerial Leadership," p. 269.

46 N. M. Tichy and M. A. Devanna, *The Transformational Leader* (New York: Wiley 1986).

47 Seltzer and Bass, p. 694.

48 Deluga, p. 457.

49 Frances Yamarino and Bernard Bass, "Transformational Leadership and Multiple Levels of Analysis," Human Relations, vol. 43, no. 10 (1990), p. 976; See also David Walman, "CEO Charismatic Leadership: Levels of Management and Levels of Analysis Effects," *Academy of Management Review*, April 1999, pp. 266–268.

50 J. A. Conger, "Inspiring Others: The Language of Leadership," *Academy of Management Executive* vol. 5, (1991), pp. 31–45; See also Linda Hill, "Charismatic Leadership in Organizations," *Personnel Psychology*, October 1999, pp. 767–768.

51 Bernard Bass, *Leadership and Performance Beyond Expectations* (New York: The Free Press, 1985); and Deluga, pp. 457–458; See also Boas Shamir, "Correlates of Charismatic Leader Behavior in Military Units: Subordinates Attitudes, Unit of Characteristics, and Superiors Appraisals of Leader Performance," *Academy of Management Journal*, August 1998, pp. 387–410.

52 Deluga, p. 457.

53 Ibid.

54 Yamarino and Bass, p. 981.

55 For a review, see Robert Keller, "Transformational Leadership and the Performance of Research and Development Project Groups," *Journal of Management*, vol. 18, no. 3 (1992), pp. 489–501.

56 J. J. Hater and Bernard Bass, "Superiors' Evaluations and Subordinates' Perceptions of Transformational and Transactional Leadership," *Journal of Applied Psychology*, vol. 73 (1988), pp. 695–702.

57 J. M. Howell and C. A. Higgins, "Champions of Technological Innovation," *Administrative Science Quarterly*, vol. 35 (1990), pp. 317–341.

58 Yamarino and Bass, p. 981.

59 C. M. Solomon, "Careers Under Glass," *Personnel Journal*, vol. 69, no. 4 (1990), pp. 96–105.

60 See, for example, James Bowditch and Anthony Buono, *A Primer on Organizational Behavior* (New York: John Wiley, 1994), p. 238.

61 Russell Kent and Sherry Moss, "Effects of Sex and Gender Role on Leader Emergence," *Academy of Management Journal*, vol. 37, no. 5 (1994), pp. 1335–46; Jane Baack, Norma Carr-Ruffino, and Monica Pelletier, "Making It to the Top: Specific Leadership Skills," *Women in Management Review*, vol. 8, no. 2 (1993), pp. 17–23.

62 S. M. Donnel and J. Hall, "Men and Women as Managers: A Significant Case of No Significant Difference," *Organizational Dynamics*, vol. 8, (1980), pp. 60–77. See also Jennifer L. Berdahl, "Gender and Leadership in Work Groups: Six Alternative Models," *Leadership Quarterly*, Spring 1996, pp. 21–40.

63 M. A. Hatcher, "The Corporate Woman of the 1990s: Maverick or Innovator?" *Psychology of Women Quarterly*, vol. 5, (1991), pp. 251–259.

64 D. G. Winter, *The Power Motive* (New York: The Free Press, 1975).

65 L. McFarland Shore and G. C. Thornton, "Effects of Gender on Self and Supervisory Ratings," *Academy of Management Journal*, vol. 29, no. 1 (1986), pp. 115–129; quoted in Bowditch and Buono, p. 238.

66 G. H. Dobbins and S. J. Paltz, "Sex Differences in Leadership: How Real Are They?" *Academy of Management Review*, vol. 11 (1986), pp. 118–127; R. Drazin and E. R. Auster, "Wage Differences Between Men and Women: Performance Appraisal Ratings versus Salary Allocation as the Locus of Bias," *Human Resource Management*, vol. 26 (1987):157–168. See also Nancy DiTomaso and Robert Hooijberg, "Diversity and the Demands of Leadership," *Leadership Quarterly*, Summer 1996, pp. 163–187 and Chao C. Chen and Ellen Van Velsor, "New Directions for Research and Practice in Diversity Leadership," *Leadership Quarterly*, Summer 1996, pp. 285–302.

67 M. Jelinek and N. J. Alder, "Women: World-Class Managers for Global Competition," *Academy of Management Executive*, vol. 2, no. 1 (1988), pp. 11–19; J. Grant, "Women as Managers: What Can They Offer to Organizations?" *Organizational Dynamics*, vol. 16, no. 3 (1988), pp. 56–63. On the other hand, one author suggests that women should be more Machiavellian: "War favors the dangerous woman. Women may love peace and seek stability, but these conditions seldom serve them." Harriet Rubin, *The Princessa: Machiavelli for Women* (New York: Doubleday/Currenly, 1997), quoted in Anne Fisher, "What Women Can Learn from Machiavelli," *Fortune*, April 1997, p. 162.

68 Frederick E. Fiedler, *A Theory of Leadership Effectiveness* (New York: McGraw-Hill, 1967), p. 147; See also David Stauffer, "Once a Leader, Always a Leader?," *Across the Board*, April 1999, pp. 14–19.

69 Ibid.

70 See, for example, Robert J. House and J. V. Singh, "Organizational Behavior: Some New Directions for I/O Psychology," *Annual Review of Psychology*, vol. 38, (1987), pp. 669–718; L. H. Peters, D. D. Hartke, and J. T. Pohlmann, "Fiedler's Contingency Theory of Leadership: An Application of the Meta-Analytic Procedures of Schmidt and Hunter," *Psychological Bulletin*, vol. 97, (1985), pp. 274–285.

71 Fred Fiedler and J. E. Garcia, *New Approaches to Effective Leadership: Cognitive Resources and Organizational Performance* (New York: John Wiley and Sons, 1987); and Robert T. Vecchio, "Theoretical and Empirical Examination of Cognitive Resource Theory," *Journal of Applied Psychology*, April 1990, pp.

141–147. See also Robert Vecchio, "Cognitive Resource Theory: Issues for Specifying a Test of the Theory" *Journal of Applied Psychology*, June 1992.

72 Robert J. House and Terrence Mitchell, "Path-Goal Theory of Leadership," *Contemporary Business*, vol. 3 (1974), pp. 81–98; and Abraham Sagie and Meni Koslowsky, "Organizational Attitudes and Behaviors as a Function of Participation in Strategic and Tactical Change Decisions: An Application of Path-Goal Theory," *Journal of Organizational Behavior*, January 1994, pp. 37–48.

73 J. Fulk and E. R. Wendler, "Dimensionality of Leader-Subordinate Interactions: A Path-Goal Investigation," *Organizational Behavior and Human Performance* vol. 30 (1982), pp. 241–264.

74 G. B. Graen and T. A. Scandura, "Toward a Psychology of Daidic Organizing." L. L. Cummings and B. M. Staw (eds.) *Research in Organizational Behavior,* vol. 9 (Greenwich, CT: J.A.I. Press, 1987), p. 208; See also David Schneider and Charles Goldwasser, "Be a Model Leader of Change," *Management Review*, March 1998, pp. 41–48.

75 Antoinette Phillips and Arthur Bedeian, "Leader-Follower Exchange Quality: The Role of Personal and Interpersonal Attributes," *Academy of Management Journal*, vol. 37, no. 4 (1994), pp. 990–1001; see also Nancy Boyd and Robert Taylor, "A Developmental Approach to the Examination of Friendship in Leader and Follower Relationships," *Leadership Quarterly*, vol. 9, no. 1, 1998, pp. 1–25; Jaesub Lee, "Leader Member Exchange: The "Pelz Effect" and Cooperative Communication Between Group Members," *Management Communications Quarterly*, November 1997, pp. 266–287; and Christopher Avery, "All Power to You: Collaborative Leadership Works," *Journal for Quality and Participation*, March–April 1999, pp. 36–41.

76 Jerald Greenberg, *Managing Behavior in Organizations* (Upper Saddle River, NJ: Prentice-Hall, 1996), p. 215.

77 Phillips and Bedeian, "Leader-Follower Exchange Quality."

78 See Robert P. Vecchio, "Situational Leadership Theory: An Examination of a Prescriptive Theory," *Journal of Applied Psychology*, August 1987, pp. 444–451; and Jerald Greenberg, *Managing Behavior in Organizations* (Upper Saddle River, NJ: Prentice-Hall, 1996), p. 226.

79 Steve Kerr and J. M. Jermier, "Substitutes for Leadership: Their Meaning and Measurement," *Organizational Behavior and Human Performance*, vol. 22 (1978), pp. 375–403. See also Philip M. Podsakoff and Scott B. MacKenzie, "An Examination of Substitutes for Leadership Within a Levels-of-Analysis Framework," *Leadership Quarterly*, Fall 1995, pp. 289–328.

80 David Alcorn, "Dynamic Followership: Empowerment at Work," *Management Quarterly*, Spring 1992, pp. 11–13.

81 Jon Howell, David Bowen, Peter Dorfman, Steven Kerr, and Philip Podsakoff, "Substitutes for Leadership: Effective Alternatives to Ineffective Leadership," *Organizational Dynamics*, Summer 1990, p. 23.

82 Ibid.

83 "What It Means to Lead," *Fast Company*, February–March 1997.

84 Adrian Tomine, "Fast Pack 2000," *Fast Company*, March 2000, pp. 246–247.

85 Ibid., p. 268.

86 Ibid.

THE LEADER'S ROLE IN ORGANIZATIONAL AND CULTURAL CHANGE

1 Linda Grant, "Menaced Moments," *Fortune*, 27 October 1997, p. 188; and Linda Grant, "Kodak Still Is in a Fix," *Fortune*, 11 May 1998, pp. 179–181.

2   The following is based on Nadler and Tushman, pp. 77–97.
3   Ibid., p. 82.
4   Ibid., p. 85.
5   For a discussion see Julian Barling, Tom Weber, and E. Kevin Kelloway, "Effects of Transformational Leadership Training on Attitudinal and Financial Outcomes: A Field Experiment," *Journal of Applied Psychology,* December 1996, pp. 827–832.
6   Ibid.
7   See, for example, John Rizzo, Robert J. House, and Sydney I. Lirtzinian, "Role Conflict and Ambiguity in Complex Organizations,: *Administrative Science Quarterly*, 15 June 1970, pp. 150–63. For additional views on sources of conflict, see Patricia A. Gwartney-Gibbs and Denise H. Lach, "Gender Differences in Clerical Workers' Disputes Over Tasks," *Human Relations*, June 1994, pp. 611–40; and Kevin J. Williams and George Alliger, "Role Stressors, Mood Spillover, and Perceptions of Work-Family Conflict in Employed Parents,: *Academy of Management Journal*, August 1994, pp.837–869.

SECTION FIVE
MANAGING ORGANIZATIONAL
AND CULTURAL CHANGE

1   See for example, Martha Peak, "An Era of Wrenching Corporate Change," *Management Review*, July 1996, pp. 45–49. See also Elias Carayannis, "Organizational Transformation and Strategic Learning in High Risk, High Complexity Environment," *Technovation*, February 1999, pp. 87–94.
2   Melanie Warner, "Nightmare on Net Street," *Fortune*, 6 September 1999, pp. 285–288.
3   Ibid., p. 286.
4   Based on David Nadler and Michael Tushman, "Beyond the Charismatic Leader: Leadership and Organizational Change," *California Management Review*, Winter 1990, p. 80; and Alfred Marcus, "Responses to Externally Induced Innovation: To their Effects on Organizational Performance," *Strategic Management Journal*, vol. 9, (1988), pp. 194–202. See also Steve Crom, "Change Leadership: the Virtues of Obedience," *Leadership & Organization Development Journal*, March–June 1999, pp. 162–168.
5   Nadler and Tushman, p. 80.
6   Gary Dessler, *Winning Commitment: How to Build and Keep a Competitive Work Force* (New York: McGraw-Hill, 1993), p. 85.
7   Ibid., p. 85. See also Varun Grover, "From Business Reengineering to Business Process Change Management: A Longitudinal Study of Trends and Practices," *IEEE Transactions on Engineering Management*, February 1999, p. 36.
8   Denison, Corporate Culture, p. 12. For a recent discussion see also Daniel Denison, "What Is the Difference between Organizational Culture and Organizational Climate? A Native's Point of View on a Decade of Paradigm Wars," *Academy of Management Review*, July 1996, pp. 619–654.
9   Nadler and Tushman, 79.
10 Niccolo Machiavelli (trans. W. K. Marriott), *The Prince*, (London: J. M. Dent & Sons, Ltd., 1958).
11 Richard Osborne, "Core Values Statements: The Corporate Compass," *Business Horizons*, September–October 1991, pp. 28–34.
12 John Mariotti, "The Challenge of Change," *Industry Week*, 6 April 1998, p. 140.
13 Paul Lawrence, "How to Deal with Resistance to Change," *Harvard Business Review*, May–June, 1954. See also Andrew W. Schwartz, "Eight Guidelines for Managing Change," *Supervisory Management*, July 1994, pp. 3–5; Thomas J. Werner and Robert F. Lynch, "Challenges of a Change Agent" *Journal for Quality and Participation*, June 1994, pp. 50–54; Larry Reynolds, "Understand Employees' Resistance to Change,"

HR Focus, June 1994, pp. 17–18; Kenneth E. Hultman, "Scaling the Wall of Resistance," *Training & Development Journal*, October 1995, pp. 15–18; and Eric Dent, "Challenging Resistance to Change," *Journal of Applied Behavioral Science*, March 1999, p. 25.
14 Timothy Judge et al., "Managerial Coping with Organizational Change: A Dispositional Perspective," *Journal of Applied Psychology*, vol. 84, no. 1, 1999, pp. 107–122.
15 Kurt Lewin, "Group Decision and Social Change," in T. Newcomb and E. Hartley, (Eds.), *Readings in Social Psychology* (New York: Holt Rinehart & Winston, 1947). See also Thomas Cummings and Christopher Worley, *Organization Development and Change* (Minneapolis: West Publishing Company, 1993), p. 53. See also Terry Neese, "Convincing Your Employees to Accept Change," *LI Business News*, 7 March 1999, p. 41.
16 Charles Philips, "Can He Fix Philips?" *Fortune*, 31 May 1997, pp. 98–100.
17 John P. Kotter, *Leading Change* (Boston: Harvard Business School Press, 1996), pp. 40–41.
18 Ibid., p. 44.
19 Ibid., p. 57.
20 Ibid., pp. 90–91.
21 Ibid., pp. 101–102.
22 Kathryn Harris, "Mr. Sony Confronts Hollywood," *Fortune*, 23 December 1996, p. 36.
23 Noel Tichy and Ram Charan, "The CEO as Coach: An Interview with Allied Signal's Lawrence A. Bossidy," *Harvard Business Review*, March–April 1995, p. 77.
24 Suzy Wetlaufer, "Driving Change: An Interview with Ford Motor Co.'s Jacques Nasser," *Harvard Business Review*, March–April 1999, pp. 77–88.
25 Christian Ellis and E. Michael Norman, "Real Change in Real-Time," *Management Review*, February 1999, pp. 33–38.
26 Beer, Eisenstat, and Spector, 163.
27 This is based on Kotter, "Leading Change: Why Transformation Efforts Fail," pp. 61–66.
28 Ibid., p. 65.
29 Beer, Eisenstat, and Spector, p. 164.
30 Erin Brown, "Big Business Meets the E World," *Fortune*, 8 November 1999, p. 88.
31 Ibid., p. 91.
32 Ibid.
33 David Baum, "Running the Rapids," *Profit Magazine*, November 1999, p. 54.
34 Ibid.
35 Stewart Alsop, "E or Be Eaten," *Fortune*, 8 November 1999, pp. 94–95.
36 Laurie Windham, "Exec Help Wanted," *Profit Magazine*, November 1999, pp. 13–15.

CONTROLLING AND BUILDING
COMMITMENT

1   Tim McCullom, "Getting Control of All That Paper," *Nation's Business*, 1 November 1998, p. 30.
2   Kenneth Merchant, "The Control Function of Management," *Sloan Management Review*, Summer 1982, p. 44.
3   This section is based on William Newman, *Constructive Control* (Upper Saddle River, NJ: Prentice Hall, 1995), pp. 6–9.
4   Kristina Sullivan, "Boeing Achieves Internet Liftoff," *PC Week*, 10 May 1999, p. 67.
5   Ibid.
6   Glenn A. Welsch, *Budgeting: Profit Planning and Control* (Upper Saddle River, NJ: Prentice Hall, 1988), p. 16.
7   Thomas Connellan, *How to Improve Human Performance: Behaviorism in Business and Industry* (New York: Harper & Row, 1978), pp. 68–73.

8 For a discussion, see Joan Woodward, *Industrial Organization: Behavior and Control* (London: Oxford, 1970), pp. 37–56.

9 Robert Simons, *Levers of Control: How Managers Use Innovative Control Systems to Drive Strategic Renewal* (Boston: Harvard Business School Press, 1995), p. 80.

10 This classification is based on Simons, p. 81.

11 For example, see Simons, p. 82.

12 Daniel Wren, *The Evolution of Management Thought* (John Wiley & Sons, 1994), p. 115.

13 Based on Kenneth Merchant, *Modern Management Control Systems* (Upper Saddle River, NJ: Prentice Hall, 1998), p. 642.

14 For a discussion, see Kenneth Merchant, *Modern Management Control Systems* (Upper Saddle River, NJ: Prentice Hall, 1998), pp. 542–545.

15 Ibid., p. 304.

16 Joel Kurtzman, "Is Your Company off Course? Now You Can Find Out Why," *Fortune*, 17 February 1997, pp. 128–130.

17 See for example Matt Hicks, "Tuning to the Big Picture for a Better Business," *PC Week*, 15 July 1999, p. 69.

18 Hicks, p. 69.

19 "The Software War," *Fortune*, 7 December 1998, p. 102.

20 Guy Bolton, "Enterprise Resource Planning Software Creates Supply Business Revolution," *Knight Ridder/Tribune Business News*, 9 November 1998.

21 "The Software War," *Fortune*, 7 December 1998, p. 102.

22 Robin Cooper and Tobert Kaplan, "The Promise and Peril of Integrated Costs Systems," *Harvard Business Review*, July–August 1998, p. 109.

23 Stephen Baker and Steve Hamm, "A Belated Rush to the Net," *Business Week*, 25 October 1999, pp. 152–158.

24 Simons, p. 81.

25 Ibid., p. 84.

26 Ibid., pp. 84–95.

27 Ibid., p. 86.

28 These characteristics are based on Simons, p. 87.

29 This discussion is based on Simons, pp. 87–88.

30 The following, except as noted, is based on Kenneth Merchant, *Control in Business Organizations* (Boston: Pitman, 1985), pp. 71–120. See also Robert Kaplan, "New Systems for Measurement and Control," *The Engineering Economist*, Spring 1991, pp. 201–218.

31 This is based on Simons, pp. 81–82.

32 Merchant, p. 98.

33 "Did Warner-Lambert Make a $468 Million Mistake?" *Business Week*, 21 November 1983, p. 123; quoted in Merchant, pp. 98–99.

34 Chris Argyris, "Human Problems with Budgets," *Harvard Business Review*, January–February 1953, pp. 97–110.

35 Peter Coy, "Big Brother, Pinned to Your Chest," *Business Week*, 17 August 1992, p. 38.

36 Jeffrey Stanton and Janet Barnes-Farrell, "Effects of Electronic Performance Monitoring on Personal Control, Task Satisfaction, and Task Performance," *Journal of Applied Psychology*, December 1996, p. 738; and Paul Greenlaw, "The Impact of Federal Legislation to Limit Electronic Monitoring," *Public Personnel Management*, Summer 1997, pp. 227–245.

37 Stanton and Barnes-Farrell, pp. 738–745.

38 Ibid., p. 738.

39 Norihiko Shirouzu and Jon Bigness, "'7-Eleven' Operators Resist System to Monitor Managers," *Wall Street Journal*, 16 June 1997, pp. B-1–6.

40 Tom Peters, *Liberation Management* (New York: Alfred A. Knopf, 1992), pp. 465–466.

41 Tom Burns and G. M. Stalker, *The Management of Innovation* (London: Tavistock, 1961), p. 119.

42 This quote is based on William Taylor, "Control in an Age of Chaos," *Harvard Business Review*, (November–December 1994), pp. 70–71. James Collins and Jerry Porras, *Built to Last: Successful Habits of Visionary Companies* (New York: Harper and Row, 1994).

43 Ibid., p. 71

44 J. Newcomb, 1998 letter to employees, 17 May 1999.

45 Gary Dessler, "How to Earn Your Employees Commitment," *Academy of Management Executive*, vol. 13, no. 2, 1999, pp. 58–67.

46 Personal interview. See Gary Dessler, Winning Commitment: How to Build and Keep a Competitive Work Force (New York: McGraw-Hill, 1993), pp. 27–28.

47 Ibid., p. 28.

48 Ibid., p. 30.

49 Rosabeth Moss Kanter, *Commitment and Community* (Cambridge, MA: Harvard University Press, 1972), pp. 24–25.

50 See Dessler, p. 64.

51 JoAnn Davy, "Online at the Office: Virtual Communities Go to Work," *Managing Office Technology*, July–August 1998, pp. 9–11.

52 Ibid.

53 Dessler, p. 69.

54 Kanter, p. 91.

55 Abraham Maslow, *Motivation and Personality* (New York: Harper & Row, 1954), p. 336.

56 Interview with assembler Dan Dise, March 1992.

57 Personal interview, March 1992.

58 Address to the Academy of Management, 9 August 1996.

MANAGING WITH INFORMATION TECHNOLOGY

1 James Senn, *Information Systems in Management* (Belmont, CA: Wadsworth Publishing Co., 1990), p. 58.

2 Peter F. Drucker, "The Coming of the New Organization," *Harvard Business Review* (January–February 1988), p. 45.

3 Carroll Frenzel, *Management of Information Technology* (Boston: Boyd & Fraser, 1992), p. 10.

4 See, for example, David Kroenke and Richard Hatch, *Management Information Systems* (New York: McGraw-Hill, 1994), p. 20.

5 Senn, p. 58.

6 Kenneth Laudon and Jane Price Laudon, *Management Information Systems, 5th edition* (Upper Saddle River, NJ: Prentice Hall, 1998), p. 5.

7 The following is based on Kenneth Laudon and Jane Price Laudon, *Management Information Systems, 4th edition* (Upper Saddle River, NJ: Prentice Hall, 1996), pp. 11, 41–46. See also John Verity, "Coaxing Meaning out of Raw Data," *Business Week*, 3 February 1997, pp. 134, 138.

8 Jenny McCune, "Thirst for Knowledge," *Management Review*, April 1999, p. 10.

9 Louisa Wah, "Behind the Buzz," *Management Review*, April 1999, p. 17.

10 McCune, p. 11.

11 Frenzel, p. 11.

12 Based on Senn, 8; and Laudon and Laudon, *Management Information Systems, 5th Edition*, p. 5.

13 Kenneth Laudon and Jane Laudon, *Essentials of Management Information Systems, 4th edition* (Upper Saddle River, NJ: Prentice-Hall, 1997), p. 73.

14 Laudon and Laudon, *Management Information Systems, 4th edition*, p. 7.

15 Senn, pp. 14–15.

16 See, for example, Kroenke and Hatch, p. 51.

17 Laudon and Laudon, *Management Information Systems, 4th edition*, p. 24.

18 Laudon and Laudon, *Essentials of Management Information Systems*, p. 405.

19 See, for example, Laudon and Laudon, *Management Information Systems*, p. 24.

20 Larry Long and Nancy Long, *Computers* (Upper Saddle River, NJ: Prentice-Hall, 1996), p. 18.

21 Senn, p. 576.

22 This discussion is based on Senn, pp. 576–577.

23 Bill Gates, *Business @ the Speed of Thought* (New York: Warner Books, 1999), p. 22.

24 Emily Nelson and Evan Ramstad, "Hershey's Biggest Dud Has Turned Out to Be New Computer System," *Wall Street Journal*, 29 October 1999, p. A1.

25 Senn, p. 415.

26 See, for example, Senn, p. 418.

27 Ibid., p. 427.

28 Microsoft Corp., special informational advertising, *Fortune*, 8 November 1999.

29 Kenneth Laudon and Jane Laudon, *Management Information Systems, 5th Edition* (Upper Saddle River, NJ: Prentice Hall, 1998), p. 608.

30 Ibid., p. 608.